D0961317

THE LEGACY OF RUTH BADER GINSBURG

Ruth Bader Ginsburg is a legal icon. In more than four decades as a lawyer, professor, appellate judge, and associate justice of the U.S. Supreme Court, Ginsburg has influenced the law and society in real and permanent ways.

This book chronicles and evaluates the remarkable achievements Ruth Bader Ginsburg has made over the past half-century. Including chapters written by prominent court watchers and leading scholars from law, political science, and history, it offers diverse perspectives on an array of doctrinal areas and on different time periods in Ginsburg's career. Together, these perspectives document the impressive — and continuing — legacy of one of the most important figures in modern law.

Scott Dodson is Harry & Lillian Hastings Research Chair and Professor of Law at the University of California Hastings College of the Law. An expert in civil procedure and federal courts, Dodson has authored more than thirty-five articles appearing in the *Stanford, Michigan, California, University of Pennsylvania,* and *Virginia* law reviews, among others. He is the author of *New Pleading in the Twenty-First Century* (2013) and *Civil Procedure: Model Problems and Outstanding Answers* (2011, 2d ed. 2012). His writings have been cited by the Fourth, Fifth, Seventh, Ninth, Tenth, and Eleventh circuits. Dodson is a frequent commentator in various news media and has blogged at *SCOTUSblog, Civil Procedure & Federal Courts Blog,* and *PrawfsBlawg.*

The Legacy of Ruth Bader Ginsburg

Edited by

SCOTT DODSON

University of California Hastings College of the Law

CAMBRIDGE
UNIVERSITY PRESS

CAMBRIDGE
UNIVERSITY PRESS

32 Avenue of the Americas, New York, NY 10013-2473, USA

Cambridge University Press is part of the University of Cambridge.

It furthers the University's mission by disseminating knowledge in the pursuit of education, learning, and research at the highest international levels of excellence.

www.cambridge.org
Information on this title: www.cambridge.org/9781107062467

© Cambridge University Press 2015

First published 2015

Printed in the United States of America

A catalog record for this publication is available from the British Library.

Library of Congress Cataloging in Publication data
The legacy of Ruth Bader Ginsburg / edited by Scott Dodson, University of California Hastings College of the Law
  pages cm
Includes bibliographical references and index.
ISBN 978-1-107-06246-7 (hardback)
1. Ginsburg, Ruth Bader   2. Judges – United States – Biography.
3. Law – United States.   I. Dodson, Scott, editor.
KF8745.G56.L44   2015
347.73'2634–dc23   2014043082

ISBN 978-1-107-06246-7 Hardback

Contents

Contributors

Paul Schiff Berman – Manatt/Ahn Professor of Law; and Vice Provost for Online Education and Academic Innovation, The George Washington University

Stephen B. Cohen – Professor of Law, Georgetown Law Center

Scott Dodson – Professor of Law and Harry & Lillian Hastings Research Chair, UC Hastings College of the Law

Cary Franklin – Assistant Professor of Law, University of Texas School of Law

Tom Goldstein – Partner, Goldstein & Russell, P.C.; Publisher, *SCOTUSblog*

Lisa Kern Griffin – Professor of Law, Duke Law School

Lani Guinier – Bennett Boskey Professor of Law, Harvard Law School

Aziz Z. Huq – Professor of Law, University of Chicago Law School

Robert A. Katzmann – Chief Judge, United States Court of Appeals for the Second Circuit

Herma Hill Kay – Barbara Nachtrieb Armstrong Professor of Law, UC Berkeley Law School

Linda K. Kerber – May Brodbeck Professor in the Liberal Arts and Professor of History, Emerita, University of Iowa

Dahlia Lithwick – Senior Editor, *Slate Magazine*

Deborah Jones Merritt – John Deaver Drinko-Baker & Hostetler Chair in Law, The Ohio State University Moritz College of Law

Neil S. Siegel – David W. Ichel Professor of Law; Professor of Political Science; Co-Director, Program in Public Law, Duke Law School

Reva B. Siegel – Nicholas deB. Katzenbach Professor of Law, Yale Law School

Nina Totenberg – Legal Affairs Correspondent, National Public Radio

Joan C. Williams – Distinguished Professor of Law and UC Hastings Foundation Chair; Founding Director of the Center for WorkLife Law, UC Hastings College of the Law

Preface

Now in her eighties, Ruth Bader Ginsburg has spent more than twenty years as an associate justice on the U.S. Supreme Court, thirteen years as a judge on the U.S. Court of Appeals for the District of Columbia Circuit, and seventeen years as law professor. During her teaching years, she was also general counsel for the ACLU's Women's Rights Project, which she co-founded. Her impact on the law over the last half-century cannot be overstated. Yet no book on Ginsburg's legacy exists. This book will be the first to fill that gaping void.

As the second woman appointed to the Supreme Court, Justice Ginsburg's jurisprudence is perhaps best known for influencing the law on women's rights. In particular, her landmark opinion for the Court in *United States v. Virginia* established heightened scrutiny for gender segregation in state schools, and her dissenting opinion in *Ledbetter v. Goodyear Tire & Rubber Co.* helped motivate Congress to pass the Lilly Ledbetter Fair Pay Act of 2009, which abrogated the Court's cramped interpretation of federal gender-discrimination laws. In 1937, a Gallup poll asked, "Would you vote for a woman presidential candidate?" and received only 33 percent of answers in the affirmative. In 2012, the percentage had risen to 95 percent. We've come a long way, baby, and Ginsburg's monumental efforts as a justice have contributed to those social changes.

Her victories on the Court have come at the tail end of a much larger project of how the law respects gender equality that Ginsburg and others began in earnest more than forty years ago. As the chief litigator for the ACLU's Women's Rights Project, Ginsburg litigated and won several pathmarking (as she might call them) decisions at the Supreme Court, each of which became another wave eroding the sands of antiquated notions of a woman's place in society and in the eyes of the law. When Ginsburg was done, few doubted that the tide had turned; those waves would continue until the erosion had made the shore flat – an even playing field.

Ginsburg is no one-trick pony. As the resident proceduralist on the Court, her opinions have fundamentally affected matters of federal procedure and jurisdiction. She also has written notable opinions in the fields of federalism, international law, criminal procedure, racial equality, abortion, congressional power, and even tax. In some ways, her impact in these areas is even more important to celebrate, if only because it has been overshadowed by her triumphs in gender equality.

The person behind the bench is often seen as a source of contradiction. Dimunitive yet forceful. Passionate yet rational. Strategic yet direct. Dear friend to her ideological antithesis, Justice Antonin Scalia. A daughter, student, professor, lawyer, judge, wife, and mother, she is a lover of music, opera, and fine company. Details of her character and personal life will be memorialized in biographies to come, but the way they intersect with her legal accomplishments is its own story.

This book chronicles and evaluates the remarkable achievements Ruth Bader Ginsburg has made over the last half-century. The chapters, written by prominent court watchers and leading scholars from law, political science, and history, offer diverse perspectives on an array of doctrinal areas and different time periods in Ginsburg's career. Together, these perspectives document the impressive legacy of one of the most important figures in modern law.

Acknowledgments

This book was my idea, but it is the product of many. The all-star lineup of contributors has resulted in a picture of Ruth Bader Ginsburg that is unparalleled. I thank those who encouraged me to pursue the project, including the anonymous reviewers solicited by Cambridge University Press, whose suggestions also helped shape the book. John Berger, longtime Cambridge editor, offered his experience and knowledge to its development. I am grateful to UC Hastings College of the Law for supporting the project. As always, my wife, Ami, offered a keen eye, gentle guidance, and quiet patience throughout the effort.

Acknowledgments usually start with the phrase "this book would not be possible without." For this book, there's really only one true end to that phrase, and it is an obvious one: Ruth Bader Ginsburg. Her remarkable life and career have made producing this book both easy and a pleasure.

PART I

SHAPING A LEGACY

1

Notes on a Life

Nina Totenberg

Early in the fall of 1971, I was pretty new to the Supreme Court beat, and I came upon a brief that I simply could not understand. The brief argued that the Fourteenth Amendment guarantee of equal protection of the law applied not just to racial minorities, but also to women.[1] "How can that be?" I wondered, since the Fourteenth Amendment was enacted after the Civil War specifically to protect African Americans.

I flipped to the front of the brief and saw it had been written by one Ruth Bader Ginsburg, a Rutgers Law School professor. So, I called her. The short answer to my question was that the Fourteenth Amendment says no "person" shall be denied the equal protection of the law,[2] and women, after all, are people.

But I got a lot more than that. She spent an hour filling me in, teaching me, and answering my undoubtedly very stupid questions. I emerged from a tiny phone booth in the Supreme Court press room like a goose primed to have her liver removed for foie gras. We soon became phone friends.

I *met* RBG, as she is known inside the Court, at some rather boring legal conference in New York. It was so boring, in fact, that we undertook a different task – shopping.

I have a vivid memory of our cab ride in New York that day. Ginsburg had applied for a federal district-court judgeship, and the New York senators' screening committee had interviewed her, telling her she was not qualified because she had not handled any major securities litigation. I remember Ginsburg, flinty-eyed, muttering, "And I wonder how many gender-discrimination cases they have handled."

It was classic RBG – tough and to the point, with a touch of gallows humor.

The other authors in this book will tell you much about Ruth Bader Ginsburg's career, background, legal journey, and jurisprudence. I want to hit just a few highlights, and add a few stories you won't hear elsewhere.

Ruth Bader Ginsburg is the leading liberal voice of dissent on the modern Supreme Court. But she arguably made her most profound mark on the law before becoming a judge, as a pioneer for women's rights. Put simply, she changed the way the world is for American women.

For more than a decade, until her first judicial appointment in 1980, she led the fight in the courts for gender equality. When she began her legal crusade, women were treated, by law, differently from men. Thousands of state and federal laws restricted what women could do, barring them from jobs, and even from jury service. By the time she donned judicial robes, however, Ruth Ginsburg had worked a revolution.

For those readers not familiar with the Ginsburg bio, let me reprise it quickly. She has lived a life that is both blessed and benighted. Born and raised in Brooklyn, Ruth Joan Bader lived a comfortable, though hardly plush, life as the daughter of a not very successful furrier-turned-haberdasher. She went to public schools and excelled as a student – and a baton twirler and a majorette. (She still keeps a baton in her chambers still and will, on occasion, twirl it for a visitor.)

By all accounts, her mother was the driving force in her life, and when Ruth was thirteen, her mother fell ill with cancer. Mrs. Bader remained sick, often bedridden, until her death the day before her daughter's graduation as valedictorian from high school. At Cornell, Ruth Bader, then seventeen, met Martin (a.k.a. Marty) Ginsburg, the well-off, happy-go-lucky son of a corporate executive. She often said that he was the only person she dated who was interested in her brain. Cornell, in those days, was something of a party school. The future justice did a fair amount of studying in the bathroom back then to avoid being seen as a grunt. She again finished first in her class.

Ruth and Marty were married at his parents' home. His mother would become like a second mother to her daughter-in-law, and on the wedding day, the senior Mrs. Ginsburg offered some advice on the secret of a happy marriage: "It is simply that every now and then it helps to be a little deaf." The advice was so good, recalls RBG, that she followed it "not just in dealing with my dearly beloved spouse but with my colleagues at the Court."

By 1958 the young Ginsburgs were at Harvard Law School, juggling schedules and their three-year-old daughter Jane.

We all think of Justice Ginsburg as the tiny, elegant octogenarian she is today. But back then she was "exotically and ravishingly beautiful," in the words of one of her male classmates. So much so that when school opened, and a professor, in one of those giant classrooms, first called on "*Mrs.* Ginsburg," there was an audible and collective "groan" of male disappointment in the room.

Then terror struck. Marty Ginsburg was diagnosed with testicular cancer. It had spread to four lymph nodes, and doctors told the couple that his chances of survival were almost nil. The Ginsburgs decided to try everything, including two draconian operations and daily radiation therapy. As Marty later put it, "that left Ruth with a three-year-old child, a sick husband, and Law Review," all of which she did with aplomb, as well as collecting notes from Marty's classes (he was a year ahead of her) and typing his papers. The happy ending of this story is that Marty Ginsburg survived, graduated with honors, and went to New York to join a big law firm.

The couple, however, was not sure yet that he would live for long, so wife and daughter moved with Marty, with Ruth doing her last year of law school at Columbia, where she again graduated at the top of her class. Harvard refused to give her a degree, and when it sought to amend that many years later, Ginsburg said no.

It is hard today to imagine the kind of discrimination Ginsburg endured because of her sex. How, despite her top place at Columbia, she could not find a job with a law firm. How she was recommended for a Supreme Court clerkship, but Justice Felix Frankfurter wouldn't even interview her. How she wore loose clothes to hide her pregnancy while teaching at Rutgers for fear she would not get tenure if they knew she was pregnant, and how she was the first woman to teach at Harvard Law School but was not offered a permanent position.

Ginsburg views those experiences with some grace, observing that if she had been able to follow a more traditional career path, she might not have had the headline-grabbing career she ended up with.

She tells some pretty funny stories about her life as a young lawyer. She finally got a clerkship with Judge Edmund L. Palmieri, having been turned down by, among others, Judge Learned Hand, who told a mutual friend he couldn't hire a woman because he couldn't swear in front of her. As it turned out though, Ginsburg's boss, Judge Palmieri, would often give Hand a ride home from work, and Hand would sit in the front seat singing sea shanties and swearing up a storm. Ginsburg, sitting in the backseat, was transfixed. She finally asked why, if Hand said "whatever came into his head" in the car, he had refused to consider her as a law clerk on grounds that he wouldn't feel free to speak without censoring himself? Replied Hand: "Young lady, I am not *looking* at you."

Bucking her up on the sidelines during all such madness was Ginsburg's husband Marty. The Ginsburg marriage was one of those marvels of life, a fifty-six-year marathon of love and support.

Before law school Marty was drafted, and they spent two years at Fort Sill, Oklahoma, a diversion that he would later say proved a stroke of good fortune.

"We had nearly two whole years far from school, far from career pressure, and far from relatives, to learn about each other and begin to build a life," he later said.

Among the things he learned was that "Ruth was a fairly terrible cook, and for lack of interest, unlikely to improve." So Marty, "out of self preservation" learned to cook. He took the Escoffier cookbook the couple had received as a wedding present and started at the beginning, working all the way through it.

Marty Ginsburg, in addition to becoming a famous tax lawyer, became a famous chef. The couple's children, at an early age, banished their mother from the kitchen.

James, their second, was an unexpected surprise ten years after Jane was born, since Marty had been told his radiation treatments had likely made him sterile.

Ruth and Marty Ginsburg complemented each other in ways too numerous to list. She was shy, introverted, and soft-spoken. He was witty and outgoing. Typical was his puckish description of why, after becoming a law professor, he moved teaching posts, from Columbia Law School to Georgetown Law School. His wife, he deadpanned, had gotten "a good job" in Washington.

Marty Ginsburg was always promoting his wife. Clinton administration officials said it was his relentless and artful behind-the-scenes lobbying that brought RBG's name into the mix of potential Supreme Court nominees in 1993.

At the end of his life, facing a losing battle with cancer, Marty wrote to his wife that he had "admired and loved" her almost from the moment they met. Turning introspective about his own life, he told a friend, "I think the most important thing I've done is to enable Ruth to do what she has done."

The day after Marty died, an ashen-faced Justice Ginsburg announced her opinion for the Court in one of the Term's major cases. She was on the bench, she told colleagues, "because Marty would have wanted it this way."

The Ginsburgs were partners not just in marriage but also in law. Fittingly, it was a tax case that Marty came across that led his wife into the area of law for which she became so famous.

The case involved a traveling salesman in Oklahoma named Charles Moritz who had claimed a dependent-care deduction on his taxes for money spent to take care of his eighty-nine-year-old mother while he was on the road. The IRS had disallowed the deduction, noting that Congress had allowed it only for women and divorced or widowed men. Charles Moritz was single and had never been married, so the IRS said he was ineligible. Moritz represented himself in the tax court, arguing that if he were a dutiful daughter instead of a dutiful son, he would be allowed the deduction.

The tax court concluded that the Internal Revenue Code was immune from constitutional challenge – a proposition that Marty Ginsburg, tax lawyer extraordinaire, found "preposterous."

Walking into his wife's workroom at home, he dropped the decision on to her desk, suggesting that she might find it "interesting." Soon she emerged with three words: "Let's take it." Marty called Moritz, and the couple began working on the brief, he from the tax perspective, she from the constitutional-law perspective.

According to Marty Ginsburg, for his wife, this was "the mother brief." She had to sit down and think through the issues and the remedy. The solution was to ask the court not to invalidate the statute but to apply it equally to both sexes. The Ginsburgs won in the lower court, and the government appealed to the Supreme Court. In its petition for certiorari, the government said that the lower court's decision cast a cloud of unconstitutionality over literally hundreds of federal statutes. And to prove its point, the government appended to its brief a list of these hundreds of statutes.[3] The government had no idea it was handing Ginsburg a road map, for these were the very laws that she would target to litigate and challenge over the next decade.

By the 1970s, now a professor at Columbia, Ginsburg had founded a special project on women's rights at the American Civil Liberties Union (ACLU) and was leading the battle in the courts against sex discrimination.

Her battle plan was characteristically cautious, precise, and single-mindedly aimed at one goal – winning. Knowing that she had to persuade male, establishment-oriented judges, she often picked male plaintiffs, and she particularly liked Social-Security cases because they illustrated how discrimination against women can harm men too. For example, in 1975, she persuaded a unanimous Supreme Court to strike down a law that denied survivors benefits to widowers but allowed them for widows.[4]

As an advocate in court, Ginsburg was a diminutive, even-toned powerhouse. She was organized, thoroughly prepared, and as one observer put it, "tough as nails." After one argument at the Supreme Court, a colleague asked her why she had twice avoided answering a question put to her by Justice John Paul Stevens. "Because," she replied coolly, "if I had answered him, my answer might have lost Justice [Lewis] Powell's vote, and if I didn't answer Stevens, I was going to get his vote anyway."

By the end of the 1970s, Ginsburg had argued six cases in the Supreme Court, won five, and written briefs in dozens of other cases. She revolutionized the law.

In her own life, too, Ginsburg was fearless about pressing the cause for women. When she was teaching at Rutgers, she pointed out to the dean that the women faculty members were not paid as well as the men. The dean demurred, noting that her husband, after all, "had a good job." So Ginsburg joined a class-action suit against Rutgers, resulting in enormous salary increases in settlement of the suit. A couple of years later, while on the Columbia law faculty, she gave the Columbia administration fits too. When school officials decided to save money by sending layoff notices to twenty-five maids but not a single janitor, Professor Ginsburg entered the fray. As a result, no maids were laid off.

And if those weren't enough, she joined a class action against the university over disparate pensions for female and male faculty.

Over the years there have been many occasions in which Ginsburg, through actions, not words, has stood up for something she felt strongly about. Most recently, after the Supreme Court ruled in two gay marriage cases, she became the first sitting Supreme Court justice to preside at a same-sex marriage ceremony.

When Justice Antonin Scalia calls her "fearless," he means not just intellectually fearless, but physically as well. Scalia vividly remembers being with Ginsburg at one of those flossy summer teaching gigs justices get invited to. This one was on the French Riviera. "And she went parasailing!" he recalls in amazement. "This little, skinny thing. You'd think she'd never come down. She was sailing off a motor boat ... way up in the sky. My God, I would never do that."[5]

Being a judge was always Ginsburg's objective, as far back as when I first knew her when she was in her thirties, but getting there took a while. In 1980 she was appointed to the Court of Appeals for the District of Columbia, where she served with distinction for more than a dozen years. And then, in 1993, there was a Supreme Court vacancy.

In the beginning of President Bill Clinton's search for a nominee, she was not at the top of his list. Mario Cuomo, George Mitchell, and Stephen Breyer (later to get the nod) were all ahead of her initially. But one of the things that people greatly underrate about Ginsburg is her ability to perform. She may be quiet, shy, even hard to talk to, but put her on a stage, and this woman knows how to deliver. That's what she did in her interview with Clinton, and his aides said he quite simply was "smitten."

Ginsburg has another trait that few appreciate. She knows how to handle the press, even use it when she wants to. In her two bouts with cancer, she knew that hiding her condition or treatment would only provoke speculation, so she was relatively forthcoming (for a Supreme Court justice) in releasing information.

Conversely, in the summer of 2013, after she turned eighty, she knew speculation would soon accelerate over her possible retirement. So, she embarked on a not-so-quiet campaign to head off such speculation by granting a bunch of interviews. Time after time, she responded that she had no intention of retiring, unless and until her health prevented her from doing the job. Yes, she admitted, there were some things she had given up – water skiing, for example – but not her court work.

Indeed, if anything, Ginsburg seems to have found a voice stronger than ever. It is the voice of dissent.

She has acknowledged that she regrets going along with the 2009 decision that upheld the Voting Rights Act but sowed the seeds for overturning it.[6] And when the Court four years later did in fact overturn the key section of the law requiring preclearance for certain states, her dissent was full throated.

"The sad irony of today's decision lies in its utter failure to grasp why the [Voting Rights Act] has proven effective.... Throwing out preclearance when it has worked and is continuing to work to stop discriminatory changes [in voting procedures] is like throwing away your umbrella in a rainstorm because you are not getting wet."[7]

"Some of my favorite opinions are dissenting opinions," she once told me. "I will not live to see what becomes of them, but I remain hopeful."

In one case she did live to see her dissent become the law of the land. In the 2007 case of *Ledbetter v. Goodyear Tire & Rubber Co.*,[8] the Court, by a 5-to-4 vote, gutted a major provision of the civil rights law barring employment discrimination. Ginsburg's dissent blasting the majority essentially called on Congress to overrule the decision. Presidential candidate Barack Obama campaigned on the promise to do just that, and when he was elected, with large democratic majorities in both houses, the Lilly Ledbetter Fair Pay Act was the first statute enacted by the new Congress and signed by the new president.[9] Ginsburg has a framed copy of the act in her chambers.

Ginsburg is not without victories. At least one had to be seen to be fully appreciated. The case involved the strip-search of a teenage girl named Savana Redding after a classmate told the school vice principal that Redding was carrying unauthorized prescription-strength ibuprofen. Redding's mother sued the school district for violating Savana's right to be free from unreasonable searches. School officials found no drugs on the girl.

The Court's conservatives seemed to think there was no big deal to this. And fellow Clinton appointee, Stephen Breyer, opined, "I'm trying to work out why this is a major thing to, say, strip down to your underclothes, which children do when they change for gym.... How bad is this?"[10]

Every woman in the press section could hardly believe her ears, remembering what it is like to be a pubescent and shy teenage girl, with a developing body.

As for Ginsburg, she looked like she might explode. She interrupted, her voice dripping with exasperation, to note that Redding had been forced to "shake (her) bra out, shake, (and stretch) the top of her underpants" and, even after school officials found nothing, they made Redding sit outside the vice principal's office for two hours, putting her in a "humiliating position."[11] Ginsburg's fury seemed to turn the tide, and when the decision came out, the Court held, 8 to 1, that the search violated the Fourth Amendment.[12]

Ginsburg's most notable majority opinion came just three years after her appointment to the Supreme Court: her 7-to-1 opinion declaring that the Virginia Military Institute (VMI) could no longer remain an all-male institution.[13] True, said Ginsburg, most women, indeed most men, would not want to meet the rigorous demands of VMI, but the state, she said, could not exclude women who could pass muster.

"[The state] may not rely on overbroad generalizations about the different talents, capacities, or preferences of males and females," she wrote. "[G]eneralizations about 'the way women are,' estimates of what is appropriate for *most women*, no longer justify denying opportunity to women whose talent and capacity place them outside the average description."[14]

Let me say here that in all the years I have known Ginsburg, I have failed to pry out of her any exclusive information, with one exception. I learned from her quite recently that Justice Sandra Day O'Connor was originally assigned the VMI opinion, but she declined, telling the senior assigning justice, John Paul Stevens, that the opinion, by right, should go to Ginsburg.

Ginsburg was forever grateful to O'Connor, loved serving with her, viewed her as a kind of sister "in law," and was amused by the high-powered lawyers who confused the two women justices – despite the fact that the two have never looked anything like each other.

People often find it odd that she also loves the company of Justice Antonin Scalia, despite their more than frequent disagreements and sometimes vituperous footnote battles. But Ginsburg served with Scalia on the D.C. appeals court, and she loves that he makes her laugh. They share a love of opera, and they often have spent New Year's Eve together.

Ginsburg has been a generous friend to me, especially when my late husband was terribly ill for nearly five years. She often would scoop me up and take me somewhere with her to get rid of my blues. But she and I know the boundaries.

On one occasion in 2010, I really felt obligated to push them. I was interviewing Ginsburg at the 92nd St. Y in New York on stage. It was just days after President Obama had excoriated the conservative Court majority for its campaign-finance decision, *Citizens United v. FEC*.[15] Justice Samuel Alito, sitting in the audience with other justices, had shaken his head at the president's message and mouthed the words "not true."

So, I observed to Ginsburg, that given the fact I *am* a reporter, I just had to ask her about all this and what she thought of it.

She paused for several seconds. (Ginsburg does not speak without thinking first.)

Alito had been sitting behind her, she said, so she didn't see what happened. But, she added that she did have a problem that night: staying awake. The justices, she explained, had eaten dinner together at the Court beforehand. She had a cocktail followed by wine. "And I'm kind of a little person, so sitting there while everyone around is bobbing up and down and we have to sit there sober as judges ..."

It was, she conceded, rather hard to keep her eyes open. Justice Breyer would give her a "gentle push," she said, whenever she started to "lean over," but he was not as good as the retired Justice David Souter had been. "He knew the first sign," she confessed, "and would give me a pinch."

Classic RBG. The audience loved her self-deprecating remarks, but my reporter's heart sank. I knew she was going to tell me absolutely nothing that would make news.

2

Ruth Bader Ginsburg:
Law Professor Extraordinaire

Herma Hill Kay

On August 10, 1993, for the first time in U.S. history, a female attorney general (Janet Reno) presented the commission of a president (William Clinton) to seat a female justice (Ruth Bader Ginsburg) on the United States Supreme Court.[1] Ginsburg, a tireless advocate for equality between men and women, joined Sandra Day O'Connor as the second woman and the 107th justice on the high court. Ginsburg's professional life before becoming a justice was unusual because she did not come from the public or private practice of law. Rather, she had spent the first seventeen years of her career as a law professor before accepting President Carter's appointment to the United States Court of Appeals for the District of Columbia Circuit in 1980. With her elevation to the Supreme Court, she became only the sixth justice and the first female to have held a tenured appointment on a law school faculty.[2] This chapter presents an overview of her academic background as a prelude to examining how that experience might have influenced her work on the Court.

BACKGROUND AND LEGAL TRAINING

Born in Brooklyn on March 15, 1933, to Jewish-American parents of Central European and Russian ancestry, Ginsburg credits her mother, Celia Bader, for encouraging her intellectual development.[3] She amply repaid that investment by graduating first among the women in her class and being elected to Phi Beta Kappa at Cornell University in 1954. At Cornell, she met and married an upper-classman, Martin D. Ginsburg; both decided to study law. She later recalled that she had been inspired to become a lawyer "because of my horror at what Joe McCarthy, who saw a communist in every corner, was doing to the country."[4] She saw the "brave lawyers, standing up for the people who were called before the Senate Internal Security Committee, the House Un-American Activities Committee"[5] and wanted to prepare herself to fill a similar role.

Her husband entered Harvard Law School in 1953 but was called to military service after his first year. The Ginsburgs spent the next two years in Fort Sill, Oklahoma. In 1956, she entered Harvard and her husband resumed his studies there. Their daughter, Jane, born on July 21, 1955, was then fourteen months old.

Harvard Law School had not admitted women students until 1950, and they were still an oddity in 1956. Ginsburg's entering class of 552 Harvard students contained only nine women. The professors knew all of them, and so did Dean Erwin Griswold, who gave a reception for them and pointedly asked each woman why she occupied a place that would otherwise have gone to a man – a question that was received with resentment by his guests, but which he later explained as a misunderstood attempt to "encourage the women to make full use of their legal training."[6]

Despite this chilly atmosphere, Ginsburg proved herself an outstanding student and was elected to the *Harvard Law Review.* Her husband graduated in 1958, having kept up his studies with his wife's help while successfully battling cancer, and accepted a position in New York City with Weil, Gotshal & Manges. Wanting to join him there with their daughter, she applied to Harvard for permission to complete her third year at Columbia. Despite the school's practice of frequently granting male students such permission, Dean Griswold told her that she had not made out a case of "exigent personal circumstances" to justify the move and denied her request.[7] Ginsburg thereupon withdrew from Harvard and transferred to Columbia, where she found a warmer reception: "Dean Warren didn't ask any questions. He just accepted me."[8] Some years after her graduation from Columbia, Ginsburg recalled that Harvard "finally thought me worthy of a degree." Her response to the offer extended by Dean Albert Sacks in 1971, which conditioned the grant of a Harvard diploma upon her renunciation of her Columbia degree, was swift and unequivocal: "I hold only one *earned* degree," she pointed out; "[i]t is from Columbia. I treasure it and will have no other."[9]

At Columbia, as at Harvard, she was elected to the *Law Review* and graduated in 1959, tied for first place in the class. She clerked for District Court Judge Edmund L. Palmieri, who was persuaded by Professor Gerald Gunther to give her a "trial run" despite his reluctance to hire a woman with a young child. Gunther secured the job by a threat and a promise. He warned Palmieri that his future supply of Columbia clerks would dry up if he refused to hire Ginsburg, but he also guaranteed the judge a male replacement clerk if the relationship did not work out. For her part, Ginsburg was grateful for the opportunity, recognizing that her "status as 'a woman, a Jew, and a mother to boot' was a bit much for prospective employers in those days."[10]

Following her two-year clerkship with Palmieri, another mentor appeared. Hans Smit, a 1958 Columbia graduate, had returned to the school in 1960 as the founding director of its Project on International Procedure. He hired Ginsburg in 1961 to work on the project for two years. She served as a research associate in 1961–2 and as associate director in 1962–3. During her work on the project, Ginsburg traveled to Sweden, where she undertook a study of Swedish civil procedure together with Anders Bruzelius, a city court judge in Lund, Sweden. Their joint effort was published as a book in 1965.[11] Four years later, in recognition of this work, the co-authors received honorary degrees from the University of Lund.

GINSBURG AT RUTGERS, NEWARK, LAW SCHOOL, 1963–1972

Another of Ginsburg's Columbia professors, Walter Gellhorn, was instrumental in securing her appointment at Rutgers.[12] She was hired to replace one of the early African American law professors, Clyde Ferguson, who had left Rutgers to accept the deanship at Howard Law School. She later told a Columbia student reporter that "the school might have said, 'If we can't get a black to replace Clyde, let's get a woman.'"[13] Her appointment was not a novelty at Rutgers. She had been preceded by Eva Hanks who had joined the faculty the year before Ginsburg arrived in 1963. With Ginsburg's appointment, Rutgers joined the small band of two other law schools – the University of Miami and Howard University – that had two women serving at the same time. Jeanette Ozanne Smith and Maria Minnette Massey taught at Miami, while Alessandra del Russo and Patricia Roberts Harris were at Howard. These three schools exhibited some diversity in the backgrounds of their female law professors: although the two at Miami were both graduates of that school, none of the other four had been hired by their alma maters. The Miami pattern was the normal one for most of the women law professors hired before 1960, while that of Howard and Rutgers was more typical of those hired later.

During her first three years in law teaching, from 1963 to 1966, Assistant Professor Ginsburg was able to develop her scholarly interest in civil procedure by teaching three courses in the area: Remedies, Civil Procedure, and a Comparative Procedure seminar, which focused on the work she had done in Sweden following her clerkship. Her publications during this period were devoted to the same field. She also contributed chapters on the Scandinavian countries (with co-authors) to a book on international judicial assistance edited by Hans Smit of Columbia who had hired her for the research project in Sweden.

Ginsburg's personal experience of encountering sex-based obstacles to her professional career, begun at Harvard, continued at Rutgers. She later publicly revealed that she had been paid less than her male colleagues when she was hired in 1963:

> Dean Willard Heckel, one of the kindest, finest men I have ever known, carefully explained about the State University's limited resources, and then added it was only fair to pay me modestly, because my husband had a very good job.[14]

She found the dean's frankness "somewhat surprising," particularly because the Equal Pay Act had become effective in 1963, the year she was hired. Although that federal statute did not immediately apply to academic employment, its purpose was clear enough: women should not be paid less than men for doing the same work. Ginsburg added that "some seven years later, I was part of a class of women from all faculties at Rutgers, Newark, each of whom received an enormous raise in settlement of an Equal Pay claim."[15]

In addition to unequal pay, Ginsburg initially lacked job security at Rutgers, instead holding a contract that could be renewed annually. When she became pregnant during her second year of teaching, she feared that her contract would not be renewed for a third year if she revealed her condition. Her apprehension may have stemmed from the fact that when her first child was born, "it was understood [by her Oklahoma employers] that I would leave work and not come back." At Rutgers, she developed an effective strategy to conceal her pregnancy. As she explained, "I said nothing, but borrowed clothes from my ever supportive, one size larger mother-in-law. With her wardrobe at my disposal, I managed to make it through the spring semester."[16] Once her contract had been renewed, Ginsburg felt free to announce the good news to a few of her colleagues that she was expecting a second child. Her son, James Steven Ginsburg, was born on September 8, 1965.

Based on a substantial record of publication, teaching, and professional service, Ginsburg was promoted to associate professor in 1966. In that year, she added the basic Comparative Law course to her teaching schedule, as well as courses on the Conflict of Laws and Federal Jurisdiction. She published her still-classic tenure article on the Full Faith and Credit Clause in 1969[17] and was promoted to professor the following year.

PROFESSOR GINSBURG'S POST-TENURE SCHOLARLY FOCUS

In a stunning reversal of field following her promotion, Ginsburg never published another major article on civil procedure after 1970. Instead, beginning in 1971, she focused her energies and scholarly attention on the legal status of women. The seeds for this new direction had been laid during her two years of research in Sweden. Looking back on those years in 2012, Ginsburg explained their formative influence on her later career:

> My eyes were opened up in Sweden. This was in '62 and '63 – women were about a quarter of the law students there, perhaps three percent in the United States. It was already accepted that a family should have two wage earners. A woman named Eva Moberg wrote a column in the *Stockholm Daily* paper with the headline, "Why should the woman have two jobs and the man only one?" And the thrust of it was, yes, she is expected to have a paying job, but she should also have dinner on the table at seven, take her children to buy new shoes, to their medical check-ups, and the rest. The notion that he should do more than take out the garbage sparked debates that were very interesting to me.... Well, that was at the start of the '60s. I put it all on a back burner until the late '60s when the women's movement came alive in the United States.[18]

Ginsburg herself played a prominent role in helping the women's movement "come alive" in the legal profession in 1969, when she and three colleagues undertook to persuade the Association of American Law Schools (AALS) to protect their women law students against overt discrimination by major law firms.[19] The AALS is the national membership organization for law schools, and given the relatively small number of women law professors and professors of color in 1969, the faculties of its member schools were overwhelmingly white and male. The organization had amended its membership requirements in 1951 by prohibiting member schools from discrimination in admissions based on race following the United States Supreme Court's decision in *Sweatt v. Painter*,[20] which had ordered the University of Texas Law School to admit black students. Significantly, the impetus for action in the case of sex discrimination, like that of race discrimination, was treatment of law students rather than law faculty. By the mid-1960s, the number of women law students had become significant, but the number of women lawyers in practice remained small.

Professor Frank "Tom" Read of Duke Law School, who was also an assistant dean in charge of student admission and placement, soon recognized what his peers in other major law schools like Harvard, Yale, and Columbia also were learning: They all had "women students who had very good records, and should have been interviewed as part of the top of the class, but they were just having a terrible time getting jobs, principally with the major law firms."[21] Ginsburg, Read, and two assistant deans from Harvard and Yale met in her New York apartment on a Sunday afternoon in 1969 to "cobble together a statement"; it ultimately became the AALS position on nondiscrimination based on sex, adopted by the organization at its December 1969 meeting:

1. The Association urges that members of the legal profession provide equal employment opportunities for female applicants for legal positions.
2. The Association urges that member schools take steps within their power to eradicate sex-based discrimination within law schools and particularly in the placement process.[22]

In March 1970, the AALS appointed a Special Committee on Women in Legal Education partly in response to petitions by women law students. The Special Committee met in April 1970 and formally proposed that the Association amend its articles of incorporation to require law schools to deny use of their placement facilities to prospective employers who discriminate on the basis of sex. The AALS Executive Committee approved the proposal, but broadened it to cover all forms of discrimination based on "race, color, sex, or national origin" and set it for action at the 1970 Annual Meeting.

The Special Committee's 1970 Report went beyond placement to act on several other matters, including urging member law schools to adopt recruitment programs, both for women law students – "to let women know that the legal profession is open to them" – and for women law professors, stating its belief that "lack of women faculty members has a serious adverse effect on recruitment, education and placement of women students."[23]

The Special Committee was reappointed in 1971, and as a symbol of its permanent place in the AALS Committee structure, it became the Standing Committee on Equality for Women in Legal Education with Professor Ruth Bader Ginsburg as a member. It called upon the AALS to sponsor a Symposium on the Law School Curriculum and the Legal Rights of Women to be held at N.Y.U. Law School in October 1972. By the time the Symposium took place, Ginsburg had left Rutgers for Columbia, and the AALS had created a new Section on Women in Legal Education.

Thereafter, matters moved swiftly. In 1972, Ginsburg served as chair of both the Standing Committee and the Section, a role she continued to perform as co-chair in 1973 with Professor Shirley R. Bysiewicz, law librarian at the University of Connecticut. By 1974, the Standing Committee had been consolidated into the Section. What had begun at Ruth Bader Ginsburg's kitchen table in 1969 as an effort to prevent law firm discrimination against women law students had evolved into an effort to create teaching materials dealing with the broader issues of sex discrimination and to recruit women law faculty.

In addition to her work with the AALS, Ginsburg undertook two new projects also dealing with sex discrimination: the first was to offer a seminar on the subject, and the second – growing out of the first – was to prepare a casebook to support the new course. She described both in a 1995 speech at Rutgers:

> Around 1970, women students whose conscience had awakened at least as much as mine, women encouraged by a vibrant movement for racial equality, asked for a seminar on Women and the Law. I repaired to the Library. There, in the space of a month, I read every federal decision *ever* published involving women's legal status, and every law review article. That was no grand feat. There were not many decisions, and not much in the way of commentary. Probably less altogether than today accumulates in six months time.
>
> I was engaged in preparing materials for the seminar when Frank Askin had a visitor in his constitutional law class or constitutional litigation seminar. The visitor was Mel Wulf, then Legal Director of ACLU's National Office. The Supreme Court had just noted probable jurisdiction in a case called *Reed* v. *Reed*. The complainant, Sally Reed, had challenged an Idaho statute that read: As between persons "equally entitled to administer" a decedent's estate, "males must be preferred to females." The ACLU had filed the Jurisdictional Statement in *Reed* and I asked Mel if I could write the Brief for Appellant. We will write the brief, Mel said, and so we did, Mel and I together, with the grand aid of students from Yale, NYU, and Rutgers.[24]

Those two events led to Ginsburg's deeper immersion in women's rights. That, in turn, resulted in her decisions to help found the ACLU Women's Rights Project, designed to advance "public understanding, legislative change, and change in judicial doctrine," in 1972, her collaboration with me and Kenneth Davidson of Buffalo to publish the country's first comprehensive casebook on sex-based discrimination in 1974, and her advocacy in support of the Equal Rights Amendment (ERA) between 1974 and 1978. In all three undertakings, her cause was a grand one: to put women into the U.S. Constitution and thereby equate women's rights with human rights. All are discussed later in this chapter.[25]

GINSBURG AT COLUMBIA, 1972

Ginsburg joined the Columbia law faculty as its first tenured woman professor in 1972. By that time, Title VII of the Civil Rights Act of 1964 had been extended to cover university faculty.[26] Thereafter, a law school's refusal to hire an otherwise qualified woman to teach law because of her sex was not only an infraction of AALS membership requirements[27] but also a violation of federal law.[28] She recalled the circumstances of her appointment as remarkably low key: "I was not subjected to any examination or asked to show and tell. The faculty simply held a cocktail party in my honor to say welcome home."[29]

Ginsburg may have experienced her appointment as "uneventful," but her new dean, Michael Sovern, reportedly expressed "glee" in an interview about the school's success in recruiting her to its faculty, in part because of her "distinguished scholarship"[30] but also, in the reporter's view, because Columbia had beaten out some of its rivals in hiring her.[31]

In any event, Ginsburg's new colleagues soon discovered that they had welcomed an activist into their midst. She became a prominent leader in the struggle to end sex discrimination in the university's compensation policies:

> My very first month on campus, Columbia sought to save money in the housekeeping department. The University sent lay off notices to 25 maids – and no janitors. I entered that fray, which happily ended with no lay offs. I also supported (as the Law School's representative to the University Senate) the request of the campus Commission on the Status of Women for a comprehensive equal pay salary review.

> Hardest for my University and Law School colleagues to bear was the litigation that followed a tea Madam Wu, a world-renowned physics professor, held at her Claremont Avenue apartment on a clear winter day, for all the senior women at Columbia. (Eleven women had achieved that rank in the mid-1970s, compared to over one thousand men.) One of the eleven, Carol Meyer, Professor at the School of Social Work, wrote about the meeting years later. She reported having been more than a little suspicious when she received the invitation, which came from me. "Women meeting together? Was this to be a cell meeting of some kind," she wondered. To the contrary, reported Ginsburg, what was discussed was the sex differential then part of the University's TIAA-CREF plan, under which women received lower monthly retirement benefits because on average, women live longer than men. Eventually, a federal case was filed, with some one hundred Columbia women – teachers and administrators – as named plaintiffs. . . . In that matter, as in many others – I recall particularly an earlier episode involving a request to extend health benefits to cover pregnant employees – I was shielded from accusations of disloyalty to the University by law school deans (first Michael Sovern, then Albert Rosenthal) and colleagues who – although they did not inevitably agree with me on the merits – recognized the value of having the questions fully aired.[32]

A CASEBOOK ON SEX-BASED DISCRIMINATION

The 1972 NYU Symposium was the time and place where the plan to coauthor a law school casebook on sex-based discrimination was conceived by me, Ginsburg, and Kenneth Davidson.[33] Ken and I, like Ginsburg, had both responded to requests from our law students to create "Women and the Law" courses. In 1971, Davidson offered such a course at SUNY Buffalo, and was beginning to put together teaching materials for it. Berkeley women students brought a similar request to me around the same time, and I helped them persuade a practitioner, Colquit Meacham Walker, to offer such a course by promising to attend all of the class sessions.

No casebooks existed for such a course in 1971. Professor Leo Kanowitz of Hastings published a coursebook in 1973 based on a series of essays he had published together in 1969.[34] Davidson wanted to turn his materials, then limited to women in the workplace, into a casebook, but he also wanted to recruit others to collaborate by adding relevant coverage from other areas where sex discrimination was beginning to make itself felt. He sent his unpublished materials to me. I read them and was immediately struck by how well a chapter on family law would work with the employment materials. Even at that early point, the connection between the stereotypes ingrained in the roles of "wife" and "office wife" were too clear to be overlooked. Ken welcomed my participation, and we agreed that the project would need the collaboration of a constitutional law expert. Ruth Bader Ginsburg was the obvious choice. She was, by that time, the director of the ACLU's Women Rights Project and was already litigating the pathbreaking Equal Protection cases before the United States Supreme Court that would ultimately create a firm place for women in the Constitution for the first time in its history. We decided to pitch the project to her at the NYU conference, which she had helped to organize.

A major topic of discussion at the conference was whether the subject of Women and the Law should remain a stand-alone course or whether coverage of the subject should be distributed more broadly across the curriculum. The preliminary announcement for the conference had expressed a clear preference for the latter option. While acknowledging that "dedicated faculty members" had taught such courses to "students who have a special interest in the subject," it cautioned that "unless information on the legal rights and disabilities of women is included in the most basic law school courses, the nation's law graduates will continue to have scant understanding of the legal restrictions under which 53 percent of the population lives."[35] The three of us were among the "dedicated faculty" who had been engaged in the former course, and when the conference was over, we concluded that both options were viable and should be pursued independently. For ourselves, we elected to prepare a casebook for a stand-alone course on what we would call "Sex-Based Discrimination," rather than "Women and the Law."

The first edition of the book was published in 1974. In the Foreword, we cited the noted anthropologist, Margaret Mead, for the proposition that no known culture had failed to establish a division of roles based on sex. We cited the noted writer, Simone de Beauvoir, for the insight that "man is the creator and controller of culture and its norms, while woman is the Other whose place is fixed by him."[36] We observed that although men have thereby gained "the greater share of power and prestige, [they] are no less trapped in their assigned roles," going on to explain our decision to focus on the laws that facilitate and regulate those "assigned roles" in the hope of creating a tool for their ultimate destruction. In words written by Ginsburg, we declared that

> we believe that, as an initial device the law is likely to be more effective as an aid in opening arenas for personal action.... Hopefully in aid of men and women who are willing to explore their potential as human beings, we have directed our attention to the support law has provided for traditional roles, as well as the stimulus law might provide toward a society in which the members of both sexes are free to develop their individual talents.[37]

Ginsburg did double duty, contributing to the book not only as a co-author, but also as a litigator for the ACLU Women's Rights Project. In the first edition appeared three cases she had argued before the United States Supreme Court: *Reed v. Reed, Frontiero v. Richardson,* and *Commissioner v. Moritz.*[38] Between 1972 and 1980, Ginsburg filed briefs in nine major Supreme Court sex-discrimination cases, personally arguing six and winning five. She also filed *amicus curiae* briefs in fifteen related cases. In describing her goal and litigation strategy, Ginsburg noted that while there was nothing subtle about the classifications based on sex that riddled the statute books, there was a problem of perception: laws treating women differently from men were regarded not as harmful but as benignly favoring women. To overcome this belief, she sought to teach legislators, judges, and the public that their daughters and granddaughters could be disadvantaged by their attitude. Her strategy led the Court to adopt a heightened "intermediate" constitutional standard and created the intellectual foundations of sex-discrimination law. All of these cases were incorporated into subsequent editions of the casebook.[39]

THE EQUAL RIGHTS AMENDMENT

Ruth Bader Ginsburg did her most significant law-reform work at Columbia. Not content with relying on her own considerable skills at advocacy to persuade the United States Supreme Court to adopt a new interpretation of the Equal Protection Clause, she energetically threw herself into the effort to solidify the case law with a new Amendment to the Constitution: the Equal Rights Amendment.

The ERA was first introduced in Congress in 1923,[40] sponsored by Alice
Paul and her National Women's Party in the hope of achieving the broad constitutional base of support for women's rights that the suffragists had expected,
but failed, to get from the Nineteenth Amendment.[41] In 1972 Congresswoman
Martha Griffiths, the principal House of Representatives proponent of the ERA,
predicted that it would "be ratified almost immediately."[42] Between 1972 and
1978, a year before the seven-year ratification period expired, Ginsburg made a
number of speeches and wrote articles in support of the ERA. Illustrative of the
articles are two published in the *American Bar Association Journal*[43] and one in
the first issue of the *Harvard Women's Law Journal*.[44] In the first ABA piece, she
traced the history of the proposed amendment, noting that the objections to its
adoption voiced in 1973 were "solidly answered" during the 1920s debate[45] but
nonetheless answering them once more[46] and going on to make the affirmative
case for ratification. Her second ABA piece, published four years later as the
time for ratification was running out, took the ABA to task for failing to carry
out its 1974 undertaking "to play an active role in educating the public" about
why "the E.R.A. is the way for a society that believes in the essential human
dignity ... of each man and each woman."[47] Writing in the *Harvard Women's
Law Journal* a year later, her response to the critics was more succinct:

> The ERA is not a "unisex" amendment. It does not stamp man and woman
> as one (the old common law did that); it does not label them the same; it
> does not require similarity in result, parity or proportional representation. It
> simply prohibits government from allocating rights, responsibilities or oppor-
> tunities among individuals solely on the basis of sex.[48]

In the end, however, Representative Griffith's prediction of swift passage
proved overly optimistic, and by 1978 Ginsburg was invited to testify before
both chambers of Congress in support of an extension of the initial 1979 ERA
ratification deadline. Reflecting her expertise as a proceduralist, she began by
addressing four contested issues about the extension process. She argued, first,
that Congress had authority to extend the deadline; second, that it could do so
by a simple majority vote; third, that the president's signature was unnecessary
to validate the measure; and fourth, that extension of the ratification period
would not, standing alone, empower the states to rescind a prior ratification.[49]
Next, she addressed the merits by supporting the need for additional time.
She placed the responsibility squarely on the Supreme Court's failure to act
decisively in setting a new course for interpretation of the Equal Protection
Clause as it applies to sex-based classifications:

> Arbitrary gender lines still clutter the lawbooks and regulations of the nation
> and states, the Supreme Court vacillates insecurely from one decision to the

next, and is sometimes disarmed from reaching any decision, as it holds back doctrinal development and awaits the signal the Equal Rights Amendment would supply.[50]

Congress responded by extending the deadline for ratification until June 30, 1982.[51] In refashioning her arguments in 1979 for the Orgain Lecture at the University of Texas Law School, Ginsburg offered a milder, but still critical assessment of the Court's equal protection precedents:

> Since 1971, the Supreme Court has taken significant steps in a new direction, but generally, it has done so insecurely, with divided opinions, and without crisp doctrinal development. The longing of lower courts for firmer guidance was well expressed in a 1975 opinion by Judge Newcomer of the Eastern District of Pennsylvania: In dealing with recent high court gender discrimination precedent, Judge Newcomer said, trial judges feel like players at "a shell game who [are] not absolutely sure there is a pea."[52]

PROFESSOR GINSBURG'S INFLUENCE ON JUSTICE GINSBURG

Although Justice Ginsburg's notable opinions range far beyond those encompassed by the law school subjects she taught in Sex-Based Discrimination and Civil Procedure courses,[53] her scholarly expertise has made itself felt most keenly in those areas. Other contributors to this volume cover her opinions in depth. Here it seems appropriate simply to identify some of the opinions (and dissents) that showcase her strengths as a teacher.

High on this list, of course, are her sex-discrimination opinions, dealing either with constitutional claims under the Equal Protection Clause and the Due Process Clause or statutory claims under the Equal Pay Act of 1963 or Title VII of the Civil Rights Act of 1964. The most significant among the former group is her opinion for the majority in *United States v. Virginia*,[54] handed down in 1996, in which she elevated the "intermediate" level of scrutiny established in one of the cases she had litigated twenty years earlier to become a heightened "skeptical" scrutiny just a shade lower than "strict" scrutiny:

> Focusing on the differential treatment or denial of opportunity for which relief is sought, the reviewing court must determine whether the proffered justification is "exceedingly persuasive." The burden of justification is demanding and it rests entirely on the State. . . . The State must show "at least that the [challenged] classification serves important governmental objectives and that the discriminatory means employed are 'substantially related to the achievement of those objectives.'" The justification must be genuine, not hypothesized or invented post hoc in response to the litigation. And it must

not rely on overbroad generalizations about the different talents, capacities, or preferences of males and females.[55]

Among the latter is her influential dissent in *Ledbetter v. Goodyear Tire & Rubber Co.*,[56] written in 2007, a wage discrimination suit brought by Lilly Ledbetter in which she claimed that her raises as a Goodyear area manager had deliberately been slowed or denied because of sex discrimination. Although her compensation was comparable to that of male managers when she was hired as the only female manager in 1979, by the time she retired in 1998, she was earning substantially less than the lowest paid male manager: her salary was $3,727 per month, while that of the lowest-paid male was $4,286.

The Court held that her recovery was limited to pay periods that fell within the 180-day statute of limitations for Title VII claims. The ruling effectively barred Ledbetter from recovering for discrimination before September 26, 1997. Ginsburg's dissent, which charged the majority with a "cramped interpretation" of Title VII, made clear why she thought "pay disparities are significantly different" from adverse treatment claims like termination, failure to promote, or refusal to hire:

> Pay disparities often occur, as they did in Ledbetter's case, in small increments; cause to suspect that discrimination is at work develops only over time. Comparative pay information, moreover, is often hidden from the employee's view. Employers may keep under wraps the pay differentials maintained among supervisors, no less the reasons for those differentials. Small initial discrepancies may not be seen as meet for a federal case, particularly when the employee, trying to succeed in a nontraditional environment, is averse to making waves.[57]

Ginsburg ended with a pointed suggestion for Congress: "Once again, the ball is in Congress' court. As in 1991, the Legislature may act to correct this Court's parsimonious reading of Title VII."[58] Congress was receptive: it enacted an amendment to Title VII called the Lilly Ledbetter Fair Pay Act of 2009, which specified that "an unlawful employment practice occurs, with respect to discrimination in compensation in violation of this title ... each time wages, benefits, or other compensation is paid, resulting in whole or in part from such a decision or other practice."[59] The act was the first signed by President Barack Obama upon taking office in 2009.

Although Justice O'Connor, rather than Justice Ginsburg, led the way in shaping the Court's abortion jurisprudence, Ginsburg took over that role after O'Connor had retired, but with a crucial difference. While O'Connor had most often been in the majority, the changes in Court personnel that came with President George W. Bush's appointments of Chief Justice Roberts and Justice Alito to replace Chief Justice Rehnquist and Justice O'Connor, Ginsburg was forced to pen dissents.

Her stirring dissent in *Carhart v. Gonzalez*[60] ("*Carhart II*") is a prime example. Justice Kennedy authored the Court's 5–4 decision in *Carhart II*, citing the government's interest in protecting fetal life to uphold Congress's Partial-Birth Abortion Act despite its failure to include an exception protecting the woman's health. He distinguished the Court's prior decision in *Stenberg v. Carhart*,[61] which had invalidated a similar Nebraska statute (over his dissent) because the act prohibited only intact dilation and evacuation (D&E), leaving available dilation and extraction (D&X) in which the fetus was dismembered, thus protecting the woman's health by preserving a safe alternative procedure.

Dissenting, Ginsburg called the decision in *Carhart II* "alarming," saying, "the Court upholds a law that, while doing nothing to 'preserve fetal life,' bars a woman from choosing intact D&E although her doctor 'reasonably believes [that procedure] will best protect [her].'" She dismissed as "reflect[ing] ancient notions about women's place … that have long since been discredited" the Court's concern for the mental and emotional health of women whose doctors might fail to describe the "gruesome" procedure in detail in order to spare their feelings. She singled out for rejection the majority's conclusion that

> while we find no reliable data to measure the phenomenon, it seems unexceptional to conclude some women come to regret the choice they made to abort the infant life they once created and sustained.... The State has an interest in ensuring that such a grave choice is well informed. It is self-evident that a mother who comes to regret her choice to abort must struggle with grief more anguished and sorrow more profound when she learns, only after the event, what she once did not know: that she allowed a doctor to pierce the skull and vacuum the rapidly-developing brain of her unborn child, a child assuming human form.[62]

Ginsburg pointedly observed that the Court had chosen to protect women rather than to require doctors to inform their patients accurately and adequately of the different procedures and their attendant risks. In taking that course, Ginsburg charged, "the Court deprives women of the right to make an autonomous choice, even at the expense of their safety." She concluded, echoing her confirmation testimony, "In candor, the Act, and the Court's defense of it, cannot be understood as anything other than an effort to chip away at a right declared again and again by this Court – and with increasing comprehension of its centrality to women's lives."[63]

Ginsburg's mastery in civil procedure was displayed in three cases the Court handed down between 2010 and 2014, dealing with constitutional limitations

on state-court jurisdiction over nonresident defendants that marked its first rulings in the area since the mid-1980s.[64] Justice Ginsburg, the Court's procedural
expert, wrote the majority opinion or the principal dissent in all three, and she
plainly collaborated with *Professor* Ginsburg in fashioning her approach.

The first was *Goodyear Dunlop Tires v. Brown*,[65] a case concerning "general
jurisdiction" over foreign corporations under which a state court may entertain any and all claims against the defendant if its affiliations with the forum
state are sufficiently continuous and systematic. The second, in which she
dissented, was *J. McIntyre Machinery, Ltd., v. Nicastro*,[66] a case involving "specific jurisdiction" which is limited to the adjudication of issues arising from
or connected with the very controversy that gave rise to the litigation. The
third case, *Daimler AG v. Bauman*,[67] written in 2014 by Justice Ginsburg for a
Court unanimous in denying jurisdiction, also featured an opinion by Justice
Sotomayor concurring in the judgment, while disagreeing with "the path the
Court takes to arrive at that result."[68]

Dunlop Tires arose from a bus accident outside Paris, France, that caused the
death of two thirteen-year-old boys from North Carolina. Their parents, alleg-
ing that the accident was caused by a defective tire manufactured in Turkey at
the plant of a foreign subsidiary of Goodyear USA, filed a wrongful death suit
for damages in North Carolina against Goodyear USA and its subsidiaries in
Turkey, Luxembourg, and France. The foreign subsidiaries objected to North
Carolina's assertion of jurisdiction over them. Reversing the judgment of the
North Carolina Supreme Court, which had upheld jurisdiction, the Supreme
Court ruled that "foreign subsidiaries of a United States parent corporation
[are not] amenable to suit in state court on claims unrelated to any activity of
the subsidiaries in the forum State."[69]

Reviewing the Court's earlier decisions on general jurisdiction, Ginsburg
thus summarized the typical cases fitting that category: "For an individual,
the paradigm forum for the exercise of general jurisdiction is the individual's
domicile; for a corporation, it is an equivalent place, one in which the corporation is fairly regarded as at home."[70] Noting that unlike the parent company,
Goodyear USA, which did not contest jurisdiction over it, the foreign subsidiaries "are not registered to do business in North Carolina ... have no place
of business, employees, or bank accounts in North Carolina ... do not design,
manufacture, or advertise their products in North Carolina ... and they do
not solicit business in North Carolina or themselves sell or ship tires to North
Carolina."[71] Summing up what this absence of affiliation meant, Ginsburg
observed that petitioners are in no sense "at home" in North Carolina. Their
attenuated connections to the state fall far short of "the continuous and systematic general business contacts" necessary to empower North Carolina to

entertain suit against them on claims unrelated to anything that connects them to the state.[72]

In *McIntyre*, there were more connections between the British manufacturer corporation and the plaintiff's injury in New Jersey than there had been in *Goodyear Tires*, but New Jersey's contacts were still held insufficient to justify jurisdiction. Unlike its unanimous decision in *Goodyear Tires*, however, the Court split 4-2-3 in *McIntyre*. Justice Kennedy's plurality opinion for himself and three others stated that McIntyre had not "engaged in conduct purposefully directed at New Jersey" in spite of the fact that it had manufactured and sold to plaintiff's employer through a U.S. distributor the scrap metal machine that injured the plaintiff in New Jersey. He reasoned that although McIntyre's activities, including the sale of its machines to a U.S. distributor and attendance at several trade shows in states other than New Jersey, "may reveal an intent to serve the U.S. market, ... they do not show that J. McIntyre purposefully availed itself of the New Jersey market."[73]

Justices Breyer and Alito concurred in the judgment, but not in the plurality's reasoning, noting that "on the record present here, resolving this case requires no more than adhering to our precedents." Doing so yielded the conclusion that the plaintiff had not proven his case because he had not shown that McIntyre had "purposefully availed itself of the privilege of conducting activities within New Jersey, or that it delivered its goods in the stream of commerce with the expectation that they will be purchased by New Jersey users," adding that the Court, in earlier separate opinions, "has strongly suggested that a single sale of a product in a State does not constitute an adequate basis for asserting jurisdiction over an out-of-state defendant, even if that defendant places his goods in the stream of commerce, fully aware (and hoping) that such a sale will take place."[74] The concurring justices refused to agree either with "the plurality's seemingly strict no-jurisdiction rule" or with "the absolute approach adopted by the New Jersey Supreme Court ... [under which] a producer is subject to jurisdiction for a products-liability action so long as it 'knows or reasonably should know that its products are distributed through a nationwide distribution system that *might* lead to those products being sold in any of the fifty states.'"[75]

Justice Ginsburg, joined by Justices Sotomayor and Kagan, ridiculed the plurality's opinion in two scathing opening paragraphs:

> A foreign industrialist seeks to develop a market in the United States for machines it manufactures. It hopes to derive substantial revenue from sales it makes to United States purchasers. Where in the United States buyers reside does not matter to this manufacturer. Its goal is simply to sell as much as it can, wherever it can. It excludes no region or State from the market it wishes

to reach. But, all things considered, it prefers to avoid products liability litigation in the United States. To that end, it engages a U.S. distributor to ship its machines stateside. Has it succeeded in escaping personal jurisdiction in a State where one of its products is sold and causes injury or even death to a local user?

Under this Court's pathmarking precedent[s], ... one would expect the answer to be unequivocally, "No." But instead, six Justices of this Court, in divergent opinions, tell us that the manufacturer has avoided the jurisdiction of our state courts, except perhaps in States where its products are sold in sizeable quantities. Inconceivable as it may have seemed yesterday, the splintered majority today "turn[s] the clock back to the days before modern long-arm statutes when a manufacturer, to avoid being haled into court where a user is injured, need only Pilate-like wash its hands of a product by having independent distributors market it.[76]

Ginsburg concluded on a hopeful note: "While I dissent from the Court's judgment, I take heart that the plurality opinion does not speak for the Court, for that opinion would take a giant step away from the 'notions of fair play and substantial justice' underlying [long-standing precedent] *International Shoe* [*v. Washington*, 326 U.S. 310, 316 (1945)]."[77]

Daimler AG v. Bauman[78] was a suit brought in the Federal District Court for the Northern District of California by citizens and residents of Argentina against a German public stock company to recover for human rights violations that took place entirely outside the United States. The Court unanimously held that California lacked jurisdiction over the nonresident defendant. In response to Justice Sotomayor's concurring opinion, Justice Ginsburg undertook to provide a comprehensive analysis of the Court's personal jurisdiction precedents from 1877 to 1952, beginning with the strict territorial rule of *Pennoyer v. Neff*,[79] through the "canonical opinion in this area" that established a more qualitative approach in specific jurisdiction cases, *International Shoe v. Washington*,[80] and finally focusing on the post-*International Shoe* "textbook case of general jurisdiction appropriately exercised over a foreign corporation that has not consented to suit in the forum," *Perkins v. Benguet Consolidated Mining Co.*[81] Her conclusion was straightforward:

> General and specific jurisdiction have followed markedly different trajectories post-*International Shoe*. Specific jurisdiction has been cut loose from *Pennoyer*'s sway, but we have declined to stretch general jurisdiction beyond limits traditionally recognized.[82]

Like a patient classroom teacher justifying her reasoning to a doubting student, Ginsburg painstakingly explained how her position in *Daimler* was consistent with precedent and supported by jurisdictional policy, devoting four lengthy footnotes to responding in detail to Sotomayor's objections.[83] Needless to say, Ginsburg's careful analysis of the Court's entire personal jurisdiction output in *Goodyear Tire* and *Daimler* provides a tour de force for current Civil Procedure teachers and goes far to marginalize the plurality's opinion in *Nicastro*, which she cited only once in *Daimler*, and then only to her own dissent (which Sotomayor had joined).

Justice Ginsburg's collaboration with Professor Ginsburg is well illustrated by these six examples: Justice Ginsburg clarifies the law and often breaks new ground – especially in the *VMI* case, where she led the Court to adopt a higher, "skeptical scrutiny" standard of review for constitutional sex discrimination cases – and Professor Ginsburg places those decisions in precedential context and lays the foundation for building upon them in future cases. In this way, her work is reminiscent of that done earlier by a law professor turned state court judge: Chief Justice Roger J. Traynor of the California Supreme Court. In the days before computer-assisted legal research, his opinions went well beyond what was absolutely necessary to decide the particular dispute before him, instead organizing the common law field it represented, citing relevant supporting cases from a multitude of other states, distinguishing those opposed to his result, and in the process clarified the law for other courts, law professors, and law students. A particularly significant example of his influence on the academy lies in his collaboration with Professor Brainerd Currie in the development of Currie's "governmental interest" analysis to choice of law.[84] Here, as elsewhere, his opinions became classics of the genre and found their way into law school casebooks in many fields. Similarly, Ginsburg's *VMI* opinion has been seen as pivotal in discussions of constitutional law, sex-based discrimination, feminist legal theory, education and the law, same-sex marriage, and military law, among others. WestLaw's list of the cases, administrative rulings, and secondary sources that cite *VMI* contained 5,166 listings on October 21, 2014.

Ginsburg's dissents featured here were all written after she became the senior liberal justice who decides, in cases where the four liberals oppose the five conservatives, which of the four should have the responsibility of writing the liberal dissent. As Professor Garrett Epps recently pointed out, "the purpose of such a dissent is to discredit the majority's reasoning and offer future courts grounds to distinguish or overrule the case. Ginsburg often assigns that duty to herself; her major dissents are masterpieces of the genre."[85] Those purposes also make her dissents valuable to law professors and law students. Her dissents in *Carhart II* and *Ledbetter* have already been recognized as influential. I have no doubt that her dissent in *Daimler* will be so recognized as well.

CONCLUSION: GINSBURG'S COMBINED INSTITUTIONAL ROLES AS A
LAW PROFESSOR AND AS THE SECOND WOMAN JUSTICE

Professor Ginsburg's scholarship and advocacy in the 1970s guided the Court
to a new interpretation of the Equal Protection Clause in its application to
claims of sex-based discrimination. As a justice, she has strengthened that
interpretation and expanded it to other areas. Like Justice Thurgood Marshall
before her, Ginsburg understands the perspectives of individuals seeking to
overcome barriers to full citizenship. In her life as a law professor she set an
example of the possibility of melding scholarship and inspirational classroom
teaching with real-world advocacy. During her first thirteen years as a justice,
she helped the Court develop more progressive positions on many issues. In
her fourteenth year, with Chief Justice Roberts and Justice Alito providing a
new conservative majority, she has become the conscience of the Court on
many of those same issues. Her womanhood continues to inspire other women
to believe in and act upon the possibility of great achievements, but her lasting
jurisprudential contributions to the nation and the world rest not on her sex
but on her thoroughly documented and carefully articulated opinions.

3

Before *Frontiero* There Was *Reed*:
Ruth Bader Ginsburg and the Constitutional
Transformation of the Twentieth Century

Linda K. Kerber

What's fair? The cries of the playground – "that's fair," "that's not fair" – echo throughout our adult lives. Sometimes an entire society's understanding of what's fair shifts in a decade, a year, even a single day. Children of Jehovah's Witnesses refuse to salute the flag in school and change the way a nation views the First Amendment.[1] Oliver Brown thinks it's unfair that his daughter can't attend her neighborhood school. Rosa Parks refuses to give up her seat on a Montgomery bus. Together they change definitions of what counts as equality.[2] Sometimes you go to sleep one night, and when you wake up, the rules have changed. That happened on November 22, 1971, when the U.S. Supreme Court ruled for the first time that arbitrary discrimination on the basis of sex could be a denial of equal protection of the laws.

The case that triggered this shift was a modest one. It came from a small state (Idaho) and involved hardly any money ($930, which lawyers' fees completely consumed). To most people, the dispute seemed merely a family squabble, hardly worth the expensive attention it would get. It is the rare constitutional law casebook in which it figures in more than a footnote. Yet Sally Reed's complaint was far from trivial. It disrupted well-established rules of fairness and spurred broad social transformation in the ways that both men and women make some of the most important choices in their lives.

In the usual telling, women enter the narrative of U.S. constitutional history when it touches on the right to vote: when the Seneca Falls 1848 "Declaration of Sentiments" claimed for women the right to vote; when the word "male" was placed in the Fourteenth Amendment in 1868; when the word *sex* was omitted from the Fifteenth Amendment in 1870; and when the U.S. Supreme Court ruled in 1875 that women had no constitutional right to vote.[3] Then follows the long struggle for a federal suffrage amendment, resulting in the passage of the Nineteenth Amendment in 1920. After a gap, the story picks up with the efforts to pass the Equal Rights Amendment in the 1970s and early 1980s. All this is appropriate and not wrong.

But there is a richer and far more complex story of women's relationship to the Constitution. It starts at the beginning, when the original Constitution of 1789 promised that "the Citizens of each State shall be entitled to all the privileges and immunities of Citizens in the several states."[4] Who are citizens? What are their privileges and immunities? How do we know when a privilege or immunity is denied? The Constitution doesn't specify. It awaits our interpretation.

Long after 1868, when the Fourteenth Amendment explicitly promised all persons "equal protection of the laws,"[5] the principle of equality needed defending. On what terms can a person claim to have been denied equal protection of the laws? In 1873, the U.S. Supreme Court told Myra Bradwell that denying her the right to practice law was not a denial of the equal protection of the laws.[6] In 1875, the Court unanimously told Virginia Minor that denying her the right to vote was not a denial of the equal protection of the laws.[7] And in 1970, the Idaho Supreme Court told Sally Reed that denying her the right to serve as executor of her young son's estate was not a denial of the equal protection of the laws.[8] But as it turned out, Reed's case was a watershed moment.

The Reeds were a family of modest resources. Cecil Reed, a mechanic, worked for the state highway department. His wife, Sally, had more education; she worked white-collar jobs as a secretary or bookkeeper. When the Reeds divorced in 1958, Sally was awarded custody of their adopted son, Richard. But when Richard grew into a rambunctious teenager, breaking curfew and generally getting into trouble, the county court removed him from Sally's care, placed him briefly in the local Children's Home, and then sent him to live with Cecil. In March 1967, sixteen-year-old Richard committed suicide in the basement of his father's house using one of his father's guns.

The estate Richard Reed left behind included his beloved cornet – he'd planned to study music in college – and the small savings account his mother had set up for his college education. Sally Reed began the process of administering the estate – she had, after all, established the account – and petitioned the probate court to name her its administrator. Cecil Reed also applied to the probate court to administer the estate, telling Sally that she was "too dumb" to handle it.

Under an Idaho law dating back to 1864, when a person died without a will, the probate court was directed to assign an administrator in the following order: surviving husband or wife, children, father or mother, brothers or sisters. (Until 1919, married women were excluded from this list.) The law also provided that "of the several persons equally entitled, males must be preferred to females"[9] – or, as one legal wit later put it, "All people are equal, but male people are more equal than female people." Because Sally could not show that her ex-husband was incompetent, the probate court promptly appointed Cecil administrator of his son's estate. Idaho's rules were not peculiar; similar statutes were in force in Arizona, Nevada, South Dakota, Wyoming, and the District of Columbia.

Sally Reed was outraged. Hindsight makes it easy to see that the ingredients for her outrage were easily at hand. For the previous four years, women throughout the country had been naming the discrimination they faced. In 1963, Congress had decided that men and women hired for the same job should receive the same pay. (As one judge said famously when considering the differences between maids and janitors, "Dusting is dusting is dusting.")[10] Also in 1963, the President's Commission on the Status of Women (whose honorary chair was Eleanor Roosevelt) published a stunning report, outlining the disparities in treatment men and women received throughout American law and society. And finally that year, Betty Friedan published her best-selling manifesto, *The Feminine Mystique*, which exposed as degrading to women a wide range of behaviors once seen as mere courtesy and innocent social practice.[11] Then in 1964, after what can only be described as a quirky congressional debate, Title VII of the Civil Rights Act became law. This statute listed sex along with race as inherited characteristics that could not be used to exclude people from jobs (not even to "protect" them from overwork).

Sally Reed had never counted herself a feminist, but living in Boise she was surrounded by the sounds of the women's liberation movement. In Boise (as throughout the country), pregnant teachers were complaining that they were being forced to take unpaid leave as soon as their pregnancies became discernible; girls were resentful of rules that barred them from taking part in programs open only to boys; and women student-athletes were grumbling that they had to hold bake sales to raise travel money while the travel expenses of collegiate male teams were being paid for with student activity fees (to which women were required to contribute). Rules like these had long been considered fair – an aspect of the social structure that, it was believed, privileged girls and women by protecting them from the competition of a "man's world." By the late 1960s, though, what most women considered fair was changing.

Sally Reed decided to get a new lawyer. Friends brought her to Allen Derr – forty-three years old, in general practice for a dozen years. Derr needed no persuading. As a young marine serving in China late in World War II, he had been troubled by the discrimination he saw practiced against African American corpsmen. Back in civilian life, he encountered even more discrimination while working as assistant executive secretary of his college fraternity, Tau Kappa Epsilon (TKE). "We had chapters who wanted to take in colored pledges," he recalled; "we had alumni who disagreed." During the early 1950s, Derr spent four years traveling to TKE chapters around the country, working to make sure that chapters could "pledge who they wanted to pledge." In the process, he found himself fighting racism. Thinking about his eleven-year-old daughter, he remembered later, it became easy for him to transfer those feelings to the cause of women's civil rights.[12]

Arguing that the 1864 probate law violated promises of equal protection of the laws in Idaho's state constitution and also in the Fourteenth Amendment, Derr helped Sally Reed appeal the probate court's decision to Idaho's Fourth Judicial District Court. Agreeing with Derr's argument, the judges there sent the case back to the probate court for a new determination on the merits of the issue. (The probate court would have to decide, for example, whether Sally's bookkeeping experience made her a more suitable administrator than Cecil.) But Cecil appealed the district court ruling to the Idaho Supreme Court, which ruled unanimously in his favor. "Philosophically," the decision read, "it can be argued that the [statute does] discriminate against women on the basis of sex. However, *nature itself has established the distinction....* The legislature ... evidently concluded that in general men are better qualified to act as an administrator than are women."[13]

It was now February 1970. Thirty-eight-year-old Ruth Bader Ginsburg had just taken up an appointment at Columbia Law School that allowed her to spend half her time leading the American Civil Liberties Union's new Women's Rights Project (WRP), whose basic principle was that discrimination on the basis of sex was neither benign nor harmless.

Ginsburg prepared a short list of four classic cases, ranging over a century, which the WRP was committed to overturning: *Bradwell v. Illinois* (1872),[14] which had denied a married woman the right to practice law; *Muller v. Oregon* (1908),[15] which had justified protective labor legislation on the grounds of women's maternal function; *Goesaert v. Cleary* (1948),[16] which had upheld a state's exclusion of women entirely from a line of work; and the recently decided *Hoyt v. Florida* (1961),[17] upholding the near complete exclusion of women from jury service.

The Fourteenth Amendment, ratified in 1868 in the aftermath of the Civil War, had promised "equal protection of the laws" to "all persons." But every time a woman had challenged disparities of treatment based solely on sex – from Myra Bradwell in 1873, challenging Illinois's exclusion of women from the practice of law, to Gwendolyn Hoyt in 1961, challenging Florida's opt-in law for women's jury service – the Supreme Court had responded that different treatment was reasonable, based (as the Idaho Supreme Court had said) on distinctions that "nature itself has established." The Court's decisions all reflected what most American believed to be the common sense of the matter.

Legally, the decisions were based on the English law of domestic relations – and the elaborate system of coverture (the legal state women entered upon marriage) that flowed from it – which men of the founding generation had made the ominous choice to adopt for the United States virtually unchanged. As a result, the new republic was committed to different systems of fairness for men and women (and especially married women). Beginning with the premise that, from the moment of marriage, husbands controlled the physical bodies of their wives, the original law of domestic relations placed sharp limits on the extent to which married women could own property and make economic and social choices for themselves.[18] Idaho's probate law, like Florida's jury service law, was one of many remnants of this system still in force throughout the United States in 1971. Given this history, prospects were grim. Ginsburg recalled, "the possibility of getting a favorable decision seemed nil. The Supreme Court had held the line so long."[19]

Nevertheless, she hoped for a chance to destabilize one of the four classic decisions. She especially wanted the opportunity to challenge the exclusion of women from jury service. "It has," she mused, "both the rights aspect and the obligation."[20] As it turned out, however, the *Reed* case presented itself first. When Ginsburg spotted Derr's appeal to the Supreme Court, she saw a way to challenge all four cases at once, and she pounced. ACLU director Melvin Wulf joined in enthusiastically, and Derr agreed to accept the ACLU's help, provided that he conduct the oral argument if the Court agreed to hear the case.

The Court did agree to hear the case, and, on Tuesday, October 19, 1971, Derr opened his oral argument with a broad request: "We are here today to ask you to do something that this Court has never done since the Fourteenth Amendment was adopted in 1868, and that is to declare a State statute that distinguishes between males and females as unconstitutional. We feel that this case could have a significance for women somewhat akin to what *Brown v. Board of Education* had for the Colored People."[21]

Derr directly implicated the two classic cases of *Muller v. Oregon* and *Goesaert v. Cleary*. For more than a century, Derr argued, discrimination on the basis of sex had been respectable so long as some legitimate public interest was invoked (as the protection of women's reproductive health had been invoked in *Muller* in 1908). *Muller* and similar cases had sustained the situation, Derr insisted, "that wherever there has been a classification on the basis of sex, anything goes."[22]

Derr also raised the 1948 case of *Goesaert v. Cleary*. That case concerned a Michigan law, enacted at the urging of an all-male bartender's union, that forbade a woman to tend bar unless she was the wife or daughter of the owner. Margaret Goesaert, the widow of a bar owner, had brought the case because she couldn't sustain the family business unless she and her daughter Valentine continued to tend bar as they had when Valentine's father was still alive. The salary they would have to pay a male bartender was more than the small tavern could afford. The Michigan law thus burdened their occupational choice and denied them equal protection of the law. They were joined by twenty-six other women bar owners or barmaids, and represented by Anne R. Davidow, an experienced feminist and labor litigator. Yet Justice Felix Frankfurter believed, as he remarked in his opinion for the Court ruling against them, Michigan had a legitimate interest in keeping order in bars, and the Court did not think it was irrational for the state legislature to believe that "bartending by women may ... give a rise to moral and social problems" because the practice lacked "the protecting oversight" provided by a man. (Frankfurter chose to ignore a deposition submitted along with Goesaert's brief in which another woman bar owner reported that male bartenders "would drink upon the premises, and she has not had any of this difficulty with a barmaid.") This test of "rationality," Derr argued, was for women "almost as bad as the separate-but-equal test of *Plessy v. Ferguson*, holding back women ... from their entitlements under the Fourteenth Amendment, the Equal Protection Clause."[23]

Ginsburg, Wulf, and Derr were hoping the Court would write a decision broad enough to overturn not only *Muller v. Oregon* and *Goesaert v. Cleary* but also the more recent 1961 opinion handed down in *Hoyt v. Florida*. In that case, the Court upheld rules adopted by the state of Florida that made it far less likely for women than men to be called for jury service on the grounds that a "woman is still regarded as the center of home and family life."[24] The Court thus denied murder defendant Gwendolyn Hoyt a jury drawn from a full cross section of the community. In doing so, the Court sustained the practice of defining a woman's civic obligations primarily in terms of her service to her husband.

Derr was backed by a formidable eighty-eight-page brief, carefully prepared by Ginsburg and Wulf, that laid out what would become the standard line of argument against discrimination on the basis of sex. Unafraid to invoke feminism, Ginsburg and Wulf wrote that "a new appreciation of women's place has been generated in the United States.... Courts and legislatures have begun to recognize the claim of women to full membership in the class 'persons' entitled to due process guarantees of life and liberty and equal protection of the laws." Leaning on Pauli Murray's classic essay "Jane Crow and the Law," Ginsburg emphasized the similarities between discrimination on the basis of race and on the basis of sex: both misused "congenital and unalterable biological traits of birth" to justify prejudice. "Once thought normal, proper and ordained in the very nature of things," the brief continued, "sex discrimination may soon be seen as a sham, not unlike that perpetrated in the name of racial superiority ... and based on inaccurate stereotypes of the capacities and sensibilities of women."[25] Between Ginsburg's brief and Derr's argument, the team hoped to entice the Court into a major erosion of its antiquated decisions on sex-based discrimination.

The momentum seemed to be with them. The New York City Human Rights Commission filed an amicus brief in *Reed*, noting the flood of unfairness complaints it had been receiving from women and urging the Court to declare sex discrimination unconstitutional. It argued, in other words, that what New York City women now considered fair had changed. During the fall of 1971, while the justices deliberated Sally Reed's appeal, the Senate Judiciary Committee took up the Equal Rights Amendment (ERA) already approved by the House. The text of the ERA was simple: "Equality of rights under the law shall not be denied or abridged by the United States or by any state on account of sex." North Carolina senator Sam Ervin's energetic efforts to rewrite it into inadequacy stirred debate over the amendment.[26]

Meanwhile, courts had begun to question the basic traditions of coverture that still applied to women. In 1960, the U.S. Supreme Court had held in *Wyatt v. United States* that, under certain circumstances, a wife could be compelled to testify against her husband.[27] Lower courts, such as the Fourth Judicial District Court in Idaho that had found for Sally Reed, also were reconsidering old assumptions. In 1968, courts in Pennsylvania and Connecticut invalidated sentences for women that were longer than those given men who had committed the same crimes; in 1969, a federal district court in Kentucky held that women could not be excluded from juries even if discussions in jury rooms were likely to embarrass them; in 1970, Faith Seidenberg and Karen DeCrow of the National Organization for Women's New York City chapter persuaded a federal district court that it was indeed unconstitutional for bars to exclude women patrons who were unaccompanied by men (a practice originally intended to keep out prostitutes, because it was believed that only a prostitute would enter a bar without a male escort). And only a few months before the Supreme Court began its consideration of *Reed*, the California Supreme Court, urged by Wendy Webster Williams, then a young law clerk and a recent graduate of the University of California's law school, and persuaded by a feisty brief drafted by law students Mary Dunlap and Margaret Kemp, overturned a *Goesaert*-style law forbidding women to tend bar.[28]

Given these developments, few legal arguments remained for Cecil Reed's attorney, Charles Stout, to make. He could only splutter that Idaho women were voters (they had been since 1896), and if they didn't like the probate law, they could elect new legislators to change it:

> The legislators in enacting this statute knew that men were as a rule more conversant with business affairs than were women.... One has but to look around and it is still a matter of common knowledge that women still are not engaged in politics, the professions, business, or industry to the extent that men are.... In all species ... nature protects the female and the offspring to propagate the species and not because the female is inferior. The pill and the conception of children in a laboratory and incubation in a test tube, if this occurs, ... cannot get away from this prime necessity if the race is to be continued, and there will still remain a difference and the necessity for a different treatment.[29]

On November 22, 1971, though, the Supreme Court decided differently. The *Reed* ruling was unanimous: Idaho's preference for males was arbitrary, and mere administrative convenience was not sufficient to justify the discrimination. The Court sent the case back to Idaho to be decided on the merits, but a new trial was avoided when Sally Reed agreed to serve as a co-executor with Cecil. More important, Ginsburg would later observe, the *Reed* decision "was the turning-point case" – the first time the Supreme Court sustained a woman's complaint that she had suffered unconstitutional gender discrimination.[30] "Before that," Ruth Bader Ginsburg observed recently, "the Supreme Court never saw a sex classification it didn't like."[31]

Yet much of what the Court thought was left to inference. In its ruling, the Court never mentioned *Goesaert* or *Hoyt*, nor did it offer comprehensive principles for the decision. *Reed* was not the sweeping triumph for which Ginsburg and Wulf had hoped. Indeed, the California Supreme Court had already gone much further in *Sail'er Inn*, unanimously declaring discrimination on the basis of sex as suspect as discrimination practiced on the basis of race. After *Reed*, many sex-based preferences fell, but because *Reed* offered no broader mandate, more than four decades of often bitter argument have followed, with legislators and courts having to define what constitutes sex discrimination point by point, issue by issue, case by case.

Reed did make it more difficult for states to ground their laws, and Americans to ground their social practices, in stereotypes about men's and women's differences. No longer could it be assumed that men had "a better head for numbers," that women were too weak to be police officers, or even that workmen's compensation death benefits should automatically go to surviving wives but not to surviving husbands (unless they could show they had been economically dependent on their wives). At the time *Reed* was decided, a man charged with rape in most states could defend himself by claiming that the victim had dressed provocatively; no state yet believed it was possible to charge a married man with the rape of his wife; in five states, if a wife committed adultery, her husband could kill her lover and plead – it was considered a reasonable defense – that the murder had been a crime of passion.

In the next few years, Ruth Bader Ginsburg would offer a dazzling series of arguments in what are now regarded as a classic series of Supreme Court decisions establishing a simple principle: even when stereotypes about women's behavior might accurately predict what might be expected from a *majority* of women, those women who did not fit the stereotype ought not be ignored or unprotected. Indeed, "archaic and overbroad" generalizations about women regularly harm men whose own behavior or situation do not fit expected stereotypes about what could be expected of men. Among these cases would be *Frontiero v. Richardson* (1973),[32] in which the Court's opinion was wide ranging, although some of the justices wanted to wait to see whether the ERA passed; and *Weinberger v. Weisenfeld* (1975),[33] a case to which Ginsburg would often refer proudly, in which she persuaded a unanimous Supreme Court to agree that a provision of the Social Security Act that offered widow's benefits to women with small children but ignored widowers with small children was based on the stereotype that imagined only bereft mothers, not bereft fathers. The principle that stereotypes could not be used as shorthand to deny equal protection continued to be central to subsequent equal-protection decisions, including *United States v. Virginia* (1996)[34] and *Nevada Department of Natural Resources v. Hibbs* (2003).[35]

One would think that the principle would be, by now, the common sense of the matter. But as late as 2010, when the Court heard argument in *Flores-Villar v. United States*, testing asymmetrical requirements for the nonmarital children born abroad to U.S.-citizen men and women, several justices seemed unconvinced. "What separates a stereotype from a reality?" Justice Antonin Scalia asked Flores-Villar's attorney. "Do you say it is not true that if there is an … illegitimate child, it is much more likely that the woman will end up caring for it than that the father would?" The attorney embarked on a complex explanation; Justice Ginsburg jumped in to clarify, for all the world as though she were back in her classroom at Rutgers Law School in 1971: "There are people who don't fit the mold. So a stereotype is true for maybe the majority of women. [But that is not to say] this is the way women are, this is the way men are."[36]

Although it has taken decades to litigate these and similar issues, they are the easy ones. More difficult have been those cases in which the situations of the men and women concerned were not precisely the same and the matters to be decided involve not only equality but what the law calls "equity" – that is, fairness when the circumstances of the parties differ. Questions of equity have been painfully difficult to resolve, because the answer to the question "What's fair?" is rarely obvious.

Only slowly have gay men and lesbians been included in the legal understanding of equal protection. The first state statutes prohibiting employment discrimination on the basis of sexual orientation were passed in Wisconsin in 1982; at this writing, twenty-nine states and the federal government still lack such prohibitions.[37] In the mid-1990s, as states were being asked to recognize civil unions and same-sex marriage, Congress passed the Defense of Marriage Act (DOMA), specifying that when the word "marriage" was used in any federal statute or regulation, it was to be interpreted to mean "only a legal union between one man and one woman as husband and wife, and the word 'spouse' refers only to a person of the opposite sex who is a husband or a wife."[38] Advocates of the change insisted that they were stabilizing linguistics and protecting traditional understandings of marriage, dating to time immemorial, from gay and lesbian disruption. They did not understand themselves to be undermining the general principle of equal protection when they linked marriage to heterosexuality. They understood gay men to be essentially different from heterosexual men; lesbians essentially different from heterosexual women. At worst, they understood themselves to be subjecting gays and lesbians to legal inconvenience.

But when Hilary and Julie Goodridge and six other same-sex couples sued the Massachusetts Department of Public Health for denying them marriage licenses, Chief Justice Margaret Marshall, writing for the Massachusetts Supreme Judicial Court, went straight to the question of whether same-sex couples denied marriage had also been denied equal protection.[39] As Marshall made those arguments, she quoted Justice Ginsburg in *United States v. Virginia* to the effect that the history of constitutional law is itself "the story of the extension of constitutional rights and protections to people once ignored or excluded."[40] Marshall repeatedly invoked historical knowledge and the changes in understandings of the meanings of equal protection and of marriage that have been developed since the founding generation. As Marshall tells the history of marriage in Massachusetts, civil marriage has changed in three major ways since the early republic. First, the rules of coverture, once so controlling, have been broken: "Marriage no longer merges the civil identity of a woman in that of her husband." Second, ideas about what constitutes an appropriate marriage have changed over time: miscegenation statutes have been abolished. Third, children have been unburdened "from the stigma and the disadvantages heretofore attendance upon the status of illegitimacy" and decisions about the best interests of the child no longer turn "on a parent's sexual orientation or marital status."[41] Now that hundreds of state benefits are filtered through marriage, it is no longer reasonable to exclude gay men and lesbians from them.

Marshall acknowledged that the decision to embrace homosexual couples in the same legal space as heterosexual couples "marks a change in the history of our marriage law." Yet in the years since 2003, her reasoning has become common sense: subsequent state supreme courts based their own decisions where Marshall had placed hers – on the principle of equal protection of the law guaranteed in the Fourteenth Amendment and in their own state constitutions.[42]

By the time Edith Windsor turned to the U.S. Supreme Court in 2012, the issue was framed squarely as a matter of equal protection, and the majority opinion written by Justice Kennedy, which Ruth Bader Ginsburg joined, devoted three pages to listing some of the most grievous burdens that DOMA placed on same-sex couples.[43] The descent of *Windsor* from *Reed* is not hard to trace. After *Windsor*, state bans on same-sex marriage have continued to fall: federal judges in Utah, Oklahoma, Texas, Virginia, and Michigan ruled them unconstitutional as a matter of equal protection. (At this writing, same-sex marriage is legal in nineteen states and the District of Columbia.) Today's widespread support for gay rights is grounded in Ginsburg's career-long expansive redefinition of equal protection to embrace sex and gender equality.

Another large question remains: How does "equal protection of the laws" apply to reproductive rights and access to abortion? Justice Harry Blackmun grounded *Roe v. Wade* in a right of privacy, balanced against a compelling state interest in the health of the fetus in the late stages of pregnancy.[44] It has been left to Justice Ginsburg (and Justices Brennan, Douglas, and Thurgood Marshall before her) to give abortion rights an equal-protection context: pregnancy is woman-specific. Is pregnancy leave vacation time? Is it sick leave? Is the denial of insurance benefits for work loss resulting from a normal pregnancy sex discrimination? Or does the commitment to equal protection require the law to make it possible for women to be both parents and workers on the same terms as men? In 1974, dissenting in *Geduldig v. Aiello*, Justices Brennan, Douglas, and Marshall insisted that California's failure to cover pregnancy-related disabilities threatened "to return men and women to a time when 'traditional' equal protection analysis sustained legislative classifications that treated differently members of a particular sex solely because of their sex," and they cited three of Ginsburg's benchmark cases: *Muller, Goesaert,* and *Hoyt*.[45]

But resistance to recognizing access to abortion – a medical procedure that men do not need – as a matter of equal protection (men confront no similar law limiting their choice of medical procedures) continues and strengthens. Forty years after *Roe*, states have enacted more than 200 statutes limiting abortion, such as Oklahoma's mandatory pre-abortion sonograms, and outright prohibition, such as North Dakota's statute forbidding abortion when the fetal heartbeat can be detected (within six to eight weeks of conception). Nearly 90 percent of U.S. counties lack an abortion provider. And under the federal Affordable Care Act, health plans cannot be required to include abortion coverage.[46]

The principle of equal protection lurks within every abortion argument. The failure to ground the decriminalization of abortion in equal protection and to specify the end of coverture has had major consequences. Nowhere is the argument that access to abortion is a matter of equal protection made more eloquently than in Ruth Bader Ginsburg's 2007 dissent in *Carhart v. Gonzales*.[47] The Court supported a federal ban on late-term abortion – a ban opposed by the American College of Obstetricians and Gynecologists, which found the procedure necessary and proper in certain cases, and a ban that lacked an exception for the health of the mother. Justice Ginsburg – who was joined in dissent by Justices John Paul Stevens, David Souter, and Stephen Breyer – took the unusual step of reading her emphatic dissent from the bench. She began by restating *Roe*'s promise, emphasizing not only "the right of the woman to choose to have an abortion before viability," but also that the "State's legitimate interests … in protecting … the life of the fetus that may become a child" were limited by its interests "in protecting *the health of the woman.*" Relying on misleading information about the risks, "the Court deprives women of the right to make an autonomous choice, even at the expense of their safety." And she asserted that what is "at stake in cases challenging abortion restrictions is a woman's control over her own destiny."[48]

She ended by citing lines from the *Hoyt* decision that had been rejected by the Court in *Planned Parenthood of Southeastern Pennsylvania v. Casey*:

"There was a time, not so long ago, when women were regarded as the center of home and family life, with attendant special responsibilities that precluded full and independent status under the Constitution." In the *Casey* decision, the Court made clear that these views "are no longer consistent with our understanding of the family, the individual, and the Nation. Their ability to realize their full potential, the Court [had] recognized, is intimately connected to "their ability to control their reproductive lives." Thus legal challenges to undue restrictions on abortion procedures do not seek to vindicate some generalized notion of privacy; rather they center on a woman's autonomy to determine her life's course, and thus to enjoy equal citizenship stature.[49]

Ginsburg possessed a finely honed appreciation of her own historical debt. On the brief that she filed with the Supreme Court in *Reed*, along with her own name and those of Melvin Wulf and Allen Derr, she placed two more: Dorothy Kenyon, who had been arguing for equal treatment of women since her graduation from New York University School of Law in 1917, and Pauli Murray, the great-granddaughter of both slave and slave master who did as much as anyone of her generation to link sexism with racism. Only the year before, at the age of eighty-two, Kenyon had walked in the New York parade commemorating the fiftieth anniversary of suffrage. She had been offered an open car in which to ride but she insisted on walking; she had wanted the young women "to know I was with them," she told reporters. While Ginsburg was working on the brief, Kenyon was dying of cancer; Pauli Murray would give her eulogy. Neither woman had written a word of the brief, yet it bore their names because Ruth Bader Ginsburg understood more clearly than almost anyone of her time the debt that the women of her generation – and, I would add, our own generations – owed to those of preceding generations. Without their efforts, she would never have been able to challenge successfully a century's worth of law and social practice – a century's misunderstanding of what fairness and equality really mean.

Sally Reed died in 2002, but not before she and Derr had enjoyed a triumphal visit with Ruth Bader Ginsburg in her chambers in the Supreme Court.[50] Reed, Derr, and Ginsburg – along with all the women and men who made the social movement we call Women's Liberation and encouraged Sally Reed to challenge an unjust Idaho law – opened a door, tested a legal argument, and validated a new set of assumptions about what equal protection of the law reasonably means. Ginsburg's brilliant *Reed* brief became a template for many more lawsuits, many more arguments, and much more complex reasoning about the elements of fairness.

4

Struck by Stereotype: Ruth Bader Ginsburg on Pregnancy Discrimination as Sex Discrimination

Neil S. Siegel and Reva B. Siegel

It was always recognition that one thing that conspicuously distinguishes women from men is that only women become pregnant; and if you subject a woman to disadvantageous treatment on the basis of her pregnant status, which was what was happening to Captain Struck, you would be denying her equal treatment under the law.[1]

INTRODUCTION

This chapter invites consideration of Ruth Bader Ginsburg's 1972 merits brief[2] in *Struck v. Secretary of Defense*.[3] The brief is little known because the Supreme Court of the United States eventually declined to decide the case.[4] But anyone seeking to understand the origins and nature of Justice Ginsburg's views on sex discrimination would be well advised to read this brief. So would anyone interested in deepening an appreciation of how the Constitution speaks to gender equality.

In her capacity as general counsel for the Women's Rights Project of the American Civil Liberties Union, Ginsburg filed the *Struck* brief a little more than a year after the Court decided *Reed v. Reed*[5] but before the Court began to shape liberty and equality doctrine concerning the regulation of pregnant women in cases such as *Roe v. Wade*,[6] *Frontiero v. Richardson*,[7] and *Geduldig v. Aiello*.[8] Ginsburg wrote the brief on behalf of an Air Force officer, Captain Susan Struck, whose pregnancy – and whose refusal on religious grounds to have an abortion – subjected her to automatic discharge from military service.[9]

This chapter revises and updates an essay that was published as Neil S. Siegel & Reva B. Siegel, Struck by Stereotype: Ruth Bader Ginsburg on Pregnancy Discrimination as Sex Discrimination, 59 *Duke L.J.* 771 (2010). We thank Justice Ginsburg for illuminating comments, and Natalie Bedoya and Jennifer Bennett for able research assistance.

The brief demonstrates that along with several other feminist lawyers of the era, Justice Ginsburg has always viewed discrimination against pregnant women as a core case of sex discrimination.[10] In 1972, Ginsburg understood pregnancy discrimination as sex discrimination because she has long viewed laws enforcing sex roles of the separate-spheres tradition as compromising the "equal citizenship stature" of women.[11] One of us has described Justice Ginsburg's commitment to "equal citizenship stature" as the defining characteristic of her inclusive constitutional vision.[12] The *Struck* brief illuminates the origins and contents of this vision.

In the brief, Ginsburg argued that excluding a pregnant woman from the Air Force when men otherwise similarly situated in their capacity or incapacity to work are provided sick leave is a core case of sex discrimination; she argued that the distinction "reflects arbitrary notions of woman's place wholly at odds with contemporary legislative and judicial recognition that individual potential must not be restrained, nor equal opportunity limited, by law-sanctioned stereotypical prejudgments."[13] The brief opened by emphasizing that laws imposing traditional sex roles on pregnant women deny individuals equal opportunity *and* perpetuate the secondary social status of women:

> Heading the list of arbitrary barriers that have plagued women seeking equal opportunity is disadvantaged treatment based on their unique childbearing function. Until very recent years, jurists have regarded any discrimination in the treatment of pregnant women and mothers as "benignly in their favor." But in fact, restrictive rules, and particularly discharge for pregnancy rules, operate as "built-in headwinds" that drastically curtail women's opportunities. Decisions of this Court that span a century have contributed to this anomaly: *presumably well-meaning exaltation of woman's unique role in bearing children has, in effect, restrained women from developing their individual talents and capacities and has impelled them to accept a dependent, subordinate status in society.*[14]

Ginsburg thus argued that traditions of regulating women during pregnancy are not in fact benign but instead play a key role in imposing on women "subordinate" social status.

As this chapter shows, Ginsburg's equal protection argument in *Struck* anticipates views that she would subsequently express on the bench.[15] Prominent among them is her account of intermediate scrutiny for the Court in *United States v. Virginia*.[16] That account requires the judiciary closely to examine laws that classify on the basis of sex but allows government to differentiate between men and women so long as "such classifications [are] not ... used, as they once were, to create or perpetuate the legal, social, and economic inferiority of women."[17]

Ginsburg's understanding of pregnancy discrimination in *Struck* calls into question certain feminist characterizations of her as a proponent of formal equality – a criticism advanced by those who viewed Ginsburg's repeated representation of male plaintiffs in the early sex-discrimination cases as narrowly reflecting a concern with arbitrary sex-based classification only.[18] Rather than expressing a commitment to formal equality, Ginsburg argued that laws differentiating on the basis of sex are unconstitutional when they enforce traditional sex stereotypes because such laws wrongfully restrict individual opportunity and contribute to the subordinate status of women. Ginsburg was able to perceive social subordination in the exclusion of a pregnant woman from military service, even though pregnancy had long been understood as justifying differential treatment of the sexes, because she saw that government regulation was enforcing traditional sex stereotypes.[19]

As interesting and consequential as Ginsburg's own views have been, recovery of the *Struck* brief is even more important for what it illuminates about the present. In the immediate aftermath of *Struck*, the Court acknowledged that pregnancy discrimination might be an invidious expression of sex discrimination but did not seriously consider the account that Ginsburg and other feminist litigators offered of how laws discriminating against pregnant women could enforce traditional sex stereotypes and so deny women the equal protection of the laws.[20] Nor did the Court scrutinize the relationship to which the *Struck* brief pointed – between cases protecting women's right to equal protection and protecting their autonomy in deciding whether to bear children.[21] Decades later, however, through a series of incremental changes that have not yet been fully recognized,[22] the Court began to reason from something like Ginsburg's position without quite embracing it.

Part I recounts the facts of *Struck*. Part II details the arguments Ginsburg made in her merits brief in the case. Part III explores what *Struck* suggests about Ginsburg's views on constitutional equality. Part IV shows that, although the Court did not initially embrace the understanding of pregnancy discrimination that Ginsburg expressed in *Struck*, over time the Court has begun to internalize the concerns of the feminist movement about the stereotyping pregnant women face. The Court has incorporated these concerns into equal protection and due process doctrines regarding the regulation of pregnant women.

I. THE FACTS OF *STRUCK*

The facts of *Struck v. Secretary of Defense* are straightforward.[23] Captain Susan Struck was a career officer in the United States Air Force who served as a nurse in the Vietnam War.[24] In 1970, she became pregnant.[25] She was ordered to an Air Force base in the state of Washington, where a disposition board hearing was held.[26] She declared her intent to give the child up for adoption as soon as she gave birth, and she stated that her accrued leave time of sixty days was more than sufficient to cover the temporary period of disability that she anticipated at the time of childbirth.[27] The Air Force, however, pursuant to a regulation then in effect, gave her this choice: have an abortion on the base or leave the Service.[28] Because Captain Struck was a practicing Roman Catholic, abortion was not an option for her.[29] But neither did she quietly accept the termination of her chosen career.[30] She instead sued to fend off the discharge, securing able representation from lawyers for the American Civil Liberties Union in Washington.

Captain Struck was able to obtain a stay of her discharge each month, but she lost on the merits both in the district court and in the United States Court of Appeals for the Ninth Circuit.[31] In the view of these courts, it was constitutionally irrelevant that no other physical condition occasioning a temporary period of disability – whether a broken leg or drug and alcohol abuse (which might not be temporary) – resulted in mandatory discharge. Nor did it matter that a male officer who participated in conceiving a child was free – indeed, encouraged – to continue his service career as a parent.[32]

The Supreme Court agreed to entertain Captain Struck's claims to constitutional attention. Ginsburg challenged the Air Force regulation at bar as a violation of (1) equal protection, (2) Captain Struck's right to privacy in the conduct of her personal life, and (3) her free exercise of religion.[33] Solicitor General Erwin Griswold was apparently concerned about the government's chances before the Court. As Ginsburg later recounted, "he recommended that the Air Force waive Captain Struck's discharge and abandon its policy of automatically discharging women for pregnancy."[34] The Air Force agreed, and General Griswold moved to dismiss the case as moot.[35]

The Supreme Court never heard oral argument. It elected to vacate the judgment of the Ninth Circuit and remand the case to that court "to consider the issue of mootness in light of the position presently asserted by the Government."[36]

II. GINSBURG'S ARGUMENTS IN *STRUCK*

Ginsburg's *Struck* brief has been neglected[37] not only because the Court did not decide the merits of the case, but also because, shortly thereafter, the justices rejected an equal protection challenge to a pregnancy-discrimination claim.[38] The brief's neglect is unfortunate. Among its other virtues, the *Struck* brief richly illustrates Justice Ginsburg's approach to sex discrimination. During her Supreme Court confirmation hearing, then-Judge Ginsburg sought "to explain how [her] own thinking developed on [the] issue" of sex discrimination. To do so, she recalled Captain Struck's story, "a case involving a woman's choice for birth rather than the termination of her pregnancy."[39] "The *Struck* brief," she recalled, "marks the time when I first thought long and hard about this question [of sex discrimination]."[40]

In the brief, Ginsburg argued that government regulation of pregnant women was presumptively unconstitutional when such regulation enforced the sex roles and stereotypes of the separate-spheres tradition – the familiar structuring of sex roles in which men are expected to perform as breadwinners and women are expected to perform as economically dependent caregivers. Ginsburg challenged the plaintiff's discharge for pregnancy on the grounds that it perpetuated this tradition:

> The central question raised in this case is whether the Air Force, consistent with the equal protection principle inherent in the due process clause of the fifth amendment, may call for immediate discharge of pregnant women officers (whether detection of pregnancy occurs at 8 days or 8 months), unless pregnancy terminates soon after detection, while granting sick leave for all other physical conditions occasioning a period of temporary disability. *It is petitioner's position that this distinction reflects arbitrary notions of woman's place wholly at odds with contemporary legislative and judicial recognition that individual potential must not be restrained, nor equal opportunity limited, by law-sanctioned stereotypical prejudgments.* Captain Struck seeks no favors or special protection. She simply asks to be judged on the basis of her individual capacities and qualifications, and not on the basis of characteristics assumed to typify pregnant women.[41]

As Ginsburg presented it, the government's discrimination against pregnant officers was a paradigmatic case of the sex-role restrictions that subordinated women. Because the Air Force viewed pregnant officers through traditional sex stereotypes, it excluded all pregnant women from employment, rather than conditioning eligibility on capacity to work.[42] The very case at bar illustrated that "many women are capable of working effectively during pregnancy and require only a brief period of absence immediately before and after childbirth."[43] The government, however, did not make such an individualized determination. Instead, it barred all pregnant women from serving, putatively to protect them.[44] Regulations that purport to protect pregnant women by forcing them to stop working, the *Struck* brief sharply observed, "have in practice deprived working women of the protection they most need: protection of their right to work to support themselves and, in many cases, their families as well."[45] Thus, "mandatory pregnancy discharge reinforces societal pressure to relinquish career aspirations for a hearth-centered existence."[46]

The sex-role stereotypes shaping the Air Force regulation was perhaps most visible in its sex-differentiated approach to parenting. The regulation defined the terms of service in such a way as to require a choice between employment and parenthood – for women only.[47] Fathers were allowed to serve in the Air Force while mothers were not. Although "men in the Air Force are not constrained to avoid the pleasures and responsibilities of procreation and parenthood,"[48] Ginsburg's brief observed, Captain Struck "was presumed unfit for service under a regulation that declares, without regard to fact, that she fits into the stereotyped vision ... of the 'correct' female response to pregnancy."[49]

The regulation challenged in *Struck* assessed pregnant women as a group rather than as individuals, and it prohibited the employment of officers who became mothers, while allowing the employment of officers who became fathers. The regulation's prescriptive assumptions about pregnant women reflected and reinforced the sex roles of the separate-spheres tradition,[50] defining women's family role in such a way as to make women dependents and second-class participants in core activities associated with citizenship. "Presumably well-meaning exaltation of woman's unique role in bearing children has, in effect, denied women equal opportunity to develop their individual talents and capacities and has impelled them to accept a dependent, subordinate status in society."[51] Increasingly, Americans were recognizing that laws imposing this traditional role on women violate women's right to the equal protection of the laws.[52] "In very recent years," Ginsburg explained, "a new appreciation of women's place has been generated in the United States. Activated by feminists of both sexes, legislatures and courts have begun to recognize and respond to the subordinate position of women in our society and the second-class status our institutions historically have imposed upon them."[53]

Although focusing most heavily on the equal protection argument, Ginsburg advanced two additional constitutional objections to the Air Force regulation. First, she urged that the regulation violated Captain Struck's right to privacy.[54] Relying on *Griswold v. Connecticut*[55] and *Eisenstadt v. Baird*,[56] she argued that the regulation "substantially infringes upon her right to sexual privacy, and her autonomy in deciding 'whether to bear ... a child.'"[57] In response to the Air Force's suggestion that it was aiming to discourage reproduction by service members, Ginsburg noted that the Air Force provided additional benefits to service members who become fathers in order to encourage them to continue serving.[58] "The woman," by stark contrast, "serves subject to 'regulation'; her pursuit of an Air Force career requires that she decide not to bear a child."[59]

Ginsburg also asserted a free exercise claim, "stress[ing] that the challenged regulation operates with particularly brutal force against women of [Captain Struck's Roman Catholic] faith."[60] This was because "termination of pregnancy prior to the birth of a living child was not an option [she] could choose."[61] In sum, "the regulation pitted her Air Force career against ... her religious conscience."[62]

III. THE LIGHT *STRUCK* SHEDS

What does Ruth Bader Ginsburg's merits brief in *Struck* suggest about her understanding of constitutional equality? Her brief makes clear that "disadvantageous treatment because of pregnancy is indeed sex discrimination."[63] She views some, but not all, regulation of pregnancy as discriminatory, just as she opposes most, but not all, forms of gender differentiation by the government as a violation of equal protection. Ginsburg neither mechanically rejects the potential relevance of differences between the sexes nor invariably embraces them. At bottom, the *Struck* brief suggests, Ginsburg contests legally enforced sex-role differentiation because she views the prevailing system of sex-role differentiation as perpetuating the subordinate status of women.[64] "Heading the list of arbitrary barriers that have plagued women seeking equal opportunity," she thus insisted, "is disadvantaged treatment based on their unique childbearing function."[65] The harm is not simply the restriction imposed on one woman's opportunities, but the "disadvantaged treatment" regularly inflicted on women because of their childbearing capacity. Ginsburg was concerned with a practice harming a group.

In *Struck*, Ginsburg highlighted the forms of group disadvantage that discrimination can impose, and she repeatedly related concerns about stereotyping and subordination. For example, Ginsburg emphasized that laws enforcing traditional sex stereotypes inflict harm because they reinforce "the subordinate position of women in our society and the second-class status our institutions historically have imposed upon them."[66] This antisubordination perspective would shape Ginsburg's approach to equal protection on the Court as well. For example, in her majority opinion in *United States v. Virginia*, she would distinguish sharply between efforts to exclude women from institutions or opportunities in American society and efforts to include them by taking relevant differences (such as pregnancy) into account.[67]

More specifically, the *Struck* brief exemplifies that antisubordination values (1) define Ginsburg's understanding of constitutional equality, and thus guide her determination of when and how equality values are implicated; (2) lead her to consider equality questions from the perspective of members of historically excluded groups; and (3) render her commitments to equality and liberty mutually reinforcing. This Part considers each dimension of her thinking in turn.

First, Ginsburg does not regard an antisubordination approach as an alternative to equality analysis. Rather, she regards antisubordination *as* equality – that is, as equal standing and respect. She insists that sex discrimination exists even when a regulation is purportedly based on physical differences between the sexes, or "when its impact concentrates on a portion of the protected class, for example, married women, mothers, or pregnant women."[68] Her perspective deems constitutionally pertinent not only the existence of a formal sex classification or intentional discrimination but also the effects and social meanings of government regulation of women. These concerns define an antisubordination understanding of equality,[69] which guides determination of when and how equality values are implicated. As illustrated by *Struck*, such guidance is critical in determining when sex differentiation implicates equality.

Second, the *Struck* brief illustrates how, in determining whether equality values are implicated, Ginsburg adopts an antisubordination perspective. She takes into consideration the standpoint of members of historically excluded groups rather than reasoning only from the perspective of members of included groups – as did the majority in *Plessy v. Ferguson*[70] and *Bradwell v. Illinois*.[71] Thus, Ginsburg continually presents the case from Captain Struck's point of view. She draws from the "petitioner's experience" to substantiate her assertion that "many women are capable of working effectively during pregnancy and require only a brief period of absence immediately before and after childbirth."[72] She underscores the devastating impact of the Air Force regulation on the career prospects of a military woman and the lack of any justification for the regulation that did not sound most plausibly in traditional stereotypes about how women are "supposed" to respond to a pregnancy.[73]

Third, although Ginsburg stresses the equality dimension of discharge-for-pregnancy regulations in her *Struck* brief,[74] she also asserts a substantive due process claim and advances it in a way that reveals the link between her views on constitutional equality and constitutional liberty.[75] (At the time of *Roe*, feminists understood *Struck* as both an equality and a liberty case – just as they understood *Roe*.)[76] In making the due process argument, Ginsburg continues to speak in part in terms of "discrimination" and social subordination.[77] This is not because she is conceptually confused, but because she registers that laws intervening in major life decisions and enforcing status roles may simultaneously implicate both equality and liberty – equal protection and due process. Restricting women's liberty may be a means to the end of communicating inequality, and discriminating against women may diminish their opportunities to fashion fulfilling lives.[78] For Ginsburg, it seems less important to disentangle these two clusters of constitutional commitments than it is to emphasize the ways in which they are intertwined.[79]

Some feminists, however, have criticized Justice Ginsburg for advocating a sex-blind formal equality in sex-discrimination cases; they depict her as only and overly concerned with arbitrary sex-based differentiation[80] – in substantial part because she championed the causes of male plaintiffs in certain such cases.[81] Much of this criticism occurred in an era of backlash, when an increasingly conservative Court was employing a formalist conception of classification to make equal protection law blind to problems of disparate impact and hostile to affirmative action, in sex as well as race cases.[82] In such an era, it was possible to (mis)construe Ginsburg's selection of male sex-discrimination plaintiffs as of a piece with the formalist reasoning of the Burger Court.

As the *Struck* brief shows, however, it was not. Ginsburg's selection of a *pregnant* plaintiff to advance the equal protection claims of women demonstrates that she is no formalist. In *Struck* itself, Ginsburg explains that she is challenging laws that enforce traditional sex-role stereotypes because such laws lead to the subordination of women: "presumably well-meaning exaltation of woman's unique role in bearing children has, in effect, denied women equal opportunity to develop their individual talents and capacities and has impelled them to accept a dependent, subordinate status in society."[83] Captain Struck "was presumed unfit for service under a regulation that declares, without regard to fact, that she fits into the stereotyped vision ... of the 'correct' female response to pregnancy."[84] Ginsburg's message is clear: sex-role stereotypes of the separate-spheres tradition subordinate women by denying them an equal chance to make their own meaning of their lives.

In an important article, Cary Franklin has reconstructed the social theory on which Ginsburg's early litigation strategy was premised. As Franklin shows, Ginsburg understood that the stereotypes contested by the male plaintiffs she represented were part of a dyadic system of gender roles that defined men as breadwinners and women as dependent caregivers in ways that subordinated women.[85] Ginsburg's anti-stereotyping approach was not simply hostile to sex classification or sex differentiation; she opposed traditional sex stereotypes insofar as they were part of a system of social roles and understandings that anchored women's inequality.

Ginsburg's effort to defend a pregnant member of the Air Force is of a piece with her interest in bringing cases on behalf of caregiving men. Neither reflects a formal view of equality. Instead, Ginsburg challenged laws enforcing traditional sex stereotypes because she understood them as part of a larger set of social arrangements that ultimately subordinated women.

Ginsburg's articulation of an antisubordination perspective in *Struck* is even more remarkable when the brief is situated in historical context. Today, antisubordination arguments tend to be associated with Owen Fiss's 1976 expression of antisubordination themes in *Groups and the Equal Protection Clause*[86] and Catherine MacKinnon's 1979 use of an antisubordination analytic in *Sexual Harassment of Working Women*.[87] The *Struck* brief evidences Ginsburg speaking in an antisubordination register in 1972, carrying into the sex-equality context concerns about status inequality expressed in debates over *Brown v. Board of Education*.[88] One cannot help but be struck (so to speak) by the timing of this brief. Although Ginsburg was by no means the only legal feminist at the time to conceive sex equality from an antisubordination perspective, she did play an early and leading role in showing how concerns about social subordination illuminate the problem of sex discrimination. Her prescience in the brief has not been sufficiently recognized.

The timing of Ginsburg's *Struck* brief is noteworthy for another reason. Ginsburg persuasively urged the Court to view pregnancy discrimination as a form of sex discrimination, and to view sex discrimination as inextricably intertwined with women's autonomy to decide whether to bear children, at a time when the entire landscape of modern sex discrimination law and substantive due process law had yet to be worked out. Ginsburg and the women's movement talked about pregnancy discrimination in a way that ties together pregnancy discrimination and women's equality, and women's equality and reproductive freedom,[89] before the Court split them apart in cases such as *Roe v. Wade, Frontiero v. Richardson,* and *Geduldig v. Aiello.* The Court made some fateful choices in these cases: to focus its sex-equality jurisprudence on cases other than pregnancy, and so to develop its sex-equality jurisprudence in isolation from its abortion jurisprudence.[90] Only by apprehending where the law was and where it was about to go when *Struck* was litigated can one fully appreciate the momentousness, the audacity, and the profundity of this brief – as well as the implications of its erasure. In 1976, the Court embraced the intermediate scrutiny standard for sex-discrimination claims in a case involving men who sought to purchase beer – and 3.2 percent beer at that.[91] How would our understanding of sex discrimination and substantive due process law differ had the Court recognized the equal protection claim of a pregnant service woman who challenged the government's requirement that she have an abortion or lose her position in the military?

IV. BACK TO THE FUTURE

This chapter has not recovered all of the virtues of Ruth Bader Ginsburg's merits brief in *Struck v. Secretary of Defense.* Nor has it identified all of the interesting questions and ironies that it implicates.[92] The brief is a veritable treasure trove of accurate predictions, subtle insights, and effective advocacy.

Among other things, it mentions the possibility of intermediate scrutiny for sex classifications,[93] leaves the door open for "compensatory treatment" of women "in special situations,"[94] underscores the men who have adopted Ginsburg's position,[95] gently gestures in the direction of the link between sex discrimination and burdensome regulations of abortion,[96] and emphasizes themes of sexual intimacy and privacy,[97] which decades later would find expression in the Court's dawning, and increasingly robust, recognition of the equal-citizenship stature of gay people.[98] Throughout the brief, Ginsburg's distinct and powerful voice is present. For legal academics who care about the development of Justice Ginsburg's views on sex discrimination, the brief is essential reading.

Most significantly, however, the brief deserves a wide readership because of what it instructs about the present. It may soon be time to reimagine what is possible in this corner of constitutional law. In 1972, Ginsburg's *Struck* brief made a compelling argument that pregnancy discrimination is sex discrimination because of the social understandings about women that pregnancy discrimination reflects and the profound limitations on their lives that it enforces. Although the Court eventually accepted much of her general vision of sex equality, it was slow to recognize discrimination against pregnant women as a paradigmatic form of sex discrimination. In 1974, the Court in *Geduldig* acknowledged that discrimination against pregnant women might be animated by invidious judgments about women, but found the exclusion of pregnancy benefits from otherwise comprehensive disability insurance to be a rational method of saving taxpayer monies.[99] The Court did, however, yield to the instruction of Congress that discrimination against pregnant women can violate federal employment discrimination law, and it began to enforce the 1978 Pregnancy Discrimination Amendment (PDA) to Title VII of the 1964 Civil Rights Act.[100] After three decades of PDA litigation, Americans are more receptive to the claim that discrimination against pregnant women is sex discrimination, and they have come to view it as a claim of fundamental – even constitutional – magnitude.[101] With these changes, the Court has begun to move closer to Ginsburg's understanding of sex discrimination without wholeheartedly embracing her point of view.[102]

For example, Chief Justice Rehnquist – Rehnquist! – wrote the majority opinion in *Nevada Department of Human Resources v. Hibbs*.[103] *Hibbs* upholds the leave for family care provided by the Family and Medical Leave Act of 1993 (FMLA)[104] as a valid exercise of Congress's power under Section 5 of the Fourteenth Amendment to combat unconstitutional sex discrimination.[105] Remarkably, *Hibbs* expressly registers the sometimes deep divide between formal equality and substantive equality. In an America in which women are still required to serve as the principal caregivers in their families, mere formal equality in the administration of family-leave benefits – for example, allowing no leave time for any employees – would "exclude far more women than men from the workplace"[106] and therefore would not effectively "combat the stereotypes about the roles of male and female employees that Congress sought to eliminate" in passing the FMLA.[107]

Hibbs reflects the understanding that new mothers and pregnant women face intense stereotyping in the workplace. Quoting Congress, *Hibbs* observes:

> Historically, denial or curtailment of women's employment opportunities has been traceable directly to the pervasive presumption that women are mothers first, and workers second. This prevailing ideology about women's roles has in turn justified discrimination against women when they are mothers or mothers-to-be.[108]

In these and other passages, *Hibbs* clearly indicates that regulation of pregnant women can amount to constitutionally actionable sex discrimination; for example, the Court suggests that laws giving benefits to pregnant employees that are premised on traditional sex-role stereotypes violate equal protection.[109] The *Hibbs* Court had no occasion to reconcile its reasoning with *Geduldig*,[110] but the reasoning in *Hibbs* parallels Ginsburg's reasoning in *Struck*, not the Burger Court's reasoning in *Geduldig*.[111]

Geduldig is commonly read as holding that discrimination against pregnant women can never be sex discrimination. After *Hibbs*, however, it is time to read *Geduldig* more precisely, as holding that discrimination against a pregnant woman is not always sex discrimination – but sometimes can be.[112] The *Geduldig* Court acknowledged that "distinctions involving pregnancy" might inflict "an invidious discrimination against the members of one sex or the other."[113] *Geduldig*'s reference to invidiousness is best understood in the way that Wendy Williams's brief in *Geduldig* used the term "invidious" – namely, as referring to traditional sex-role stereotypes.[114] The modern Court sometimes, but not always, recognizes that regulation concerning pregnancy can, as Ginsburg's *Struck* brief urged many years ago, unconstitutionally reflect or reinforce sex-role stereotyping.[115]

In addition to arguing that pregnancy discrimination is sex discrimination, Ginsburg's *Struck* brief showed that women's equality and reproductive freedom are inextricably linked. The brief noted that many lower courts, including the federal district court in *Roe v. Wade*, had read the Court's contraception decisions as "holding that women have a right to determine for themselves, free from unwarranted governmental intrusion, whether or not to bear children."[116] The Court invoked but did not elaborate this understanding in *Roe*, which tended to reason about childbearing decisions from the perspective of a woman's physician.[117] But after two decades of national debate over abortion, a majority of the Court came to address decisions concerning childbearing with attention to questions of women's liberty and equality. *Planned Parenthood of Southeastern Pennsylvania v. Casey*[118] protects the liberty of the pregnant woman,[119] while reasoning about the sex-equality implications of intrusive restrictions on abortion.[120] Though the Court in *Gonzales v. Carhart* may have taken a step in a different direction,[121] Justice Ginsburg spoke for four justices in *Carhart* when she emphasized that "legal challenges to undue restrictions on abortion procedures do not seek to vindicate some generalized notion of privacy; rather, they center on a woman's autonomy to determine her life's course, and thus to enjoy equal citizenship stature."[122]

CONCLUSION

For reasons intellectual, historical, and jurisprudential, Ruth Bader Ginsburg's skillful advocacy on behalf of Captain Susan Struck warrants the attention that it has long been denied. The *Struck* brief shows that in 1972 Ginsburg viewed laws imposing traditional sex stereotypical roles on pregnant women as a core case of sex discrimination; she argued that such laws violated equal protection because they denied individual women equal opportunity and imposed on women as a group a dependent, subordinate status in American society. Today, many in the nation and on the Court have come to adopt her perspective as their own. The revolution in constitutional understanding for which she called in *Struck* has been achieved to a striking extent – and may yet be realized more completely within the lifetimes of those graduating from law school today.

A Postscript to Struck *by Stereotype*

Ruth Bader Ginsburg

Reading the account of Captain Susan Struck's case, vibrantly told by Neil S. Siegel and Reva B. Siegel, brought me back to the summer of 1972. ACLU Legal Office staff counsel Joel M. Gora and I spent many hours in June and July of that year preparing a petition for certiorari, one we hoped would engage the Court's attention. In the preceding year, the ACLU had taken on, along with *Struck*, several other cases challenging the rule, then maintained by all the Armed Forces, requiring pregnant service members to choose between abortion and ouster from the military. But Captain Struck's case was our front-runner. We aimed to present the issue of reproductive choice through her eyes and experience. Captain Struck chose birth, but her Government made that choice a mandatory ground for discharge. We filed the petition on July 31, 1972 and were elated that fall, when the Court, on October 24, granted certiorari.

From the end of October until December 4, when we filed our brief on the merits, the full presentation of Captain Struck's case was my principal project. But as if synchronized, the Air Force waived Captain Struck's discharge on the eve of our submission. It was the right decision for the Air Force, and good news for Captain Struck and other service members caught in the same bind. But an ideal case to argue the sex equality dimension of laws and regulations governing pregnancy and childbirth had slipped from our grasp.

Perhaps it is indulgence in wishful thinking, but I remain of this view: Had the Court considered Captain Struck's case, with the benefit of full briefing and oral argument, a dreadful mistake might have been avoided. After homing in on Captain Struck's plight, what rational jurist could have declared adverse discrimination based on pregnancy not sex-based discrimination at all![123]

Associate Justice, Supreme Court of the United States. Copyright © 2010 by Ruth Bader Ginsburg. This Postscript was originally published as Ruth Bader Ginsburg, *A Postscript to Struck by Stereotype*, 59 DUKE L.J. 799 (2010), and is reprinted here with the consent of Justice Ginsburg and *Duke Law Journal*.

Great constitutional law scholar Paul Freund observed that "judges ... should not be[] influenced by the weather of the day, but they are necessarily influenced by the climate of the age."[124] An apt example is the case featured in the concluding portion of Struck *by Stereotype* – *Nevada Department of Human Resources v. Hibbs*,[125] in which Chief Justice Rehnquist led the Court in upholding against heavy assault the family-care leave provision of the Family and Medical Leave Act of 1993.

I appreciate beyond measure the intelligence and caring evident in every page of Struck by *Stereotype*. The authors have captured just what was on my mind and in my heart while composing the plea that will no longer rest, unnoticed, in the Supreme Court Library's collection of briefs.

5

Beyond the Tough Guise:
Justice Ginsburg's Reconstructive Feminism

Joan C. Williams

For someone who has been called the Thurgood Marshall of women,[1] Justice Ginsburg has received remarkably little attention from legal feminists.[2] Indeed, for decades, she has been consigned to the dustbin of Formal Equality, as someone obsessed with treating men and women the same under the law, to women's detriment, even when the two groups were clearly different.[3]

Those wishing to salvage Ginsburg's reputation recently have defended her as an "antisubordination" feminist, applying to Ginsburg a term invented by legal theorist Catharine MacKinnon to describe her own approach. In this essay, I argue that associating Ginsburg with MacKinnon's "feminism unmodified"[4] ultimately proves confusing because it glosses over important differences between the two women. Ginsburg is more fruitfully seen as a reconstructive feminist whose goal is to reconstruct breadwinner and caregiver roles and, more generally, the relationship of market work and family work. This chapter ends by taking reconstructive feminism the next step: it proposes to jumpstart the stalled gender revolution by placing masculinity's "tough guise" at the center of feminist analysis.

IS GINSBURG AN ANTISUBORDINATION THEORIST?

Pointing to her brief in *Struck v. Secretary of Defense*, Neil Siegel and Reva Siegel argue that Justice Ginsburg should be seen through an antisubordination lens.[5] The *Struck* brief's antisubordination rhetoric is not an aberration. In fact, the briefs from the landmark 1970s cases Ginsburg was involved with under the auspices of the ACLU Women's Rights Project are chockfull of antisubordination rhetoric.

This chapter draws from and adapts two of my previous works, *Tough Guise*, 9(2) ISSUES IN LEGAL SCHOLARSHIP (2011), and *Jumpstarting the Stalled Gender Revolution*, 63 HASTINGS L.J. 1267 (2012).

The 1971 amicus brief Ginsburg co-wrote in *Reed v. Reed* uses the terms "inferior," "subordinate," "subordination," and "second-class" fifteen times.[6] "A person born female," the brief states, "continues to be branded inferior for this congenital and unalterable condition of birth."[7] The brief brings in historical evidence, quoting a nineteenth-century editorial to the effect that just as "Negroes" are "doomed to subjection" because they are inferior to the white race, woman, too, is happier "subject to man" "because it is the law of her nature."[8] This brief also quotes at length from the antisubordination rhetoric in the 1848 Declaration of Sentiments from Seneca Falls.[9]

Later that same year, in the case that was to become *Frontiero v. Richardson*, Ginsburg co-authored a brief that used terminology of subordination or inferiority twelve times, reiterating that "Historically, women have been treated as subordinate and inferior to men."[10] Relying heavily on the new social history, the brief recalls that "The common law heritage, a source of pride for men, marked the wife as her husband's chattel, 'something better than his dog, a little dearer than his horse.'"[11]

The *Struck* brief two years later sounds many of the same notes, decrying "the subordinate position of women in our society and the second-class status our institutions historically have imposed upon them."[12] Women are "relegated to an inferior legal status"[13]; they have "the stigma of inferiority and second-class citizenship associated with them."[14] This brief again relies heavily on nonlegal materials: "For if women only have a place, clearly the rest of the world must belong to someone else and, therefore, in default of God, to men."[15] The "presumably well-meaning exultation" of women "has impelled them to accept a dependent subordinate status in society."[16] "Men's domination of women" is referred to as an "historic fact."[17]

Ginsburg's 1973 brief in *Kahn v. Shevin* continues the antisubordination theme. Following the "grandmother brief," it again asserts that "Historically, women have been treated subordinate and inferior to men."[18] *Kahn* involved a tax exemption offered to widows but not widowers. Ginsburg and company warned that "favors of this kind come at an exorbitant price," citing Sarah Grimke's famous line (beloved of MacKinnon): "We ask no favors for our sex. All we ask of our brethren is that they take their feet off our necks."[19] The tax-exemption rule, ostensibly to benefit women, "perpetuates sex stereotypes and thereby retards women's access to equal opportunity and economic life."[20] Shielding women from politics ensures that "laws are drafted from masculine perspective."[21]

I could go on and on. Suffice it to say that the notion that Ginsburg wanted lily-liver formal equality is woefully ill informed. In retrospect, I am shocked that so many of us – myself included – read the Supreme Court opinions in early Equal Protection cases as evidence of what feminists wanted rather than as evidence of what they could get Eight White Guys to accept.[22]

The early legal feminists not only embraced antisubordination language but also kept on using it even after it became clear that the antisubordination strategy did not appeal to the Supreme Court. In 1979, Ginsburg wrote (along with a lawyer at her husband's firm, Weil, Gotshal & Manges) a brief in *Wengler v. Druggists Mutual Insurance Co.*, which involved a challenge to a Missouri workers-compensation law that offered death benefits automatically for the spouse of a male worker but required proof of incapacity or dependence for spouses of female workers.[23] Statutes that offer "purported favors to females as men's appendages," said the brief, "downgrade women's status as workers and, in the cumulative effect, dampen women's aspirations and limit their opportunities"[24] by perpetuating a "familiar stereotype – the dominant, independent man/subordinate, dependent woman."[25] The brief complains that the equation of "widow" with "dependent surviving spouse … reflects a traditional way of thinking about females as inferior to males"[26] and that the statute reflects "archaic and overbroad generalizations about men as breadwinners and women as dependents" dating from an era when "those in positions of power accepted as axiomatic women's subordination to men."[27] Ginsburg and her co-author decry "the old accepted rules and customs of purportedly favoring women [as] do[ing] so only in conjunction with a few of them as men's appendages."[28] These gals were antisubordination firebrands.

But not firebrands like MacKinnon. Just ask MacKinnon herself: "I think the fatal error of the legal arm of feminism has been its failure to understand that the mainstream of sex inequality is misogyny and the mainstream of misogyny is sexual sadism."[29] MacKinnon's focus is on sex – one particularly unhealthy kind of sex: the eroticizing of dominance, whether through sexual harassment[30] or pornography[31] or rape.[32] In MacKinnon's view, "the eroticization of dominance and submission [is what] creates gender."[33] Or, more famously, "sexuality is to feminism what work is to marxism."[34]

These concerns are a far cry from Ginsburg's. MacKinnon and Ginsburg are quite literally not talking about the same subject: MacKinnon focuses on the linkage of sexuality and dominance, while Ginsburg's focus is on separate spheres' organizations of work and family. Virtually all of the cases in which Ginsburg involved the ACLU Women's Rights Project involved challenges to the breadwinner-homemaker dyad. By my quick count, twelve out of fourteen of these early cases aimed at disestablishing those separate spheres.[35] In cases that did not directly involve the breadwinner/homemaker dyad, the ACLU briefs focus on deconstructing the descriptions of men and women that justify the breadwinner as the "natural" role for men and the caregiver as the "natural" role for women.[36] Ginsburg's message was, and has always been, that men can be caregivers and women can be breadwinners, and (to quote her former clerks Susan and David Williams) "we can be full human beings with a full emotional palette even in the workplace, and we are thinking, analyzing people, even at home."[37]

The second important difference between Ginsburg and MacKinnon is their attitude toward men. MacKinnon typically paints men as oppressors, pure and simple. Men, MacKinnon tells us, do not want to hear that Linda Lovelace (of *Deep Throat*) didn't like the sex; "men believe what turns them on" (i.e., eroticized violence).[38] Occasionally, MacKinnon acknowledges differences among men (those "who do not rape women" or "who are made sick by pornography"),[39] but these moments are rare and fleeting. MacKinnon pays little attention to distinguishing between *men* and the unhealthy *traditions of masculinity* she critiques so searingly well; MacKinnon's view is that "what turns men on, what men find beautiful, is what degrades women."[40] When men sexually harass women, she notes, "it doesn't mean they all want to fuck us, they just want to hurt us, dominate us, and control us and that *is* fucking us."[41] No wonder MacKinnon's view is that women are "born, degraded, and die."[42]

Ginsburg's view of men couldn't be more different. Ginsburg brought her views on gender over from the Sweden of the 1960s, where a full-fledged assault aimed to deconstruct the separate spheres' dichotomy between the definition of men as beings whose natures suited them perfectly for market work and public life and the definition of women as beings whose natures suited them perfectly for family work and private life.[43] The goal in Sweden was to make structural changes in the organization of market work and family work and in the ideology of what men and women are "really like," in order to enable both men and women to live up to their full human potential, freed from the straitjacket of the breadwinner/homemaker roles.[44] Swedish advocates argued "that imprisonment in the masculine role is at least as great a problem to men as conformity to a feminine ideal is to women" and "that debate about liberation and equality must be about how men as well as women are forced to act out socially determined stereotypes."[45] For MacKinnon, women's liberation entails a freedom from the violence (and the sexuality?) of men. For Ginsburg, women's liberation is contingent on the mirror-image liberation of men.

JUSTICE GINSBURG AS A RECONSTRUCTIVE FEMINIST

Unlike MacKinnon, whose chief strength is her eloquence in excoriating current outrages, Justice Ginsburg offers a clear reconstructive vision.

Were I Queen, my principal affirmative action plan would have three legs. First, it would promote equal educational opportunity, and effective job training for women, so they would not be reduced to dependency on a man or the state. Second, my plan would give men encouragement and incentives to share more evenly with women the joys, responsibilities, worries, upsets, and sometimes tedium of raising children from infancy to adulthood. (This, I admit, is the most challenging part of the plan to make concrete and implement.) Third, the plan would make quality daycare available from infancy on. Children in my ideal world would not be women's priorities, they would be human priorities.[46]

Ginsburg's vision embeds a central ambiguity. Often she speaks of her ideal as one in which both parents participate simultaneously in market work and family work. At other times, though, she seems more focused on making the world safe for role switching – for men to be caregivers and women to be breadwinners. She has often said that *Weinberger v. Wiesenfeld* is her favorite case, and that Stephen Wiesenfeld's devotion to his son deeply touched her. She wrote in the brief: "Just as Paula Wiesenfeld's status as a breadwinner is devalued so Stephen Wiesenfeld's parental status is denigrated."[47] Judges who heard the case were extremely skeptical, or downright certain, that Stephen Wiesenfeld actually did not want to be a stay-at-home dad. The brief expressed outrage:

> Equally myopic, but impossible to explain in light of his own contemporaneous pronouncements is appellant's reference in this Court, as in the court below, to appellant's advanced degrees in his ability to command a substantial salary. If Jason Paul's surviving parent were a woman, any suggestion that her academic degrees and intellectual capacity indicated she should choose remunerative employment over personal attention to her new newborn child would undoubtedly be dismissed with alacrity.[48]

Whether Ginsburg wants to deconstruct separate spheres or simply to populate them with humans of a different body shape, one thing is clear: like Olaf Palme in the 1960s, her goal is to work in coalition with men, placing masculinity at center stage.[49] When asked why she had chosen to work through the ACLU rather than through a women's organization, Justice Ginsburg replied, "I always thought that there was nothing an antifeminist would want more than to have women only in women's organizations, in their own little corner, empathizing with each other and not touching a man's world. If you're going to change things, you have to be with the people who hold the levers."[50] A *Washington Post* reporter who interviewed Ginsburg in 1993 noted a photograph of her son-in-law gazing adoringly at his newborn child. The reporter quotes her as telling visitors, "This is my dream for society.... Fathers loving and caring for and helping to raise their kids."[51]

Ginsburg's focus on men explains her opposition to "special treatment" for women. "Special benefits for women ... result in discriminatory treatment of similarly situated men, themselves victims of male sex-role stereotypes," asserted the Women's Rights Project 1973 brief in *Kahn v. Shevin*,[52] which also noted that "gender-based discrimination frequently impacts adversely on both sexes" and decried the "fundamental unfairness to men as well as women of legislative lines based on sex stereotypes."[53] This theme emerged again in *Orr v. Orr*, the case that challenged an alimony statute that limited alimony to women.

> The Alabama alimony statute unfairly and unconstitutionally discriminates against husbands who elect to stay at home and care for the family, or who, relying on their wives' ability and desire to make the major contribution to the financial support of the family, select a less remunerative career, or who, because of involuntary disability, are necessarily dependent on their wives.... Thus, for example, a husband who would like to be a poet or a painter and whose family can maintain an adequate living standard on his wife's earnings, is discouraged by the Alabama alimony statute from fully developing his talent and pursuing his aspiration.[54]

That brief noted that "far more clearly, the discrimination visited upon the husband by the Alabama alimony statute stamps women as persons assigned a special place in a world controlled by men. By steering the husband out of the home, it steers the wife into it and keeps her there, thus discouraging wives from achieving economic self-sufficiency."[55]

In the light of Ginsburg's early briefs, it becomes clear that her greatest Supreme Court triumph was not *Virginia v. United States*,[56] as is often assumed. It was *Nevada Department of Human Resources v. Hibbs*,[57] written by Chief Justice Rehnquist, which upheld the constitutionality of the Family and Medical Leave Act (FMLA) as applied to state governments.[58] *Hibbs* can be seen as channeling Ginsburg's reconstructive vision, virtually unchanged since the 1960s. Like many of the cases in which the Women's Rights Project became involved, *Hibbs* involved a man who wanted to care for a family member. Williams Hibbs, who worked for the state welfare department, was fired when he took time off to care for his wife, who had been very seriously injured in an auto accident.[59] Much to the astonishment of constitutional law scholars, Rehnquist limited the federalism doctrine he himself had championed, which used the Tenth Amendment to rein in congressional power.[60]

Ginsburg's handprints are all over *Hibbs*.[61] The case involved a statute Ginsburg cared deeply about, championed by Judith Lichtman's Women's Legal Defense Fund (now the National Partnership for Women and Families).

Lichtman had co-authored some of the early Women's Rights Project briefs with Ginsburg and had hung tough, resisting pressure to accept a national maternity leave statute, in favor of a statute that applied to men as well as women.[62] This was a controversial move, one Ginsburg has defended. For her, the FMLA expresses a key tenet of reconstructive feminism: not a commitment to treat men and women the same, but a commitment to change existing masculine norms, and to substitute new norms that include the experience of women.[63] The FMLA does this, she would argue, because it changes the definition of the ideal worker, by sending the message that caregiving – both self-care and care of others – naturally plays a role in adults' lives whatever gender, and that employers should be prohibited from penalizing adults, whatever gender, who need time off for caregiving.[64]

Ginsburg has been making this argument since 1975, when her *Gender and the Constitution* article argued that women needed "affirmative action" in order to achieve true equality.[65] The "overriding objective must be an end to role delineation by gender, and in its place, conduct at every school level, [and] later in the job market, signaling that in all fields of endeavor females are welcomed as enthusiastically as males are."[66] What this entailed was hardly to treat men and women the same in the fact of norms designed around men, or, as she put it, "eliminating institutional practices that limit or discourage female participation."[67] For example, "deferral of an education to raise a family or to finance the education of a spouse might be regarded with the same favor as accomplishments of college athletes or politicians."[68] Or, "extended study programs might be provided for students unable to undertake full-time study because of special family obligations that cannot be met by customary financial aid (notably, care of preschool children)."[69] Later in the same article, Ginsburg wrote: "If we are genuinely committed to the eradication of gender-based discrimination, the problem of job and income security for childbearing women workers must be confronted and resolved head-on."[70] She advocated (in the politest possible terms) "comprehensive income protection and medical benefits for pregnancy and childbirth, financed through compulsory social insurance," parental leaves that can be taken by men or women, and comprehensive, non-means-tested child care.[71]

Ginsburg argued (as have I)[72] that it is inconsistent with a commitment to gender equality to force the costs of childrearing onto mothers, and that mothers' "choice" to quit is less of a choice than a response to a workplace designed around an ideal worker who takes no time off for childbearing, childrearing, or anything else: someone with a man's body and men's traditional (breadwinner) life pattern.[73] "We will continue to shortchange parents," she wrote, "particularly mothers, and children until childrearing burdens are distributed more evenly among parents, their employers and the tax-paying public."[74] In other words, Ginsburg – like a true reconstructive feminist – defines equality as treating men and women the same, but only after deconstructing the existing norms defined by and around men and masculinity and reconstructing existing institutions in ways that include the bodies and traditional life patterns of women.[75]

This is the theoretical framework the Court adopted in *Hibbs*.[76] It took what seemed at first glance a workers' rights statute that gives all eligible employees up to twelve weeks off a year to care for a family member with a serious health condition,[77] and defended it as a gender-bias statute, thereby allowing the Court to uphold its constitutionality.[78] Both Rehnquist's language and his logic come right out of the Women's Rights Project briefs of thirty years earlier. He decried the "stereotype-based beliefs about the allocation of family duties [that have] remained firmly rooted" and noted that seven states' leave statutes reinforced stereotypes by offering maternity leave for women but no leave for men, "reinforcing the very stereotypes that Congress sought to remedy through the FMLA."[79] Like Ginsburg before him, Rehnquist focused on men, noting that "parental leave for fathers ... is rare. Even ... [w]here child-care leave policies do exist, men ... receive notoriously discriminatory treatment."[80] Rehnquist decried "the pervasive presumption that women are mothers first, and workers second,"[81] concluding that

> stereotypes about women's domestic roles are reinforced by parallel stereotypes presuming a lack of domestic responsibilities for men.... These mutually reinforcing stereotypes created a self-fulfilling cycle of discrimination that forced women to continue to assume the role of primary caregiver, and fostered employers' stereotypical views about women's commitment to work and their value as employees."[82]

I do not doubt that Chief Justice Rehnquist had his own life experiences that led him to recognize the importance of family caregiving. His wife died of cancer when she was still relatively young, and he sometimes took off early from the Supreme Court to pick up his grandchild from day care in order to help his divorced daughter.[83] But I have little doubt that Ruth Bader Ginsburg helped him interpret these experiences in a reconstructive vein: she is one charming and persuasive lady.

Ginsburg is a reconstructive feminist, dedicated to deconstructing separate spheres in order to substitute a reconstructive vision of a world where masculine norms are replaced with norms that include the experience of women as well as that of men; of a world where men and women share both employment and the work of the family; of a society where men and women are not stereotyped as "naturally" agentic and "naturally" communal.[84]

THE WAY FORWARD

The revolution in gender roles Ginsburg sought to spark largely stalled out in the mid-1990s.[85] Further change in women's roles is being blocked by an unmoving massif: unchanging gender pressures on men. It is therefore time to act on Ginsburg's insistence that opening up new roles for women requires opening up healthier masculinities for men.

New social science evidence offers insights on manhood. Manhood is precarious, notes social psychologist Joseph Vandello and his colleagues. Unlike womanhood, which is generally seen as a biological inevitability, manhood has to be earned – over and over again and in public.[86] This leads to "gender role stress": chronic anxiety over whether one is a "real" man.[87] Actions that provide temporary relief from anxiety include "drinking heavily, driving fast, excelling at sports, making lots of money, bragging about their sexual exploits, and fathering many children."[88]

Particularly important is the fact that manhood remains intertwined with breadwinning. Ironically, Americans see being a good provider as an integral part of being a good father: gender pressures on men to be good fathers propel them away from home, rather than toward it.[89]

Gender pressures on men to perform as breadwinners without caregiving responsibilities have actually *intensified*, as compared to the time when Ginsburg was putting the finishing touches on the grandmother brief. Marianne Cooper's important study reveals how the tech sector valorizes men who literally do nothing but work.[90] She quotes one Silicon Valley engineer:

> Guys try to out-macho each other, but in engineering it's really perverted because out-machoing someone means being more of a nerd than the other person.... It's not like being a brave firefighter and going up one more flight than your friend. There's a lot of see how many hours I can work, whether or not you have a kid.... He's a real man; he works 90-hour weeks. He's a slacker; he works 50 hours a week.[91]

Long hours are nothing new. What's changed is that heroic manliness now requires that men – far from taking time out to care for children – don't even sleep. Another engineer explained:

> Even under normal circumstances, when there are no extraordinary demands, you see people working 36 hours straight just because they are going to meet the deadline. They are going to get it done, and everybody walks around being proud of how exhausted they were last week and conspicuously putting in wild hours. It's a status thing to have pizza delivered to the office. So I don't know why it happens, but I really feel like it is kind of a machismo thing: I'm tough. I can do this. Yeah, I'm tired, but I'm on top of it. You guys

don't worry about me.... The people who conspicuously overwork are guys, and I think it's usually for the benefit of other guys.[92]

Cooper concludes: "The successful enactment of this masculinity involves displaying one's exhaustion, physically and verbally, in order to convey the depth of one's commitment, stamina, and virility."[93]

During the era when Ginsburg first embraced Olaf Palme's vision, no one had documented the backlash that goose-steps men back into line if they attempt to share caregiving responsibilities. Social scientists have now done so. Joseph Vandello and his colleagues studied job evaluations of professional men who chose to work part time to take care of an infant.[94] They found that although men and women value workplace flexibility equally, men were less likely to say they expected to use flexibility policies to the extent they believed (as many did) that others would see them as less masculine if they used such policies.[95] The research also found that use of flexibility policies also caused both men and women to be evaluated more negatively and recommended for smaller raises.[96] Men were not penalized more than women on objective measures, but they faced harsher character judgments.[97] Both men and women who used flexibility policies were seen as more feminine and less masculine, but this evaluation hurt the men more because they were seen as gender deviants.[98]

A study by Laurie Rudman and Kris Mescher confirmed that the flexibility stigma is a femininity stigma.[99] Using experimental vignettes, Rudman and Mescher measured the extent to which taking a twelve-week family leave to care for a sick child or ailing mother was seen as indicative of poor organizational citizens ("poor worker stigma") and feminine ("femininity stigma").[100] Introducing both race and gender into the equation, they found that women were more likely than men to see men who took leave as poor workers; poor worker stigma was associated with organizational penalties.[101] Men who took leave were seen as more feminine, making them more likely to be penalized and less likely to be given organizational rewards.[102] The femininity stigma fully accounted for the effect of the poor worker stigma on penalties, suggesting that male workers tend to be seen as poor workers precisely *because* they are seen as feminine.

A third study is even more sobering: it shows that men who deviate from traditional breadwinner roles encounter backlash from women as well as men. Jennifer Berdahl and Sue Moon found that in a traditionally male workplace (a large metropolitan police force with a majority of male officers), fathers who made caregiving responsibilities salient on the job suffered the highest levels of general mistreatment.[103] In the traditionally female workplace, fathers fared no better: those who made caregiving responsibilities salient suffered the highest levels of masculinity harassment (based on the perception that they were insufficiently masculine).[104]

How can we change these depressing findings? Changing workplace culture is not impossible, as evidenced by an important study by Robin Ely and Debra Myerson of an organizational change initiative on oil platforms. When the study began, these jobs enshrined the "tough guise":[105] they "rewarded men for masculine displays of bravado and for interactions centered on proving masculinity,"[106] which entails "masculine identity centered on appearing physically tough, technically infallible, and emotionally detached."[107] Ely and Myerson quote one man:

> [Back then] the field foremen were kind of like a pack of lions. The guy that was in charge was the one who could basically outperform and out-shout and out-intimidate all the others. That's just how it worked out here on drilling rigs and in production. So those people went to the top, over other people's bodies in some cases. Intimidation was the name of the game.... They decided who the driller was by fighting. If the job came open, the one that was left standing was the driller. It was that rowdy.[108]

Because this masculine script led to high accident rates, management called in a team to change company culture. "We were more and more frustrated with the fact that people kept getting hurt.... In the early nineties we made the commitment [to reduce injuries] that became known as Safety 2000."[109] A manager who had worked for the company for twenty-seven years described a resulting shift: "But it's not like that at all now. I mean we don't even horseplay like we used to. There's no physical practical jokes anymore. Most stuff now is just good-natured joking."[110] An electrician matched this with a description of a shift away from the ideal of the "strong silent type":

> Ten, twelve years ago I just couldn't imagine sitting down with somebody like you and talking about these kinds of things. It was way more macho then than it is now. It was like, "Hey, this is a man's world. If you can't cut it here, boy, you don't need to be here." Now there's a little bit more of, "Let's learn what people are about," a little bit more about the personal and interpersonal relationship and that kind of stuff.[111]

In other words, under the new regime, definitions of competence and leadership changed. Before the culture shift, any expression of vulnerability or acknowledgment of physical limitations, much less a request for help (or even for information!) was a sign of weakness. The result was a history of mistakes and a culture of cover-ups. Under the new regime, workers were trained to acknowledge their own physical limitations, to ask for help when they needed it, and to openly attend to feelings – their own and others'. A production operator described the new ideal worker as someone who "knows what he's doing, or if he doesn't, he'll take the time to do the research to understand what he's doing.... They take time to learn."[112] Workers learned to talk things through and learn from past mistakes. When a seventeen-year-old accidentally shut down all production by throwing a switch, subsequent discussion revealed he had done so on the advice of a co-worker who was a six-foot-four former Chicago cop. The younger man acknowledged that he felt intimidated by the older man. "This exchange led to a larger team discussion about the need to watch out for one's potential to intimidate – however unwittingly – or to be intimidated."[113] The tough guise came to be seen as a workplace detriment.

Workplace culture can change – it *has* changed since the period when Ginsburg was developing her reconstructive vision in the 1970s. Now the challenge is to make sure it changes for the better. What worked on the oil platforms, not surprisingly, was to redefine the desired qualities as the *real* marks of manhood. Thus when one company leader held "fireside chats" – on-site meetings in which he listened to workers' concerns – the blue-collar guys talked "about how brave he is to do this."[114] Note that he was not just "being a good listener" (a feminine quality); he was demonstrating "bravery" (coded masculine).

All this holds important messages for moving feminism closer to Ginsburg's reconstructive vision. If manhood often is forged on the job, then changing the tough guise at work is a crucial feminist agenda. No easy answers – but that's a very different agenda than currently exists in American feminism. It's time to stop blaming women for their failure to bargain for gender equality within the family. So long as gender pressures on men remain unchanged, and schedules remain a key metric in the mine-bigger-than-yours dynamic so central to conventional masculinity, women's kitchen-table bargaining is fated to fail. Feminists need to take up Ginsburg's mantle and open up a conversation about how to change gender pressures on men.

PART II

RIGHTS AND REMEDIES

6

"Seg Academies," Taxes, and *Judge* Ginsburg

Stephen B. Cohen

On the U.S. Court of Appeals for the District of Columbia, then-Judge Ruth Bader Ginsburg authored an opinion with profound implications not only for the law of taxation but also for the role of courts in ending racial discrimination in education. The case, *Wright v. Regan*,[1] involved the dramatic intersection of the income tax law and equal protection obligations of federal authorities under the Constitution's Fifth and Fourteenth Amendments. The precise technical legal issue before her was procedural – whether parents of black schoolchildren had standing to challenge the grant of federal tax-exempt status to racially segregated private schools – but it was hardly arcane or narrow.[2] In affirming that standing existed and reversing the contrary decision of the District Court below, Judge Ginsburg opined that the tax benefits of exempt status constituted significant financial assistance and that the provision of such assistance to racially segregated private schools – so-called "seg academies" – violated equal protection obligations imposed by the Constitution.

Judge Ginsburg's decision was unfortunately reversed on appeal by a divided Supreme Court, which ruled that the plaintiffs did not have standing because they lacked a sufficiently concrete interest in the outcome of the litigation. She nevertheless provided a persuasive and coherent defense of the right of victims of racial discrimination in education to seek redress in the courts, and strong dissents from Justices Brennan and Stevens (joined by Justice Blackmun) supported her position. She thus created a benchmark that future Supreme Courts may use to revise a Supreme Court majority decision that appears, at least to this observer, as fundamentally wrong and fundamentally flawed. Her opinion in *Wright* also offers ways of understanding the later development of educational equal protection doctrine, including Ginsburg's seminal decision in the *Virginia Military Institute* case.

This chapter recounts the historical, political, and legal context in which Judge Ginsburg's ruling in the *Wright* case arose. The context explains the

importance of her decision to the battle against segregated education and
highlights as well the repeated efforts of powerful political forces, including
the Reagan administration and congressional conservatives, to cripple efforts
to prohibit racially discriminatory private schools from receiving federal subsidies through the tax system. This essay also aims to highlight *Wright*'s place in
the modern doctrine of educational discrimination.

I. "SEG ACADEMIES" AND TAX-EXEMPT STATUS

A. *The Importance of Tax-Exempt Status*

For over a century, Congress has provided tax-exempt status to private schools
that operate on a "not for profit" basis. The corporation income tax of 1894
specifically excluded from its coverage a broad array of nonprofit organizations, including educational institutions.[3] In 1917, the individual income tax
(enacted in 1913) was amended to give an additional advantage to a narrower
class of nonprofit entities – primarily schools, churches, hospitals, and organizations for relief of the poor – by permitting their donors to deduct charitable
contributions.[4] In later years, nonprofit organizations were also permitted to
abstain from paying social security and unemployment taxes.[5]

The conflict over tax exemptions for segregated private schools first emerged
after the 1954 Supreme Court holding in *Brown v. Board of Education* that
public school segregation is unconstitutional.[6] Segregation academies, private schools formed to avoid the mandate of *Brown*, sought and received federal tax-exempt status.[7] Civil rights groups sued to prevent these schools from
receiving federal tax benefits.[8]

Throughout the controversy, segregated private schools fought hard to
retain exempt status.[9] Yet most of these schools lacked net income, because
receipts are generally more than offset by expenses. While the exemption does
confer immunity from social security and unemployment taxes, this benefit
was not usually cited as important.[10] According to the IRS, the primary reason for seeking exempt status was so that gifts to a school can be deducted as
charitable donations.[11]

The deduction of claimed contributions, however, is proper only if the
payments are truly charitable donations and are not made in payment for
educational services. If the payment is required, explicitly or informally, as a
condition of a student's enrollment, then its formal designation as a "contribution" is not controlling; the payment is treated as tuition and nondeductible.[12] In general, courts have regarded whether such a payment is "voluntary"
and without "expectation of commensurate benefit" as a matter of subjective

intent and have stated that the determination of intent depends on the facts and circumstances of each particular case.[13]

In 1979, however, the IRS announced a new objective test for charitable contributions to private schools in Revenue Ruling 79–99,[14] based on a decision by the First Circuit Court of Appeals.[15] To the extent that the value of educational services to the donor's children exceeded designated tuition, a contribution was to be treated as nondeductible. The new revenue ruling was protested by the entire private school community, which complained about the automatic disqualification of parents as donors to the extent that the real costs of educating their children exceeded tuition.[16]

In December 1980, the Treasury Department told Congress that secular and sectarian private schools had agreed on a compromise that would supersede Revenue Ruling 79–99.[17] The compromise accepted the subjective standard, but then set forth objective criteria from which subjective intent could be more easily inferred. Certain enumerated factors, alone or in combination, would imply that the contribution was made "in expectation of obtaining educational benefits" for the donor and therefore was not deductible: for example, the denial of admission to children of taxpayers who do not contribute; or the absence of a significant tuition in a school that places unusual pressure on parents to contribute.[18]

At the time, this controversy over disguised tuition was not connected with the ongoing conflict over exemptions for private schools that discriminate. Yet the segregated private schools (unlike most other private institutions) strongly opposed the compromise reached between the IRS and most other private institutions. Their opposition suggests that they benefited significantly, not only from bona fide donations but also from charitable deductions taken for disguised tuition.[19] Thus, the ability of parents to deduct disguised tuition may have been the critical advantage of exempt status for segregated schools, perhaps as or even more important than the deduction for bona fide charitable donations.

B. The Green Principle: Denying Tax-Exempt Status to Racially Segregated Private Schools

Not until 1970, under the pressure of litigation instituted by civil rights groups, did the IRS accept the principle that racially segregated schools may not lawfully receive tax-exempt status.[20] In 1969, the Lawyers' Committee for Civil Rights filed *Green v. Kennedy*, an action on behalf of black schoolchildren in Mississippi, challenging the constitutionality under the equal protection clause of the grant of tax exemptions to racially discriminatory private schools.[21] Because of the claim that a federal statute was being applied in violation of the Constitution, a three-judge federal court was convened.[22] On January 12, 1970, the court issued a preliminary injunction ordering the IRS to withhold exemptions from segregated schools in Mississippi.[23] In July 1970, the IRS announced a policy of denying exempt status to all segregated private schools nationwide.[24]

One year later, the *Green* court issued a final opinion interpreting the Internal Revenue Code as not granting exemptions to racially discriminatory private schools.[25] Writing for a unanimous panel, Judge Harold Leventhal gave three reasons for this conclusion. First, under the common law, an organization whose activities are illegal or contrary to public policy is not entitled to privileges and immunities ordinarily afforded to charities.[26] If Fagin's school for pickpockets could not qualify as a charitable trust, then neither should a segregated private school.[27] Thus, "if we were to follow the common law approach," the Code would be interpreted to deny exempt status in such cases.[28] Second, the Internal Revenue Code "must be construed and applied in consonance with the Federal public policy against support for racial segregation of schools, public or private."[29] The numerous "sources and evidences of that Federal public policy" included the Thirteenth and Fourteenth Amendments, *Brown* and its progeny, and the 1964 Civil Rights Act.[30] Third, any other construction "would raise serious constitutional questions" and "it would be difficult indeed to establish that such [tax] support can be provided consistently with the Constitution."[31]

In addition, a permanent injunction was issued against the government, even though the IRS had acquiesced in the preliminary order,[32] because of the need to prevent future administrations from changing course:

> The July 1970 [IRS] Press Release does not indicate whether the new construction is considered mandatory or merely within the sound discretion available to the IRS in construction of the Code. If defendants' construction were discretionary, it could be changed in the future. We think plaintiffs are entitled to a declaration of relief on an enduring, permanent basis, not on a basis that could be withdrawn with a shift in the tides of administration, or changing perceptions of sound discretion.[33]

The injunction applied only to Mississippi because, under equitable principles, such relief had to be limited to the plaintiffs before the court. However, Judge Leventhal emphasized that, notwithstanding the restricted geographical scope of his order, the legal principle enunciated in construction of the Internal Revenue Code applied nationally:

> To obviate any possible confusion the court is not to be misunderstood as laying down a special rule for schools located in Mississippi. The underlying

principle is broader, and is applicable to schools outside Mississippi with the same or similar badge of doubt.[34]

On appeal, *Green* was affirmed (albeit summarily) by the Supreme Court.[35] *Green* was also cited in four decisions of U.S. Courts of Appeals, upholding IRS authority to deny exemptions to racially discriminatory schools.[36] In addition, Congress appears to have ratified the *Green* decision in 1976 by explicitly amending the Code to deny tax-exempt status to social clubs that discriminate on the basis of race.[37] By prohibiting exemptions to segregated social clubs, Congress signaled its understanding that exemptions for segregated schools already were disallowed.[38] Both House and Senate reports specifically cited *Green* as establishing that "discrimination on account of race is inconsistent with an educational institution's tax-exempt status."[39]

The *Green* principle – construing the IRC to prohibit the grant of exempt status to whites only private schools – has been subject to only one significant (and, as it turned out, short-lived) challenge since 1970. Late in the afternoon of Friday, January 8, 1982, the Reagan administration made two startling announcements.[40] First, the Internal Revenue Service, reversing an eleven-year-old policy, said it would henceforth grant tax exemptions to segregated private schools, because, in the view of the Reagan administration, the IRS had no legal authority to deny them. Second, the government asked the Supreme Court to vacate, as "moot," *Bob Jones University v. United States*[41] and *Goldsboro Christian Schools, Inc. v. United States*,[42] two cases in which racially discriminatory private schools were challenging prior denials of tax-exempt status.[43]

After critical public reaction,[44] however, the Reagan administration swiftly backed off and changed course. It said that it favored and would submit to Congress legislation to authorize the IRS to deny exemptions to private schools that discriminate.[45] Pending congressional action, moreover, the IRS would continue to deny them in all such cases, save for *Bob Jones* and *Goldsboro*, to which exempt status would be restored.[46] Five weeks later, the D.C. Circuit enjoined the IRS from granting exemptions to any segregated school, including *Bob Jones* and *Goldsboro*.[47] The government then withdrew the "suggestion of mootness" in the two Supreme Court cases,[48] and oral argument occurred later that fall.

The Supreme Court issued its near unanimous decision a few months later. In *Bob Jones University v. United States*, Chief Justice Burger, writing for an 8 to 1 majority, held, as did the earlier three-judge panel in *Green*, that the Internal Revenue Code should be construed to deny exempt status to racially segregated private schools.[49] The lone dissenter was Justice William Rehnquist.

When all these actions are put together – the Supreme Court's affirmance of the *Green* decision, congressional endorsement of *Green* through the legislative denial of tax-exempt status to segregated social clubs, and the Supreme Court's decision in *Bob Jones* – the *Green* principle appeared firmly entrenched.

C. Lax Enforcement

Despite the ringing affirmation of the *Green* principle – that exempt status must be withheld from racially discriminatory private schools – enforcement of that principle in practice was lax. In the thirteen-year period, following the first order in *Green* and preceding then-Judge Ginsburg's opinion in *Wright v. Regan*, tax-exempt status was withheld from only 111 schools that enrolled probably no more than 50,000 students.[50]

The Southern Regional Council (an organization of southern business, labor, religious, and professional leaders interested in race relations) estimated that in 1970 about 400,000 white students were attending segregated schools and that by 1972 this figure had grown to 535,000.[51] One organization of private schools, affiliated with segregationist white citizen councils, reported its 1971 membership as including 396 academies with 176,000 students.[52] In 1978, the U.S. Civil Rights Commission counted 3,500 schools that were created or substantially expanded at the time of local school desegregation.[53] (All 3,500 may not have discriminated, but it was reasonable to assume that a substantial proportion did, given the propinquity in time of the schools' creation or expansion to desegregation efforts.) Perhaps the most pointed evidence of nonenforcement was that a number of private schools adjudged by federal courts to be discriminatory, and therefore ineligible for direct aid to education, continued to enjoy federal income-tax exemptions.[54] While there was no consensus as to the total number of segregated private schools, even the lowest estimate indicated that only a tiny fraction was denied exemption.

The gap between principle and practice resulted from implementing procedures, under which a school obtained a tax-exemption merely by declaring that it did not discriminate. Once the required declaration was made, the school was presumed nondiscriminatory, and the presumption was rarely challenged.

The first enforcement guidelines,[55] contained in the July 1970 IRS press release, accepted the *Green* principle but made declaration of nondiscrimination easy. Tax exemptions would be "available to private schools announcing racially nondiscriminatory admissions policies," and "in most instances evidence of a nondiscriminatory policy can be supplied by reference to published statements of policy."[56] The manner of publication was left to the school's discretion.

The permanent injunction issued in *Green* in 1971 specified that Mississippi schools were to include the policy statement in all brochures, catalogues, and printed advertising and to "bring it to the attention of ... minority groups."[57] In response, the IRS formally announced nationwide publicity standards in 1972. Revenue Procedure 72-54 listed acceptable methods, in the alternative, as (1) publication in a "newspaper of general circulation that serves all racial segments of the locality"; (2) "broadcast media" that reach "all segments of the community the school serves"; (3) "school brochures and catalogues" if "distributed ... to all segments of the community that the school serves"; or (4) advising "leaders of racial minorities ... so that they in turn will make this policy known to other members of their race."[58]

After the U.S. Civil Rights Commission challenged the adequacy of these standards,[59] the IRS adopted somewhat more stringent guidelines in 1975. Revenue Procedure 75-50 sets out three basic requirements, all of which must be met. First, the nondiscrimination policy must be stated in the school's charter or by-laws, in all brochures and catalogues, and all written advertising. Second, the policy has to be publicized either in a "newspaper" or through the "broadcast media." Third, the publicity has to occur "during the period of ... solicitation for students ... during the school's registration period."[60] The 1975 guidelines remain in effect today.

These four approaches – the 1970 IRS press release, the 1971 *Green* injunction, the 1972 Revenue Procedure, and the 1975 Revenue Procedure – assumed that a mere declaration of policy was adequate to enforce the *Green* principle. Yet according to the U.S. Civil Rights Commission, the Justice Department under Presidents Ford and Carter, and a congressional study, schools that in fact practiced racial discrimination easily met even the heavier burden of publication imposed in 1975.[61] Most simply declared that they did not discriminate and thus obtained exemptions.[62] Only the handful that openly acknowledged their discriminatory practices lost exempt status.

In 1976, *Green* was reopened, and, at the same time, a class action on behalf of parents of black schoolchildren nationwide sued the IRS for stricter enforcement of the *Green* principle in *Wright v. Regan*.[63] Both suits were consolidated, but the proceedings were suspended in 1978, when the IRS published its own proposal for stricter enforcement.[64] The proposal was derived from criteria developed by federal district courts for identifying segregated private schools ineligible for state textbook aid.[65]

The new IRS enforcement proposal focused not on self-serving declarations but on two objective factors: the propinquity in time of a private school's formation or expansion to public school desegregation, and the private school's proportion of minority enrollment. Any private school formed or substantially expanded at the time of local public school desegregation would be presumed discriminatory unless its minority enrollment was at least 20 percent of the proportion of minorities in the local community's school age population.[66] The presumption could be rebutted only by engaging in four of five specified practices designed to attract minority students and faculty.[67]

Public reaction to the 1978 proposal was overwhelmingly negative. The IRS received over 150,000 letters, virtually all in opposition, and the public was invited to comment during three days of hearings at the IRS national office.[68] As a result of the criticism, the proposal was made substantially less rigid and was republished in 1979.[69] Under the revised proposal, the presumption of discrimination would arise only if minority enrollment was "insignificant" (in addition to the school being founded or expanded at the time of local public school desegregation), and rebuttal of an unfavorable presumption was made considerably easier.[70] These changes, however, were not sufficient to overcome the negative public reaction.[71]

After hearings in the House and Senate on the revised proposal,[72] Congress froze enforcement in the mold of the 1975 Revenue Procedure by attaching two riders to the Treasury Appropriations Bill for 1980. One, the Dornan amendment, specifically denied funds for enforcement of either the original 1978 proposal or the 1979 revision.[73] The other, the Ashbrook amendment, prohibited the use of appropriated funds to enforce any Treasury or IRS guidelines not in effect before August 22, 1978 (the date on which the IRS published its 1978 enforcement proposal).[74] Both the Dornan and Ashbrook amendments continued in effect for several subsequent fiscal years.[75]

These congressional efforts undermined the IRS attempt to strengthen its enforcement rules. As a result of the Ashbrook and Dornan amendments, the ineffective enforcement protocol of the 1975 Revenue Procedure remained the only vehicle for implementing the principle of *Green*.[76]

II. LITIGATION RESUMES: THE STRENGTHENED *GREEN* ORDER AND *WRIGHT V. REGAN*

A. *The District Court*

In 1979, following passage of the Ashbrook and Dornan amendments, the Lawyers' Committee for Civil Rights reopened the suspended proceedings in *Green* and *Wright*, seeking a court order of more vigorous enforcement of the *Green* principle. In November, District Court Judge Hart dismissed the *Wright* component on jurisdictional grounds,[77] primarily because the plaintiffs were held to lack standing under the 1975 Supreme Court opinion in *Simon v. Eastern Kentucky Welfare Rights Organization (EKWRO).*[78]

In *EKWRO*, indigent plaintiffs challenged a Revenue Ruling permitting a hospital to receive tax-exempt status regardless of whether it provided free or below cost service to the poor. The plaintiffs lacked standing, the Supreme Court declared, because it "is purely speculative whether the denials of service specified in the complaint fairly can be traced to (the Ruling) or instead result from decisions made by the hospitals without regard to the tax implications."[79] Similarly, in the *Wright* litigation, Judge Hart concluded, it was purely speculative whether racial discrimination by segregated private schools could be traced to IRS enforcement practices or resulted from decisions made by the schools without regard to taxes.

Judge Hart, however, rejected an identical argument with respect to the *Green* component because standing had already been found by the original three-judge panel in 1970.[80] After trial on the merits, in May 1980, Judge Hart granted the kind of substantive relief requested by the *Green* plaintiffs by ordering stricter enforcement. He enjoined the IRS from granting exempt status to Mississippi schools that were "established or expanded at the time of local school desegregation, unless the schools clearly and convincingly demonstrate that they do not discriminate."[81]

In July 1980, following Judge Hart's order in the Mississippi litigation, Congress acted to prevent the IRS from denying exemptions to private schools under his strengthened *Green* injunction or any other future judicial rules. It expanded the Ashbrook rider, which already banned spending to enforce any rule made by the Executive after August 22, 1978, to include in addition "any ... court order."[82] Meanwhile, during this same period, the dismissal of *Wright* was on appeal to the D.C. Circuit.

B. The Appeal: Judge Ginsburg's Opinion

In June 1981, the Court of Appeals, in an opinion by Judge Ginsburg, reversed Judge Hart and ruled that the *Wright* plaintiffs did have standing.[83] Her opinion began by reviewing in detail the history of both the *Green* and *Wright* litigation.[84] She emphasized "the anomalous result" of the district court decision.[85] To obey both court decree and congressional stop order, the IRS must apply one set of guidelines to schools in Mississippi and another, less stringent set of procedures to schools outside Mississippi, even schools bearing 'the same or similar badge of doubt.'"[86]

Acknowledging that the 1975 Supreme Court opinion in *EKWRO* stands for the proposition that "litigation concerning tax liability is a matter between taxpayer and IRS, with the door barely ajar for third party challenges,"[87] Judge Ginsburg cited other Supreme Court precedents pointing in the opposite direction, affirming that parents of black schoolchildren do have standing to challenge government assistance to private schools practicing race discrimination. In particular, Judge Ginsburg noted that in the companion *Green* litigation, *Norwood v. Harrison,*[88] and *Gilmore v. City of Montgomery,*[89] the Supreme Court upheld the standing of the plaintiffs to challenge government conduct as "inconsistent with an overriding, constitutionally rooted national policy against racial discrimination in United States educational facilities."[90]

In *Norwood,* parents of black schoolchildren challenged aid to segregated private schools under a Mississippi program begun in 1940, which furnished free textbooks for students at all public and private elementary and secondary schools in the state.[91] In a unanimous decision, the justices found for the parents and ordered the Federal District Court in Mississippi to establish procedures for identifying private schools that were racially discriminatory and therefore ineligible for free textbooks.[92]

One year later, in *Gilmore,* parents of black students sought an injunction against "the use of city owned and operated recreational facilities by any private school group ... which is racially segregated."[93] Citing *Norwood,* the Supreme Court again unanimously affirmed an order against the exclusive use of certain facilities, because that constituted "tangible state assistance outside generalized services."[94]

Given these precedents, Judge Ginsburg concluded:

> *Green, Norwood,* and *Gilmore* presented plaintiffs whose standing seems to us indistinguishable on any principled ground from the standing of the plaintiffs in this action. If the plaintiffs before us are not entitled to question the IRS practices at issue here, it is difficult to comprehend why the *Green, Norwood,* and *Gilmore* plaintiffs were entitled to challenge the tax exemptions, textbook loans, and specially reserved park facilities at issue in those cases.[95]

Thus, Judge Ginsburg's opinion in *Wright* provided a persuasive defense of the right of parents of back schoolchildren to challenge the provision of government assistance, include tax-exempt status, to racially segregated private schools. She affirmed the *Green* principle that "seg academies" may not receive tax-exempt status. She offered an important vehicle, litigation by private individuals, for curing the woeful underenforcement of *Green* when more vigorous implementation was blocked by congressional enactment of the Ashbrook and Dornan amendments.

C. The Supreme Court Reverses

In 1984, three years later, a 5-3 Supreme Court majority reversed Judge Ginsburg's decision on grounds similar to those cited by Judge Hart.[96] The opinion of the Court by Justice Sandra Day O'Connor stated:

> The diminished ability of respondents' children to receive a desegregated education would be fairly traceable to unlawful IRS grants of tax exemptions only if there were enough racially discriminatory private schools receiving tax exemptions in respondents' communities for withdrawal of those exemptions to make an appreciable difference in public school integration. Respondents have made no such allegation. It is, first, uncertain how many racially discriminatory private schools are in fact receiving tax exemptions. Moreover, it is entirely speculative … whether withdrawal of a tax-exemption from any particular school would lead the school to change its policies.[97]

Thus, Justice O'Connor concluded:

> The links in the chain of causation between the challenged Government conduct and the asserted injury are far too weak for the chain as a whole to sustain respondents' standing. In Simon v. Eastern Kentucky Welfare Rights Org … the Court held that standing to challenge a Government grant of a tax-exemption to hospitals could not be founded on the asserted connection between the grant of tax-exempt status and the hospitals' policy concerning the provision of medical services to indigents.[98]

Justice William Brennan, endorsing Judge Ginsburg's reasoning, issued a stinging dissent:

> Once again, the Court "uses 'standing to slam the courthouse door against plaintiffs who are entitled to full consideration of their claims on the merits.'"[99]
>
> [T]he Court displays a startling insensitivity to the historical role played by the federal courts in eradicating race discrimination from our Nation's schools – a role that has played a prominent part in this Court's decisions from Brown v. Board of Education.[100]

Moreover, Justice Brennan continued, the allegations in the complaint were more than sufficient to satisfy standing requirements:

> The respondents have alleged a direct causal relationship between the Government action they challenge and the injury they suffer: their inability to receive an education in a racially integrated school is directly and adversely affected by the tax-exempt status granted by the IRS to racially discriminatory schools in their respective school districts. Common sense alone would

recognize that the elimination of tax-exempt status for racially discriminatory private schools would serve to lessen the impact that those institutions have in defeating efforts to desegregate the public schools.[101]

Justice Stevens, whose separate dissent was joined by Justice Blackmun, also emphasized the majority's "untenable assumption that the granting of preferential tax treatment to segregated schools does not make those schools more attractive to white students and hence does not inhibit the process of desegregation."[102]

III. THE LEGACY OF *WRIGHT*

A. *Segregated Private Schools since the Supreme Court Decision*

During the thirty years since the Supreme Court's decision in *Wright*, there have been numerous studies of the de facto resegregation of America's public school systems but surprisingly no systematic examination of the contribution of private segregated education to this phenomenon. What evidence exists is anecdotal.

For example, in 2002, the *Birmingham News* reported on the Wilcox Academy in rural Alabama as "100 percent white, a typical link in the chain of private Black Belt academies erected in the late 1960s and 1970s to circumvent federal integration orders."[103] However, the newspaper also noted, "The chain is weakening by the year. Beset with dwindling enrollments, internal conflicts and an inability to pay teachers' salaries, so-called 'seg academies' close down regularly in this rural stretch of central Alabama."[104]

There are reports, however, that all-white private academies in the South continue to receive federal tax-exempt status, even in Mississippi, where Judge Hart's strengthened enforcement order may have had little or no effect. In 2012, an article in the *Atlantic* magazine described one such school in Indianola, Mississippi, that continues to benefit from federal tax-exempt status.[105] The *Atlantic* also claimed that at least thirty-five such schools continue to operate in the Mississippi Delta.[106]

B. *Echoes of* Wright *in the Virginia Military Institute Case*

There were echoes of *Wright* in the much later 1996 Supreme Court decision in *United States v. Virginia*[107] (VMI) for which Justice Ginsburg also wrote the opinion of the Court. In *Wright*, Judge Ginsburg expressed serious doubt that the equal protection clause of the Constitution permits the federal government to grant tax-exempt status to racially segregated private schools. In *VMI*, Justice Ginsburg held that the equal protection clause does not permit the state to finance a military college, the Virginia Military Institute, open only to male applicants.

It was of course direct state funding rather than tax-exempt status that raised the equal protection issue in *VMI*. Nevertheless, during oral argument, counsel for the state argued that if the Constitution requires a military college financed and controlled by the state of Virginia to admit women, then it also requires Wellesley College to admit men or lose its federal tax-exempt status.[108] Similarly, in dissenting from the Court's decision in *VMI*, Justice Scalia wrote: "It is certainly not beyond the Court that rendered today's decision to hold that a [tax deductible] donation to a single-sex college should be deemed contrary to public policy and therefore not deductible if the college discriminates on the basis of sex."[109]

Notwithstanding the conclusion that the Fifth and Fourteenth Amendments prohibit exempt status for racially segregated private schools, and notwithstanding the Supreme Court's decision in *VMI*, can exempt status be constitutionally provided to single-sex private educational institutions? The constitutional status of whites-only private schools is vastly different from that of single-sex educational institutions. Although in *Bob Jones*, the Supreme Court cited the "unmistakably clear" agreement among "all three branches of the Federal Government" that racial discrimination must be eliminated,[110] there is no evidence of a similar hostility to single-sex educational institutions. Thus, an amicus brief in the *VMI* case contrasted racially segregated education with single-sex education to counter the suggestion that if a military college financed by, and subject to the control of, the state of Virginia is required to admit female applicants, then Wellesley College must admit men or lose its federal tax-exempt status:

> The three branches of the federal government have not, acting independently or in concert, articulated a position against, much less launched a crusade to dismantle, private single-sex colleges.... In short, there is no "fundamental public policy" or "declared position of the whole Government" which the maintenance or establishment of private single-gender undergraduate college programs contravenes.... Moreover ... the evidence is clear and well-established that single-sex education for women is particularly effective in preparing them for leadership and success, generally, and in male-dominated fields, more particularly.[111]

As Justice Ginsburg noted in *VMI*, the Supreme Court has "reserved most stringent judicial scrutiny for classifications based on race or national origin."[112]

In addition, there is a vast difference between the kind of support afforded the Virginia Military Institute – the college was largely financed and controlled by the state of Virginia – and the less extensive and intrusive support afforded by tax-exempt status. Justice Ginsburg's opinion in *VMI* noted the special circumstances of the case, addressing "specifically and only an educational opportunity recognized ... as 'unique,' ... an opportunity available only at Virginia's premier military institute, the Commonwealth's sole single-sex public university or college."[113]

In the absence of special circumstances, however, the Equal Protection Clause Fourteenth Amendment should permit an all-men's (as well as an all-women's) college to benefit from tax-exempt status, even though more intrusive government financing and control of the kind in the *VMI* case would raise equal protection issues and despite the fact that racially segregated private schools should ordinarily not be permitted to receive exempt status given the especially high constitutional value placed on ending racial discrimination in education.

Judge Ginsburg's consideration of *Wright* – where the underlying issue involved the strict scrutiny of racial classifications under the equal protection clause – may have influenced Justice Ginsburg's articulation of the intermediate scrutiny of gender classifications in cases like *VMI*. Indeed, together *VMI* and *Wright* present an integrated and balanced approach to equal protection challenges that considers differences between race and gender discrimination and between different kinds of government assistance. Thus, tax-exempt status for racially segregated private schools would be constitutionally suspect while tax-exempt status for an all male institution presumably would not.

Of course, depending on the context and the myriad different ways that single-sex education might be implemented, it is conceivable that in special circumstances, tax-exempt status for single-sex private education might offend the Equal Protection Clause. Justice Ginsburg's tax expert husband, Professor Martin G. Ginsburg, suggested one such circumstance more than thirty years ago in 1977.[114] The IRS had ruled that a charitable deduction was available for contributions to a males-only college scholarship for graduates of a coeducational high school.[115] Professor Ginsburg conceded that contributions to a scholarship for students at a single-sex institution could be deductible. He forcefully argued, however, that the IRS ruling on a males-only scholarship at a coeducational institution was inconsistent with applicable federal law, Supreme Court precedents, and possibly even the Constitution.[116]

> The Supreme Court has declared invidiously discriminatory gender-based classifications that denigrate women or deny them equal opportunity. Such

classification ... is inconsistent with the equal protection requirement of the fifth and fourteenth amendments. The decade's precedent solidly establishes an elevated review standard for gender-based allocation of benefits or opportunities. A "legitimate" objective will not save a sex classification; a "rational" means/end relationship will not suffice. In the Court's words: "To withstand [constitutional] scrutiny ... classifications by gender must serve important governmental objectives and must be substantially related to those objectives."[117]

Strongest condemnation has been expressed by the Court for the gender criterion used to preserve for males special advantage in "the marketplace and the world of ideas." Distinguishing "between [boy and girl] on educational grounds," the Court has emphasized, is "self-serving" and "coincides with the role typing society has long imposed."[118]

7

A More Perfect Union:
Sex, Race, and the *VMI* Case

Cary Franklin

May 17, 2014, marked the sixtieth anniversary of *Brown v. Board of Education.*[1] On that day, President Obama issued a proclamation commemorating the decision as "a turning point in America's journey toward a more perfect Union."[2] The president noted that *Brown* not only breathed life into the Equal Protection Clause of the Fourteenth Amendment but also provided impetus for the landmark civil rights statutes of the 1960s, most notably, the Civil Rights Act of 1964 and the Voting Rights Act of 1965. In so doing, the president declared, the decision "shifted the legal and moral compass of our Nation."[3]

Yet for all these words of praise, there was an undercurrent running through the president's proclamation: a suggestion that for too many Americans, the promise of *Brown* remains just that. The president left it to the First Lady and Secretary of Education Arne Duncan to make this point more explicitly. In a commencement address to graduating high school seniors in *Brown's* home city of Topeka, Kansas, Michelle Obama observed that "our schools are as segregated [today] as they were back when Dr. King gave his final speech," and that "many districts in this country have actually pulled back on efforts to integrate" – with the result that American children are once again attending school "with kids who look just like them."[4] Arne Duncan echoed these observations. He noted that although *Brown* ended de jure segregation, it did not end de facto segregation; in fact, many school districts that desegregated in the 1960s and 1970s have since resegregated.[5] Today, 40 percent of black and Latino students attend "intensely segregated schools," and white students are similarly isolated: only 14 percent attend truly integrated schools.[6] Thus, Duncan concluded that although *Brown* may once "have seemed like the end of a long struggle for educational equality,"[7] it was actually just the beginning of a struggle that continues to this day.

The Executive Branch's not-entirely-sanguine assessment of racial progress in the decades since *Brown* stands in stark contrast to the message emanating from the Supreme Court in recent years in regard to the status of racial equality in the United States. While the Executive commemorated *Brown's* anniversary by calling attention to the ongoing struggle to overcome our nation's long history of racial subordination, the Roberts Court has, in its recent decisions involving race discrimination, emphasized our emancipation from this history. Several years ago, the Court invalidated race-based school desegregation plans voluntarily adopted by Louisville and Seattle on the ground that those cities had already "removed the vestiges of past segregation"[8] (or were innocent of de jure segregation in the first place) – and thus had nothing to remedy. More recently, the Court invalidated a key provision of the Voting Rights Act after finding that the United States had overcome the history of race discrimination that initially justified the act's passage.[9] "History did not end in 1965,"[10] Chief Justice Roberts declared: "things have changed dramatically since then."[11] He asserted that Congress had no business trying to protect racial minorities in the twenty-first century based on decades-old "facts having no logical relation to the present day."[12]

In fact, the Court has suggested – in these and other cases – that we have come so far in surmounting our history of race discrimination that measures designed to combat discrimination or "help" racial minorities are now often the true barriers to equality. On this view, such measures – whether they take the form of school integration plans, civil rights statutes, or affirmative action – are preventing us from achieving the genuine and original promise of the Fourteenth Amendment: a color-blind society in which the state refrains from classifying individuals on the basis of race.[13]

Of course, not all of the justices subscribe to this "color-blind" constitutionalism. In her twenty-one years on the Court, Ruth Bader Ginsburg has been a powerful proponent of a different understanding of equal protection and the aims of the Fourteenth Amendment. This understanding is not blind to race but attentive to the ways in which it affects people's lived experiences. It does not assume that we have overcome our long history of race discrimination but instead examines the ways in which this history continues to shape institutional structures and curtail opportunity. It is an understanding that has animated not only Ginsburg's service on the Court but her entire career as a lawyer. It has formed a central part of her life's work.

Thus, it is not surprising that (what is perhaps) Ginsburg's most famous opinion should be the one that most fully articulates this understanding. The opinion is a sweeping meditation on the meaning of the Fourteenth Amendment's equality guarantee, the role of history in constitutional interpretation, and the lengthy and ongoing efforts of the American people to form a "more perfect Union." As such, it ranks as one of the most important commentaries on *Brown*, and on the entire strain of equal protection law that grew out of *Brown*, to issue from the Court in decades – even though it never once mentions that decision. In fact, the opinion is not even (on its face, at least) about race at all.

I. THE *VMI* CASE

Ruth Bader Ginsburg was a very junior justice on the Supreme Court when she was assigned to write the majority opinion in *United States v. Virginia*.[14] At issue in the case was the admissions policy of the Virginia Military Institute, a highly regarded, public, all-male military academy. By the 1990s, VMI had been a single-sex school for more than a century and a half, and those in charge of the school wished it to remain that way. Thus, when a female high school student seeking admission to the school filed a complaint about its admissions policy with a sympathetic Justice Department, VMI found itself in court.

A large part of VMI's appeal – to a certain breed of teenagers and their parents – is its unusually rough and rigorous pedagogical style. To achieve its goal of transforming sophomoric youngsters into "citizen-soldiers," the school relies on an "'adversative method' modeled on English public schools and once characteristic of military instruction."[15] Entering students are subjected to a "rat line" comparable in intensity to Marine Corps boot camp; for their entire first year, they are incessantly tormented and punished by upperclassmen. The goal of this particular brand of pedagogy is to show new cadets what they are capable of when pushed to their physical and psychological limits, to bind them to "their fellow sufferers,"[16] and to forge a unified corps of disciplined and highly regimented young men. To this end, VMI has long required cadets to wear uniforms, eat together, adhere to the same schedule, and live in spartan barracks where surveillance is ubiquitous and privacy nonexistent. Relatively few of these "citizen-soldiers" actually go on to join the United States military,[17] but many – through some combination of skills acquired at VMI and the help of the school's remarkably cohesive and loyal alumni network[18] – enter the upper echelons of the state's business and political communities.[19]

The "rat line" is not a standard element in most teenagers' vision of college life, but VMI's militaristic ethos does appeal to some young men and, as it turns out, to some young women as well. In the two years before the Justice Department brought suit against VMI, hundreds of teenage girls had inquired (but received no reply) about possible admission to the school.[20] The Justice Department filed its suit on behalf of these women and others like them. It argued that some women would want to attend VMI, given the chance, and that some women were capable of meeting all of the school's admissions standards save the sex requirement.[21] Although the framers of the Fourteenth Amendment may not have recognized Virginia's maintenance of an all-male military institute as a violation of equal protection, the Justice Department argued, the state's ongoing restriction of this valuable and unusual opportunity to men did not comport with contemporary understandings of citizenship and equality.[22]

Virginia responded to these claims by arguing that an all-male environment was integral to VMI's ability to accomplish its mission – that VMI simply would not be VMI if it were forced to admit female cadets.[23] For a start, the state asserted that the incorporation of women would undermine the adversative method, which depended on a complete lack of privacy and personal space, and demanded a kind of physical closeness that would be inappropriate between men and women.[24] The school simply could not continue to function as it had been functioning, with great success, for most of the nation's history, if it were required to make the sort of accommodations that an influx of female cadets would require. Moreover, the state argued, the adversative method did not constitute a suitable approach to the education of women, most of whom "tend to thrive in a cooperative atmosphere"[25] rather than one that involves being berated on a regular basis. Thus, the state proposed to remedy the educational inequality caused by its maintenance of an all-male military academy not by permitting women to attend VMI but by creating a separate "leadership" program for women at a nearby women's college.[26] Instead of seeking to push female students to their physical and psychological breaking point, this program would aim to support and encourage them – and it would do so by sparing them almost all of the extreme lifestyle elements characteristic of education at VMI.[27]

It seems fair to say that when *United States v. Virginia* reached the Supreme Court in the mid-1990s, no justice had thought more deeply about the constitutional questions implicated by this set of arguments than Ruth Bader Ginsburg. Long before she became a Supreme Court Justice, Ginsburg had been a litigator of constitutional sex discrimination cases. She co-founded the ACLU Women's Rights Project in the early 1970s with the aim of convincing the Court that discrimination on the basis of sex was no less a violation of equal protection than discrimination on the basis of race. Her campaign was fantastically successful. Within a few years of bringing her first case, Ginsburg had persuaded the Court that discrimination on the basis of sex implicated constitutional equality concerns and warranted heightened scrutiny under the Fourteenth Amendment. In 1993, when President Clinton nominated Ginsburg to the high court, he acknowledged this achievement by referring to her as the "Thurgood Marshall of gender equality law."[28]

The *VMI* case provided Ginsburg with her first opportunity to speak about sex discrimination as a justice, and on behalf of the Court – and she made the most of it. Her opinion in *United States v. Virginia* answers the question at issue, of course: whether the state of Virginia may continue to operate a military institute exclusively for men. But the opinion does more than that. It explicates, much more fully than the Court had in previous opinions, the "mediating principle"[29] that guides the application of the Fourteenth Amendment in cases involving sex-based state action. In other words, Ginsburg's opinion in *United States v. Virginia* does not simply resolve the contest over VMI's admissions policy. It articulates a "guide for decision"[30] – an interpretive principle the Court has used (and in Ginsburg's view, ought to continue to use) to apply the broad generalities of the Constitution, such as "equal protection," to actual cases on the ground.

United States v. Virginia explicitly rejects blindness – in this case, sex-blindness – as the guiding principle in constitutional equality law. In the course of her opinion, Ginsburg provides multiple examples of sex classifications that are likely consistent with equal protection. She suggests, for instance, that a sex-specific recruitment program aimed at achieving "a sufficient 'critical mass' to provide female cadets with a positive educational experience"[31] at VMI would pass constitutional muster, despite the fact that such a program might be construed as treating women differently than men. She suggests, in addition, that the admission of women would require VMI to make "accommodations, primarily in arranging housing assignments and physical training programs for female cadets"[32] – and that such sex-specific accommodations would not run afoul of equal protection. Indeed, Ginsburg goes so far as to suggest that some single-sex schools (and here she cites a collection of private women's colleges) may advance, rather than impede, the pursuit of sex equality and thus satisfy legal requirements regarding the equal treatment of the sexes.[33] Yet she strikes down VMI's admissions policy, holding in no uncertain terms that *this* classification violates the Equal Protection Clause. The operative principle here is obviously not sex-blindness, or anti-classification. So what is the principle guiding the Court's determination that VMI is constitutionally compelled to admit women?

United States v. Virginia holds that the Fourteenth Amendment permits sex-based state action that "dissipate[s]"[34] traditional sex stereotypes but disallows sex-based state action that reflects or reinforces such stereotypes. Unlike the anti-classification principle, this anti-stereotyping principle is contextually grounded. To implement this principle, one needs to know something about the history of stereotyping and discrimination a group has faced before determining whether a given action by the state has deprived that group of equal protection. To this end – and to a greater extent than any other opinion in the canon of constitutional sex discrimination law – *United States v. Virginia* excavates and analyzes the particular forms of discrimination women have historically faced in the American legal system.

Ginsburg's opinion points out that from the time of the founding until 1920, "women did not count among voters composing 'We the People.'"[35] Thomas Jefferson was merely stating the prevailing wisdom of his day when he observed that even if the United States were "a pure democracy," women would still be excluded from decision-making councils because propriety demanded that they refrain from "mix[ing] promiscuously in the public meetings of men."[36] Politics was not the only public pursuit from which women were historically excluded. Ginsburg notes that women were barred from a wide range of occupations, including law, medicine, policing, and bartending.[37] They were also systematically denied entrée to educational institutions that would have prepared them for most desirable and remunerative forms of work.[38] Underwriting all of these instances of discrimination, Ginsburg observes, was a stereotyped conception of women's (and men's) sex and family roles. Historically, sex-based regulation reflected the idea that women were, at best, secondary players in the public sphere, and it reinforced the notion that their proper place was in the home, caring for their children and families.[39]

Justice Scalia did not see the point of this lengthy foray into the history of sex discrimination. In his dissenting opinion, he accused Justice Ginsburg of gratuitously "deprecating the closed-mindedness of our forebears"[40] by invoking a litany of historical examples of discrimination that had little bearing on the constitutionality of VMI's admissions policy. Indeed, Scalia noted that many of Ginsburg's historical examples involve "the treatment of women in areas that have nothing to do with education."[41] But her aim, in invoking all of this history, was not to disparage previous generations of Americans but to make a point about equal protection: namely, that the past is not entirely past, and that history is relevant to the adjudication of contemporary discrimination claims under the Fourteenth Amendment. To determine whether a given regulation violates equal protection, it is necessary to assess whether it perpetuates a history of discrimination that has deprived the members of a particular group of full and equal citizenship. Thus, Ginsburg holds, the problem with VMI's all-male admissions policy is not that it classifies individuals on the basis of their sex but that it reflects and reinforces the set of stereotypes that have incited and justified discrimination against women for most of American history. The exclusion of women from VMI – and the hastily conceived women's "leadership" institute that was supposed to make up for it – perpetuate traditional stereotyped conceptions of men as soldiers, protectors, and public citizens, and of women as passive, domestic creatures, more suited to caring than combat. It does not simply do this in the abstract: it reinforces inequality in practice by depriving women of access to a valuable educational opportunity and a career pipeline that feeds into positions of influence in the state of Virginia.

This is what differentiates VMI's all-male admissions policy from the other forms of sex-based state action Ginsburg seems to condone in *United States v. Virginia*. VMI's exclusion of women reinforces a long history of exclusion; it perpetuates a tradition in which women were denied equal access to the public sphere and deprived of educational and professional opportunities on the basis of stereotypes about their proper maternal and domestic roles. By contrast, targeted efforts to recruit female cadets and modest sex-specific accommodations in housing aim to end this history of exclusion. They are designed to integrate women into VMI and to help female cadets and the institution itself overcome the wall of stereotypes that long barred half the state's population from reaping the rewards of a VMI education. Ginsburg articulated this distinction quite succinctly in her opinion when she wrote that "sex classifications may be used to compensate women for particular economic disabilities [they have] suffered, to promot[e] equal employment opportunity, [and] to advance full development of the talent and capacities of our Nation's people. But such classifications may not be used, as they once were, to create or perpetuate the legal, social, and economic inferiority of women."[42]

This approach to equal protection reflects a broader conception of the meaning and purpose of the Fourteenth Amendment. Ginsburg concludes her opinion in *VMI* by citing the observation of historian Richard Morris that "a prime part of the history of our Constitution ... is the story of the extension of constitutional rights and protections to people once ignored or excluded."[43] *United States v. Virginia* suggests this history ought to serve as a guide for applying the Equal Protection Clause to today's constitutional controversies. It is likely true that a VMI with female cadets is different from a VMI without female cadets. As Ginsburg observes in her opinion, VMI after racial integration was not the same as it was before it integrated.[44] But in neither instance, she opines, was there reason to believe that a move toward greater inclusion "would destroy the institution rather than enhance its capacity to serve the 'more perfect Union.'"[45]

II. *VMI* AS A MODEL FOR EQUAL PROTECTION

Justice Scalia dissented vigorously from almost all aspects of Ginsburg's majority opinion in *United States v. Virginia*. His central objection was to the level of scrutiny it seemed to apply to sex-based state action. Scalia asserted that the Court had long applied intermediate scrutiny in the context of sex, asking whether the discrimination was "substantially related to an important government objective."[46] He argued that the tougher test of strict scrutiny was reserved for cases involving race discrimination.[47] Yet, the majority opinion in *United States v. Virginia* seemed to collapse this distinction. It seemed to treat sex discrimination the same as race discrimination for purposes of equal protection, subjecting it to a higher level of scrutiny than Scalia believed was warranted.[48]

Justice Scalia may be right that *United States v. Virginia* does not leave much room between the levels of scrutiny that apply in cases involving sex- and race-based state action. The Court repeatedly declares that sex-based state action requires an "exceedingly persuasive justification"[49]; it subjects the state's asserted justifications for VMI's all-male admissions policy to a fairly intense form of scrutiny. But in accusing the Court of subjecting sex discrimination to the same standard of review as race discrimination, Scalia overlooks what is almost certainly the bolder move Ginsburg makes in *VMI*, which is to suggest that race discrimination is, or ought to be, evaluated under the same set of constitutional principles that apply in the context of sex discrimination. Some of the most profound implications of Ginsburg's opinion in *VMI* concern how we ought to understand the constitutional project of equal protection – as much in the context of race as in the context of sex.

To say that *VMI* has these broader constitutional implications is not to say that the opinion does not make important observations about sex in particular. One of Ginsburg's most daunting and significant challenges as a litigator in the 1970s was to make the history of sex discrimination visible to a Court that had not previously demonstrated any familiarity with the subject. It was not an easy task. The Court was accustomed, by then, to hearing race discrimination claims, but it had far less experience adjudicating legal controversies that implicated sex. It sometimes struggled on the latter front, particularly in cases where the analogy to race was weakest, such as those involving pregnancy. In 1974, for instance, the Court failed to recognize pregnancy discrimination as sex discrimination, reasoning that not all women are pregnant: having a child is just something some women do.[50]

Ginsburg's opinion in *United States v. Virginia* seeks to rectify these early missteps. It provides an unprecedentedly comprehensive account of the history of women's experiences in the American legal system, making visible aspects of that history the Court had previously overlooked. Most striking, in this regard, is the opinion's treatment of "supposed 'inherent differences'"[51] between men and women. "We have come to appreciate" that physical differences between the sexes "remain cause for celebration,"[52] Ginsburg wrote. But, she observed, we have also come to appreciate that such differences may not be used, as they once were, "for denigration of the members of either sex or for artificial constraints on an individual's opportunity."[53] As Ginsburg notes in *VMI*, the Court does not generally confront the issue of "inherent differences" in the context of race, where such "differences" ceased long ago to serve as a legitimate justification for race-based state action.[54] But women's capacity to become pregnant is "enduring,"[55] and Ginsburg's opinion in *VMI* makes an important contribution to the Court's understanding of its constitutional significance. It suggests not that the state should ignore pregnancy, but that it may not regulate pregnancy in ways that reflect or reinforce traditional stereotyped conceptions of women's sex and family roles. This is, undoubtedly, an important clarification of the Court's earlier constitutional reasoning regarding physical differences between the sexes.[56]

Yet in focusing on the particular – the history of sex discrimination and the regulation of "supposed 'inherent differences'" between the sexes – Ginsburg's opinion in *United States v. Virginia* also makes important observations about equal protection law more generally. It suggests that judges ought to remain cognizant of the aims of the Fourteenth Amendment – to foster social inclusion and remedy group-based inequality – when interpreting the Equal Protection Clause. The only way to do this, the opinion suggests, is to attend to history, and to the particular experiences of different groups in the American legal system. Armed with such awareness, it becomes possible to determine whether a contested form of state action perpetuates or ameliorates the kinds of inequality the Fourteenth Amendment was designed to combat. *VMI* teaches that, sometimes, state action that helps to ameliorate inequality will take the form of group-based classifications. Classifications of this kind – though they sort people on the basis of a group characteristic – do not violate equal protection: they are equal protection.

Because *United States v. Virginia* engages in these broader forms of reasoning about the Fourteenth Amendment, its implications are not confined to the context of sex.[57] Indeed, in the nearly two decades that have passed since *VMI*, Ginsburg has consistently applied the principles articulated in that case to constitutional questions involving race.[58] She has, for instance, repeatedly voted to uphold race-based educational affirmative action programs – for much the same reason she condoned sex-based recruitment programs designed to achieve a "critical mass" of female cadets at VMI. Ginsburg observed in *Grutter* and *Gratz*, the 2003 University of Michigan affirmative action decisions, that despite our ostensible commitment to *Brown*, the American education system remains plagued by vast race-based disparities.[59] Such disparities are also present in housing, employment, government contracting, and health care; and in all of these contexts, she argued, race-based disparities reflect historical and ongoing discrimination against racial minorities.[60] Affirmative action programs, like the ones employed by the University of Michigan, are designed to ameliorate these disparities and to distribute opportunities to communities that have long been denied them. They also serve, Ginsburg noted, to dissipate racial stereotypes – to challenge the "traditional and unexamined habits of thought"[61] that continue to deprive racial minorities of equal standing in American society. "Were our Nation free of the vestiges of rank discrimination long reinforced by law," it might make sense to treat all race-based classifications the same.[62] But, she argued, "we are not far distant from an overtly discriminatory past, and the effects of centuries of law-sanctioned inequality remain painfully evident in our communities and schools."[63] In light of these historical realities, "consistency"[64] in the form of color-blindness impedes, rather than speeds, the realization of equal protection.

Ginsburg echoed this point a decade later in her tour de force dissent in *Shelby County v. Holder*,[65] a decision that gutted the preclearance requirement of the Voting Rights Act.[66] As noted earlier, the Court in *Shelby County* chided Congress for failing to recognize that "history did not end in 1965,"[67] and that Americans today have substantially overcome their taste for discrimination. Ginsburg responded to this assessment of the state of racial affairs circa 2013 by asserting that "the Court ignores that 'what's past is prologue,'"[68] and that "those who cannot remember the past are condemned to repeat it."[69] Certainly, she acknowledged, times have changed, and jurisdictions that once blocked most racial minorities from voting do not do so today. But instances of blatant race discrimination in voting continue to occur, and perhaps even more ominously, Ginsburg noted, older forms of discrimination have "evolved into subtler second-generation barriers."[70] Sometimes, such barriers can be difficult to recognize as such without appreciating the history that gave rise to them – which is why Ginsburg called attention to the Court's whitewashing of the nation's long and ongoing struggle with race discrimination in the context of voting. Just because these second-generation barriers are harder to see does not mean they are any easier to overcome – which is why Ginsburg argues that it makes no sense to interpret the Fourteenth Amendment as a bar to anti-discrimination measures. Race-consciousness in the pursuit of racial equality is not, and has never been, she argues in *Shelby County*, a problem under the Equal Protection Clause.

III. *VMI* AND THE PRESERVATION OF A CONSTITUTIONAL TRADITION

Ginsburg has frequently observed that this way of thinking about race-consciousness and equality has broad support around the globe. She notes in the Michigan affirmative action cases, for instance, that the United Nations–initiated Conventions on the Elimination of All Forms of Racial Discrimination and on the Elimination of All Forms of Discrimination against Women explicitly "distinguish between policies of oppression and measures designed to accelerate *de facto* equality."[71] But this dividing line between group-based classifications that serve to oppress and group-based classifications that serve to rectify injustice is not just part of a contemporary global conversation about equality. It has deep roots in our own constitutional tradition. The Court has long treated race as a "suspect category," Ginsburg has explained, "'not because [race] is inevitably an impermissible classification, but because it is one which usually, to our national shame, has been drawn for the purpose of maintaining racial inequality.'"[72] She has noted that "the Court's once lax review of sex classifications demonstrates the need for such suspicion."[73] But strict scrutiny was not intended, and has not been deployed, as an automatic proscription of all group-based classifications. Its purpose is not to eliminate classifications as such but "to ferret out classifications in reality malign, but masquerading as benign."[74] Thus, Ginsburg has argued, the recent suggestion by some of her colleagues that strict scrutiny is fatal even for classifications designed to ameliorate racial inequality is a new departure with little precedent in the history of American equal protection law.

Ginsburg has an unusually broad and deep understanding of this aspect of our constitutional tradition because she has been thinking and writing about it for over four decades. When Ginsburg first turned her attention to sex-based equal protection law, in 1970, there was very little of it.[75] Given the dearth of legal materials on sex discrimination, she and other legal feminists often looked to race-based equal protection law as a foundation for their claims.[76] What they found was not a doctrine that barred all racial classifications, but one that precluded the state from regulating race in ways that perpetuated the secondary status of racial minorities.

Courts in the late 1960s were often quite receptive to race-based state action that worked to dismantle traditional racial hierarchies. This was the period in which courts and legislatures began genuinely to implement *Brown*, which they typically interpreted as a command to eradicate a "system of segregation and its effects."[77] In 1968, in *Green v. New Kent County School Board*, the Court read *Brown* as a directive to school districts "to take whatever steps might be necessary" to "convert promptly to a system without a 'white' school and a 'Negro' school, but just schools."[78] The Court amplified this point three years later in *Swann v. Charlotte-Mecklenburg Board of Education*,[79] which upheld a race-based busing plan designed to better integrate the district's schools. *Swann* involved a court-ordered busing plan, and the Court suggested there might be limits on the judiciary's power to order such plans. But regarding busing and other race-based integration plans voluntarily adopted by school districts, the Court made the following observation:

> School authorities are traditionally charged with broad power to formulate and implement educational policy and might well conclude, for example, that in order to prepare students to live in a pluralistic society each school should have a prescribed ratio of Negro to white students reflecting the proportion for the district as a whole. To do this as an educational policy is within the broad discretionary powers of school authorities.[80]

These decisions made clear that classification was not synonymous with discrimination in the context of race; what mattered, for purposes of equal protection law, were the ends to which the classification was directed.

Education was not the only context in which the Court suggested there was a difference between classification and discrimination. The Court made the same point, from a different angle, in *Griggs v. Duke Power Company*.[81] *Griggs* held that facially neutral employment policies that have a disparate impact on racial minorities constitute discrimination on the basis of race unless justified as a business necessity. Though "fair in form," the Court held, such policies are "discriminatory in operation"[82]; they cement a system of racial exclusion inconsistent with modern conceptions of equality. The Court in *Griggs* was interpreting the race provision of Title VII of the 1964 Civil Rights Act. But numerous federal appeals courts in the 1970s held that the same rule applied in the context of equal protection.[83] These holdings reflected the prevailing understanding in this period, which was that the form of the law (whether or not it explicitly classified on the basis of race) was less relevant to its constitutionality than its effect on the ground. Courts did not treat state action that had an integrative effect and worked to counteract race discrimination the same as state action that perpetuated segregation and inequality.

In fact, the Court's willingness to permit racial classifications designed to combat traditional forms of racial inequality at one point proved something of a problem for Ginsburg. One of her early cases for the ACLU Women's Rights Project, *Kahn v. Shevin*,[84] arrived at the Court at the same time as an early race-based affirmative action case, *DeFunis v. Odegaard*.[85] *Kahn* involved a Florida statute that granted widows, but not widowers, a property-tax exemption. Ginsburg's concern was that the Court would uphold the affirmative action program in *DeFunis* on the ground that group-based classifications designed to combat discrimination were permissible under equal protection – and that it would mistakenly place the classification in *Kahn* in the same category.[86] Ginsburg worked hard in her brief to try to explain the difference between the two cases, arguing that affirmative action dissipated racial stereotypes, while Florida's tax law reinforced stereotypes of men as breadwinners and women as their dependents.[87] Her concerns proved prescient, however. The Court upheld the statute in *Kahn*, reasoning that equal protection did not bar all sex classifications and that this one seemed to help women, who faced greater challenges than men in the job market.[88]

Kahn did not end up having great precedential value (nor did *DeFunis*, which the Court declared moot).[89] But this episode provides a striking illustration of the prevailing conception of group-based classifications in the early 1970s. For nearly a century after the Fourteenth Amendment was enacted, courts routinely upheld race- and sex-based classifications. That changed with *Brown* and the race- and sex-equality cases that followed in its wake. But the new rule did not dictate that all group-based classifications were impermissible; it held such classifications impermissible when they perpetuated a history of stereotyping and discrimination. It is only relatively recently that an appreciable number of justices have begun to suggest that equal protection makes no distinction "'between a "No Trespassing" sign and a welcome mat.'"[90] Indeed, this strict anti-classificationist view has really only emerged in full force during Ginsburg's time on the Court.

Against this backdrop, *United States v. Virginia* assumes a heightened constitutional significance. Ginsburg's opinion makes an important contribution to constitutional sex discrimination law by clarifying how the state may regulate "inherent differences" between men and women: namely, in ways that promote equal opportunity and dismantle sex-based hierarchies, but not in ways that perpetuate conventional stereotypes about men's and women's sex and family roles. But *United States v. Virginia* is just as important for what it preserves as for what it innovates. Ginsburg's opinion powerfully reasserts a long-standing conception of equal protection: one that is alert to histories of group-based discrimination, sensitive to law's effects on the ground, and tolerant of state action that seeks to foster equality while disallowing state action that perpetuates traditional patterns of injustice.

It has become commonplace today to divide Supreme Court justices into two camps: "originalists" and "living constitutionalists." In some ways, these labels are fair enough. Justice Ginsburg *is* a living constitutionalist, in the sense that she believes new generations of Americans may invoke the broad generalities of the Constitution to combat forms of inequality only dimly perceived by their ancestors. But too much emphasis on the progressive or forward-looking nature of living constitutionalism can obscure the degree to which Ginsburg's jurisprudence engages with the past. Her opinions often recount neglected stories – histories of discrimination that illuminate important aspects of contemporary questions in equal protection law. But this is not all they do. In addition to describing traditions of injustice we are striving to overcome, Ginsburg's opinions seek to preserve a constitutional tradition of which we might be proud – a tradition that has long recognized that "'the Constitution is color conscious to prevent discrimination being perpetuated and to undo the effects of past discrimination.'"[91] This tradition is currently under threat, as the Court increasingly subscribes to a "color-blind" constitutionalism that makes no distinction between measures designed to oppress and measures designed to defeat oppression. Justice Ginsburg has made many contributions to American law in the decades she has served on the Court. But the greatest of these may be her preservation, for future generations of Americans, of a constitutional tradition that is capable of distinguishing between "actions designed to burden groups long denied full citizenship stature"[92] and those designed to include such groups, on equal terms, in the life of the nation.

8

Barriers to Entry and Justice Ginsburg's Criminal Procedure Jurisprudence

Lisa Kern Griffin

INTRODUCTION

In her twenty plus years on the United States Supreme Court, Justice Ruth Bader Ginsburg has issued momentous decisions and significant dissents concerning constitutional guarantees of equality. She is best known for her leadership – as an advocate, scholar, judge, and justice – on issues of gender discrimination.[1] Although one might expect related commitments to civil liberties to shape cases concerning the criminal justice process, Justice Ginsburg's mark on constitutional criminal procedure appears comparatively faint. Her contributions have been subtle,[2] and her cautious opinions at first seem disconnected from the clear principles established in the discrimination cases.[3]

Yet when Justice Ginsburg's criminal procedure decisions are considered through the lens of her broader jurisprudence on equality, some common commitments emerge. The argument for "equal citizenship stature"[4] relates to her efforts to remove the systematic barriers to entry that preclude access to the courts in criminal cases. Here too she seeks to protect the dignity of defendants facing official power. And through careful engagement with the facts of each case and a consistent focus on the prerequisites to fair adjudication, she has highlighted the due process obligations of prosecutors, demanded adequate representation of defendants, expanded the right to confront witnesses, and increased the jury's control over sentencing determinations.

This chapter reconsiders Justice Ginsburg's understated but important criminal procedure legacy. Notably, a comprehensive bibliography documenting her own prolific writings, together with the academic commentary and assorted tributes published through her first ten years on the Court, lists

I am grateful to Sara Sun Beale, Sam Buell, Neil Siegel, and Christopher Slobogin for valuable comments and conversations; to Katelyn Saner for excellent research assistance; and to Scott Dodson for helpful editorial suggestions.

hundreds of publications, but not a single one concerning criminal procedure.[5] Part I assesses the perception of Justice Ginsburg's muted voice in the field. It describes her role in protecting existing trial rights from encroachment and articulating new requirements of procedural equality, and also characterizes those cases as consonant with her incremental approach. Justice Ginsburg's contributions have received little attention in part because her disposition to caution often produces outcomes that appear to favor the government, at least in the short term. Her opinion for the Court in *Perry v. New Hampshire*,[6] for example, surprised some observers by rejecting any special reliability screening for suggestive eyewitness identifications,[7] and Part I concludes with a discussion of that case.

When Justice Ginsburg writes from an internal perspective on the courts, however, and shifts her focus from reliability to opportunity, the volume of her voice increases. Part II describes Justice Ginsburg's efforts to ensure meaningful access to the criminal courts. Her opinions appear most animated when they concern an aspect of the criminal justice process that reinforces inequality. And that concern may have found its fullest expression in a civil case: *Connick v. Thompson*.[8] In *Connick*, Justice Ginsburg issued a fierce dissent from the Court's decision to vacate a damages award in favor of a defendant who was wrongfully convicted after prosecutors suppressed exculpatory evidence.[9]

Part III connects Justice Ginsburg's advocacy for meaningful access to the criminal courts to her dedication to fair treatment in other realms. Intellectual history and personal experience complicate any justice's jurisprudence, and it can be difficult to trace beliefs in one area to decisions in another. Legacies are not always linear, but this chapter suggests that Justice Ginsburg's legacy is more integrated than previously thought. There is an unexplored connection between her perception of the role of the courts in remedying unfairness in the discrimination cases, and lowering barriers to entry in the criminal justice process.

I. INCREMENTAL PROTECTIONS AND RESTRAINED DECISIONS

Justice Ginsburg's criminal procedure jurisprudence appears mild because she has acted primarily to preserve existing liberties rather than to expand constitutional protections. By and large, she seems less active on behalf of criminal defendants than "one might expect from a Justice appointed by a Democratic president and hailing from the ACLU."[10] This perception is in keeping with "progressive criticism of Justice Ginsburg as an excessively cautious jurist."[11] And some commentators report the defense bar's assessment that her "support of defense-oriented positions is somewhat lacking in intensity" and thus has not had a significant impact.[12] Though she has in fact voted more frequently to protect defendants than most of her colleagues on the Rehnquist and Roberts Courts, Justice Ginsburg's record does not appear to favor defendants as much as the decisions of progressive icons such as Justices Brennan and Marshall did.[13]

This is so in part because Justice Ginsburg's intellectual instincts on the Court, as with her earlier litigation strategies, have been incremental across substantive areas of the law. As an advocate, she challenged classifications based on gender discrimination one at a time rather than attempting to prevail on a new constitutional theory aimed at broad social change. Often celebrated for these measured steps in the direction of what were ultimately historic advances in gender equality, Justice Ginsburg has repeatedly cited slow but steady forward motion as her preferred speed on the bench as well.[14] Indeed, she has self-identified as given to interstitial action, an approach that she believes "affords the most responsible room for creative, important judicial contributions."[15] She favors narrow rules, adheres closely to established precedents, and generally avoids grand pronouncements.[16] Her conception of the judicial role, as she stated in her confirmation hearings, is to "get it right and keep it tight."[17] This layered, gradual, common-law approach to social progress extends to abortion rights, and Justice Ginsburg has famously expressed concern that the landmark *Roe v. Wade*[18] decision was an ill-timed sudden move that "ventured too far."[19]

Pragmatism characterizes many of Justice Ginsburg's criminal procedure decisions as well. She has employed her incremental approach not only to slowly advance social change but also to defend the remnants of Warren Court precedents. The Warren Court extended the right to counsel to indigent defendants charged with felonies, required that suspects undergoing custodial interrogation be advised of their right to remain silent and consult an attorney, and applied the exclusionary rule to state-court suppression of evidence seized in violation of the Fourth Amendment.[20] Justice Ginsburg has served on the Court during an era of erosion in those and other criminal procedure rights. Although approximately half of her decisions could be categorized as favoring the government, she often carefully constructs a narrow majority ruling, drafts a concurrence that mitigates the impact of the decision, or dissents to lay down a marker against future encroachment.[21] As Christopher Slobogin has observed, "rather than lambasting the majority for its blindness or illogic in broad and far-reaching language, [her] concurrences pay close attention to precedent and rely on precise 'lawyerly' analysis detailing how narrow the majority ruling is, or could be construed to be."[22]

In relation to other areas of the law, Justice Ginsburg has garnered few marquee opinion assignments concerning criminal procedure. Some of the majority opinions that she has authored fit within this narrow, cautious genre. One closely followed decision, *Perry v. New Hampshire*,[23] concerned eyewitness identifications. Members of the defense community hoped the Court would address growing skepticism of eyewitness testimony, which is often persuasive evidence against criminal defendants but flawed in terms of reliability. The Court, however, concluded that a fair opportunity for the defense to raise the soundness of an identification before a jury was sufficient to assure due process, even if the identification was made under suggestive circumstances.[24]

The witness in the *Perry* case had called the police to report seeing an African American man allegedly breaking into cars in the parking lot of her apartment complex. When the police arrived and questioned the witness in her apartment, the witness pointed out her kitchen window at a suspect, Barion Perry, standing in the parking lot. A month later, however, the witness could not identify Perry in a photo array. And at the time of the initial identification, Perry was standing next to a police officer in the still-dark parking lot, and was the only African American person there. Perry was charged with theft by unauthorized taking and criminal mischief, and he moved to suppress the parking lot identification on the ground that admission of a suggestive one-person show-up would violate due process. The New Hampshire trial court denied the motion and admitted the identification. Perry was convicted of theft and appealed through the state courts to the Supreme Court.

The Supreme Court affirmed. Due process concerns, it reasoned, arise only when law enforcement officers introduce the suggestive element themselves, and the improper police conduct creates a "substantial likelihood of misidentification."[25] In reaching that decision, Justice Ginsburg frustrated some observers by disregarding the mounting social science evidence calling the reliability of eyewitness identifications into question.[26] She reasoned, however, that the Constitution protected the defendant not by excluding the evidence but by affording an opportunity to persuade the jury that it is not credible.

Perry exemplifies Justice Ginsburg's emphasis on in-court process over on-the-street policing. She generally views law enforcement from a practical perspective, and she has imposed few new constraints on investigative practices. Justice Sotomayor presents something of a contrast, with notable decisions advancing a more expansive and technologically savvy understanding of privacy under the Fourth Amendment,[27] objecting to the narrowing scope of Fifth Amendment *Miranda* protections in custodial interrogations,[28] and dissenting from the Court's due process analysis in *Perry* itself.[29]

Justice Ginsburg's *Perry* opinion also reveals the way in which she privileges the context of the adversarial process over content-based exclusions. It is in keeping, for example, with her alliance with Justice Scalia to establish

a reinvigorated Sixth Amendment right to confront witnesses, no longer tethered to the reliability of the hearsay statement a witness made.[30] "The potential unreliability of a type of evidence," she wrote in *Perry*, "does not alone
render its introduction at the defendant's trial fundamentally unfair."[31] Justice
Ginsburg further deferred to state and lower federal courts on the question of
whether evidence is sufficiently reliable to be admitted.

Where Justice Ginsburg does act to strengthen protections against law
enforcement intrusion, it is often because she perceives a need to discourage
misconduct. In *Perry*, for example, she noted the limited deterrence value of a
contrary ruling, concluding that it would be difficult to dissuade law enforcement from engineering identifications through a case where only external
facts and circumstances gave rise to the suggestiveness.[32] In other cases, however, she has resisted unfair manipulation of investigations and objected to
governmental end-runs around the rules.

For example, Justice Ginsburg has often advocated rules designed to prevent
law enforcement from gaming encounters with suspects. As she acknowledged
in *Perry*, police misconduct represents a systematic failure that raises a due
process problem and may require an exclusionary remedy. In a recent Fourth
Amendment case, *Kentucky v. King*,[33] she dissented to underscore the dangers
of police-created exigencies.[34] Likewise, she has been vigilant about police
manipulation when it comes to the requirement of *Miranda* warnings, favoring
a broad definition of "custody."[35] In addition, she has insisted that something
more than an anonymous tip is required before an officer can claim reasonable suspicion for a stop,[36] and she recently expressed concern that police may
dodge the warrant requirement by removing a party who refuses to consent
to a search from the premises.[37] She has also opposed efforts to "constrict the
domain of the exclusionary rule" to deterrence, fearing that would create perverse incentives for law enforcement to neglect the electronic databases that
"form the nervous system of contemporary criminal justice operations."[38]

Overall, however, Justice Ginsburg proceeds from the premise that what
happens in court matters more than how defendants got there. Her opinions
suggest that individuals can best confront the power of the state from within
the criminal justice process. And where the right to be heard has been vindicated,[39] then the adversarial system adequately protects equality and fairness.
Perry helps to illuminate where her commitments lie. The core of her reasoning in *Perry* is that the trial process – including the right to counsel, the right
to cross examine witnesses, the rules of evidence, expert testimony, carefully
crafted jury instructions, and the requirement of proof beyond a reasonable
doubt – suffices to caution juries against placing undue weight on flawed eyewitness testimony.[40]

II. OPPORTUNITY JURISPRUDENCE AND AN INTERNAL
PERSPECTIVE ON THE COURTS

Justice Ginsburg's contributions to criminal procedure stem primarily from her attention to the power of individual defendants within the trial process rather than constraints on the power of the state. Where she perceives a fair playing field, Justice Ginsburg has often authored or joined pro-government decisions.[41] It is true that those decisions exist in some tension with her progressive instincts in other contexts.[42] But adjudicative criminal procedure often upends expectations in this way because it can create unusual affinities. For example, although Justice Ginsburg and Justice Sotomayor vote together often, they diverge in many criminal procedure cases. Justice Sotomayor's focus on expanding constitutional rights can put her at odds with Justice Ginsburg's trial-process approach. In contrast, Justice Ginsburg's vigilance about procedural safeguards has led her to support a less-frequent ally, Justice Scalia, in his decisions redefining the Confrontation Clause and expanding the domain of the jury.[43]

Moreover, Justice Ginsburg shares with some of her colleagues an internal perspective and a commitment to ensuring fairness within the existing system of criminal adjudication rather than changing its parameters. Even on a Court composed almost entirely of former appellate judges,[44] Justice Ginsburg stands out as a "lawyer's lawyer" and "judge's judge."[45] Whether appellate judges bring common temperaments and techniques to the docket is an open question. When William Rehnquist joined the Court in 1972, former federal judges were in the minority, and earlier Courts had members with substantially more experience as governors, legislators, and cabinet members.[46] Empirical studies have questioned Chief Justice Roberts's contention that appellate judges on the Court are more likely to follow precedent and set aside policy preferences.[47] But he has recently made more nuanced statements about the justices' shared internal perspective on the Court's place in the American political process. In a 2013 appearance before the United States Court of Appeals for the Fourth Circuit, Chief Justice Roberts acknowledged that some of the questions before the Court might benefit from a broader view of public policy but could only be evaluated by the current Court through a "focused way of drilling in on the law."[48]

A hallmark of Justice Ginsburg's jurisprudence is that she is indeed adept at "drilling in on the law," and even more so at closely reading the factual record.[49] A meticulous review of the details of a case and the procedural complexities comports with her deliberate approach. But even through that lawyerly lens, Justice Ginsburg has a long view. She fully understands how litigation relates to policy and how to patiently pursue a principle through individual cases that are sometimes many years apart. She is not only one of the most seasoned litigators on the current Court but also the Court's most significant social movement advocate at present. She has firsthand experience of the eventual interplay between judicial decision making and increased opportunity.[50]

Accordingly, over time, her constitutional criminal procedure decisions have helped to balance the government's power in the trial process. Even where she has not actively expanded defendant's rights, she has identified the "practical obstacles" to protecting those rights and has advocated the removal of those barriers.[51] She has, for example, rejected executive branch attempts to shift prosecutions arising from the war on terror away from the purview of the federal courts.[52] And she has guarded the right to be heard and mount a defense,[53] and the opportunity to cross examine witnesses and present facts to a jury.[54]

Perhaps Justice Ginsburg's primary concern in criminal cases has been ensuring that neither lack of means nor limited procedural prowess shuts defendants out of court. She has been particularly dedicated to preserving the right to counsel.[55] In *Alabama v. Shelton*,[56] she extended the right to counsel to proceedings where the defendant receives a suspended sentence.[57] Defendants who decide to appeal from a guilty plea also require counsel, as she argued in *Halbert v. Michigan*.[58] The state should never, she wrote, "bolt the door to equal justice" when indigent defendants seek appellate review of criminal convictions.[59] Nor should defendants be left without counsel when confronted with the complexities of the adversarial system. Ever practical, Justice Ginsburg has noted that 68 percent of the prison population did not complete high school and may lack basic literacy skills, and that alone can bar entry to the courts.[60] She also has written separately to underscore that procedural requirements are "a tall order for a defendant of marginal literacy,"[61] to express concern about uncounseled convictions for driving under the influence,[62] and to suggest that judges are obligated to warn pro se litigants about the consequences of their legal decisions.[63]

The right-to-counsel cases fundamentally implicate Justice Ginsburg's commitment to fair access, and she views the function of public defenders broadly. She recognizes that there are "systematic failures across the country in the provision of defense counsel services to the indigent."[64] To begin to address those problems, she has argued for "expanding the situations in which the right to counsel obtains" and "policing the implementation of the right."[65] In *Maples v. Thomas*,[66] for example, she wrote a spare but searing description of the minimal resources and training supporting defense lawyers in capital cases in Alabama.[67] In that light, she found no procedural default when an attorney's abandonment of a client resulted in a missed deadline, which would have arbitrarily denied the defendant his "day in court."[68] And in *Vermont v. Brillon*,[69] she concluded that "delay resulting from a systematic breakdown in the public defender system" could be charged to the state.[70] She has also stated that she has "yet to see a death case, among the dozens coming to the Supreme Court on eve-of-execution stay applications, in which the defendant was well represented at trial."[71] Because she entrusts defense lawyers with maintaining some balance in the adversarial process, Justice Ginsburg has also held counsel to a high standard.[72]

Furthermore, a robust view of the jury's role follows from Justice Ginsburg's belief that safeguards in the adversarial trial best ensure fairness.[73] She has dissented in death penalty cases to underscore the importance of clear instructions to juries on the choices they confront.[74] And she allied herself with Justice Scalia in a series of decisions on jury determinations of sentencing facts. She voted with the majority in *Apprendi v. New Jersey*,[75] which requires jury findings of aggravating factors that increase criminal sentences beyond statutory maximums.[76] She later authored related opinions requiring that facts supporting a capital sentence be found by a jury,[77] and prohibiting judges from making factual findings giving rise to higher potential sentences.[78] In a 2005 sentencing case, *United States v. Booker*,[79] Justice Ginsburg's concern with mandatory sentencing guidelines encountered her resistance to abrupt systematic change.[80] She was the only justice to join the majority opinions on both substance and remedy, first agreeing that the mandatory federal Sentencing Guidelines violated the jury trial guarantees of the Sixth Amendment, but then joining with four different colleagues to conclude that the appropriate remedy was to give judges the discretion to apply them. Despite the decisive impact of switching her vote, she did not write at all in the case.

What may be the most telling criminal procedure opinion authored by Justice Ginsburg actually came in a civil case. Her dissent from the Court's decision in *Connick v. Thompson*[81] highlights the connection between fair play by prosecutors and the right to be heard. It involves a defendant first denied access to exculpatory evidence necessary to his criminal trial and then stripped of the remedy he received in civil court for his related constitutional claim.

The case arises from the wrongful conviction of John Thompson for robbery and murder. Thompson spent eighteen years in prison for those convictions, fourteen of them on death row in solitary confinement twenty-three hours a day.[82] During his robbery trial, prosecutors withheld several pieces of exculpatory evidence, including a blood sample from the robbery crime scene establishing that the perpetrator's blood type was B.[83] Though prosecutors did not test Thompson's blood (which is type O), neither did they disclose to the defense that the forensic evidence, and a lab report conclusively identifying the perpetrator's blood type, existed. In fact, they took pains to conceal it by removing it from the property room during pretrial discovery. Prosecutors then used the robbery conviction to seek the death penalty in the subsequent murder trial, and to preclude Thompson from testifying in his own defense because of the impeachment effect of the prior conviction.

A defense investigator came across a microfiche copy of the laboratory report in police archives just before Thompson's sixth scheduled execution date in 2003.[84] The blood evidence ruled out Thompson's involvement in the robbery, and the trial court vacated that conviction. Thompson was also granted a new trial on the murder charge because the prosecution's "egregious" misconduct and intentional concealment of exculpatory evidence had prevented him from presenting a defense and testifying at trial. Upon retrial, Thompson was acquitted of the murder and released.

Thompson then sued for the violation of his federal civil rights under 42 U.S.C. § 1983. Pursuant to *Brady v. Maryland*,[85] due process requires the government to disclose to the defense any evidence in its possession that is both favorable and material to the defendant's guilt or punishment.[86] Thompson alleged that the New Orleans District Attorney's deliberate indifference to the need to train prosecutors on their constitutional obligations caused a constitutional violation. The central question was whether the harm to Thompson resulted from the District Attorney acting in his official capacity, or from the individual and independent violations of rogue prosecutors.[87] A jury found the District Attorney's Office liable and awarded Thompson $14 million in damages. The Fifth Circuit sustained the award, but in a 5-4 decision authored by Justice Thomas, the Supreme Court concluded that the District Attorney's Office could not be held liable for a single incident of wrongdoing.

In order to prevail, Thompson needed to demonstrate that the District Attorney was deliberately indifferent to the need to train his prosecutors about *Brady's* command, and that the lack of training led to the *Brady* violation. An earlier case, *Canton v. Harris*,[88] had established that deliberate indifference may be shown when a policymaker ignores a pattern of similar constitutional violations by untrained employees.[89] The Court in *Thompson* held, however, that the District Attorney was entitled to rely on prosecutors' general professional training and ethical obligations. Although the case was the third before the Supreme Court concerning misconduct by the New Orleans District Attorney's Office,[90] the Court also concluded that Thompson failed to show the necessary pattern of deliberate indifference to the constitutional obligation.[91]

Justice Ginsburg would have upheld the damages award in light of the "gross, deliberately indifferent, and long-continuing violation of [Thompson's] fair trial right."[92] The case serves as a self-contained demonstration of both the importance of enforcing *Brady* requirements and the role of section 1983 liability in doing so. Accordingly, Justice Ginsburg let the facts speak for themselves and dedicated her dissent – joined by Justices Breyer, Sotomayor, and Kagan – to a "lengthy excavation of the trial record."[93]

By exposing the root causes and net effects of pervasive noncompliance with *Brady* violations, she refuted the majority's conclusions that only a single violation occurred, and that the District Attorney was anything but deliberately indifferent to it:

> From the top down, the evidence showed, members of the District Attorney's Office, including the District Attorney himself, misperceived *Brady*'s compass and therefore inadequately attended to their disclosure obligations. Throughout the pretrial and trial proceedings against Thompson, the team of four engaged in prosecuting him for armed robbery and murder hid from the defense and the court exculpatory information Thompson requested and had a constitutional right to receive. The prosecutors did so despite multiple opportunities, spanning nearly two decades, to set the record straight. Based on the prosecutor's conduct relating to Thompson's trials, a fact trier could reasonably conclude that inattention to *Brady* was standard operating procedure at the District Attorney's Office.[94]

Although the evidence at issue was one crime lab report regarding blood-type evidence, several prosecutors over many years engaged in various acts to suppress it. The only thing isolated or unitary about the constitutional violation was "the sense that it culminated in the wrongful conviction and near execution of only a single man."[95] Moreover, the District Attorney's cavalier attitude toward training was not just "deliberate" but "flagrant."[96] When the supervisor had long ago "stopped reading law books," and the office had never disciplined a single prosecutor despite "one of the worst records" in the country concerning *Brady* violations, then breaches were not just predictable but inevitable. According to Justice Ginsburg, "the *Brady* violations in Thompson's prosecutions were not singular and they were not aberrational. They were just what one would expect given the attitude toward *Brady* pervasive in the District Attorney's Office."[97] To conclude that a "culture of inattention" does not constitute disregard for "a known or obvious consequence" simply ignores the facts.[98]

Justice Ginsburg's dissent is an effort to bring those facts to light, not only to expose the injustice to Thompson but also to explain the broader hindrance to enforcement that the Court's decision created. Lax training and monitoring allow, or even encourage, prosecutors to ignore a right "fundamental to a fair trial."[99] Because "explicitly illegal policies are rarely put in place," insisting that "liability flows only from an explicit policy essentially immunizes policymakers who simply adopt a facially constitutional policy, or institute no policy at all, and then fail to prevent or implicitly condone unconstitutional conduct."[100] And prosecutorial concealment "is bound to be repeated unless municipal agencies bear responsibility – made tangible by § 1983 liability."[101]

The intensity with which Justice Ginsburg writes in *Connick* emphasizes her faith in the rigor of the adversarial system, and her view that it can only function if defendants have full and fair access to court. For Justice Ginsburg, *Brady* "is among the most basic safeguards brigading a criminal defendant's fair trial right," and a *Brady* violation "by its nature, causes suppression of evidence beyond the defendant's capacity to ferret out."[102] Because the absence of the withheld evidence may result in the conviction of an innocent defendant, "it is unconscionable not to impose reasonable controls impelling prosecutors to bring the information to light."[103] If a defendant does not know of a defense he might raise, then he has not been "let in" to court in the way that Justice Ginsburg envisions. Common sense dictates that defendants should not be compelled to "scavenge for hints of undisclosed *Brady* material when the prosecution represents that all such material has been disclosed."[104] Moreover, narrowing definitions of prerequisites like "indifference" unduly restrict liability, and again deprive the defendant of legal recourse. Arising together, those issues yielded Justice Ginsburg's most forceful piece of writing surrounding a question of criminal procedure.

III. COMMON COMMITMENTS AND UNEXPLORED CONNECTIONS

There is an unrecognized connection between remedying unfairness to individual defendants and Justice Ginsburg's resistance to "built-in headwinds" that have discriminatory effect.[105] At several points, links appear between the right to participate and be heard in the criminal justice process and her legacy on equality. Indeed, an opinion emphasizing prosecutors' duty to give defendants a fair opportunity to present a defense fits within Justice Ginsburg's small but significant collection of impassioned dissents.

Justice Ginsburg has stated that she writes separate opinions only where she believes them to be "really necessary."[106] She carefully "[c]hooses her ground" when dissenting,[107] and thus the decision to write at all is noteworthy. And *Connick* belongs in the even more select group of dissents so expressive of Justice Ginsburg's core constitutional concerns that she read from the bench to underline the objection to the majority's decision. An oral dissent, she has explained, indicates "more than ordinary disagreement."[108] Most often she does not "announce," but when she wants to "emphasize that the court not only got it wrong, but egregiously so," reading a dissent can serve an "immediate objective."[109] It signals that the dissenter views the majority as "importantly and grievously misguided."[110]

Ledbetter v. Goodyear,[111] in which Justice Ginsburg delivered perhaps her best known dissent from the bench, sounds some of the same notes as her *Connick* opinion. The majority decision in *Ledbetter,* authored by Justice Alito, held that a woman had waited too long to sue for pay discrimination even though she was unaware for years that she was earning substantially less than her male coworkers at a tire plant. Justice Ginsburg emphasized that private sector employees do not ordinarily know what their colleagues are making:

> Pay disparities often occur, as they did in Ledbetter's case, in small increments; cause to suspect that discrimination is at work develops only over time. Comparative pay information, moreover, is often hidden from the employee's view. Employers may keep under wraps the pay differentials maintained among supervisors, no less the reasons for those differentials. Small initial discrepancies may not be seen as meet for a federal case, particularly when the employee, trying to succeed in a nontraditional environment, is averse to making waves.[112]

Because employees cannot "comprehend [their] plight," neither can they complain until the disparity becomes apparent. And as a result of the Court's decision, an employee's "initial readiness to give [the] employer the benefit of the doubt" would preclude a later challenge.[113]

What struck Justice Ginsburg about *Connick* relates to her central objection in *Ledbetter.* There, the plaintiff first suffered exclusion from full and fair participation in the workplace, and then was barred from court when she sought a remedy for that harm. Ledbetter did not know that she was paid less than her male counterparts until time extinguished her claim. Thompson's dilemma is substantively distinct but structurally similar. Thompson was unaware of exculpatory evidence that could exonerate him while he spent eighteen years in prison on a wrongful conviction. Then, though there was no question that he suffered a deprivation of his constitutional rights, the Court constructed a procedural impediment that precluded prosecutorial liability. Justice Ginsburg also understood and expressed in both cases how foreclosing a remedy would affect future employees seeking equal pay, or future defendants exposed to similar unfairness.[114]

Congress subsequently passed the Lilly Ledbetter Fair Pay Act of 2009, accepting an invitation that Justice Ginsburg extended from the bench and adopting the position she took in dissent. It is too soon to say whether her *Connick* dissent might similarly inspire new standards on the *Brady* front, but at a minimum the decision has generated substantial commentary about the need to reconsider the mechanisms through which *Brady* is enforced.[115]

Justice Ginsburg's oral dissents have gathered strength across substantive areas,[116] and their broader strokes connect to her criminal procedure decisions. Recently, she has engaged in some negative incrementalism on both affirmative action and abortion rights.[117] In *Fisher v. University of Texas*,[118] she agreed that the University of Texas's admissions plan should stay in place but objected to the decision to send it back for the lower court to judge it against a more demanding standard, expressing some concern about the majority's strategy to diminish affirmative action over time.[119] Moreover, in *Gonzalez v. Carhart*,[120] she argued that treating women as incapable of making the difficult choices surrounding second-trimester abortions denied them equal protection.[121] And she read her dissent aloud to emphasize what she called the majority's "alarming" ruling and "effort to chip away" at abortion rights.[122]

Furthermore, Justice Ginsburg continues to make her strongest arguments through a scrupulous understanding of the record and a common sense view of the facts.[123] Her dissent in *Vance v. Ball State University*[124] challenged a restrictive definition of "supervisor," which in turn narrowed the conduct prohibited under Title VII of the Civil Rights Act of 1964.[125] In Justice Ginsburg's view, the majority's definition of supervisor – limited to the person with the authority to hire, fire, demote, promote, transfer or discipline an employee[126] – exhibited "remarkable resistance" to "workplace realities" and would leave many employees defenseless against those in their chain of command who could make their work life miserable without having "tangible" authority.[127] The following day, in *Shelby County v. Holder*,[128] Justice Ginsburg read a dissent from the bench objecting that to conclude from the nation's progress in protecting minority voters that the voting rights law was no longer needed was like "throwing away your umbrella in a rainstorm because you are not getting wet."[129]

Insisting on the realities – not only of workplaces and voting districts but of public defenders' and prosecutors' offices – has been a key feature of Justice Ginsburg's dissents. Employees do not ordinarily inquire about the salaries of their counterparts,[130] supervisory power is not confined to the individual who hires and fires,[131] constitutional protections can achieve some gains and remain necessary at the same time.[132] Nor do prosecutors suppress exculpatory evidence in coordination with several colleagues unless the office in which they work broadly tolerates circumvention of constitutional rights.[133] The *Connick* Court simply ignored the basic realities of a functioning District Attorney's Office to conclude that there was no deliberate indifference and that two decades of conduct involving many prosecutors constituted a single act.[134] A defendant deprived of the essential facts necessary to his defense, and then precluded from seeking recourse for that violation in court, has twice been excluded from the system. And when the Court relies on these fictions to hinder judicial enforcement of constitutional rights, Justice Ginsburg views that as yet another failure of process.

There is thus an extent to which Justice Ginsburg's criminal procedure decisions harmonize with the underlying commitment of her broader juris-prudence. She is dedicated, she has said, to "the idea of essential human dig-nity, that we are all people entitled to respect from our Government as persons of full human stature, and must not be treated as lesser creatures."[135] According to Neil Siegel, this belief in "equal citizenship stature"[136] defines Justice Ginsburg's vision for "how government power should be exercised and how individual rights should be protected in the American constitutional order."[137] Her criminal procedure opinions are neither entirely consistent with each other nor perfectly consonant with the discrimination decisions, but there is an intriguing and important relationship between them.

Both sets of decisions, moreover, weave together fair process and equal access. In the gender discrimination cases, Justice Ginsburg has treated lib-erty and equality as interconnected values that "inform one another."[138] At times, she has used liberty arguments to protect equality,[139] and in the criminal procedure realm, she has shown how equality concerns can safeguard liberty interests. In a majority opinion in *M.L.B. v. S.L.J.*,[140] written early in her ten-ure on the Court, Justice Ginsburg recognized the relationship between equal protection and the illegitimacy of "fencing out would-be appellants based solely on their inability to pay core costs."[141] There, she held that indigent par-ents must be afforded an opportunity to appeal termination of parental rights whether or not they can pay for preparation of the trial record.[142] The rationale in the opinion was self-consciously imprecise because it comprehended more to the "essential fairness of the state-ordered proceedings anterior to adverse state action" than due process.[143]

Justice Ginsburg also perceives some shortcomings to criminal procedure rights conceptualized as constraints and instead concentrates on the gov-ernment's affirmative obligations to ensure fair process.[144] She recognizes, however, that fundamental liberty interests sometimes provide the strongest support for access to the courts.[145] Consequently, neither the canonical gender discrimination decisions nor the quieter criminal procedure opinions can be described through "resort to easy slogans or pigeonhole analysis."[146] The two groups of cases, however, seem to coalesce around an ideal of opportunity, and an understanding of the importance of a fair playing field.[147]

CONCLUSION

Though they have received less attention than other areas of her jurisprudence, Justice Ginsburg's criminal procedure opinions resonate with her work against discrimination. Her conception of a fair criminal justice process is infused with equality principles, and particularly with the conviction that the government should not foster inequality, and should work to remedy the effects of past injustices. She has focused on expanding opportunity within adjudication, more than on ensuring reliability or enlarging privacy in the ways that her progressive predecessors did. Once criminal defendants have access – to the exculpatory information that might allow them to mount a defense, to the attorneys necessary to do so, and to a duly empowered jury – then she believes that the adversarial process safeguards constitutional rights. That commitment is an insufficiently appreciated dimension of Justice Ginsburg's criminal procedure jurisprudence, and a connection that both informs and amplifies her other contributions.

9

A Liberal Justice's Limits:
Justice Ruth Bader Ginsburg and the
American Criminal Justice System

Aziz Z. Huq

INTRODUCTION

No observer of Justice Ruth Bader Ginsburg's career in the law can miss the tension between her unflinching support for substantive justice and her tempered view of the "measured" judicial steps possible under that flag.[1] That contrast is starkly posed by a snapshot comparison between her praxis as a lawyer and her praxis as a judge. Though the 1970s and 1980s, Ginsburg exercised a guiding hand in roughly sixty cases concerning gender equality, including a dozen at the high court, in her capacity as co-founder of the American Civil Liberties Union's Women's Rights Project.[2] These cases crystallized a novel principle that the state cannot regulate based on stereotypes "about the way women are" so as to "create or perpetuate the legal, social, and economic inferiority of women."[3] This supple, historically sensitive understanding of antidiscrimination, once installed, marked a dramatic departure from American law's anterior treatment of women.[4] It also stood as a remarkable foil to the failure of the then-pending Equal Rights Amendment to the Constitution – a contentious political process that might well have caused the Court to stay its hand had it been dealing with less skilled advocates.[5]

By contrast, Ginsburg has insisted upon a more chastened role for federal judges in controversial domains of social policy during her time on the federal bench. Rather than boldly venturing where popular majorities fear to tread, she has warned, federal courts should rarely and hesitantly "step ahead" of democratic sentiment as articulated by the national political branches.[6] Instead, she explained, judges should write "modestly" by opening "a dialogue" with the

I am grateful to Scott Dodson for the invitation to write and for insightful edits. I am also pleased to acknowledge the support of the Frank Cicero, Jr. Faculty Fund. This chapter is respectfully dedicated to Justice Ruth Bader Ginsburg. If only every lawyer could learn the craft of law from so unstintingly skilled and so wisely humane a mentor.

political branches.[7] Courts, she has explained in a later majority opinion, "do not, or should not, sally forth each day looking for wrongs to right."[8] As befits a legatee of the Legal Process School associated with Henry Hart and Albert Sacks of the Harvard Law School, Ginsburg glosses her judicial restraint by focusing on the reticulated institutional dynamics of our federal system.[9] Invoking concerns with both institutional competence and political-feedback effects, she has highlighted the impediments any single federal judge must navigate to secure conformity with constitutional principles. That judge, she cautioned, must persuade not only a majority of her multimember Court but also the coordinate branches of government, as well as a national public ready to rally against over-reaching judgments and "turn the legislative tide in the opposition direction."[10]

It bears emphasis that her restraint is not underwritten by doubt about the virtues of her legal positions. Instead, it reflects practical concern about the realization of such positions against social and political resistance. The Court, Ginsburg is quite aware, does not have a final a say on the substance of the law as many like to believe. She is also cognizant that the "counter-majoritarian difficulty" provides no powerful motivation for limiting judicial review on behalf of vulnerable classes.[11] In this regard, her thinking is closely aligned with Alexander Bickel's observation that "in a society which in all other respects rests on [democratic] theory, judicial review cannot ultimately be *effective*."[12]

Nor, for Ginsburg, is the admonition to incrementalism mere cant that decorates the storefront and hides the spoilage of wares. Scholarly assessments of her jurisprudence routinely rank the justice as a "minimalist"[13] and as a jurist who successfully steers a "middle course" between methodological poles.[14] A 2007 empirical study further concluded that Ginsburg voted to alter precedent less often than any of her then colleagues with the exception of Justice Souter.[15] And a recent study of her Fourth Amendment jurisprudence finds a pattern of "negative gradualism," in which the justice exploits her ability to read precedent closely and carefully to offer narrowing glosses of her conservative colleagues' aggressive reimagining of the law.[16] Contra the stereotypical view of her attitude toward the states, moreover, Ginsburg has also exercised a meticulous care about the preservation of room for state courts' exercise of decisional authority.[17]

This chapter considers how that tension between high principle and low politics is resolved in a domain of law rarely associated with Justice Ginsburg's name – the constitutional and statutory regulation of criminal justice. Across her three-decade-plus tenure on the Supreme Court, Ginsburg has penned an array of opinions about American criminal justice. These address a range of topics, including the scope of federal criminal liability, the state's investigative reach into individuals' quotidian lives, the division of labor between judges and the jury, and the nature and availability of post-conviction remedies. Without question, the range of these opinions maps imprecisely onto the range of criminal justice problems that the Court routinely confronts.[18] It is also underinclusive in relation to the array of problems routinely encountered in our criminal justice system. Indeed, constitutional doctrine more generally has little to say about many important questions implicated in that domain. These include the evolution of policing strategies and technologies; the shift from trials to plea bargaining, with a concomitant rise in prosecutorial power; and the fiscal infrastructure of state or federal criminal litigation. Indeed, even with respect to the critical interaction of race in criminal justice, the Court's doctrine is most fairly characterized as inattentive or even negligent.[19]

Notwithstanding these limitations, Ginsburg's criminal justice jurisprudence is a useful perch from which to analyze the avenues a liberal justice has for reformist change.[20] By specifying that opportunity set, I strive for fine-grained insight into the nature of institutional constraints on federal courts' enforcement of individual rights.

For this purpose, criminal justice is a more fruitful field to till than gender equality. At least today, the tug-of-war between constitutional principle and institutional constraint is more sharply contested in the criminal domain than in that equality-related arena. There are a number of reasons for this. Women, Ginsburg once explained, could ease the pathways to change because they are proximate partners and intimates of men who adjudicate their constitutional stature.[21] Her observation proved prescient. As a historical matter, moreover, Ginsburg qua advocate was swimming with the historical tide of changing gender mores during the 1970s. As a result, while the Court remains inconstantly sensitive to calcified gender roles,[22] and while gender inequalities still striate both public and private spheres,[23] American society writ large has traveled some way in the last half-century on gender equality. We are no longer in an era in which a Supreme Court justice would turn away the highest-ranking student in her Columbia and Harvard law school classes based on gender.[24] Aside from abortion-related claims, moreover, gender inequality is rarely a theme today for political candidates. Female votes are instead increasingly important for electoral success.[25] In contrast, the politics of crime have been consistently fraught over the past four decades in ways that seem unlikely to fade.[26] Prevailing attitudes to criminal suspects generally remain minatory. In contrast, prosecutors and crime victims tend to be politically potent interest groups. The institutional circumstances of judicial intervention on behalf of criminal suspects therefore remain fragile and vulnerable to legislative backlash. This poses a problem for those – including Ginsburg herself – who take seriously the Constitution's concern with limiting the leviathan's coercive use of criminal law tools.

The central conclusions of this inquiry are easily summarized. In the first instance, both opportunity and constraint for a liberal justice's reform agenda in respect to criminal justice emerge endogenously from the federal judiciary to an extent that has not been appreciated. In contrast to leading accounts of the judiciary's role in social change, I point to ways in which a liberal justice can be hemmed in by the dispersed coterie of federal judges surrounding her. I do not mean to suggest that such endogenous constraints are the only frictions on judicially motivated reform. Rather, my point is that they are much more salient than the exogenous factors more often picked out by scholars. Flipping the analysis around, I further suggest how that justice can leverage those same judges toward reform-minded goals. Acutely aware of these constraints, Ginsburg has adroitly navigated the tension between aspiration and institutional fact to the large benefit of constitutional-rights holders.

To motivate my analysis, I begin by sketching very briefly some of the "pathologies" of our criminal justice system.[27] The point is not to be comprehensive. I rather aim to underscore the simple point that this system falls far short of even minimal constitutional aspirations. That stage set, I describe four lines of jurisprudence wherein Ginsburg's opinions have played important functions. By situating her choices within this case law, I hope to illuminate the constrained opportunities for liberal justices seeking to shield individual liberty against the burdens imposed by the criminal process and by consequent punishment.

I. THE CHALLENGE OF AMERICAN CRIMINAL JUSTICE

American criminal justice subsists in crisis. That crisis is peripheral to our ordinary political discourse. Perhaps this is because criminal justice's pathologies are so entrenched, so much the guilty product of our democratic preferences, and so likely to burden disproportionately the politically marginal.[28] The crisis's two central facts are America's asymptotically high levels of incarceration (at least in comparison to other democracies) and its disproportionate burdening of racial minorities. After a century of stability, American incarceration rates rose from 158 to 635 per 100,000 between 1970 and 2000.[29] Between 1970 and 2010, the U.S. prison population also grew by 705 percent.[30] Ethnic and racial minorities today comprise an increasingly large share of that population.[31]

Our criminal justice system is not a measured response to changing patterns of criminality. To the contrary, especially at the national political level, those responses have been the work of partisan entrepreneurs exploiting the fear of crime to motivate turnout, not the result of changes to the actual crime rate.[32] As a result, policy responses have been and continue to be deeply flawed.

Lapses in accuracy, fairness, and even-handedness hound criminal justice from the first contacts between police and suspects to the end of adjudication and beyond. At its entry points are a network of policing practices that often have racially disparate effects and sometimes race-based motivations.[33] Even in serious criminal investigations, a nontrivial number of false convictions occur.[34] Most criminal cases, though, are not serious but involve misdemeanor charges. In this domain, the rate of false positives is likely higher still.[35] Error rates are high across the board because of two weaknesses in the adjudicative process. First, most criminal defendants are disadvantaged by the severe and pervasive deficiencies in criminal-defense funding.[36] Public defenders are often asked to represent thousands of defenders per year. Few defendants represented on the state's dime receive sufficient time. Second, even those who secure more than a scintilla of attention from their overstretched public defender then must gamble on state adjudicative mechanisms that too often fail to conform to basic constitutional requirements.[37] Trials, with the panoply of procedural entitlements of the Bill of Rights, have long ceased to be a dominant mode of sorting between guilty and innocent.[38] Today, plea bargaining dominates jury adjudication, in part because of a decades-long fiscal vise in which state judiciaries have been squeezed.[39] As a result of these trends, the finely crafted procedural entitlements of the Bill of Rights are largely irrelevant to most defendants, who "plead guilty and thus cannot appeal, lack a viable legal claim, or lack the time needed to pursue those procedures."[40]

Finally, the effects of this dysfunctional system endure long after defendants leave the courtroom and prison house. Formal and informal limitations on housing and employment mean convicts face considerable difficulties securing new employment and instead find themselves trapped in a "'closed circuit' of perpetual social and legal marginality."[41] Whatever its deterrence value, exposure to the criminal justice system undermines families,[42] destroys the social fabric of communities,[43] skews political participation,[44] and entrenches poverty.[45] All these spillover effects are even more troublesome to the real and grave extent that politicians are inclined to "disproportionately subject to ... harsh sanctions ... African American offenders."[46]

The sheer magnitude and complexity of criminal justice's problems cast an ambiguous shadow on the Supreme Court's role as the body primarily responsible for the articulation of constitutional rules in the U.S. political system.[47] Indeed, so immense are these problems that they might compromise the federal judiciary's constitutional mission. To see this, consider the double bind that criminal justice reform inflicts on federal judges. On the one hand, a constitutional court that blinks at the pervasive constitutional harms inflicted in the name of criminal justice would hardly seem defensible or credible. On the other hand, the discrete, common-law mode of adjudication of the Supreme Court, coupled with the fragile "political foundations" of judicial review,[48] mean that federal courts often lack either the incentives or the tools to make large changes to the criminal justice system. This is so also because the latter is embedded in larger "policy regimes" that include welfare systems and market policies.[49] Hence, their unconstitutional features cannot be dismantled without some disentangling from the immanent institutional complex. Even in the teeth of such rebarbative complexity, judicial quietude might be taken as an implicit normative endorsement of criminal justice arrangements in a political regime that locates constitutional thinking principally in the Court. Rather than a lubricant for change, the Court's dominant role in constitutional review would be an impediment to those seeking reform. If this were so, the Court's mandate for constitutional review, along with its impotence in respect to most margins of the criminal justice system, would aggravate the system's deleterious spillover effects. Rather than an opportunity for intervention, this account suggests that the criminal justice system is likely to be the Achilles heel of a liberal Court committed to enforcing constitutional entitlements.

At the very least then, criminal justice sharply presents the conflict between constitutional principle and cold institutional reality that has troubled Justice Ginsburg elsewhere. Her contributions to the Court's jurisprudence in the field hence provide an opportunity to reflect upon how that difficult passage can be navigated in the absence of prevailing social headwinds.

II. JUSTICE GINSBURG'S CRIMINAL JUSTICE JURISPRUDENCE

Judicial doctrine, at least as produced by the Supreme Court, stands at several removes from the brute empirics of the criminal justice system. The latter's operation can be captured only by eschewing granular detail in favor of wide-angle, institutional analysis. In contrast, American-style judicial review tends to work at the retail level, at least to the extent that it formally requires a narrowly pitched controversy between two parties who stand in adverse positions to each other.[50] Courts are supposed to focus on the facts about the specific parties before them. Even when they benefit from amicus briefing on the wider, systemic effects of a decision, the justices lack any direct fact-finding authority.[51] Their impressions of the criminal justice system, accordingly, are necessarily third- or fourth-hand, and so often hostage to the political economy of amicus participation.

Not only is the flow of information from the real world of criminal justice to the high court exiguous, but also the channel in reverse is equally narrow. In criminal cases, available effectual relief is typically limited. Neither class-wide relief nor injunctive remedies are ordinarily available.[52] It is only when the Supreme Court announces a new, generally applicable rule of constitutional law, binding on the states and their tribunals under the Supremacy Clause, that a specific controversy has even the potential for systemic effects. Opportunities for such intervention, furthermore, are carefully titrated through a series of institutional screens. Typically, the production of a new rule will depend on the state to move first – an unenforced criminal law generally will produce no justiciable cases[53] – and then on the existence of a defendant willing and able to litigate the question to decision. Even then, no single justice acting alone can force the Court to exercise its discretionary certiorari jurisdiction.[54]

It is within this tightly constrained context that the role of a liberal justice endeavoring to vindicate faithfully the interests denominated in the constitutional text must be understood. In what follows, I highlight four lines of cases in which Justice Ginsburg has made substantial contributions as an opinion author to criminal justice jurisprudence: the substantive definition of federal crimes, remedies for Fourth Amendment violations, the division of labor at trial between judge and jury, and the availability of post-conviction remedies. At the outset, it bears emphasis that Justice Ginsburg has (of course) voted in almost all of the criminal law and procedure cases that have come before the Court, and that her opinion at the Court's conference or her vote has been decisive in other occasions. My focus on her *opinions* is nevertheless warranted as a lens onto the distinctive opportunity set for a liberal justice seeking to press a large, unruly, and recalcitrant criminal justice system into conformity with constitutional norms.

A. *The Substantive Reach of Federal Criminal Law*

The scope of substantive criminal law matters because it determines how far into private conduct a government can reach for punitive and coercive ends. At present, "a great deal of conduct is criminalized, and of that conduct, a large proportion is criminalized many times over."[55] Outside of the rare case in which a criminal prohibition trenches on a substantive constitutional right,[56] the Supreme Court has the power to speak directly to the contours of federal criminal law through statutory construction, but not to the content of state criminal law that generates the lion's share of criminal sentences.[57] Federal felonies, however, make up only 5 percent of felonies nationally, a proportion that has remained stable for decades.[58] Even within this limited bailiwick, the Court has generally failed to develop bulwarks against overcriminalization either via constitutional rulings or by the consistent narrow construction of penal statutes. One consequence of this dynamic is that Congress and state legislatures can always respond to constitutional criminal procedure constraints by expanding the reach and depth of substantive criminal law.[59] The large scope of criminal liability is thus plausibly viewed not just as a keystone of contemporary criminal justice but also a potential counterweight to common judicial remedial strategies.

In a first series of cases, Ginsburg has pressed cautiously at one edge of this domain. She has deployed statutory canons of construction to narrow important federal criminal statutes. Most important here is a series of opinions restraining the availability of federal fraud liability in white-collar prosecutions. In *Ratzlaf v. United States*, for example, her majority opinion held that a federal anti-structuring crime, which aimed to promote accurate reporting of transactions with financial institutions, required knowledge that the transaction was illegal.[60] Her opinion relied on the rarely used canon of lenity, which counsels for reading criminal statutes against the government.[61] Six years later, in *Cleveland v. United States*, she penned a unanimous opinion construing the mail-fraud statute not to apply to a fraudulent license application to a state gaming agency, flagging concern about "a sweeping expansion of federal criminal jurisdiction in the absence of a clear statement by Congress."[62] Finally, in the 2010 case of *Skilling v. United States*, she confined the federal prohibition on fraudulent deprivations of the "intangible right of honest services" to instances of kickbacks and bribery, a class that did not include the defendant's actions in that case.[63] *Skilling*'s construction of the honest services statute constrained federal pursuit of public corruption, derailed existing prosecutions, and cast into doubt extant convictions.[64]

At a minimum, these cases suggest that judicial intervention in criminal justice matters is not limited to measures that leave "politicians ... freest to regulate where regulation is most likely to be one-sided and punitive."[65] Rather, the Court can deploy canons and purposive readings to head off "sweeping expansion[s] of federal criminal jurisdiction."[66] The extent of missed opportunities here is hard to quantify. But cases like *Ratzlaf*, *Cleveland*, and *Skilling* do not appear to be typical of the Court's treatment of substantive criminal law. Moreover, the deployment of statutory interpretation tools leaves open the possibility that Congress might respond with amendatory measures. Legislative reaction to judicial construction of a federal statute is hardly guaranteed though, and may indeed be increasingly rare due to political polarization in national institutions.[67] The result is that lenity-driven shrinkage of the criminal law's domain is not impossible, and at the very least, is presently underexploited.

B. Regulating Police Investigations

A second line of Ginsburg opinions concerns the consequences of Fourth Amendment violations. Since 1961, the Court has required evidence to be excluded from state-court proceedings when that evidence was gathered in violation of the Fourth Amendment.[68] Since its inception, the exclusionary rule has had influential critics, who point to its cost to accuracy[69] and its perverse tendency to reward only guilty objects of police misconduct.[70] More recently, conservative justices have voted successfully to limit the availability of exclusion to instances in which the Fourth Amendment violation is intentional, as opposed to being caused by either police or administrative negligence, or, alternatively, reliance on later-overruled Supreme Court precedent.[71] As a result of these decisions, police can now rely on erroneously filed warrants and mistaken database entries to make arrests. Ginsburg has taken the laboring pen in dissenting from this retrenchment.[72] Her dissents are animated by bewilderment that the Court in these cases can baldly claim that negligence by police cannot be deterred, a "suggestion [that] runs counter to a premise underlying all of negligence law."[73] The Court, in contrast to Ginsburg, often simply assumes that officials have sufficient incentive to comply with the Fourth Amendment absent its routine enforcement[74] – an assumption that runs hard against the predicate assumptions animating the Fourth Amendment.

A parallel concern with the risks of limiting the effectual scope of the Fourth Amendment has led Justice Ginsburg to take a rare lone dissenting stand against the Court's recent narrowing of its substantive scope. In *Kentucky v. King*, she was the only justice to protest the Court's endorsement of police behavior strategically designed to elicit the behavioral predicate for a warrantless entry of a home.[75] Justice Ginsburg's *King* dissent seems to be a retreat from her decision to join the Court's unanimous 1995 opinion in *Whren v. United States*, which endorsed the pretextual use of investigative strategies and eschewed inquiry into the presence of impermissible police motives.[76] That shift suggests a concern with the need for some effective mechanism to curb the manipulative use of police discretion for prohibited reasons.[77]

In one regard, these cases seem of mere technical interest. After all, the unavailability of certain Fourth Amendment remedies when officials act in good faith might not leave any given defendant without any remedy or stymie the development of general rules. But the emergent good-faith exception to the exclusionary rule must be understood against the backdrop of a larger judicial assault on Fourth Amendment remedial mechanisms. The Court has already announced that post-conviction review in federal court provides no venue for vindicating Fourth Amendment privacy interests.[78] In addition, constitutional-tort actions only rarely yield condemnations of new police tactics because the so-called qualified-immunity defense often requires dismissal.[79] In practical terms, the good-faith exception targets the one remedial device that reliably promotes doctrinal evolution to keep up with shifting police tactics.

The Ginsburg dissents in these cases are noteworthy for a second reason. They perceptively track an evolving trajectory of threats to Fourth Amendment privacy in an age of rapid technological change. In a 1995 opinion, Ginsburg cautioned that "widespread reliance on computers to store and convey information generates ... new possibilities of error, ... greatly amplifies an error's effect, and correspondingly intensifies the need for prompt correction."[80] Recent leaks from the National Security Agency confirm that the government's exploitation of "big-data" algorithmic tools to analyze large pools of data to make inferences about discrete individuals is far greater than many had previously appreciated.[81] As federal courts increasingly recognize, moreover, individualized harms can and do flow from even the collection and analysis of otherwise innocuous data by way of flawed inferences.[82] The Court's separation of intentional police misconduct from negligent police or administrative action eliminates at least one mechanism for regulating such governmental exploitation of databases to target coercive actions against individuals. Ginsburg's clear-eyed attention to the manner in which technological change catalyzes new threats to privacy contrasts sharply with other justices' reliance on incomplete and misleading analogies to eighteenth-century common law to the same end.[83]

C. *The Division of Labor between Judge and Jury*

Beginning with a 2000 decision called *Apprendi v. New Jersey*, the Court has construed the Sixth Amendment to prohibit judges in criminal proceedings from making factual determinations that increase a criminal sentence beyond the statutorily prescribed maximum.[84] Ginsburg penned an important early application of *Apprendi*'s Sixth Amendment rule to capital cases in 2002.[85] Her real contribution, though, was in the 2005 case *United States v. Booker*, which challenged the Sentencing Guidelines that apply to almost all federal criminal sentencing.[86] *Booker* contained two holdings. One five-justice majority of the Court held that mandatory guidelines violated the Sixth Amendment. Another five-justice majority held that the appropriate remedy for this constitutional flaw was to invalidate statutory provisions making the guidelines mandatory. The sole justice to join both majority opinions on substance and remedy was Justice Ginsburg. When exercising that pivotal vote, she declined to file an opinion, leaving it to Justices Stevens and Breyer to explain the rulings.[87]

Booker's net effect is somewhat odd: judges cannot be *required* by Congress or the federal Sentencing Commission to consider facts not proved to a jury, but they are nonetheless able to when they have the option of so doing. Ostensibly a vindication of the jury's role under the Sixth Amendment, *Booker* is probably better understood as opening new space for judicial discretion, especially given the background infrequency of trials. Subsequent clarifications of its rule, including two Ginsburg opinions, amplify the scope of judicial discretion. In *Ice v. Oregon,* her opinion broke from Sixth Amendment maximalism to permit judges to decide whether defendants should receive concurrent or consecutive sentences.[88] More striking is her opinion in *Kimbrough v. United States* permitting district judges to grant downward departures to sentences based on disagreement with the one-hundred-to-one sentencing ratio between crack cocaine and powder cocaine.[89] Other opinions Ginsburg has joined relax appellate scrutiny of district court sentencing decisions.[90] The net effect of these cases, empirical studies show, is an expansion of trial judges' discretion in calibrating sentences, allowing not only more interjudge variance but also a greater number of downward departures.[91]

D. Post-Conviction Remedies

Conviction and sentencing do not necessarily mark the close of the criminal adjudicative process. Defendants benefit not only from appeals but also from state and federal post-conviction processes, most commonly including habeas proceedings. The scope of post-conviction remediation for errors and lacunae in state criminal proceedings has been a central forum for contestation between liberal and conservative judges from the Warren to the Roberts Court.[92] A general trend has been toward the winnowing of post-conviction procedure, rendering trial the "main event" rather than a "tryout for the road."[93]

In this context, Ginsburg has played a central role in the rearguard fight to preserve some meaningful avenue for post-conviction relief. Consistent with her larger solicitude for the access to counsel, she has written to preserve a right to appointed counsel for discretionary state-court appellate review[94] and to permit habeas review when the state occludes exculpatory evidence from defendant's counsel.[95] Two Ginsburg opinions bear notice here. First, in *Skinner v. Switzer,* she held that the procedural vehicle used for ordinary constitutional tort actions against state officials can equally be employed to challenge a state's refusal to allow for DNA testing of biological evidence.[96] While narrowly cast, her *Skinner* opinion means a state cannot wholly foreclose a convicted defendant's efforts to secure DNA testing, as Texas strove to do in Henry Skinner's case.[97]

Second, in *Maples v. Thomas*, Ginsburg wrote for a seven-justice majority to hold that wholesale attorney failure in an appeal can dissolve ordinary forfeiture rules otherwise precluding habeas review.[98] *Maples* is one of a cluster of cases in which supermajorities of the Court have installed new safety valves to mitigate the harsh procedural barriers regulating access to habeas relief.[99] Of equal significance in *Maples* is a rare Ginsburg passage formally superfluous to its holding. In this passage, she adumbrated carefully the systemic deficiencies in Alabama's capital system.[100] So rare an excursus beyond the issue at bar prompted rebuttals from both Justice Alito and Justice Scalia.[101] Although Ginsburg did not belabor the point, it was clear that the breakdown in Maples's case ought not to be ranked as a surprise: it was, pace Alito and Scalia's protests, the product of a larger systemic breakdown.[102] Nor is *Maples* the sole occasion on which Justice Ginsburg has remarked on the scale and depth of criminal justice's pathologies. In the 2009 case of *Vermont v. Brillon*, her majority opinion held that delay resulting from a "systematic breakdown" in public defender provision could be placed at the state's door for Speedy Trial Clause purposes.[103] And writing for four dissenting justices in *Connick v. Thompson* two years later, she protested against the overturning of a damages award against a New Orleans prosecutor who had withheld exculpatory evidence in capital proceedings by writing an opinion that underscored at length the larger context of criminal justice breakdown within that Louisiana parish.[104]

To summarize, we have four lines of jurisprudence – from threshold contacts between police and suspects to post-conviction proceedings. Ginsburg has authored important opinions in all four strands of cases. Sometimes she labors for majorities, sometimes as a dissenter. In one instance (*Booker*), she did not write at all, but her vote was decisive in shaping the jurisprudence's trajectory. At the very least, these opinions should allay any inchoate sense among commentators that Ginsburg has but weak ideas or influence on constitutional rules respecting criminal justice. Rather, the question is when and how she has opportunities to play out those constitutional understandings.

III. THE JUDICIAL CONSTRAINTS ON JUDICIAL REFORM

The array of cases herein examined provides a useful sample of the ways in which a liberal justice committed to the Bill of Rights' guarantees can intervene in the pathologically troubled American criminal justice system. That sample enables consideration of two questions, one descriptive and the other normative: What institutional forces shape the opportunities for intervention in favor of constitutional interests, and do those interventions succeed in promoting those interests better than plausible alternatives?

The idea that federal judges have limited capacity to change complex state institutions is familiar from the work of political scientists such as Gerald Rosenberg and Donald Horowitz.[105] Rosenberg's work picks out the limited nature of constitutional rights, the weakness of judicial independence, and the judiciary's lack of power of implementation as constraints.[106] Horowitz's points to courts' relatively impoverished capacity to gather and analyze "social facts" as a predicate for policy-focused intervention.[107] However, the sample of cases developed here points to a different factor – the way that the federal judiciary itself, as an institutional interest group with identifiable ambitions and policy preferences, endogenously forecloses or opens channels for reform. In some instances, the avenues made available by the judiciary are meaningful. In other instances, endogenous constraints close off the most potent mechanism for social change, leaving open only devices that are at best symbolic in effect and at worst counterproductive. For a liberal justice, therefore, the most proximate brakes and accelerants for social change can easily be observed: they are sitting to her left and right, and can be met at every convening of the Judicial Conference.

Pace Rosenberg's focus on doctrine as a restraining factor for liberal reformers within the judiciary, constitutional criminal-procedure jurisprudence seems not to want for legal hooks for promoting change. The Bill of Rights abounds with open-textured provisions that can and have been inventively refashioned to unexpected ends. *Apprendi's* innovative reading of the Sixth Amendment jury-trial right is one example. More generally, no justice, liberal or conservative, need be detained long by precisely tailored constitutional text, as an examination of Eleventh Amendment or Due Process jurisprudence quickly reveals.[108] Today, moreover, a higher rate of compliance with constitutional norms might be achieved by simply declining to roll back remedial mechanisms such as the exclusionary rule or post-conviction habeas – that is, by resisting change to doctrine rather than plumbing the law for new rules.

The examples canvassed here instead point toward the federal judiciary itself as the source of both constraint and opportunity for institutional reform. To begin with, it is striking that two of the four lines of jurisprudence sketched in this chapter are at best rearguard actions by Ginsburg and her fellow liberals against the rollback of constitutional entitlements. Movement in both the exclusionary rule and the federal post-conviction contexts is toward choking off important rights. Such change has been championed by justices appointed by President Nixon and his Atwater-inspired ideological inheritors.[109] For justices who did not emerge from that political matrix, the Court's ability to select its caseload on the vote of four justices alone creates a powerful incentive to operate defensively. As Ginsburg presciently explained in 1992, "no single court of appeals judge [or Supreme Court justice] can carry the day in any case."[110] The collegial nature of Supreme Court decision making, operating in tandem with the heterogeneous preferences of justices, often appointed by different presidents, ensures that what one's colleagues believe about the law really matters.

It is not merely colleagues, however, that generate constraint on jurisprudence aimed at promoting compliance with constitutional rules. As Ginsburg observed before her appointment to the Supreme Court, it is often "district judges who are the real power holders in the federal court system."[111] This is so in more ways than one. It is not merely that the pyramidal structure of the federal judiciary means that district judges address a far greater proportion of cases than any appellate tribunal, and that they adjudicate with some finality questions of fact that cannot be reopened later. It is also that the Supreme Court acts in both a supervisory and a representational capacity in respect to the lower judiciary.[112] Conservative or liberal, justices' motivations appear to be "shaped in part by a sense of institutional duty."[113] Hence, when a decision imposes excessive labor on lower-court judges for little return, the Court has been known to do a quick volte-face.[114] At the very least, the Court is inordinately sensitive to the possibility that recognition of a claim, or some other alteration to the legal regime, might result in unwarranted difficulties for lower federal courts.[115]

This sensitivity matters because the recent expansion of the American criminal justice system has plainly outpaced federal courts' ability to maintain the same quality and quantity of per capita attention to discrete convictions. Simultaneously, legislatures have gradually defunded state courts and public defenders. One wholly predictable result of this trend has been the rise of systemic violations of constitutional rights such as the Sixth Amendment right to effective representation. Federal courts lack capacity to tackle directly such entrenched and systemic problems by the most obvious instrument – simply demanding increased state funding. Nor, even if federal judges wanted to, could they adjudicate every instance in which there was a plausible constitutional violation in a state criminal proceeding. They also lack the wherewithal to sort valid constitutional claims from the avalanche of convictions and sentences churned forth daily by state and federal courts.[116] Unsurprisingly, concerns about the administrability of any jurisprudential regime aimed at remedying criminal procedure violations in particular is almost always met with skepticism about the risk of institutional overload.[117]

Justice Ginsburg's opinions evince careful attention to judges as a constituency and its constraining power on Supreme Court rulemaking. Hence, in crafting a new path to DNA testing in *Skinner v. Switzer*, she was careful to turn aside concerns that the procedural novation would foster "any litigation flood or even rainfall."[118] Equally revealing is her approach in *Maples* to the pervasive problem of attorney incompetence. As her account of Alabama's system of capital-defense funding revealed, any effort to read the Sixth Amendment as requiring more than mere token efforts would have demanded wholesale reformist intervention into the state's criminal justice system. Consequently, *Maples* is drafted in an exquisitely narrow fashion to select only cases in which an attorney has de facto abandoned her client, as opposed to merely grossly failed to serve that client.[119] Since Ginsburg had a solid seven-justice majority in *Maples*, it is not clear that the narrow reach of the opinion was necessary to maintain a majority. The better account may be that both she and her colleagues in the majority, liberal and conservative alike, realized the institutional need to titrate judicial review of constitutional flaws in state criminal justice systems. Similarly, the procedural due process right recognized in *Skinner* is exquisitely calibrated to provide only a thin keyhole of opportunity if and only if the state forecloses all avenues in its own forums; it is not a blunderbuss to blow open dozens of extant convictions. To be institutionally tenable, that is, individual relief must be tightly tethered so as not to burst the perceived bounds of the federal judiciary's institutional capacity and open the litigation floodgates. The animating risk here is one of too much justice.

There is, though, a flip side to this coin. Lower court judges are not merely a constraint, but also a lever for change if their preferences can be channeled in the right way. The case of *Booker* and the federal sentencing guidelines is telling here. Perhaps the most important initial effect of the guidelines was to invest federal prosecutors with "indecent power relative to both defendants and judges, in large part because of prosecutors' ability to threaten full application of the severe Sentencing Guidelines."[120] *Booker* and its progeny transformed the guidelines from mandatory to advisory while installing a regime of deferential appellate scrutiny. In a world of plea bargaining, where jury trials are vanishingly rare, the net effect of these Sixth Amendment jury-trial holdings was to reinvigorate the judge as an agent in sentencing – empowering at least some district court judges to press back against prosecutors' tendency to overcharge.[121] The result has been increases in interjudge disparities[122] – albeit measured against the distorted baseline of strategic prosecutorial action – and an injection of leniency into a criminal justice system achingly short of that quality.[123] In this way, Ginsburg's key remedial intervention in *Booker,* along with her influence on the subsequent relaxation of appellate review, has added ameliorative buffering into a system previously dominated by punitive and prosecutorial interests. She has done so by deploying the very federal bench that in other contexts acts as a friction on reformist change. Endogenous institutional frictions hence operate not just as limits but also as safety valves.

No straightforward normative evaluation flows from these descriptive claims. Indeed, it is quite plausible to think that the institutional infrastructure linking police, prosecutors, trial judges, their appellate counterparts, legislators, and chief executives is too complicated and multivalent to permit facile conclusions. Any given intervention, whether judicial or electoral, will have complex and unpredictable repercussions. On this view, the best a reformer can hope for is a reasonably firm prediction and an opportunity to recalibrate her intervention as downstream consequences come into view. A correlative admonition follows: however good intentions might be, the judiciary's constrained opportunities for reform should be handled with caution.

This case for normative caution emerges by reconsidering two of the four lines of jurisprudence previously mapped. First, consider again Court's efforts to rein in the reach of substantive criminal law. Although these decisions may narrow the reach of federal criminal law, they may do so in normatively problematic ways. Most of Ginsburg's restrictive readings of substantive criminal law concern white-collar financial crime.[124] White-collar crime tends to be underenforced in comparison to the "street crimes" that dominate the criminal justice system.[125] Indeed, even white-collar crimes that impose large social costs often go unpunished. In the wake of the 2007–8 financial crisis, for example, Judge Jed Rakoff observed that "the prevailing view of many government officials (as well as others) was that the crisis was in material respects the product of intentional fraud," and yet no criminal prosecutions ensued.[126] There is a debate on whether this enforcement-related asymmetry flows from the differential social standing of white-collar offenders or the higher transaction costs of investigating such offenses.[127] However this debate is resolved, judicial obstruction of tools typically deployed against white-collar crime, without analogous treatment of other offenses, risks exacerbating the lopsidedness of enforcement patterns. At a minimum, consideration of such systemic effects should count in any evaluation of decisions such as *Ratzlaf, Cleveland,* and *Skilling.*

The second caution concerns the liberal response to limitations recently imposed on the exclusionary rule. There is a respectable argument (albeit one not yet empirically sustained) that the exclusionary rule distorts the allocation of scarce public-defender dollars toward (cheap) exclusion motions in cases where defendants are likely guilty, and away from (expensive) arguments of actual innocence where defendants committed no crime.[128] Rationing exclusion mitigates this hypothesized effect – although one might question whether good-faith exceptions are the right way to ration. This distorting effect, it should be emphasized, may well be a real cost to exclusion. An appropriately cautious liberal justice would want to account for this potential distortion when resisting expansion of the good-faith exception.

Ultimately, though, I am persuaded that Ginsburg is on the right side of this question. It is hardly clear that the downstream distortion from the exclusionary rule to defense-counsel behavior is anything but trivial given public defenders' staggering caseloads. Moreover, compliance with the Fourth Amendment would be rather underpowered absent the routine specter of exclusion, which the good-faith exception muddies. Police, who prioritize arrests, clearances, and convictions, are singularly unlikely to comply suo moto with that constitutional rule. Particularly when it comes to racial and ethnic minorities, democratic political processes may not reliably incentivize consistent constitutional compliance. Damages actions are often inaccessible to plaintiffs with constrained financial and social resources; in any case, they may not generate reliable deterrence effects.[129] A separate cluster of rules concerning litigant standing further precludes prospective injunctive relief in many other cases.[130] In the Fourth Amendment context, accordingly, it will often be the exclusionary rule or nothing.

It may well be that there are first-best judicial interventions to address all of the constitutional problems touched upon here.[131] But, as I believe Ginsburg quite well understood before being appointed to the Supreme Court, we do not live in a first-best world. The tools available in our second-best world, moreover, are flawed and sometimes dangerously double-edged. That should not result in inaction or paralysis. But it does make the challenge of navigating judicial limits in relation to the criminal justice system all the more important to take seriously. And it makes the respect owed to a judge who succeeds in passing unscathed through those shoals all the larger.

CONCLUSION

Clerks for Justice Ginsburg well know, or fast learn, that the cases in which she is most prone to write opinions are not necessarily those with the highest profile or the most glamorous. To the contrary, they were often the most procedurally obdurate of disputes, with the most imbricated twists and folds. They demanded lengthy disentangling, and hours of careful analysis. Our dysfunctional criminal justice system produces no shortage of such recondite cases. Their difficulty for a liberal justice committed to the vindication of the panoply of constitutional rights has not yet been fully appreciated.

Nor, I think, have Ginsburg's successful contributions to the field of criminal justice. In a series of subtle and strategic interventions, I have argued, Ginsburg has navigated the fraught strait between high aspiration and hard institutional reality with aplomb and grace. Her principal obstacles and opportunities in that enterprise have been her fellow federal judges, quite apart from draconian statutes and downstream resistance to rights' implementation. The case law suggests an acute awareness and subtle sense of strategy in regard to that constraining parameter. Her aplomb in traveling the course is a master class for the wise judge and the canny advocate. The law, and the constitutional liberties of Americans, are all the better for it.

PART III

STRUCTURALISM

10

A Revolution in Jurisdiction

Scott Dodson

INTRODUCTION

Most people know Ruth Bader Ginsburg as a pioneer of women's equality under the law, and for good reason. Her pathmarking work with the American Civil Liberties Union litigating gender-equality cases, her seminal opinions for the Supreme Court in gender-discrimination cases, and her social sensitivity to gender issues all have shaped both the law and America's social customs with respect to gender.

Fewer know that Ginsburg has had an enormous impact – perhaps even rivaling her impact in gender equality – on the law of civil procedure and federal jurisdiction. To be fair, civil procedure generally does not rank high on most people's favorite topics. This aversion appears to affect even Supreme Court justices. Justice David Souter, in his twenty years on the Court, wrote fewer than a dozen opinions on the civil rules.[1] And Justice Stephen Breyer openly has confessed his unfamiliarity with civil procedure.[2]

Nevertheless, the current Court as a whole seems fixated, at least far more so than in past eras, on civil procedure.[3] I'll leave it to others to speculate *why* the Court seems to have taken a proceduralist turn.[4] Here, I only mean to observe that the Court's surging interest in civil procedure has given certain justices an opportunity to show their mettle. Front and center in these cases is Justice Ginsburg, who has been regarded as the "resident proceduralist" on the Court for many years.[5]

Perhaps more so than any other justice, Ginsburg has had a special solicitude for the topic throughout her career. She taught the subject as a law professor and authored a number of scholarly works in the area, including a well-received co-authored book on Swedish procedure.[6] She remained acutely

I thank Tobias Wolff, who offered insightful reactions on an early draft.

aware of the power of procedure and its practical effects when she litigated for the ACLU.[7] And she maintained particularly close ties to her former procedure professors and other procedure and jurisdiction scholars, writing tributes to such icons as Jack Friedenthal,[8] Benjamin Kaplan (her first law professor),[9] Arthur Miller (a co-student at Harvard),[10] Allan Vestal,[11] Herbert Wechsler (also a teacher of hers),[12] and Charles Alan Wright.[13]

As a justice, she has authored many of the Court's most important procedure opinions.[14] (She even has confessed that she would write *all* of the procedure opinions for the Court if only her colleagues would let her.)[15] As a result, a large percentage of her opinions – perhaps as high as 25 percent – deals with issues of procedure and jurisdiction.[16] Professor David Shapiro has observed that those opinions exhibit "a high level of knowledge of the subject matter, lawyerly analysis of the issues at hand, a pragmatic approach ..., and an insistence that decisions not be unnecessarily broad."[17]

In this chapter, I hope to bring to light some of the enduring impact these opinions have had on the world of jurisdiction and civil procedure. The field is too wide to cover entirely; therefore, I will showcase one area of procedure in which she has spearheaded what can be fairly characterized as a revolution: federal subject-matter jurisdiction.

Subject-matter jurisdiction, often described as the "power" of a federal court, has attained a haloed status in federal jurisprudence over the years.[18] I view Ginsburg's jurisprudence in this area as a multi-pronged and multi-year attempt to desanctify subject-matter jurisdiction. She has led the charge to clarify and narrow when a limit is considered "jurisdictional," has marshaled unanimous opinions undermining its "fundamental" stature, and has explored ways to "cure" its defects, all in the name of bringing pragmatism and sensibility to jurisdictional doctrine.

In exploring these efforts, this essay makes two contributions. The first is a systematic analysis of Ginsburg's role – both as judge and justice – in pushing changes in jurisdictionality. The second is to offer some evaluative observations – mostly laudatory with a few gentle criticisms – of her efforts. Ultimately, I hope to illuminate this largely overshadowed area and give credit to the jurist whom I see as primarily responsible for its modern development.

I. THE ENSHRINEMENT OF SUBJECT-MATTER JURISDICTION

Subject-matter jurisdiction denotes the classes of cases and issues that a federal court is empowered to adjudicate. Beyond those classes, a federal court is said to "lack jurisdiction" and hence lack authority over the case.[19]

Subject-matter jurisdiction, then, is both a grant of authority and a limit of authority, and a court either has it or does not.[20]

For these reasons, subject-matter jurisdiction is said to have a unique set of effects – that it cannot be consented to or stipulated to by the parties; that its limits cannot be waived or forfeited by the parties; that its limits are not subject to judicial discretion or equitable exceptions; that defects in subject-matter jurisdiction can be raised by the court or any party at any time prior to final judgment; and that a federal court has an independent and ongoing obligation to ensure itself of proper subject-matter jurisdiction.[21]

These features of jurisdictionality come at great cost to judges, litigants, and the law.[22] A jurisdictional defect discovered late can negate years of time, effort, and cost expended in the case. Great unfairness can result if a party who loses on the merits avoids a judgment by raising lack of jurisdiction. And jurisdiction imposes work on federal judges to police their own authority and limits the ability of parties to streamline their litigation.

II. DESANCTIFYING SUBJECT-MATTER JURISDICTION

Justice Ginsburg has spearheaded an important and monumental effort to revolutionize our conceptualization of jurisdictionality by approaching jurisdictional questions with a pragmatic sensitivity to its costs. She has done so in three main areas: imposing a strong presumption against jurisdictionality in an effort to constrain "jurisdictional characterizations," allowing nonjurisdictional issues to be "resequenced" in order to be decided before jurisdictional issues, and allowing jurisdictional defects to be "cured."

A. Presumption against Jurisdictionality: Constraining Jurisdictional Characterizations

In terms of sheer volume of opinions, Justice Ginsburg's top effort in subject-matter jurisdiction has been to shrink the universe of judicial limits classified as jurisdictional. Although the effort hit some bumps along the way, she ultimately has completely reoriented the way "jurisdictionality" is conceived, and she has managed to do so through a remarkable number of unanimous opinions.

Until recently, federal courts, including the Supreme Court, gave scant consideration to the question of when a limit was jurisdictional. Careless use of the term became particularly rampant after 1960, when the Supreme Court decided a case called *United States v. Robinson*.[23] There, criminal defendants, found guilty at trial, filed notices of appeal outside of the deadline established by Criminal Rule 37(a).[24] They blamed their tardiness on excusable neglect, but the Court rejected the appeals, holding excusable neglect insufficient to relax the time stricture. Four times the Court characterized appellate deadlines as "mandatory and jurisdictional."[25] To be fair, the Court itself did not endorse that characterization but rather noted how circuits had characterized it, to see whether precedent or history might support an ability to relax the deadline. Its own discussion was primarily textual, construing the rules as disallowing enlargement, rather than basing the rigidity on attributes of jurisdictionality. Nevertheless, the repeated use of that phrase took hold in both the lower courts and the Supreme Court.[26]

For example, in *Browder v. Director, Illinois Department of Corrections*,[27] the Court held that an untimely motion for a hearing in a habeas proceeding – timely objected to – did not toll the "mandatory and jurisdictional" time to appeal.[28] In *Griggs v. Provident Consumer Discount Co.*,[29] the Court held the premature filing of a notice of appeal to be "a nullity" because "it is well settled that the requirement of a timely notice of appeal is 'mandatory and jurisdictional.'"[30] And in *Torres v. Oakland Scavenger Co.*,[31] the Court held that the failure of a notice of appeal to name an appellant deprives the Court of Appeals of jurisdiction over that appellant.[32]

It was in this milieu that Ginsburg found herself confronting questions of jurisdictionality on the D.C. Circuit, and, more than anyone else on the court, Judge Ginsburg began advocating a more careful approach.[33] In the 1986 case *Center for Nuclear Responsibility, Inc. v. NRC*,[34] her colleagues held that an untimely notice of appeal required dismissal of the appeal.[35] In dissent, Ginsburg pointed out that "Congress sometimes allocates subject matter competence (jurisdiction) with less than ideal clarity"[36] and that the overused word "jurisdiction" suffers from a "chameleon" quality.[37]

In the 1989 case *Rafeedie v. INS*,[38] the D.C. Circuit held a statutory exhaustion rule to be jurisdictional in an unusual three-opinion decision.[39] Ginsburg concurred in the judgment but disagreed with the court's jurisdictional characterization.[40] She wrote:

> Certainly, when Congress sees fit to instruct exhaustion in specific terms, courts should be especially hesitant to allow litigants to bypass administrative procedures. I cannot believe, however, that, in codifying an exhaustion rule, Congress inevitably and inexorably means to preclude early judicial review even when requiring exhaustion in a specific case would serve none of the purposes motivating the requirement and would threaten grievous harm to the person seeking review.[41]

Her sentiments provoked the dissent, which repeated the conventional wisdom: "An explicit statutory exhaustion requirement is jurisdictional; it deprives federal courts of general federal question jurisdiction to entertain an ancillary action under the APA prior to exhaustion."[42]

The following year, however, she wrote for a majority in suggesting that decoupling the standard doublet "mandatory and jurisdictional" might be appropriate: "It may be most accurate to describe as 'jurisdictional' an access-to-court rule that is in all instances unalterable, i.e., never bends, while denominating simply 'mandatory' a rule, of the kind before us here, that accommodates rare exceptions, i.e., hardly ever bends."[43] Nevertheless, as a circuit judge obligated to follow both Supreme Court and prevailing circuit decisions, she could do little more.[44]

She found more freedom on the Supreme Court, though she was slow to attract votes to her views. In the 1996 case of *Carlisle v. United States*,[45] she forcefully asserted: "It is anomalous to classify time prescriptions, even rigid ones, under the heading 'subject matter jurisdiction'"[46] because they are "less basic."[47] Still, she was new to a Court that had trended in the opposite direction, and thus her views, in that case, were confined to a concurrence.

Two years later, however, her views took root in a majority opinion called *Steel Co. v. Citizens for a Better Environment*.[48] The author was Justice Antonin Scalia, but the language and tone mirrored the sentiments that Justice Ginsburg had pushed on the Court of Appeals. "'Jurisdiction,'" the Court quoted the D.C. Circuit, "'is a word of many, too many meanings.'"[49] And, the Court followed up, "drive-by jurisdictional rulings [that do not use the concept with care] have no precedential effect."[50]

The year 2001 brought Ginsburg her first opportunity to write a majority opinion narrowing the scope of jurisdictional limitations. The case was *Becker v. Montgomery*,[51] which presented the question of whether the failure of the appellant to sign his notice of appeal rendered the Court of Appeals powerless to proceed. In a unanimous opinion, Ginsburg answered no, despite precedent such as *Griggs*, *Browder*, and *Torres* tending to impart jurisdictional stature to elements of the notice of appeal.[52] Ginsburg contained those precedents with pragmatism, explaining that "imperfections in noticing an appeal should not be fatal where no genuine doubt exists about who is appealing, from what judgment, to which appellate court."[53]

In 2004, Ginsburg wrote another unanimous opinion in *Kontrick v. Ryan*,[54] holding that the deadline of a creditor to object to a debtor's discharge is not jurisdictional, and therefore the debtor can forfeit the right to move to dismiss an untimely objection.[55] Bankruptcy Rules are for "the practice and procedure" in bankruptcy cases,[56] Ginsburg explained, just as the FRCP are "rules of practice and procedure,"[57] and "'it is axiomatic' that such rules 'do not create or withdraw federal jurisdiction."[58] Finally able to break from the care-lessness of the past, she wrote:

> Courts, including this Court, it is true, have been less than meticulous in this regard; they have more than occasionally used the term "jurisdictional" to describe emphatic time prescriptions in rules of court.... Clarity would be facilitated if courts and litigants used the label "jurisdictional" not for claim-processing rules, but only for prescriptions delineating the classes of cases (subject-matter jurisdiction) and the persons (personal jurisdiction) falling within a court's adjudicatory authority.[59]

Because the Bankruptcy Rule was a claim-processing rule, "Kontrick forfeited his right to assert the untimeliness of Ryan's amended complaint by failing to raise the issue until after that complaint was adjudicated on the merits."[60]

That same Term, Ginsburg authored *Scarborough v. Principi*,[61] a 7–2 decision holding the thirty-day deadline to cure an initial failure to allege that the government's position was not substantially justified and thus warranted fee shifting, was not jurisdictional.[62] "Rather," Ginsburg explained, "it concerns a mode of relief (costs including legal fees) ancillary to the judgment of a court that has plenary [jurisdiction]."[63]

In 2005, Ginsburg was part of a unanimous per curiam opinion in *Eberhart v. United States*,[64] which characterized as nonjurisdictional Criminal Rule 33(b)(2)'s deadline to make certain new trial motions, despite the provision in Rule 45(b)(2) that courts "may not extend" the deadline. Relying heavily on *Kontrick*, the Court held that Rule 33 is a nonjurisdictional claims-processing rule that need not be enforced when forfeited by the nonmoving party.[65] The Court expressly blamed its prior opinion in *Robinson* for "creat[ing] some confusion" by using the term "jurisdictional" four times with "imprecision."[66] "Our repetition of the phrase 'mandatory and jurisdictional,'" noted the Court, "has understandably led the lower courts to err on the side of caution by giv-ing the limitations ... the force of subject-matter jurisdiction."[67] However, the Court continued, citing *Kontrick*, *Scarborough*, and Ginsburg's concurrence in *Carlisle*, "our more recent cases have done much to clarify this point.... These claim-processing rules thus assure relief to a party properly raising them, but do not compel the same result if the party forfeits them."[68] Because of *Robinson*'s imprecision and the fact that the jurisdictional characterization was unnecessary to its disposition, its "drive-by jurisdictional" language was not controlling.[69]

The following year, Ginsburg authored yet another unanimous opinion in *Arbaugh v. Y&H Corp.*,[70] holding the employee-numerosity requirement of Title VII (making Title VII applicable only to employers with fifteen or more employees) to be a nonjurisdictional part of the merits of the claim.[71] Citing *Robinson*, the Court once again assumed blame: "This Court, no less than other courts, has sometimes been profligate in its use of the term. For example, this Court and others have occasionally described a nonextendable time limit as 'mandatory and jurisdictional.'"[72] Quoting *Steel Co.*, she wrote: "We have described such unrefined dispositions as 'drive-by jurisdictional rulings' that should be accorded 'no precedential effect' on the question of whether the federal court had authority to adjudicate the claim in suit."[73] However, she continued, citing *Kontrick, Scarborough, Eberhart,* and the *Carlisle* concurrence, "in recent decisions, we have clarified that time prescriptions, however emphatic, are not properly typed jurisdictional."[74]

Arbaugh, of course, involved not a time prescription but rather a potential merits issue in a statute, which, of course, Congress could make jurisdictional if it wished.[75] This new situation called for a more involved framework than the Court had used for deadlines. Mindful of the harsh and wasteful consequences of typing a limit jurisdictional, the Court created a "readily administrable bright line" presumption against jurisdictionality that Congress could override with a clear statement.[76] The Court then found no clear statement of jurisdictionality because the requirement did not "speak in jurisdictional terms or refer in any way to the jurisdiction of the district courts" and "appear[ed] in a separate provision" from the jurisdictional grant.[77]

After this string of unanimous or near-unanimous opinions, Ginsburg's jurisdictionality project hit a bump in 2007, when *Bowles v. Russell*[78] held that the deadline to file a notice of appeal in a civil case was jurisdictional.[79] There was no denying that the petitioner was late in his filing, and the respondent timely sought dismissal on that basis in the Court of Appeals. The narrow question was whether a court could excuse Bowles's tardiness for equitable reasons.

The Court, in an opinion by Justice Clarence Thomas, first noted a long-standing and consistent line of Supreme Court precedent calling the time to appeal "mandatory and jurisdictional."[80] While acknowledging that many of those opinions ultimately relied on *Robinson*, the Court "noted the jurisdictional significance of the fact that a time limit is set forth in a statute" and, "regardless of this Court's past careless use of terminology," cited *Griggs, Torres, Browder*, among others, in asserting that "it is indisputable that time limits for filing a notice of appeal have been treated as jurisdictional in American law for well over a century."[81] Rather than repudiate that precedent, the Court instead distinguished and expressly "call[ed] into question" the "dicta" of the more recent cases of *Kontrick, Eberhart, Arbaugh*, and *Scarborough*.[82] Because the time limit was jurisdictional, the Court held that Bowles could not rely upon equitable doctrines to excuse his tardiness.[83]

Justice Souter dissented for four justices, including Ginsburg.[84] "Although we used to call the sort of time limit at issue here 'mandatory and jurisdictional,'" he wrote, echoing Ginsburg's similar statements her own previous opinions, "we have recently and repeatedly corrected that designation as a misuse of the 'jurisdiction' label."[85] Souter accused the majority of "suddenly restor[ing] *Robinson's* indiscriminate use of the 'mandatory and jurisdictional' label to good law in the face of three unanimous repudiations."[86] Contrary to the majority, the dissenters would classify the appellate filing deadline as a claim-processing rule, not a delineation of cases.[87] And, based on its nonjurisdictional view of the appellate deadline, the dissent would find an exception to the deadline "when there is a good justification for one."[88]

Bowles provoked commentators as well.[89] Nevertheless, the Court's next decision, *John R. Sand & Gravel Co. v. United States*,[90] appeared to continue *Bowles's* trend. There, the Court held, based primarily on stare decisis, that the six-year statutory limitations period to sue the government in the Court of Federal Claims must be raised sua sponte despite the government's waiver of the issue.[91] Ginsburg was in dissent,[92] but perhaps her views nevertheless had an impact. As I later observed, the Court rephrased the question presented from whether the limitations period was "jurisdictional" to "whether a court must raise on its own the timeliness of a lawsuit filed in the Court of Federal Claims, despite the Government's waiver of the issue."[93] Indeed, the Court carefully avoided characterizing the limitations period as "jurisdictional," opting instead to characterize it as a "more absolute" bar.[94] This sensitivity offered the possibility that the Court remained open to Ginsburg's pre-*Bowles* line of cases.

In *Union Pacific Railroad Co. v. Brotherhood of Locomotive Engineers & Trainmen General Committee of Adjustment*,[95] the next case, Ginsburg steered the Court back on track with a unanimous opinion holding that the requirement that parties before the NRAB attempt settlement in conference is not jurisdictional.[96] Citing *Steel Co.*, *Arbaugh*, and *Kontrick*, the Court warned "against profligate use of the term [jurisdictional]"[97] and, applying those cases, held the requirement to be a nonjurisdictional claim-processing rule.[98] The Court distinguished *Bowles* and *John R. Sand* as resulting from "a long line of this Court's decisions left undisturbed by Congress."[99] *Union Pacific* thus reconfirmed the pre-*Bowles* precedent scaling back jurisdictionality and limited *Bowles* and *John R. Sand* as precedent-based anomalies.

In the wake of *Union Pacific*, the Court issued a series of unanimous or near-unanimous cases further entrenching the doctrine. *Reed Elsevier, Inc. v. Muchnick*[100] held the Copyright Act's registration requirement to be a nonjurisdictional precondition to filing.[101] *Henderson v. Shinseki*[102] held as nonjurisdictional the 120-day deadline for a losing veteran to file a notice of appeal with the Veteran's Court (the available administrative appellate body).[103] *Gonzalez v. Thaler*[104] held as nonjurisdictional the requirement that a timely certificate of appealability indicate the specific issue on which a habeas petitioner has made a substantial showing of the denial of a constitutional right.[105] *Sebelius v. Auburn Regional Medical Center*[106] held as nonjurisdictional the 180-day deadline for a provider to file an administrative appeal to the PRRB.[107] In these cases, the Court repeatedly reaffirmed the presumption against jurisdictionality imposed by *Kontrick* and *Arbaugh* based on the pragmatic reasons Ginsburg articulated in those opinions.[108]

Today, the precedent on jurisdictionality is fairly settled. The Court fully supports the paradigm that Ginsburg proposed in her earlier opinions – a presumption against jurisdictional characterization, based on the harsh consequences of typing a limit as jurisdictional – and it has found that presumption overcome only in the rare case in which a long line of precedent consistently holds otherwise.[109] Through this doctrine, Ginsburg has succeeded in bringing a healthy dose of pragmatism to a doctrine that tends to resist it.

B. Resequencing: Undermining the Primacy of Jurisdiction

For many years, subject-matter jurisdiction was seen as the alpha, the sine qua non, the antecedent condition without which a court can do nothing but dismiss the case.[110] More than a century ago, the Supreme Court intoned: "The rule, springing from the nature and limits of the judicial power of the United States, is inflexible and without exception.... On every writ of error or appeal, the first and fundamental question is that of jurisdiction."[111] Old precedent, along with the idea of jurisdiction as power, suggested that all questions of jurisdiction must be resolved first, before any other question was considered.

But Justice Ginsburg has been at the forefront of a modern effort to undermine the primacy of subject-matter jurisdiction by developing a doctrine that has come to be known as resequencing.

Like the doctrine of jurisdictionality, the genesis of resequencing began during her days as a judge on the D.C. Circuit. In a case called *Coker v. Sullivan*,[112] Ginsburg authored an opinion for the court resolving a statutory-jurisdiction issue before an Article III standing issue. She wrote:

> Although standing is usually a threshold inquiry, both the Supreme Court and this Circuit have long recognized the propriety of avoiding difficult, constitutionally-based justiciability issues when a case is more simply resolved on another basis. We believe this path especially appropriate here, because

the alternative rationale on which we rely is also a jurisdictional limitation, although one derived from statute rather than the Constitution.[113]

Resequencing different questions of subject-matter jurisdiction is not terribly controversial, especially when the Court has long expressed a preference for prioritizing statutory decisions over constitutional decisions. Nevertheless, the language of her opinion set the stage for broader expansion when she arrived at the Supreme Court.

In *Steel Co. v. Citizens for a Better Environment*,[114] discussed earlier in the context of jurisdictionality, one of the issues was whether courts can consider nonjurisdictional issues on the basis of "hypothetical jurisdiction."[115] Quoting the old jurisdictional-primacy cases, the Court disapproved of that approach because of the fundamental nature of jurisdiction.[116] However, the Court did acknowledge that some cases "have diluted the absolute purity of the rule that Article III jurisdiction is always an antecedent question."[117]

Justice Ginsburg concurred only in the judgment in *Steel Co.* but got her turn to set out her own views a year later in the unanimous decision *Ruhrgas AG v. Marathon Oil Co.*,[118] which considered whether a court could decide personal jurisdiction before subject-matter jurisdiction. Ginsburg's opinion characterized *Steel Co.* as holding that a court may not hypothesize subject-matter jurisdiction for the purpose of deciding the merits.[119] The distinction between subject-matter jurisdiction and merits makes sense, she wrote, but "the same principle does not dictate a sequencing of jurisdictional issues" because no assumption of law-making power is invoked when dismissing on personal-jurisdiction grounds.[120] Ginsburg acknowledged differences between subject-matter and personal jurisdiction – namely, waiver and the institutional/ personal interests – but denied "that subject-matter jurisdiction is ever and always the more 'fundamental.'"[121] In matters of jurisdiction, which includes personal jurisdiction, she concluded, "there is no unyielding jurisdictional hierarchy."[122]

The primary impetus for allowing resequencing was judicial economy and restraint. A court ought not have to slog through a difficult or novel question of subject-matter jurisdiction if the case can be dismissed on straightforward personal-jurisdiction grounds.[123] Although the Court framed its decision as resequencing only among like-jurisdictional issues, commentators interpreted *Ruhrgas* as "disaffirm[ing] the notion" that subject-matter jurisdiction is "more fundamental,"[124] and many applauded *Ruhrgas*'s attention to judicial economy in resequencing of subject-matter jurisdiction.[125]

Ginsburg took *Ruhrgas* one step further in the unanimous *Sinochem International Co. v. Malaysia International Shipping Co.*[126] There, the Court extended the *Ruhrgas* resequencing principle to issues of the judge-made doctrine of forum non conveniens; in other words, a court can dismiss under forum non conveniens without first resolving issues of subject-matter jurisdiction.[127] Rather than tying all jurisdictional doctrines together, as *Ruhrgas* did, the Court in *Sinochem* distinguished between merits and non-merits. "Jurisdiction is vital only if the court proposes to issue a judgment on the merits,"[128] Ginsburg wrote, and because forum non conveniens is not a merits determination, a court may "bypass questions of subject-matter and personal jurisdiction" to dismiss under forum non conveniens, "when considerations of convenience, fairness, and judicial economy so warrant."[129]

The doctrine of resequencing thus uses practical considerations to enable courts to resequence non-merits issues before jurisdictional issues if the result is dismissal. By grouping subject-matter jurisdiction along with nonjurisdictional issues such as forum non conveniences, resequencing erodes the primacy of subject-matter jurisdiction.

C. *"Curing" Jurisdictional Defects*

The doctrines of jurisdictionality and resequencing have resulted in strong successes for Ginsburg's vision of a more cautious and grounded idea of jurisdiction. A third Ginsburg doctrine – "curing" jurisdictional defects – has met with more opposition from other justices. The idea began with the unanimous Ginsburg opinion in *Caterpillar Inc. v. Lewis*,[130] in which the defendant removed a state case to federal court even though federal subject-matter jurisdiction was lacking at the time of removal.[131] The plaintiff timely moved to remand on the ground that the presence of a nondiverse defendant destroyed diversity, but the district court denied the motion. Later, the nondiverse defendant settled out, and the case – now completely diverse – went to trial. After judgment for the diverse defendant, the plaintiff appealed on the ground that removal was improper.[132] The Court held that the jurisdictional defect – incomplete diversity – was cured prior to judgment[133]; therefore, the only question was whether the statutory defect – removal at a time in which jurisdiction was lacking – required reversal.[134] The Court held that statutory defect could be overcome by "considerations of finality, efficiency, and economy."[135]

Caterpillar is pure Ginsburg in its consideration of jurisdiction.[136] Jurisdictional defects can be cured, and even the timely objection to those defects before the cure can be overcome by practical and pragmatic considerations.

In the subsequent case of *Grupo Dataflux v. Atlas Global Group L.P.*, however, a divided Court, with Ginsburg in dissent, drew a line at party-dropping

cures and would not extend *Caterpillar* to a single party's citizenship change.[137]
In *Grupo*, a Mexican company invoked federal alienage jurisdiction in a suit
against a limited partnership with two foreign partners. The presence of aliens
on both sides destroyed alienage jurisdiction, but the two foreign partners left
the partnership before trial, essentially changing the partnership's citizenship
from an alien to a purely domestic entity.[138] However, the Court held that
the rule that jurisdiction is considered at the time of filing allows no exception for citizenship changes, and therefore the case had to be dismissed for
lack of subject-matter jurisdiction even though the jurisdictional defect was
cured. Ginsburg dissented, seeing no difference between the dropping of partners and the dropping of parties in trimming a case down to its fully diverse
core.[139]

    Caterpillar, then, echoes the common Ginsburgian theme of circumvent-
ing jurisdictional effects. Although she was unable to convince the Court to
extend the *Caterpillar* principle in *Grupo*, *Caterpillar* remains both good law
and a modest safeguard against the costs of jurisdictional defects.

III. APPRAISALS AND OBSERVATIONS

One common theme uniting Ginsburg's efforts in each of these three jurisdictional areas is the degradation of jurisdiction through a pragmatic focus
on its harsh effects. Those effects should play more of a role in jurisdictional
doctrine, Ginsburg's opinions stress, especially in ways that limit jurisdiction's
scope and primacy.

    This focus on jurisdiction and its effects has its virtues. One great virtue is
its effort to spark critical thought in the nature and role of jurisdiction; in that
effort, Ginsburg has no doubt succeeded. The days of thoughtless, "drive-by"
jurisdictional rulings are largely over.[140] Another virtue is that the effort has
tended to produce opinions that improve judicial economy and increase litigant fairness.[141] In this regard, her efforts are quite consistent with her broader
jurisdictional and procedural jurisprudence.[142]

    But, paradoxically, the focus on jurisdiction may inhibit further profitable
development of the gains made in jurisdictional doctrine thus far. Focusing
directly on jurisdictional-characterization questions is a dichotomous trap.
The reason is that the answer to a jurisdictional-characterization question
does not necessarily say much about the effects that then flow from that
characterization.

    To illustrate, consider *Bowles v. Russell*,[143] discussed earlier. The pre-
cise question was whether a civil appellee could invoke equity to excuse
his tardy filing of the notice of appeal.[144] The majority opinion frames the

question as whether the appellate deadline is jurisdictional and assumes that a jurisdictional characterization will necessary lead to the conclusion that equitable excuses are unavailable. For its part, the dissent takes the other side, assuming that a nonjurisdictional characterization will necessarily enable equitable excuses.[145]

Both assumptions are incorrect. As I have explained elsewhere, jurisdictional boundaries can incorporate, depend upon, or be affected by questions that have attributes of nonjurisdictionality such as waiver, forfeiture, or equitable excuses.[146] Thus, it is possible for the deadline to file a notice of appeal to be "jurisdictional" and yet incorporate the equitable considerations urged by Bowles.[147]

On the flip side, nonjurisdictional boundaries can have jurisdictional effects of nonwaivability, nonforfeitability, mandatoriness, or even all of the above.[148] Thus, it would have been possible – perhaps even accurate – to characterize the deadline to file a notice of appeal as nonjurisdictional but immune from the equitable considerations urged by Bowles.[149]

The conclusion, then, is that a focus on jurisdictionality is fairly uninformative and tends to obscure the narrower and more relevant question: what *effects* does a particular rule have? Ginsburg's own emphasis on the practical ills of jurisdiction ought to drive jurisdictional doctrine toward this effects question.

For these reasons, the Court's focus on the jurisdictional-characterization question, while a marked improvement from the blasé approach to jurisdictionality reflected in cases like *Robinson* and its progeny, risks stagnation. The gains spearheaded by Justice Ginsburg's jurisdiction opinions could be built upon by transitioning the focus from jurisdictionality to effects.

There is some indication that the Court is becoming aware that the focus on jurisdictionality has reached the end of its usefulness. Ginsburg herself has acknowledged that nonjurisdictional rules can have jurisdictional attributes,[150] though these acknowledgments are often in passing fashion and are in tension with her other assertions that seem to ignore these nuances.[151] Ironically, perhaps the jurisdictionality opinion most faithful to Ginsburg's legacy is one that Ginsburg did not join: the majority opinion in *John R. Sand*.[152] There, by recasting the question presented from one focused on the jurisdictional character of the limitations period at issue to one focused on the effects of the limitations period at issue, the Court was able to focus on the more relevant and narrowest issue presented. The Court, however, has not continued *John R. Sand's* approach in subsequent cases.

Perhaps it is a bit unfair to criticize for not taking the next step. Jurisdiction has a long pedigree in Supreme Court opinions, and Ginsburg respects precedent deeply.[153] It would not be possible for her to dispense with the idea of jurisdiction altogether.[154] Still, the jurisdictional-characterization question has become a trap; in all but the most obvious of jurisdictional questions, the effects are the real issue. Decisions like *John R. Sand* suggest that tackling the effects can be workable, sensible, and respectful of precedent – in essence, a continuation of Ginsburg's legacy in this area.

Focusing on effects – in addition to producing narrower and more relevant decisions – might also spur profitable thought on those effects. Ginsburg has already made some effort on this front. For example, in *Day v. McDonough* and *Wood v. Milyard*, she wrote for the Court holding that lower courts have the authority, though not the obligation, to dismiss a habeas petition for untimeliness sua sponte despite the state's forfeiture of the defense unless the state deliberately and intelligently waived the defense.[155] Her opinion in *Wood*, in particular, tries to draw a clear line – both conceptual and doctrinal – between forfeiture and deliberate waiver.[156] Undoubtedly, more work is needed in this area,[157] but recognizing that the attention is deserved is pure Ginsburg.

CONCLUSION

In the end, credit must be given where due. Ginsburg's legacy in this area is marked by her ability to raise awareness of the importance of attending to jurisdictional issues with care and thoughtfulness. Her strides will have permanence, both for future cases within the existing doctrinal contours and for future evolution of the doctrine and understanding of jurisdiction.

11

Ruth Bader Ginsburg and the Interaction of Legal Systems

Paul Schiff Berman

From her early days writing a book on *Civil Procedure in Sweden*,[1] to her time as law professor, judge, and justice, Ruth Bader Ginsburg has always been acutely sensitive to the fact that legal systems are not hermetically sealed from each other. Always there must be ways of negotiating the interactions among such systems. In the United States, of course, such interactions often involve navigating a federalist structure of fifty-one different sovereignties, in addition to tribal governments. Internationally, the interaction of legal systems may involve the degree to which U.S. constitutional norms govern U.S. officials abroad, the impact of foreign judgments in the United States, and the potential influence of international or transnational law in domestic cases.

This chapter begins with some general observations about the reality of this legal pluralism and various possible approaches to the systemic interactions that inevitably result. Then, it surveys some of Ginsburg's key writings on the interaction of legal systems, both in law journals and in judicial opinions. This analysis reveals a consistent theme in Ginsburg's jurisprudence. Across a variety of substantive legal areas, Ginsburg often chooses a path that provides maximum play among the legal systems at issue. Beginning with her earliest scholarly writings, she has tended to oppose doctrines allowing one legal system to block another from adjudicating a dispute, and throughout her later career Ginsburg likewise tends to reject bright-line rules that choose one legal system over another. Instead, she often seems to prefer procedural arrangements that seek accommodation and flexibility in order to ensure that multiple legal systems and a variety of norms and processes are respected. These principles also carry over to Ginsburg's views about international and transnational law. A committed internationalist, Ginsburg advocates the importance

Special thanks to Sara Allawi, Ben Gottesman, and Jamie Noonan for helpful research assistance.

of seeking wisdom from others. This nondogmatic, deferential approach to plural legal systems characterizes much of her jurisprudence on intersystemic conflicts, though interestingly such deference does not always apply with as much force in Ginsburg's opinions concerning tribal communities. By taking stock of Ginsburg's navigation of legal pluralism in a set of representative writings, we can better theorize her contribution to a jurisprudential approach that seeks ongoing negotiation in an interlocking world of multiple jurisdictions and multiple legal norms.

I. POTENTIAL STRATEGIES FOR RESPONDING TO LEGAL PLURALISM

Law often operates based on the convenient fiction that human activity is only subject to the rules of one legal system at a time. Yet jurisdictional overlap is unavoidable, and so, inevitably, law must negotiate situations when multiple communities and legal authorities seek to regulate the same act or actor. Scholars studying interactions among these multiple communities have often used the term "legal pluralism" to describe the intermingling of these normative systems.[2]

The study of plural normative systems has arisen from a variety of different scholarly traditions. Perhaps the earliest studies of the clashes between state and nonstate authority were those penned by lawyers, philosophers, and theologians interested in the respective realms of church and state.[3] Likewise, historians analyzing the regulatory role of nonstate entities such as jockey clubs and stock exchanges noted that these entities often wield more power than formal state law.[4] For their part, anthropologists used the idea of legal pluralism to conceptualize the relationship between colonial and indigenous legal systems.[5] And social norms theorists and scholars in behavioral law and economics have become interested in forms of informal law that often regulate behavior as much as, or more than, official governmental pronouncements.[6]

Although legal pluralism was originally a way to broaden the scholarly lens to study the interaction between state and nonstate law, in recent years the insights of legal pluralism have also been used to analyze the more traditional interactions among formal legal systems both internationally and within one nation-state.[7] In the years following the collapse of the bipolar Cold War order, it became clear that the traditional framework of international law had expanded to include jurisdictional overlaps among many different courts, tribunals, panels, and arbitral bodies. Legal pluralism became a helpful way to analyze these complex relationships, which often lack explicit hierarchies. And even within domestic federal systems, the intersystemic interactions among states and between state and national sovereigns created fertile ground for studying pluralism in action.[8]

So, how should law respond to the reality of multiple overlapping legal systems? Often, these hybrid legal spaces have been viewed simply as a problem to be solved. This is perhaps why the possibility that parties might engage in forum shopping is so often referenced pejoratively. Thus, even when jurisdictional overlap or regulatory interdependence is undeniable, we see what Robert Ahdieh has termed "the standard dualist response."[9] Law seeks to delimit each entity's jurisdiction and authority more effectively and thereby eliminate such overlap. This paradigm of jurisdictional line drawing has been prevalent both in the international/transnational realm[10] and in discussions of federalism,[11] as courts and scholars try to demarcate distinct spheres for state and federal authority. As Ahdieh notes, "Such reactions are hardly surprising. At heart, they reflect some visceral sense of law's project as one of categorization, clear definition, and line-drawing."[12]

Yet this single-minded focus on certainty and clarity not only fails to describe a globalized world of inevitable cross-border jurisdictional overlap but also ignores the crucial question of whether leaving open space for such overlapping regulatory authority might actually be *beneficial*. Indeed, while jurisdictional overlap is frequently viewed as a problem because it potentially creates conflicting obligations and uncertainty, we might also view jurisdictional redundancy as a necessary adaptive feature of a multivariate, pluralist legal system. The very existence of overlapping jurisdictional claims often leads to a nuanced negotiation – either explicit or implicit – between or among the various communities making those claims.[13]

In focusing on the pluralist opportunities inherent in jurisdictional overlap, I echo the insights of Robert Cover's article "The Uses of Jurisdictional Redundancy."[14] Cover analyzed American federalism and celebrated the benefits that accrue from having multiple overlapping jurisdictional assertions. Such benefits include a greater possibility for error correction, a more robust field for norm articulation, and a larger space for creative innovation.[15] Moreover, when decision makers are forced to consider the existence of other possible decision makers, they may tend to adopt, over time, a more restrained view of their own power and come to see themselves as part of a larger tapestry of decision making in which they are not the only potentially relevant voice. Finally, though Cover acknowledged that it might seem perverse "to seek out a messy and indeterminate end to conflicts which may be tied neatly together by a single authoritative verdict," he nevertheless argued that we should "embrace" a system "that permits tensions and conflicts of the social order" to be played out in the jurisdictional structure of the system.[16] More recently,

Judith Resnik has noted the "multiple ports of entry" that a federalist system creates[17] and has argued that what constitutes the appropriate spheres for "local," "national," and "international" regulation and adjudication changes over time and should not be essentialized.[18]

Building on these principles, we can perhaps identify two different strategies for responding to legal pluralism. On the one hand, judges facing an issue of intersystemic complexity can seek to bring order by engaging in line-drawing and delimiting separate spheres of authority. This is what Cover calls a "jurispathic" approach because it necessarily requires the decision maker to anoint one jurisdiction as the legitimate authority and decree that all other jurisdictions are disabled from applying their norms. In doing so, the decision maker "kills off" conflicting interpretations and authorities.[19] The contrasting approach is what Cover would call "jurisgenerative."[20] This pluralist approach seeks modes of accommodation, deference, and hybridity that will allow multiple jurisdictions to continue to speak to a particular legal problem, without blocking the dialogue among systems.[21] Thus, the pluralist framework provides a way of analyzing jurisprudence concerning the interaction of legal systems in terms of whether it preserves or cuts off intersystemic dialogue. This framework also reveals patterns in Justice Ginsburg's jurisprudence across a variety of substantive legal areas.

II. POLICING COURT RULINGS THAT INTERFERE WITH THE PROCESSES OF OTHER COURTS

From the beginning of her scholarly career, Ginsburg was clearly interested in questions of intersystemic interaction and particularly the concern that one authority might cut off the ability of another authority to effectively hear a case. Indeed, one of her first major law review articles focused largely on the problem of antisuit injunctions. Entitled "Judgments in Search of Full Faith and Credit: The Last-in-Time Rule for Conflicting Judgments,"[22] Ginsburg considered in this article what should happen when a court in one state enjoins parties before it from proceeding in a lawsuit in another state. In particular, she asked whether such antisuit injunctions should receive full faith and credit in the second state, thereby blocking the litigation process in that state.

After noting the U.S. Supreme Court's silence on this issue, Ginsburg set forth the two extreme possible options in response. First, one might view the Full Faith and Credit Clause of the U.S. Constitution[23] as such an exacting command that even an antisuit injunction must be respected by the second court. Ginsburg suggested that such a rule would be "consistent with the generally strict line the Supreme Court has taken on full faith and credit to judgments," but she also observed that "state courts on the receiving end of such injunctions have not found this a palatable solution."[24] Second, there could be "a general rule denying the states authority to issue injunctions directed at proceedings in other states."[25] Although such a rule would protect the interests of the second court in pursuing its judicial process, the rule would disable the first court from issuing the relief sought by one of the parties. Thus, either option seems jurispathic, cutting off the legal process of one or the other of the courts at issue.

Significantly, Ginsburg rejected both of these jurispathic options and argued in favor of a middle ground approach: "permitting the injunction to issue but not compelling any deference outside the rendering state."[26] Thus, the initial court could still issue the injunction, but such an injunction would not be binding on the second court. Instead, the injunction *might* be accorded respect (and enforcement) by the second court, but only "as a matter of comity."[27]

Given how much this article foreshadows Ginsburg's later jurisprudence, it is worth pausing to consider her solution to the problem of antisuit injunctions. Neither court ends up wielding absolute authority independent of the other; neither court fully silences the other. Although the second court seems on the surface to retain the ultimate power to accept or reject the first court's injunction, such power cannot be wielded without significant cost because, under Ginsburg's approach, the second court would lose credibility and legitimacy if it rejected the first court's injunction without at least addressing the first court's reasoning. Thus, even if the second court retains ultimate authority, it must engage the first court's views before wielding jurispathic power. This built-in intersystemic dialogue – whereby one court asks another to refrain from litigation, and the other court then must decide how much it can defer to the first court's order – respects both courts as adjudicatory actors and leaves resolution of individual cases to a dialogic and dialectical process among courts exercising restraint, deference, and comity.

As a justice, Ginsburg has taken a similar approach to the Full Faith and Credit Clause in two U.S. Supreme Court cases. First, in *Matsushita Electric Industries Co. v. Epstein*,[28] the Court considered whether a Delaware classaction settlement should preclude litigation in a California federal court pursued by class members who argued that they were not adequately represented in Delaware. Although the Court granted preclusive effect to the Delaware settlement, thereby blocking the California litigation, Ginsburg dissented in relevant part. Ginsburg argued that the Full Faith and Credit Clause should not automatically bar the California litigation, especially given the assertion that the lawyers in Delaware did not represent the interests of all

class members.[29] Indeed, she suggested that in this case the attorneys for the
class may have too easily relinquished the class's rights to pursue the federal
litigation in order to pocket their attorneys' fees.[30] Accordingly, due process,
Ginsburg argued, required an inquiry regarding the adequacy of class representation in the first litigation before the second litigation should be blocked
by full faith and credit.[31] Thus, although preclusion doctrine is somewhat different from the antisuit injunctions discussed in her earlier article, Ginsburg
similarly rejected automatic enforcement of an injunction that would have
the effect of blocking litigation elsewhere.

Two years later, in *Baker v. General Motors Corp.*,[32] Ginsburg returned to the
realm of antisuit injunctions (even citing her own early law review article)[33] and
commanded a majority for her view regarding the proper operation of the Full
Faith and Credit Clause when one court's order aims to block the operation of
a second court's judicial process. *Baker* concerned a stipulated injunction submitted to and signed by a Michigan court in settlement of a lawsuit between
General Motors (GM) and Ronald Elwell, a former GM employee.[34] Among
other terms, the stipulated injunction purported to prevent Elwell from testifying against GM in subsequent legal proceedings.[35] The question posed before
the Supreme Court was whether, in a separate wrongful death suit brought in
a Missouri federal court by the Bakers against GM, Elwell could be called as a
plaintiff's witness or whether instead the Michigan injunction blocked Elwell
from testifying. And while it was clear that the Michigan judgment could not
preclude the *Bakers*, who were not parties to the Michigan proceedings, the
difficult question was whether it could bind *Elwell*, who obviously had been a
party in Michigan, and therefore keep him from testifying.[36] The Missouri federal district court judge ruled that allowing such a result would run counter to
public policy and therefore invoked a public policy exception to the Full Faith
and Credit Clause, whereby rendering courts would be free to ignore prior
court judgments' anathema to the rendering court's local policies.[37]

Thus, the Supreme Court appeared to be faced with a binary choice. On
the one hand, the Court could endorse the Missouri District Court's ruling
and allow courts to extricate themselves from the Full Faith and Credit Clause
simply by deeming a sister jurisdiction's judgment contrary to public policy.
On the other hand, the Court could enforce the Michigan court's order,
thereby allowing Michigan's ruling to prevent any other court in the country
from hearing Elwell's testimony in cases against GM.

Not surprisingly, as with the antisuit injunctions discussed in her article,
Ginsburg rejected both of these jurispathic options. Writing for the Court, she
first made it clear that although choice-of-law doctrines permit courts to use
public policy objections in choosing the *law* to apply in a cross-jurisdictional

case, the command of the Full Faith and Credit Clause with regard to prior *judgments* is far more "exacting" and permits no such set of broad exceptions: "A final judgment in one State, if rendered by a court with adjudicatory authority over the subject matter and persons governed by the judgment, qualifies for recognition throughout the land."[38] Thus, the Missouri court could not simply ignore the Michigan judgment based on assertions of public policy.

At the same time, the Michigan court could not automatically block the adjudication in Missouri. "Michigan's judgment," she wrote, "cannot reach beyond the Elwell–GM controversy to control proceedings against GM brought in other States, by other parties, asserting claims the merits of which Michigan has not considered."[39] The problem with the Michigan order, according to Ginsburg, was that "Michigan lacks authority to control courts elsewhere by precluding them, in actions brought by strangers to the Michigan litigation, from determining for themselves what witnesses are competent to testify and what evidence is relevant and admissible in their search for the truth."[40]

Thus, Ginsburg aimed to maintain a system in which courts respect each other's authority and judgments. Michigan's judgment could not silence Missouri in matters that Missouri had a right to adjudicate, just as Missouri could not simply ignore a lawful Michigan judgment by interposing local public policy concerns. A Full Faith and Credit Clause without a public policy exception helps ensure an interlocking system of justice whereby parties cannot evade legal judgments simply by fleeing the jurisdiction. But at the same time, Ginsburg called on courts to be restrained in the kinds of judgments they issue, remaining mindful of the prerogatives of other courts to pursue their own proceedings unfettered by foreign judgments. As a result, both the need for interdependence and independence within a federalist court system can be maintained. Her decision therefore preserves pluralist, intersystemic interaction.

Ginsburg reached a similar result in *Marshall v. Marshall*,[41] when, writing for the Court, she clarified that no broad exception to traditional jurisdictional rules should allow a state probate-court decision to divest federal bankruptcy courts of jurisdiction in a case involving claims related to an inheritance dispute. As in *Matsushita* and *Baker*, Ginsburg rejected the idea that an exercise of power by one court should be transformed into a broad assertion of *exclusive* power that would prevent other courts from litigating issues over which they would otherwise have jurisdiction. Instead, though she acknowledged that a probate court, once it exercised jurisdiction over the assets of an estate might retain exclusive jurisdiction over the distribution of those assets, she limited the scope of exclusivity only to the administration of a decedent's estate.[42] The probate court could not, she wrote, "bar federal courts from adjudicating matters outside those confines and otherwise within federal jurisdiction."[43]

In each of these instances Ginsburg opted to establish and preserve spaces of concurrent jurisdiction among multiple courts, neither foreclosing courts from speaking to issues before them, nor permitting them to foreclose subsequent courts from litigating related matters on their own. The danger, according to Ginsburg's jurisprudence, lies in decisions that usurp power over the judicial processes of other courts. Instead, these opinions suggest that mutual voice, restraint, deference, and comity are more the touchstones of her judicial vision.

III. NAVIGATING FEDERALISM

These same principles of deference carry over to areas of federalism, where Justice Ginsburg has often shown her willingness to defer to state prerogatives in interpreting state law. This deference may surprise those who focus on Justice Ginsburg's Fourteenth Amendment jurisprudence in gender-related cases. Certainly, Ginsburg supports a muscular interpretation of federal constitutional rights. After all, her most prominent pre-judicial role was as the head of the Women's Rights Project of the American Civil Liberties Union.[44] And of course her forceful advocacy in the 1970s[45] (as well as her own decision for the Supreme Court in *United States v. Virginia*)[46] has helped establish gender as a category for heightened scrutiny in equal-protection analysis.

Yet, though she is clearly a strong advocate for protecting federal rights, Ginsburg is often likely to seek ways to defer to and accommodate state interests to the extent possible. Indeed, she is far more deferential to the prerogatives of states than one might expect if one focused only on the gender cases.[47] This section first surveys four dissents in which Ginsburg argued against federal intrusion into traditional state-law domains. Then, it turns to three cases either applying the so-called *Erie* doctrine or federal preemption doctrine, two areas where courts are asked to negotiate the fault lines between state and federal law. These cases show Ginsburg seeking creative ways to effectuate both state and federal interests to the extent possible.

A. *Deference to State Law Domains*

In the 1994 case of *Honda Motor Co. v. Oberg*, the Supreme Court considered a provision of the Oregon Constitution prohibiting judicial review of the amount of punitive damages awarded by a jury "unless the court can affirmatively say there is no evidence to support the verdict."[48] The Court ruled that such a provision violated the Due Process Clause of the federal constitution.[49] Justice Ginsburg dissented, focusing on the variety of ways in which

Oregon statutory law already protected against excessive punitive-damage awards. In particular, Ginsburg noted that under Oregon law, the plaintiff in product-liability cases must prove by "clear and convincing evidence" that the defendant "show[ed] wanton disregard for the health, safety and welfare of others."[50] Moreover, the statute set forth seven substantive criteria to cabin the discretion of the factfinder.[51] And Oregon permitted judges to overturn a jury punitive-damages award "if reversible error occurred during the trial, if the jury was improperly or inadequately instructed, or if there is no evidence to support the verdict."[52] Given these protections, Ginsburg saw no reason for federal Due Process concerns to trump the Oregon constitutional provision forbidding general reexamination of a jury's punitive-damage awards.[53]

Four years later, Ginsburg again dissented from a Supreme Court decision overturning a state-law punitive-damages verdict. In *BMW v. Gore*, the Court found an Alabama jury award "grossly excessive," in violation of the Fourteenth Amendment's Due Process Clause.[54] Ginsburg, in contrast, argued that the award should be policed by the Alabama courts and that the U.S. Supreme Court should "resist unnecessary intrusion into an area dominantly of state concern."[55] Significantly, Ginsburg's dissent rested on two core arguments. First, she suggested that the Court should defer to the Alabama Supreme Court, which "report[ed] that it 'thoroughly and painstakingly'" reviewed the jury's award according to federal due process criteria.[56] According to Ginsburg, this judgment was entitled to a "presumption of legitimacy,"[57] and the U.S. Supreme Court should not "be quick to find a constitutional infirmity."[58] Second, she noted that by entering this traditional state domain with a constitutional ruling binding on all the states, the U.S. Supreme Court would be deprived of the wisdom that comes from having multiple courts develop jurisprudence in concert.[59] Indeed, she contrasted the Court's new punitive-damages review process with what typically occurs in habeas corpus review under 28 U.S.C. § 2254.[60] In contrast to such habeas cases, Ginsburg pointed out, the Court, when reviewing punitive-damages verdicts under *Gore*, "will work at this business alone. It will not be aided by the federal district courts and courts of appeals. It will be the *only* federal court policing the area."[61] Thus, by refusing to defer to states and by building its own ad hoc review process, Ginsburg opined, the Supreme Court would be left to review damage awards with neither the potential guidance of the state courts nor the potential wisdom of other federal courts. In short, she objected to the hierarchical lack of pluralism in the emerging jurisprudence.

Ginsburg has argued for greater deference to state processes in other contexts as well. *City of Chicago v. International College of Surgeons*[62] began as a case involving state court review of a municipal agency's denial of demolition permits. Such review is generally deferential under state law, limited to whether there was adequate evidence in the record to support the agency's discretionary judgment.[63] Nevertheless, the Court permitted federal courts to exercise supplemental jurisdiction – and possibly full de novo review – over such claims if appended to other federal claims.[64] While acknowledging that the "bare words" of the federal jurisdictional statute permit the exercise of jurisdiction in such cases,[65] Ginsburg dissented, arguing that the statute should not be read to extend federal jurisdiction over these sorts of state appellate reviews of state agency decisions.[66] According to Ginsburg, permitting such "cross-system appeals" would trench on areas traditionally within state authority.[67] She criticized the majority for "displac[ing] state courts as forums for on-the-record review of state and local agency actions."[68] And she worried that "after today, litigants asserting federal-question or diversity jurisdiction may routinely lodge in federal courts direct appeals from the actions of all manner of local (county and municipal) agencies, boards, and commissions. Exercising this cross-system appellate authority, federal courts may now directly superintend local agencies by affirming, reversing, or modifying their administrative rulings."[69]

One could imagine an even more pluralist approach than Ginsburg's. For example, the Court might have permitted federal jurisdiction but incorporated the state standard of deferential review. Alternatively, the Court might have developed a form of abstention doctrine that allows federal courts to proceed but only after allowing state courts first crack at resolving the issue. However, both of these avenues would be complicated given the language of the jurisdiction statute. Thus, Ginsburg's position probably goes as far as she could: denying federal supplemental jurisdiction over such claims but allowing the exercise of that authority to be checked by federal constitutional review, thereby preserving intersystemic dialogue. In contrast, the interpretation of the jurisdictional statute adopted by the majority allows the federal court to function as a fully independent alternative appellate forum in diversity cases, one that could trump state practices and standards of review.

This same concern for preserving the states' ability to interpret their own laws carries over to Ginsburg's long-held opposition to the Supreme Court's 1983 decision in *Michigan v. Long*.[70] In *Long*, the Court held that in criminal cases, when it is unclear whether a state-court decision rests on state or federal law, the federal court will assume that the state court relied on federal law, thereby subjecting the state-court decision to federal review.[71] This presumption, according to Ginsburg, gets it backward. Although she was not on the Court when *Long* was decided,[72] in a subsequent dissent she wrote: "The *Long* presumption, as I see it, impedes the States' ability to serve as laboratories for testing solutions to novel legal problems."[73] Instead, she argued that "this Court should select a jurisdictional presumption that encourages States to explore different means to secure respect for individual rights in modern times."[74]

In all four of these dissents, Ginsburg is concerned that federal courts are inappropriately displacing the ability of states to have voice regarding matters of traditional state dominion. However, that does not mean that Ginsburg always simply opts for greater state autonomy in every case. For example, she joined the dissents in both *United States v. Lopez*[75] and *United States v. Morrison*,[76] in which the Court curtailed Congress's Commerce Clause power. And of course, she has long advocated more robust federal enforcement of constitutional equal protection norms in gender discrimination cases. Thus, it might be more appropriate to view Ginsburg as a cooperative or dialogic federalist rather than a separate-spheres federalist.[77] She seems most concerned with giving states voice in a multisystem conversation rather than displacing federal authority altogether.

B. *Solomonic Effectuation of Plural Interests*

This emphasis on accommodating both state and federal authority is most easy to see in those cases in which Ginsburg has explicitly sought to effectuate both sets of interests simultaneously. As noted previously, many of the doctrines aimed at navigating the relative domains of state and federal sovereignty are built on binary decision making and clear lines of demarcation. Either a case is within state jurisdiction or federal; either state law or federal law applies, and so on. But Ginsburg tends to favor overlapping jurisdictional schemes and more deferential accommodation of multiple interests. In the three cases that follow, she works mightily to achieve this sort of pluralist resolution, even when the path for doing so is less than obvious.

The first is *Gasperini v. Center for Humanities, Inc.*[78] Here, the Court continued a line of cases considering when a federal court hearing a state claim should apply state or federal law. Ever since the Court's landmark decision in *Erie Railroad v. Tompkins*, federal courts hearing state claims are required to apply state substantive law, essentially as if the case were being decided in a state court.[79] But what happens if applying the state law conflicts with the rules governing the general operation of federal courts? These are some of the knotty problems in what has become known as the *Erie* doctrine.

Gasperini presented a particularly difficult application of the doctrine because both the state and federal interests at stake were so strong. New York had passed a tort-reform statute that sought to rein in what were perceived to be excessive jury awards.[80] Under the statute, state appellate courts were empowered to review the size of jury verdicts and to order new trials whenever the jury's award "deviates materially from what would be reasonable compensation."[81] Thus, it would seem that if such a situation happened to arise in a state-law case brought in federal court, the federal appellate court should, pursuant to *Erie* and its progeny, apply the New York law allowing appellate reexamination of the jury verdict. However, under the Seventh Amendment of the U.S. Constitution, which governs proceedings in federal court but not in state court, "the right of trial by jury shall be preserved, and no fact tried by a jury, shall be otherwise re-examined in any Court of the United States, than according to the rules of the common law."[82] This provision would normally block a federal court from conducting the sort of review mandated by the New York law. Accordingly, the Supreme Court was faced with the question of which rule would prevail in a diversity suit brought in a federal court in New York.

Justice Scalia, in dissent, took the jurispathic path, arguing categorically that federal courts must follow the Seventh Amendment's command regardless of what a New York court would do.[83] Thus, the New York law would have no impact at all in a federal diversity suit. In contrast, Justice Ginsburg worked hard to create a Solomonic solution whereby both New York's tort-reform interests and the Seventh Amendment could be accommodated.

To do this, Ginsburg construed the Seventh Amendment's Reexamination Clause to apply to federal appellate courts but not to the traditional power of federal trial judges to grant new trials notwithstanding a contrary jury verdict.[84] Thus, she reasoned that New York's law controlling compensation awards for excessiveness or inadequacy could be given effect without detriment to the Seventh Amendment, if the review standard set out in the state statute were applied by the federal trial-court judge, with appellate control of the trial court's ruling confined to "abuse of discretion."[85] Under this approach, the trial judge could apply state law reviewing the jury verdict, thereby retaining this state policy choice in state-law cases tried in federal courts,[86] while the Seventh Amendment prohibition on reexamining jury verdicts would continue to bind the federal appellate court (absent a flagrant abuse of discretion).[87]

Whatever one thinks of the soundness of Ginsburg's historical and jurisprudential analysis, what is most significant is the extraordinarily creative way in which Ginsburg worked to accommodate both state and federal interests. Had the Court adopted Justice Scalia's approach, a litigant from outside New York involved in a state-law suit with a New Yorker would be able to avoid the state's tort-reform provision simply by filing that case in, or removing that case to, federal court. On the other hand, had the Court simply applied the state law without limitations, it would have been ignoring the significant command of the U.S. Constitution regarding the sanctity of jury verdicts. By splitting the difference, the Court arguably protected the core of both state and federal interests at stake.

In *Shady Grove Orthopedic Associates, P.A. v. Allstate Insurance Co.*,[88] Ginsburg again sought to vindicate both state and federal interests in an *Erie* case. This time the question was whether, in a federal court, Rule 23 of the Federal Rules of Civil Procedure, governing class actions, would override another New York state law, this one aimed at preventing certain kinds of suits from being brought as class actions. Justice Scalia's plurality opinion took the jurispathic position that because the state law addressed class-action suits it was necessarily trumped by Rule 23 in cases heard in federal courts.[89] Ginsburg, in dissent, chose a more nuanced reading. She took Scalia to task for "relentlessly" making choices that would override state law.[90] Instead, she pointed out – in true pluralist fashion – that "before undermining state legislation" the Court should ask whether the federal and state laws truly conflict.[91] Thus, in contrast to the plurality opinion, she "would continue to interpret Federal Rules with awareness of, and sensitivity to, important state regulatory policies."[92] Taking this approach, she read Rule 23 to dictate only the *procedures* for certifying and pursuing a class-action claim. In contrast, she argued, the New York state law addressed what sort of *relief* could be pursued through the class mechanism.[93] And, as with *Gasperini*, regardless of whether one agrees with her particular way of accommodating both federal and state law, there can be no doubting her passion to pursue an approach to *Erie* that attempts to provide maximum space for the effectuation of important state policy judgments.

Ginsburg's approach to federal preemption law seems to suggest the same impulse toward mutual accommodation and splitting the difference. For example, in *American Airlines, Inc. v. Wolens*,[94] the question was whether the federal law deregulating the airline industry preempted state consumer-fraud and breach-of-contract claims brought against American Airlines related to changes the airline made unilaterally and retroactively to its frequent-flyer program. Two justices argued that federal law preempted both the fraud and contract claims,[95] while another argued that neither type of claim should be deemed preempted.[96] Ginsburg, writing for the Court, took the middle ground, holding that federal law preempted the fraud claims but not the contract claims.[97] The Airline Deregulation Act explicitly preempted state-imposed regulation "relating to [air carrier] rates, routes, or services,"[98] which would include consumer fraud claims based in state law.[99] However, the contract claims, she concluded, were based not on state regulation but on claimed breaches of terms agreed upon by the parties themselves. Thus, they could be maintained without running afoul of the Airline Deregulation Act.[100]

In each of these cases, we see Ginsburg working mightily to make subtle distinctions so as to preserve space for both federal and state interests to be vindicated. Indeed, none of the conclusions she reached were clearly dictated by the cases, rules, or statutes Ginsburg interpreted.[101] Thus, they are actually best understood as efforts to maintain a pluralist structure to American federalism, one that will allow sufficient play in the joints and overlapping jurisdiction so that all sovereignties are afforded an opportunity to weigh in with policy judgments. In short, understanding Ginsburg's pluralist jurisprudence creates a way of interpreting these cases as part of a broader approach to the interaction of legal systems.

IV. DEFERENCE TO INTERNATIONAL AND TRANSNATIONAL LAW AND PROCESS

Of course, principles of deference are often easier in domestic cases because, although federalism opens up a wide range of structural pluralism, both state and federal governments sit within one constitutional system. This section turns to Justice Ginsburg's attitude toward foreign law as interpreted and applied by courts and tribunals from around the world. Here, Justice Ginsburg shows her willingness to learn from foreign judges, her interest in comparative examples, and her efforts to build deferential principles into cases with transnational implications. Yet, at the same time, Ginsburg believes that foreign law cannot displace core U.S. constitutional principles when U.S. officials act abroad. Thus, both foreign norms and U.S. norms operate in active relationship.

Ginsburg has long been interested in comparative law. As an academic, she attended multiple gatherings of the International Academy of Comparative Law.[102] She also was affiliated with the Columbia Law School Project on International Procedure, was a member of the American Foreign Law Association, and served from 1964 to 1972 on the Board of Editors of the American Journal of Comparative Law.[103] These experiences, she has stated, "powerfully influenced" her work as a lawyer, law professor, and judge.[104]

Perhaps for this reason, she often looks to foreign law in a way that emphasizes the ongoing interaction of legal systems in dialogue with each other:

> My own view is simply this: If U.S. experience and decisions may be instructive to systems that have more recently instituted or invigorated judicial review for constitutionality, so too can we learn from others now engaged in measuring ordinary laws and executive actions against fundamental instruments of government and charters securing basic rights.[105]

Of course, as she recognizes, political, historical, and cultural contexts vary from country to country, and so the fit from system to system is imperfect. But that should not, she argues, "lead us to abandon the effort to learn what we can from the experience and wisdom foreign sources may convey."[106]

In 2011, Ginsburg went so far as to predict that the Supreme Court would over time more assiduously follow the lead of the Declaration of Independence by according "'a decent Respect to the Opinions of [Human]kind' as a matter of comity and in a spirit of humility."[107] Note those two words: comity and humility. Both are core to Ginsburg's pluralist jurisprudence. By invoking comity, she recognized that "projects vital to our well being – combating international terrorism is a prime example – require trust and cooperation of nations the world over."[108] And by focusing on humility, she suggested that legal systems should not see themselves as sealed off and unable to learn from the innovations that may exist elsewhere.[109] Thus, judges may gain wisdom and learn from the experimentation of others. As I have argued elsewhere, this is one of the core reasons that pluralist processes may sometimes be preferable to more jurispathic approaches.[110]

Ginsburg's pluralist perspective regarding the need to accommodate foreign legal processes carries over to cases involving the interlocking day-to-day functions of courts transnationally. For example, in *Intel Corp. v. Advanced Micro Devices, Inc.*,[111] Ginsburg, writing for the Court, broadly interpreted a federal statute that permits a party in a foreign or international tribunal to seek discovery in federal district courts from persons subject to the federal courts' jurisdiction. Significantly, Ginsburg rejected the broad exception urged by Intel: that federal courts should not permit such discovery if the foreign court could not itself have obtained such discovery under its local laws.[112] Instead, she reasoned that the foreign court's inability or refusal to order discovery itself says nothing about whether it would be happy to receive assistance from a U.S. court that is willing to do so.[113] Thus, a blanket prohibition on such discovery might actually thwart the wishes of the foreign jurisdiction.[114] Instead, she wrote, the best way to effectuate the aim of helping with the discovery needs of foreign jurisdictions is to permit (without requiring) such discovery, instead of imposing categorical limitations.[115] Of course, as in many Ginsburg opinions, she emphasized that district judges retain discretion to refuse or limit discovery based on a myriad of factors particular to each case.[116] But she refused to place broad prohibitions on such intersystemic discovery and thereby cabin such case-by-case discretion. In the end, this approach allows both the foreign court and the U.S. court to engage in dialogue without categorical rules either requiring or preventing discovery.

Another key aspect of intersystemic interaction is the principle that one should not be able to evade local law simply by relocating. As shown earlier,

Ginsburg is clear that, at least in the domestic context, there can be no broad public policy exceptions to the Full Faith and Credit Clause in order to prevent such evasion. But what about regulatory evasion in the transnational context, where there is no constitutionally mandated Full Faith and Credit Clause? This issue can arise if a litigant relocates abroad, but even more controversially when a U.S. governmental official acts abroad in ways that would be impermissible under the U.S. Constitution.

In this long-running debate about whether "the Constitution follows the flag,"[117] Ginsburg has taken the position that U.S. officials cannot evade constitutional limitations by acting abroad rather than on U.S. soil. For example, in *DKT Memorial Fund Ltd. v. Agency for International Development*, she wrote: "Just as our flag carries its message ... both at home and abroad, so does our Constitution and the values it expresses."[118] Accordingly, she concluded, "wherever the United States acts, it can only act in accordance with the limitations imposed by the Constitution."[119] Similarly, in *United States v. Balsys*, Ginsburg argued that "the Fifth Amendment privilege against self-incrimination prescribes a rule of conduct generally to be followed by our Nation's officialdom" and "should command the respect of United States interrogators, whether the prosecution reasonably feared by the examinee is domestic or foreign."[120]

Finally, it is significant that Ginsburg has cited, with approval, the intriguing decision in *United States v. Tiede*.[121] In *Tiede*, a foreign national accused of hijacking a Polish aircraft abroad was tried under German substantive law in Cold War Berlin in a court created by the United States. The U.S. court held that despite the use of German substantive law, the foreign national was entitled to a jury trial as a matter of U.S. constitutional right because the U.S. court must act in accordance with the Constitution even when situated beyond U.S. territorial borders.[122] According to the court, "it is a first principle of American life – not only life at home but life abroad – that everything American public officials do is governed by, measured against, and must be authorized by the United States Constitution."[123] Thus, Ginsburg appears to take very seriously the idea that the U.S. government is bound by the U.S. Constitution even beyond U.S. borders.

All of these different aspects of Ginsburg's transnational jurisprudence have a common theme: the desire to maintain a functioning global legal order characterized by respect among different systems, productive interaction among those systems, and the maintenance of cooperative efforts to cut off regulatory evasion while recognizing difference. These are core aspects of a pluralist cross-border jurisprudence. Indeed, Ginsburg's background as a comparative proceduralist make her perhaps the justice best positioned on the current Supreme Court to articulate how this sort of intersystemic perspective can work in day-to-day legal decisions.

V. DEFERENCE TO TRIBAL COURTS

In contrast to her approach to international and foreign law, Ginsburg does not appear to view tribal communities as true independent sovereignties, whose jurisdiction and legal rulings are intrinsically entitled to deference. Instead, Ginsburg, even as early as her Senate confirmation hearings, seems for the most part to have adopted the conventional view that tribes possess only the rights and privileges awarded to them by Congress.[124] As a result, this appears to be one area of Ginsburg's intersystemic jurisprudence where the focus is not so much on dialogue among communities as on the determinative law of one sovereignty over another. This is not to say that the tribes always lose in Ginsburg's decisions, but to the extent the tribes are given zones of autonomy, they are given them as an artifact of congressional largess. Thus, there is little jurisgenerative dialogue among equal sovereigns; the historically hierarchical relationship has been left largely undisturbed.

It is reasonable to ask why Ginsburg does not seem to view tribes through her usual prism of deference to another sovereign community. And while we cannot know for sure, one prominent Indian law scholar, Carole Goldberg, has suggested that Ginsburg's uneasiness with tribal community-based claims may spring from her days at the ACLU advocating for women's rights.[125] In the late 1970s the national board of the ACLU considered what position it should take in a key case then pending before the Supreme Court, *Santa Clara Pueblo v. Martinez*.[126] In this case, a female tribe member challenged a tribal law denying tribal membership to the children of women who married out of the Tribe, but granting membership to the children of men who married out.[127] Accordingly, the case raised both an Indian law question about the rights of tribes to define their own membership and an equality question about the gender distinction contained in the tribal rule.

In a 2009 memoir, Indian law attorney Alvin Ziontz recalled a debate he had with Ginsburg, then director of the ACLU Women's Rights Project, regarding the position the ACLU should take on the case. According to Ziontz, for Ginsburg, "the equal protection issue clearly trumped any tribal interest."[128] Based on Ziontz's account, Goldberg speculates that Ginsburg may have less sympathy for claims of tribal sovereignty because of concerns about potential gender discrimination in tribal communities.[129]

Turning to her actual jurisprudence on the Court, we see at times an unwillingness to treat the tribes in the generous way we saw her treat states in federalism cases. For example, in the 1997 case of *Strate v. A-1 Contractors*,[130] Ginsburg wrote an opinion for the Court disallowing tribal court jurisdiction over a car accident on a state right-of-way in Indian country. To reach this conclusion, Ginsburg relied on an earlier Supreme Court case, *Iowa Mutual Insurance Co. v. LaPlante*.[131] However, as Goldberg points out, *Iowa Mutual* only denied tribal *regulatory* jurisdiction over non-Indians *on non-Indian fee land* within a reservation.[132] Ginsburg thus was extending *Iowa Mutual* when she applied it to deny tribal *adjudicative* jurisdiction over a non-Indian on a state right-of-way *on tribally owned land* within a reservation. Moreover, Goldberg argues, "Neither the leap from regulatory to adjudicative jurisdiction, nor the leap from non-Indian fee land to a state right-of-way, was logically required or driven by congressional policy."[133] Thus, the Court's decision in *Strate* cut back on tribal court jurisdiction and therefore the potential intersystemic interaction between tribal and state courts.

Even more controversial for some Indian law scholars was Ginsburg's decision in *City of Sherrill v. Oneida Indian Nation of New York*.[134] This case derived from long-standing property claims of the Oneida, who signed a treaty with the United States after the Revolutionary War guaranteeing protection for 300,000 acres of land in upstate New York.[135] Despite federal law that prevented alienation of the land without federal consent,[136] the State of New York subsequently entered into several treaties with the Oneida that transferred almost all of this reservation land into private hands.[137] At various times during the nineteenth and twentieth centuries, the Tribe tried to recover its land, but it was not until the 1970s that federal law allowed the Tribe to sue on its own in federal court.[138] The Tribe sued for compensation for violation of its possessory rights, and in two previous suits the Supreme Court had ruled that there was federal jurisdiction over such a cause of action and that no statute of limitations defense could bar the suit.[139]

In 1997 and 1998 the Oneida purchased land that had been within its reservation originally and then claimed tribal sovereignty over the land, suing to enjoin the local government from imposing property taxes.[140] Goldberg argues that "from an Indian law perspective, the question should have been relatively straightforward: was the reacquired Oneida land properly considered Indian country, within the meaning of the federal statute defining that term?"[141] If so, according to Goldberg, then the land could not be taxed absent express federal statutory authority. Moreover, federal law defines Indian country as all land within a reservation's boundaries,[142] and relevant precedent holds that a reservation cannot be diminished absent federal permission.[143] Thus, Goldberg contends that this newly reacquired land, because it was within the boundaries of the historical reservation (which had never legally been diminished), would qualify for tax-exempt treatment as Indian country.[144]

Justice Ginsburg's opinion for the Court, however, focused instead on the fact that the land in question had been in state control for two hundred years, even if it had originally been taken illegally. According to Ginsburg,

> The wrongs of which [the Oneida Nation] complains occurred during the early years of the Republic, [whereas], [f]or the past two centuries, New York and its [local] units have continuously governed the territory.... This long lapse of time, during which the Oneidas did not seek to revive their sovereign control through equitable relief in court, and the attendant dramatic changes in the character of the properties, preclude [the Oneida Nation] from gaining the disruptive remedy it now seeks.[145]

Goldberg argues that by emphasizing the long lapse of time, the Court seems to penalize the tribe for not having had the funds to reacquire the land until recently.[146] Moreover, the focus on time suggests to Goldberg a conception of the tribes as vestigial actors, not present-day sovereign entities.[147] The Court describes the original alienation of the Oneida's land as a "grave, but ancient, wrong,"[148] and the opinion uses the word "ancient" multiple times in the opinion.[149] Goldberg argues that, by isolating the harm in the past, the Court "seems unwilling to acknowledge the ongoing struggles and survival of the Oneidas as a distinct people in contemporary America, and the ongoing nature of the wrongs that have been committed against them."[150]

Despite these opinions, it is important to note that Ginsburg's Indian law jurisprudence is certainly not invariably hostile to tribal interests. For example, in *Wagnon v. Prairie Band Potawatomi Nation*,[151] she dissented from a decision imposing state taxes on non-Indian distributors of motor fuel to on-reservation gas stations. In her dissent, she went out of her way to clarify the sovereign interests at stake: "Kansas' collection of its tax on fuel destined for the Nation Station will effectively nullify the Nation's tax, which funds critical reservation road-building programs, endeavors not aided by state funds."[152] Similarly, she largely dissented from the Court's decision in *Plains Commerce Bank v. Long Family Land & Cattle Co.*,[153] which denied tribal court jurisdiction over a mortgage-discrimination suit brought by tribal members against a non-Indian bank. Ginsburg noted that the case was not, as the Court framed it, "about 'the sale of fee land on a tribal reservation by a non-Indian bank to non-Indian individuals.'"[154] Rather, she asserted, quoting the earlier Court of Appeals decision in the case: "'this case is about the power of the Tribe to hold nonmembers like the bank to a minimum standard of fairness when they voluntarily deal with tribal members.'"[155] As Goldberg points out, the dissent also demonstrates sensitivity to the realities on the ground, "including the fact that Plains Commerce Bank often filed suit in tribal court to collect on its debts, benefited from the availability of [federal Bureau of Indian Affairs] loan guarantees, and could have included a choice-of-forum clause in its agreements had it wished to avoid tribal court."[156] Thus, it would be unfair to say that Ginsburg is always hostile to tribes. On the other hand, the reflexive deference she accords other judicial systems does not seem to carry over to tribal courts and governmental institutions as a matter of course.

CONCLUSION

It is difficult, of course, to pick out a handful of cases from decades of jurisprudence in order to spot trends. And there is always the danger of cherry-picking those cases that seem to support a thesis while ignoring other decisions that might point in a different direction. Moreover, each case presents different facts and different substantive law contexts, making broad generalizations inherently problematic.

Nevertheless, a pronounced preference for legal pluralist approaches can be discerned in Ginsburg's scholarship and in her judicial opinions. When faced with questions involving the interaction of legal systems, Ginsburg often chooses a path that emphasizes mutual accommodation, deference, and the opportunity for different systems to pursue their processes and speak to an issue. Ginsburg eschews bright-line rules that close off avenues through which a system might be allowed to articulate its norms, and she bends over backward to seek Solomonic solutions that will effectuate multiple interests. In the international arena, she humbly seeks wisdom abroad, aims to accommodate foreign processes if possible, and makes sure U.S. officials abroad follow constitutional commands. All of these jurisprudential paths aim toward making the United States a partner in the world system, not a hierarchically dominant voice. And although she seems somewhat less accommodating in cases relating to tribal sovereignty, even here she has at times shown a willingness to try to defer to tribal jurisdictional claims.

Just as important, this analysis suggests that we can evaluate judicial opinions and philosophies through the lens of legal pluralism. This interpretive lens focuses less on substantive outcome or political labels such as liberal or conservative and more on the way in which the judge understands his or her role in an interlocking, multijurisdictional legal tapestry. And given that judges inevitably face questions involving the interaction of legal systems, we can legitimately ask how each judge seeks to navigate the hybrid spaces that result. Thus, a pluralist framework provides an untapped means of considering jurisprudential legacies. In the case of Justice Ginsburg, an emphasis on mechanisms for managing pluralism illuminates tendencies in her judicial approach that otherwise may have escaped notice.

12

The Once and Future Federalist

Deborah Jones Merritt

Our Constitution established a federal system that embraces both autonomous states and a strong national government. Preserving that constitutional scheme has challenged the Supreme Court since its earliest days.[1] As Chief Justice John Roberts recently recognized, "the path of" the Court's federalism jurisprudence "has not always run smooth."[2] That path has been particularly jagged during recent years. In a series of high-profile cases, the Court has undercut both national authority and state autonomy; the results defy both the Constitution and any principled view of federalism.

Justice Ruth Bader Ginsburg has repeatedly dissented from these decisions, articulating a coherent view of federalism that honors both national power and state autonomy. Justice Ginsburg's opinions draw upon federalism principles that the Court forged during the middle decades of the twentieth century; this is the federalism that prevailed before the muddled federalism "revolution" of the Rehnquist and Roberts Courts.[3]

Justice Ginsburg, however, has refined those twentieth-century doctrines, giving them a voice of her own. As the Court's most persistent and articulate dissenter in federalism cases, she has crafted a nuanced vision of federal-state relations that serves the Constitution, national interests, and the continued vitality of state governments.

This chapter explores several of Justice Ginsburg's most notable federalism opinions. Part one examines representative cases in which Justice Ginsburg recognized Congress's power to legislate in the national interest. Part two looks at disputes in which she protected state autonomy. In part three, I explain the coherence of these doctrines and their promise for supporting the national-state balance that the Framers intended to foster. The consonance of Justice Ginsburg's dissents suggests that they are "way pavers" for the future of federalism jurisprudence on the Court.[4] Drawing on federalism precedents that once governed, Justice Ginsburg's jurisprudence offers the best path toward federalism's future.

I. THE NATIONAL INTEREST

Federalism debates often focus on state sovereignty. Justice Ginsburg, however, recognizes that the Constitution protects *both* state and national power. State autonomy is a distinctive feature of our constitutional design, but so is a strong national government. The Constitution has succeeded for more than two hundred years because it strikes a balance between those elements.

In pursuit of that balance, Justice Ginsburg has rejected several attempts by the Rehnquist and Roberts Courts to prune national authority. Her most vigorous dissents appear in two recent decisions: *National Federation of Independent Business v. Sebelius*[5] and *Shelby County v. Holder*.[6] In those cases, Justice Ginsburg defended congressional power to regulate commerce, further the national welfare through spending, and enforce the Civil War Amendments.

These dissents reveal five common threads that inform Justice Ginsburg's vision of national power. First, she stresses controlling precedent from the twentieth century. Second, Justice Ginsburg urges deference to Congress on matters that the Constitution assigns to that body. Third, she anchors her concept of balanced federalism in the Constitution's design. Fourth, Justice Ginsburg has developed a vision of complementary federalism in which state and national governments strengthen each other's work. Fifth, she relies upon the political process to backstop the Constitution's balance between state and national control. I explore each of these themes in the sections below.

A. *The Commerce Clause*

The Commerce Clause contains a scant sixteen words: it grants Congress the power "To regulate Commerce with foreign Nations, and among the several States, and with the Indian Tribes."[7] Yet those words, as Justice Ginsburg recently acknowledged, lie at the heart of the Constitution. The Framers' previous attempt to create a nation, the Articles of Confederation, left commercial regulation solely to the states.[8] This approach quickly "proved unworkable, because the individual States, understandably focused on their own economic interests, often failed to take actions critical to the success of the Nation as a whole."[9]

Responding to this failure, the Framers created a national legislature with "the authority to enact economic legislation 'in all Cases for the general Interests of the Union, and also in those Cases to which the States are separately incompetent.'"[10] The Commerce Clause thus constituted a key advance from the Articles of Confederation to the Constitution. The Framers' bold commitment to a common market, adopted almost two centuries before Europe's similar venture, fueled the new nation's economic growth.

The same constitutional commitment enabled the United States to successfully address the major economic challenges of the twentieth century. Congress responded to the worldwide Great Depression, as well as the economy's growing complexity, with a series of laws that promoted a modern, integrated economy. Although the Supreme Court initially balked at these measures, it ultimately recognized Congress's "plenary" power to "protect interstate commerce."[11] Bowing to Congress's constitutional primacy in that field, the Court embraced Congress's authority to regulate any activities "that substantially affect interstate commerce."[12]

Some jurists, however, remained uneasy about the broad scope of national power. Evoking those doubts, the Rehnquist and Roberts Courts have imposed new constraints on Congress's commerce power.[13] The most far-reaching of those limits emerged in *National Federation of Independent Business v. Sebelius*,[14] the Court's recent opinion examining the Patient Protection and Affordable Care Act of 2010 ("Affordable Care Act").[15]

In the Affordable Care Act, Congress attempted to develop a comprehensive system of health insurance that would increase consumer access and lower costs. One of the act's most controversial provisions is the individual mandate, which requires most adults to obtain "minimum essential" health insurance.[16] Congress concluded that this mandate was essential to buttress two key elements of the act: one that requires health insurers to accept all applicants, and a second that divorces pricing from preexisting conditions.[17] The latter provisions guarantee affordable health insurance to individuals who already suffer from serious health conditions. Without an individual mandate, healthy adults might defer purchasing health insurance until after they suffered illness or injury; this would make the scheme financially unsustainable for insurers.

In *Sebelius*, five justices concluded that the individual mandate exceeded Congress's Commerce Clause power. Chief Justice Roberts wrote for himself on this issue; four other justices reached the same result in a separate opinion.[18] All five observed that two reasons supported their interpretation of the Commerce Clause. First, they maintained that the Commerce Clause distinguishes between action and inaction: Congress's broad authority to regulate *"activities* that 'have a substantial effect on interstate commerce'" does not extend to regulation of *inaction*.[19] Characterizing the failure to purchase health insurance as inaction, these justices concurred that the individual mandate exceeded the Commerce Clause's grant of regulatory authority.

Second, these justices agreed that the Commerce Clause must impose some limits on congressional power. Upholding the individual mandate under the Commerce Clause, Chief Justice Roberts worried, would "extend federal power to virtually all human activity."[20] That result would violate the Framers' intent by "convert[ing] the Commerce Clause into a general authority to direct the economy."[21] Whatever the outer bounds of the Commerce Clause, these five justices reasoned, the clause must not "enable the Federal Government to regulate all private conduct."[22]

Combining these rationales, five justices concluded that the individual mandate overstepped Congress's power under the Commerce Clause. A different majority, with the Chief Justice as the swing vote, upheld the individual mandate as a valid exercise of Congress's taxing power.[23] The latter ruling may render the Commerce Clause discussion dictum,[24] but it was powerful dictum: a majority of the Court found that the Commerce Clause failed to support the individual mandate.[25]

Justice Ginsburg disagreed emphatically with the latter conclusion, stressing Congress's "capacious power" to "regulate economic activities 'that substantially affect interstate commerce.'"[26] Her opinion effectively rebutted the majority's view, while embodying the five themes that characterize her interpretations of national power.

1. Precedent

Justice Ginsburg opened her *Sebelius* opinion by protesting the majority's Commerce Clause construction as "stunningly retrogressive."[27] The interpretation, she charged, overlooked decades of Court holdings and "hark[ed] back to the era in which the Court routinely thwarted Congress' efforts to regulate the national economy in the interest of those who labor to sustain it."[28] By reviving those outdated doctrines, the Commerce Clause majority adopted a "rigid" and "crabbed" view of that clause.[29]

The majority's disregard of precedent, moreover, condemned the Court to repeating errors it had corrected seventy-five years earlier. Justice Ginsburg deftly analogized the majority's action/inaction distinction to earlier Commerce Clause doctrines that the Court had rejected as "untenable."[30] The majority's "formalistic distinction" between action and inaction, she observed, resembled the Court's ill-fated attempts to distinguish "commerce" from "production," "mining," or "manufacturing," as well as its disastrous attempt "to distinguish activities having a 'direct' effect on interstate commerce … from those having only an 'indirect' effect."[31]

Justice Ginsburg thus invoked precedent, not just as binding authority that should have governed the majority's approach, but also as hard-won lessons for the Court to heed. Reinforcing both points, she asked the Commerce Clause majority to view the Court's famous precedent, *Wickard v. Filburn*,[32] through the action/inaction lens. "Did the statute there at issue," she queried, "target activity (the growing of too much wheat) or inactivity (the farmer's failure to purchase wheat in the marketplace)?"[33] The Court's own precedents illustrated the futility of an action/inaction distinction.

The same problem plagued the Commerce Clause majority's attempt to characterize the individual mandate as regulation of inaction. The majority viewed the regulated individuals as people who were "doing nothing."[34] Justice Ginsburg, however, easily recast them as consumers whose actions substantially affected the interstate market in health insurance. "An individual who opts not to purchase insurance from a private insurer," she declared, "can be seen as actively selecting another form of insurance: self-insurance."[35]

These passages from *Sebelius* illustrate a key element of Justice Ginsburg's use of precedent: she believes that, in addition to its other roles, precedent embodies the accumulated wisdom of prior Courts. This is particularly true in areas like the Commerce Clause, where the Court can draw upon a long history of interpretation. Rather than revive the Court's ill-fated pre-1937 positions, as the majority seemed to do, Justice Ginsburg drew important lessons from the Court's more recent rulings.

2. Deference

Justice Ginsburg reminded the Commerce Clause majority that the Court owes Congress substantial deference when reviewing legislation based on the commerce power. The Court's own precedents established that it should "ask only (1) whether Congress had a 'rational basis' for concluding that the regulated activity substantially affects interstate commerce, and (2) whether there is a 'reasonable connection between the regulatory means selected and the asserted ends.'"[36]

Applying those standards, the individual mandate easily survived constitutional review. As Justice Ginsburg recounted, health care indisputably is a national concern. By 2009, health care spending already absorbed 17.6 percent of the national economy, and economists predicted that those expenditures would nearly double within a decade.[37] Congress, furthermore, had identified a key problem within that national market: uninsured Americans regularly consume health care without paying the full costs of their care. In 2008, the uninsured paid only 62.9 percent of the costs they incurred – leaving $43 billion in uncollected bills.[38]

Health care providers and insurance companies, Congress recognized, pass these costs on to consumers. Individuals who buy insurance thus subsidize health care for those who decline to purchase coverage.[39] These subsidies are far from trivial: Congress found that the average family pays more than $1,000 per year to care for the uninsured.[40] Based on these findings, Congress had a rational basis to conclude that uninsured Americans substantially affect the interstate market for health care and health insurance; indeed, it found that "the large number of individuals without health insurance ... heavily burdens the national health-care market."[41]

Responding to this burden, Justice Ginsburg continued, Congress adopted several mechanisms with a "reasonable connection" to curing the problems of noninsurance.[42] To make insurance more accessible, it required insurers to accept all applicants. To make that insurance more affordable, it forbade insurers from pricing premiums based on preexisting conditions. And to eliminate the financially disastrous effects of adverse selection, Congress required consumers to shift from self-insurance to market-based insurance.

Each of these requirements, Justice Ginsburg determined, readily passed muster under the Court's deferential standard of Commerce Clause review. The majority's action/inaction distinction, in contrast, flouted Congress's prerogative to define the market it chose to regulate.[43] The justices who attempted to draw a line between action and inaction "define[d] the health-care market as including only those transactions that will occur either in the next instant or within some (unspecified) proximity to the next instant."[44] Having defined the market narrowly, the majority labeled uninsured individuals as inactive in that market.

Justice Ginsburg, in contrast, found that "Congress reasonably ... viewed the market from a long-term perspective, encompassing all transactions virtually certain to occur over the next decade, ... not just those occurring here and now."[45] Congress's definition of the market, Justice Ginsburg continued, was particularly reasonable given three distinct features of health care: (1) all individuals eventually consume that care, (2) the timing of their consumption is unpredictable, and (3) our society provides health care even to those who cannot afford to pay for it.

Viewed from this perspective, the majority's construction of the Commerce Clause departed dramatically from the deferential review previously accorded the legislature. That deference, Justice Ginsburg stressed, rests on profound institutional and constitutional concerns. The Constitution empowers Congress, not the Court, "To regulate Commerce ... among the several States." Legislative processes, not judicial ones, are best suited to identifying economic problems and designing solutions. Deference, in other words, keeps both the Constitution and the economy strong.

3. Constitutional Design

Justice Ginsburg's jurisprudence carefully enforces the Constitution's commitment to *dual* government. As she recognizes, the national and state governments both play key roles in the federal system; undermining either one can defeat the Framers' design. In *Sebelius*, Justice Ginsburg identified two features of constitutional design that placed the Affordable Care Act squarely within Congress's power.

First, the Constitution arose out of the Framers' desire to create a national economy. They discarded the Articles of Confederation precisely because that document left economic regulation to the states, which had produced self-interested local regulation.[46] The Framers designed the Constitution and Commerce Clause, in other words, to address just the type of national economic problem covered by the Affordable Care Act. States and individuals enjoy many freedoms, but the Constitution assigns responsibility for the nation's economy to Congress.

Second, as a subset of their primary concern, the Framers recognized that the states were "separately incompetent"[47] to act "where uniform measures are necessary."[48] As Alexander Hamilton articulated the problem, "[Often] it would be beneficial to all the states to encourage, or suppress[,] a particular branch of trade, while it would be detrimental … to attempt it without the concurrence of the rest."[49] Congress, the Framers concluded, should have the power to resolve these collective action problems.

When attempting to reform the health care system, Justice Ginsburg explained, states had faced just this type of "collective-action impasse."[50] States that offered expansive health insurance attracted ailing patients who were unable to obtain coverage in other states.[51] These transient patients triggered a downward spiral of higher health care costs, larger insurance premiums, and elevated taxes.[52] Even Massachusetts, the state with the most successful reform to date, had not solved this problem. While Congress debated the Affordable Care Act, "out-of-state residents continue[d] to seek and receive millions of dollars in uncompensated care in Massachusetts hospitals, limiting the State's efforts to improve its health care system."[53]

Reform of health care insurance, therefore, presented a paradigm case for national action. By adopting the Affordable Care Act, including its individual mandate, Congress faithfully followed the Framers' design: it acted to regulate the national economy in an area that the states had proved incompetent to address.

4. Complementary Federalism

Although Congress addressed a national problem through the Affordable Care Act, it did not erase state authority in that field. While writing to uphold Congress's Commerce Clause power in *Sebelius*, Justice Ginsburg stressed two ways in which national legislators had partnered with the states to improve health care delivery.

First, Congress based the Affordable Care Act on lessons learned from state experimentation. During the late twentieth century, at least seven states had adopted laws that forbade health insurers from distinguishing between healthy applicants and those with preexisting conditions. The outcomes, unfortunately, were ominous. Each of these states "'suffered from skyrocketing insurance premium costs, reductions in individuals with coverage, and reductions in insurance products and providers.'"[54] The state experiences taught Congress that mandated coverage of preexisting conditions produces adverse selection; healthy individuals will defer buying insurance until after they suffer illness or injury.

Experimentation by Massachusetts, on the other hand, pointed to a solution: require all residents to obtain insurance.[55] The Massachusetts system, which imposed mandates on both insurers and individuals, became the model for Congress's Affordable Care Act. Innovation in the states, therefore, provided a platform for congressional action; state experience identified both pitfalls and solutions in expanding access to health insurance.

Second, when building on this knowledge, Congress explicitly chose a system that would engage state governments in an ongoing partnership with the national government. Congress, Justice Ginsburg observed, plainly had the power to adopt a "tax-and-spend federal program like Social Security."[56] But rather than nationalize health care financing, Congress designed a scheme "that retain[ed] a robust role for private insurers and state governments."[57] From the states' perspective, therefore, the majority's construction of the Commerce Clause was counterproductive.[58] The majority's reasoning pushed Congress to pursue purely federal programs rather than attempt to work with the states through ongoing partnerships.

Justice Ginsburg, in sum, described the Affordable Care Act as a prime example of the complementary roles played by state and national governments. Autonomous state governments experimented with solutions to the growing health care crisis, and Congress learned from those trials. Congress, in turn, developed an insurance scheme that would continue to embrace active experimentation by the states. That design would foster future innovation, along with programs tailored to the needs of individual states.

5. Political Process

The Commerce Clause majority in *Sebelius* expressed horror that if Congress could compel the purchase of health insurance, then it could "make mere breathing in and out the basis for federal prescription and ... extend federal power to virtually all human activity."[59] This would turn the Commerce Clause into "a font of unlimited power, or in Hamilton's words, 'the hideous monster whose devouring jaws … spare neither sex nor age, nor high nor low, nor sacred nor profane.'"[60] Among other draconian measures, what would stop Congress from "ordering everyone to buy vegetables"?[61]

Justice Ginsburg responded crisply to this "broccoli horrible."[62] The Constitution creates a "formidable check on congressional power," she wrote: "the democratic process."[63] The Commerce Clause may allow Congress to compel consumption of broccoli, but the voters will not. The political process, Justice Ginsburg reminded her colleagues, serves as the primary check on ill-conceived legislation in a democratic society.

This *Sebelius* exchange demonstrates how Justice Ginsburg integrates judicial review with the political process. She does not eschew judicial review by relying entirely on the political process; she sees a clear role for courts to play in enforcing constitutional commands. Justice Ginsburg, however, urges her colleagues to acknowledge the political process as part of their review. Proposing "outlandish" hypotheticals that would never be embraced by a democratic majority distorts the constitutional inquiry.[64]

Conversely, Justice Ginsburg charged, the willingness of five justices to overturn democratically driven legislation was "redolent of Due Process Clause arguments" that the Court had discarded decades earlier.[65] Rather than trust social and economic legislation to the political process, the Commerce Clause majority imposed its own views of individual liberty. Some of the same justices, Justice Ginsburg noted, had previously dismissed notions of substantive due process protection. "Given these Justices' reluctance to interpret the Due Process Clause as guaranteeing liberty interests," Justice Ginsburg concluded, "their willingness to plant such protections in the Commerce Clause is striking."[66]

B. *The Spending Clause*

The Spending Clause, which gives Congress the "Power To … provide for the … general Welfare of the United States,"[67] has become a major source of national power. Congress regularly taps this authority by attaching conditions to federal money shared with the states. The spending power has supported a large number of extensive federal programs, including Congress's Medicaid partnership with the states.

Congress established Medicaid almost fifty years ago to help states provide health care for the needy. Participating states qualify for sizable federal grants if they comply with Congress's minimum coverage requirements. Those requirements have changed over time, expanding both the patients served and the services covered. Congress's most recent expansion, adopted as part of the

Affordable Care Act, requires participating states to extend specified health care benefits to all adults under the age of sixty-five whose incomes fall below 133 percent of the poverty line.[68]

Congress attached both a carrot and a stick to this Medicaid expansion. States that comply with the new requirement will receive generous funds to cover the increased population.[69] States that fail to comply will forfeit these new funds and may also lose access to previously provided benefits.[70]

In *Sebelius*, the Court struck down the latter condition. Congress, the Court held, could not revoke Medicaid funds for a state's existing populations because the state refused to extend the program to a new category of patients. That condition, seven justices concluded, was too coercive to withstand scrutiny under the Spending Clause.[71]

Justice Ginsburg dissented, finding that Congress possessed ample power to expand Medicaid and change the terms of its conditional grants. In reaching this conclusion, she once again sounded themes of precedent, deference, constitutional design, complementary federalism, and political process.

1. Precedent

In *Sebelius*, Justice Ginsburg declared, the Court *"for the first time ever,"* found "an exercise of Congress' spending power unconstitutionally coercive."[72] Prior opinions had suggested "hypothetically" that Congress might tempt the states with a grant so attractive that the offer would constitute "compulsion."[73] The Court, however, had never concluded "that the terms of any grant crossed the indistinct line between temptation and coercion."[74] The Court's decision to draw that line in *Sebelius* was revolutionary.

The Court's departure from precedent was particularly regrettable, Justice Ginsburg explained, because its Spending Clause cases already protected state autonomy. Under controlling case law, Congress may impose spending conditions only if they "(a) promote the 'general welfare,' (b) 'unambiguously' inform States what is demanded of them, (c) [are] germane 'to the federal interest in particular national projects or programs,' and (d) [do] not 'induce the States to engage in activities that would themselves be unconstitutional.'"[75] Justice Ginsburg saw no reason to diverge from this existing doctrine, which the Court had devised over many decades of reviewing congressional acts.

2. Deference

Justice Ginsburg's Spending Clause jurisprudence, like her Commerce Clause doctrine, incorporates a healthy dose of judicial restraint. Courts, she counseled, should "respect ... Congress' characterization of [its] grant programs"[76] as well as the design of those programs. Courts lack the expertise and institutional capacity to craft large-scale spending programs; they must defer to congressional wisdom on those matters. Congress, rather than the Court, was entitled to define the "general Welfare" served by Medicaid.

Justice Ginsburg warned that in addition to overriding congressional authority, the Court's lack of deference had created a principle without judicially definable limits. How, she asked, will lower courts determine when congressional conditions are unduly coercive? When do states enjoy "'a legitimate choice whether to accept the federal conditions in exchange for federal funds'?"[77] Will "courts ... measure the number of dollars the Federal Government might withhold for noncompliance?"[78] Or perhaps "the portion of the State's budget at stake?"[79]

Effective judicial review, Justice Ginsburg reminded her colleagues, requires judicially enforceable lines. The majority's coercion focus, in contrast, prompted "political judgments that defy judicial calculation."[80] The Court's refusal to respect congressional judgment both undermined the legislature and set the courts on an uncharted course.

3. Constitutional Design

The *Sebelius* majority, as Justice Ginsburg recognized, overlooked a key element of the Spending Clause: Congress cannot define the "general Welfare" in a way that binds future congresses.[81] As an elected body, Congress must continuously adapt its vision to accommodate the changing views of the electorate. Without that adaptability, Congress loses its accountability to voters.

The majority's construction of the Spending Clause destroyed that constitutionally mandated accountability. Rather than honor Congress's duty to embody the electorate's current perception of the public good, the majority treated states as if they had an entitlement to Medicaid funds. "This gets things backwards," Justice Ginsburg declared. "Congress, not the States, is tasked with spending federal money in service of the general welfare. And each successive Congress is empowered to appropriate funds as it sees fit."[82]

Once again, Justice Ginsburg's analysis showed particular fidelity to the constitutional design. She understood that the Constitution gives the states no entitlement to federal funds; nor does it allow them to veto changes in congressional appropriations.[83] Individual voters, acting through their national representatives, hold sole authority to spend for the "general Welfare."

4. Complementary Federalism

The Medicaid program, Justice Ginsburg reminded her colleagues, "is a prototypical example of federal-state cooperation."[84] Rather than establish a fully federal program, as it did with Medicare, Congress has always given states an active role in designing and implementing Medicaid benefits. This partnership allows states "to tailor Medicaid grants to their particular needs, so long as they remain within bounds set by federal law."[85]

As Justice Ginsburg observed in *Sebelius*, the Medicaid partnership has been quite fruitful, profiting from local adaptations and innovation. The majority's interference with Medicaid, therefore, was particularly unfortunate; it undermined the very type of collaboration that the federal system supports. "The alternative to conditional federal spending," Justice Ginsburg cautioned the majority, "is not state autonomy but state marginalization."[86] If Congress lacks the power to alter the terms of federal-state partnerships, it might embrace exclusively national programs in the future. That would undermine the very synergies sought by a federal system.

5. Political Process

The *Sebelius* majority worried that Congress's "coercive" offer to expand Medicaid would blur lines of political accountability; the majority speculated that voters might blame (or credit) their state legislators for the Medicaid expansion. Justice Ginsburg rebutted this claim with a more pragmatic view of the political process. Congress, she noted, had partnered with the states to provide Medicaid benefits for almost fifty years; the program's "status as a federally funded, state-administered program" thus was "hardly hidden from view."[87] Debates over the Affordable Care Act, likewise, had been highly visible. Voters would have little trouble attributing the Medicaid expansion to Congress rather than state legislators.

Concern for the political process, in fact, cut strongly against the majority's position. Congress, Justice Ginsburg underscored, is accountable to individual voters – not to state governments. The majority's interpretation of the Spending Clause, which prevented Congress from allocating funds as contemporary voters preferred, severed those lines of accountability. A proper interpretation of the political process would have upheld Congress's Medicaid expansion.

C. *Enforcement of the Civil War Amendments*

The Thirteenth, Fourteenth, and Fifteenth Amendments expressly reduce the power of the states, and each grants Congress special power to "enforce" the terms of the amendment "by appropriate legislation."[88] The Supreme Court has long recognized the distinctive legislative authority conferred by these provisions: "It is the power of *Congress* which has been enlarged," the Court declared in 1879.[89] The executive and judicial branches must also honor the Civil War Amendments, but "the Framers indicated that Congress was to be chiefly responsible for implementing the rights created in" those amendments.[90]

Congress discharged that responsibility, in part, by adopting the Voting Rights Act of 1965. Among other provisions, that act requires some jurisdictions to preclear with federal authorities any proposed changes in their voting laws. The Supreme Court upheld this somewhat unusual mandate in 1966, concluding that "after enduring nearly a century of widespread resistance to the Fifteenth Amendment,"[91] Congress adopted "appropriate" legislation to combat continued, and often stealthy, suppression of voting rights.

In reaching this conclusion, the 1966 Court stressed the deference owed to Congress under the Civil War Amendments: "Congress was to be chiefly responsible for implementing the rights" recognized by those amendments, and it possessed "full remedial powers" to enforce those rights.[92] When exercising its Fifteenth Amendment power, "Congress may use any rational means to effectuate the constitutional prohibition of racial discrimination in voting."[93] The Court's only role is to assure that "Congress exercised its powers ... in an appropriate manner."[94]

Building on this endorsement of its powers, Congress reauthorized the preclearance provisions of the Voting Rights Act several times between 1970 and 1982.[95] The Supreme Court upheld each of these reauthorizations, applying the deferential standard of review that it used in its first encounter with the act.[96] In 2013, however, the Court changed course: in *Shelby County v. Holder*,[97] a majority struck down the act's coverage formula, which specified the jurisdictions subject to preclearance. Without the coverage formula, the preclearance mandate lost effect.

In embracing this result, the Court demonstrated little of the deference that it previously showed to congressional action enforcing the Civil War Amendments. Instead, the Court stressed the act's "substantial federalism costs,"[98] its conflict with "the fundamental principle of equal sovereignty,"[99] and its interference with the states' constitutionally guaranteed "autonomy in structuring their governments."[100]

Justice Ginsburg, joined by Justices Breyer, Sotomayor, and Kagan, dissented forcefully from these conclusions, striking the same notes that appear in her Commerce and Spending Clause opinions.

1. Precedent

Justice Ginsburg sharply criticized the majority's failure to follow precedent in *Shelby County*. As she stressed, it was "well established that Congress' judgment regarding exercise of its power to enforce the Fourteenth and Fifteenth

Amendments warrants substantial deference."[101] Opinions dating back almost fifty years had "repeatedly reaffirmed Congress' prerogative to use any rational means in exercise of its power in this area."[102] Rather than apply this precedent, or even acknowledge it, the Court largely sidestepped Fifteenth Amendment principles.[103]

The majority achieved this feat in two ways. First, it focused on the equal sovereignty doctrine, rather than the Fifteenth Amendment, when measuring the constitutionality of the act's coverage section. This focus, Justice Ginsburg observed, "veer[ed] away from controlling precedent ... without even acknowledging that it [was] doing so."[104] The Court had rebuffed the equal sovereignty argument almost five decades earlier, when it first upheld the preclearance and coverage provisions. In that decision, *South Carolina v. Katzenbach*,[105] "the Court held, in no uncertain terms, that the [equal sovereignty] principle '*applies only to the terms upon which States are admitted to the Union*, and not to the remedies for local evils which have subsequently appeared.'"[106] Precedent, therefore, precluded reliance on notions of equal sovereignty when assessing the Voting Rights Act.

Second, Justice Ginsburg observed, the majority drew most of its reasoning from dictum in *Northwest Austin Municipal Utility District No. One v. Holder*,[107] a 2009 case declining to rule on the constitutionality of the act's preclearance requirement. The *Shelby County* majority thus "ratchet[ed] up ... pure dictum" to produce a decision that appeared to rely upon earlier cases.[108] The Court performed this act "with nary an explanation" of its decision to invoke dictum to overrule venerable precedent, "let alone any discussion of whether *stare decisis* nonetheless counsel[ed] adherence to" the ruling in *Katzenbach*.[109]

In this way, the *Shelby County* majority endorsed a result that scorned precedent and treated dictum as controlling. For more than forty years, Congress had relied upon *Katzenbach*'s construction of the Fifteenth Amendment.[110] By unexpectedly changing its interpretation, the Court thwarted congressional attempts to end racial discrimination and enforce the fundamental right to vote. "One would expect more," Justice Ginsburg concluded acerbically, "from an opinion striking at the heart of the Nation's signal piece of civil-rights legislation."[111]

2. Deference

Justice Ginsburg framed the dispute in *Shelby County* as one of deference. "The question this case presents," she wrote in the opening paragraph of her dissent, "is who decides whether, as currently operative, § 5 [of the Voting Rights Act] remains justifiable, this Court, or a Congress charged with the obligation to enforce the post-Civil War Amendments 'by appropriate legislation.'"[112] Both the amendments' text and the Court's precedent made clear that Congress held that power.

Exercising the deferential standard of review embraced in *Katzenbach* and other precedents, Justice Ginsburg found Congress's action easy to sustain. She described the lengthy, deliberate process that Congress pursued,[113] as well as the extensive record it compiled.[114] The majority opinion, Justice Ginsburg complained, "ma[de] no genuine attempt to engage with the massive legislative record that Congress assembled."[115] Instead, the Court simply substituted its views for ones that Congress reasonably reached.

The majority, in fact, seemed impatient with Congress for disregarding the dictum it had issued in *Northwest Austin*. Chief Justice Roberts's opinion cites *Northwest Austin* more than two dozen times, stressing that the earlier opinion "expressly stated that '[t]he Act's preclearance requirement and its coverage formula raise serious constitutional questions.'"[116] In light of that language, he concluded, "Congress could have updated the coverage formula ..., but did not do so."[117] This "failure to act" left the Court "with no choice but to declare [the coverage provision] unconstitutional."[118]

This impatience, as Justice Ginsburg recognized, inverted the Fifteenth Amendment's meaning. That amendment gives *Congress* primary authority to enforce voting rights. Armed with that constitutional power, Congress should not have to monitor judicial dictum about the exercise of its authority. "Hubris," Justice Ginsburg announced, aptly described the majority's peremptory "demolition of the VRA."[119]

3. Constitutional Design

Justice Ginsburg's most passionate paragraphs in *Shelby County* feature the special role of the Civil War Amendments. "Nowhere in today's opinion," she declared, "is there clear recognition of the transformative effect the Fifteenth Amendment aimed to achieve."[120] Although the original Constitution cabined the national government's powers, the Civil War Amendments purposefully broke that mold.

"The stated purpose of the Civil War Amendments," Justice Ginsburg stressed, "was to arm Congress with the power and authority to protect all persons within the Nation from violations of their rights by the States."[121] These amendments explicitly shifted the relationship between Congress and the states, giving Congress special power to override state sovereignty when appropriate to enforce the amendments' guarantees. Although the *Shelby County* majority deplored the constraints on state autonomy that it found in the Voting Rights Act, the Civil War Amendments authorized just that type of restraint.

The majority in *Shelby County*, as Justice Ginsburg spelled out, demonstrated little awareness of the distinctive role played by the Civil War Amendments. Indeed, the Court devoted strikingly little attention – of any kind – to the Fifteenth Amendment. Chief Justice Roberts's opinion for the Court mentions the Fifteenth Amendment just five times; principles of state or equal sovereignty elicit almost twice as many mentions. Most notable, the Court's analysis opens with a discussion of equal sovereignty, the federal government's lack of any power to veto state laws, and the Tenth Amendment.[122] Without even mentioning the Fifteenth Amendment, the Court concluded that "the Voting Rights Act sharply departs from these basic principles."[123]

As Justice Ginsburg recognized, however, the *Fifteenth Amendment* departs from these principles. The majority invoked an inflated vision of state sovereignty that did not survive the Civil War – if it ever existed. In doing so, it rejected "one of the most consequential, efficacious, and amply justified exercises of federal legislative power in our Nation's history."[124] Justice Ginsburg, in contrast, faithfully adhered to the Constitution's design as amended after the Civil War.

4. Complementary Federalism

The *Shelby County* majority interpreted the preclearance provision as an oppressive burden on state and local governments. "States," the Chief Justice wrote, "must beseech the Federal Government for permission to implement laws that they would otherwise have the right to enact and execute on their own."[125] This intrusive mechanism, he asserted, had imposed heavy costs on the states.

Justice Ginsburg, in contrast, noted that preclearance offers at least one benefit to the states. Given both historical and contemporary discrimination, the covered states are particularly likely to face lawsuits filed by disgruntled voters. In that context, preclearance offers an efficient and cost-effective means of resolving disputes over voting rights. The Voting Rights Act, Justice Ginsburg concluded, thus "provided a fit solution for minority voters *as well as for States*."[126]

To back up this claim, Justice Ginsburg cited a recent example from South Carolina. That state adopted a voter-identification law in 2011, which the Department of Justice challenged through an enforcement action. After the state agreed to interpret its law in a way that would ease burdens on minority voters, the three-judge panel precleared the statute. The Voting Rights Act thus protected minority voters from discriminatory roadblocks while also shielding the state from expensive post hoc litigation.[127]

The Voting Rights Act, of course, does not offer a conventional example of cooperative federalism; the Fifteenth Amendment gives Congress broad powers to act unilaterally. As Justice Ginsburg perceived, however, the act does further some state interests. This observation exemplifies Justice Ginsburg's approach to complementary federalism: she identifies even subtle instances in which state and national interests coincide.

5. Political Process

Justice Ginsburg reinforced her *Shelby County* arguments by noting that the political process offers the best arena for addressing voter discrimination. Before adoption of the Voting Rights Act, courts failed to keep pace with discriminatory measures; as soon as judges overturned one scheme, recalcitrant election authorities adopted a substitute. For that reason, Justice Ginsburg concluded, "discrimination against minority voters was a quintessentially political problem requiring a political solution."[128] Acting on its Fifteenth Amendment authority, Congress adopted pro-active measures that the executive branch could enforce.

The political approach succeeded. The Voting Rights Act, as even the *Shelby County* majority conceded, "proved immensely successful at redressing racial discrimination and integrating the voting process."[129] Equally important, the act retained widespread congressional support. The latest reauthorization, as Justice Ginsburg documented, passed the House 390–33; in the Senate, the vote was 98–0.[130]

Given the Fifteenth Amendment's designation of Congress as primary enforcer of voting rights, the demonstrated success of the Voting Rights Act, and the strong support for that act among members of both political parties, Justice Ginsburg concluded that the Court should have left the act to the political process. Instead, the Court "err[ed] egregiously by overriding Congress' decision."[131]

II. STATE AUTONOMY

As the previous section demonstrates, Justice Ginsburg endorses the broad authority that the Constitution grants Congress to address national problems. When Congress acts under the Commerce Clause, Spending Clause, or Civil War Amendments, Justice Ginsburg stresses how those actions further the Constitution's design. Her dissents on these subjects have also emphasized the Court's departure from precedent, its failure to defer appropriately to congressional judgments, the benefits that arise from federal-state cooperation, and the role of the political process in both legitimizing and restraining legislation.

Justice Ginsburg, however, does not reflexively support national power; her opinions also recognize the value of state autonomy. When sustaining state authority, Justice Ginsburg draws upon many of the same principles that mark her opinions supporting national power. Deference, constitutional design, and complementary federalism feature prominently in these opinions. I explore these themes in two very different types of cases: preemption disputes and the Court's resolution of the 2000 presidential election.[132]

A. Preemption

As other scholars have observed, preemption cases play a pivotal role in Justice Ginsburg's federalism jurisprudence.[133] Justice Ginsburg holds Congress to a rigorous standard in these cases, requiring clear evidence that the national legislature intended to preempt state law. Other justices are more indulgent of Congress in preemption cases, placing Justice Ginsburg regularly in dissent. To illustrate Justice Ginsburg's preemption jurisprudence, I examine her opinion in *Riegel v. Medtronic, Inc.*,[134] a case in which Justice Ginsburg was the sole dissenter.

In *Riegel*, a married couple claimed that the husband had been injured by a Medtronic cardiac catheter. The couple filed a tort suit, arguing that the "catheter was designed, labeled, and manufactured in a manner that violated New York common law."[135] The trial court dismissed most of these claims, holding them preempted by Congress's Medical Device Amendments of 1976 (MDA).[136] The Supreme Court agreed with this disposition, concluding that the MDA "bars common-law claims challenging the safety and effectiveness of a medical device given premarket approval by the Food and Drug Administration (FDA)."[137]

In her dissent, Justice Ginsburg invoked three themes: the presumption against preemption, the Constitution's support of that presumption, and the merits of dual federal-state regulation. These strains echo her concerns when enforcing national power. The constitutional structure of federalism, she shows, does not solely favor national or state power; instead, it allocates authority between the two.

1. Deference
Preemption claims present a puzzle for judges committed to deference. Should a court defer to Congress, upholding the furthest plausible reach of nationally enacted laws? Or should the court defer to state courts and legislatures, preserving their regulation from national encroachment? Justice Ginsburg solves this conundrum with two complementary principles. First, congressional

purpose is "'the ultimate touchstone of pre-emption analysis.'"[138] If Congress clearly expresses a desire to preempt state law, then the Court must defer to that legislative command.

Second, and equally important, states should retain their regulatory authority unless Congress expresses a "'clear and manifest purpose'" to preempt that power.[139] The Court, in other words, should apply a strong presumption against preemption. By combining these two principles, courts achieve a proper balance between deference to Congress and respect for state autonomy.

Justice Ginsburg demonstrated her deep commitment to these principles in *Riegel*. She carefully laid out the language, context, and legislative history of the MDA, which suggested that Congress intended to preempt only premarket regulatory schemes, not consumer tort suits. The Court's contrary conclusion, Justice Ginsburg urged, was "at odds with the MDA's central purpose: to protect consumer safety."[140]

Even if Congress's intent had not been clear, Justice Ginsburg argued, the presumption against preemption should have preserved the Riegels' tort suit. Indeed, Justice Ginsburg identified three different presumptions in *Riegel*, each of which pointed to preservation of the consumers' state claims.

The first of these presumptions was the general one stated earlier: courts should always assume that Congress does not intend to preempt state law. Second, that presumption "is heightened ... 'in fields of traditional state regulation.'"[141] Finally, when Congress includes a preemption clause, as it did in the MDA, but that "clause is open to more than one plausible reading," the Court should "'accept the reading that disfavors pre-emption.'"[142]

Applying these nested presumptions, Justice Ginsburg concluded that Congress did not intend the MDA to preempt ordinary tort claims based on state law. Her analysis properly enforced congressional intent, while preserving state autonomy against inadvertent encroachment. By applying presumptions crafted in previous cases, Justice Ginsburg gave maximum deference to both congressional intent and state law. The majority, in contrast, subverted congressional intent and overrode deeply rooted principles of state law.[143]

2. Constitutional Design

The Constitution provides that "Laws of the United States ... shall be the supreme Law of the Land; and the Judges in every State shall be bound thereby, any Thing in the Constitution or Laws of any State to the Contrary notwithstanding."[144] This Supremacy Clause instructs courts to disregard state laws that conflict with national regulation. The clause, however, does not tell courts to read congressional acts expansively; nor does it require courts to invalidate state laws that supplement national acts without undercutting them.

As Justice Ginsburg argued in *Riegel* and other preemption opinions, a presumption against preemption does no violence to the Supremacy Clause. At the same time, this presumption furthers other aspects of the constitutional design: it recognizes limits on national power by forcing Congress to act definitively if it wishes to fully occupy a legislative field, and it protects state regulation until Congress takes those decisive steps.

The presumption against preemption, in fact, serves as a key mechanism promoting the dual sovereignty envisioned by the Constitution. The amorphous Tenth Amendment does not articulate an enforceable balance between state and national power; nor do some of the Court's most aggressive federalism opinions. The cautious approach to preemption embraced by Justice Ginsburg offers a surer way to protect state autonomy than any of those other avenues.

3. Complementary Federalism

Preemption claims seem to pit state and national interests against one another. Justice Ginsburg, however, views these disputes through a different lens. She recognizes that private parties may object to concurrent regulation even when the states and national government believe their regulation is complementary. The claims of self-interested litigants should not drive preemption analysis. Instead, the Court must discern Congress's intent and apply the presumptions outlined previously. In doing so, Justice Ginsburg often uncovers patterns of complementary regulation.

As Justice Ginsburg explained in *Riegel*, the MDA provided the weft for just this sort of tapestry; it built upon an existing warp of state laws that Congress intended to preserve. The federal statute responded to widely publicized deaths and injuries tied to the failure of medical devices.[145] Consumers had already filed state tort claims against the manufacturers of those devices, and Congress never displayed any intent to displace those claims. Instead, Congress adopted the MDA to expand consumer protection by adding premarket review to postmarket lawsuits.

In adopting this design, Congress built on its experience with premarket regulation of pharmaceuticals. Federal law had required premarket approval of pharmaceuticals for forty years; yet during all of those years, consumers had continued to file state tort claims against drug manufacturers.[146] Congress, therefore, understood that tort suits based on state law could complement – not threaten – federal premarket controls.

State tort law, in turn, incorporated federal premarket regulation in at least two ways. First, as Justice Ginsburg noted, a plaintiff cannot premise recovery on a theory that conflicts with the FDA's approval; premarket licensing excludes some theories of liability.[147] Second, most states regard compliance with premarket regulations as a factor for the jury to weigh in determining liability.[148] A defendant like Medtronic, therefore, could rely upon FDA approval as evidence of its appropriate care.

This entwining of state and federal law, Justice Ginsburg contended, provides the best protection for consumers. The FDA had recognized this fact, noting that "product approval and state tort liability usually operate independently, each providing a significant, yet distinct, layer of consumer protection."[149] Premarket regulation, the agency noted, cannot anticipate all possible safety risks; nor can it foresee injuries that develop over time. Tort claims, therefore, add "a significant layer of consumer protection" to regulatory schemes like the MDA.[150]

The majority's interpretation of the MDA, in contrast, left injured patients with a single tier of protection. Regardless of the extent of harm or the egregiousness of the manufacturer's conduct, consumers have no recourse for injuries caused by medical devices approved by the FDA.[151] This result was both unnecessary and contrary to congressional intent. Indeed, as Justice Ginsburg concluded, the majority's preemption ruling achieved "the 'perverse effect' of granting broad immunity 'to an entire industry that, in the judgment of Congress, needed more stringent regulation.'"[152]

B. *Bush v. Gore*

In *Bush v. Gore*,[153] the Supreme Court famously halted Florida's attempts to manually recount votes cast in the 2000 presidential election. Seven justices held that Florida's recount was "standardless" and violated the Equal Protection Clause.[154] Five of them further concluded that the only available remedy was to terminate the recount.[155] Those five votes brought the contested election to a close.

In addition to these dispositive rulings, three justices contended that Florida's recount violated Article II of the Constitution, which provides that "Each State shall appoint, in such Manner as the Legislature thereof may direct, a Number of Electors" to select the president and vice president.[156] The manual recounts ordered by the Florida courts, these justices determined, offended Article II because the courts substituted their judgment for that of the "legislature."

By stopping Florida's recount, the Supreme Court treaded on a key element of state autonomy: the state's right to administer its election process. That authority is not inviolate; the Fifteenth Amendment, for example, empowers Congress to override state election processes to enforce racial equality.[157] The election process, however, lies at the core of a state's identity. The differing opinions in *Bush v. Gore*, therefore, offer critical insights into the justices' federalism jurisprudence.[158]

Justice Ginsburg, dissenting, challenged both the Equal Protection and Article II rationales in *Bush*, stressing the Court's interference with Florida's electoral process. Her brief but powerful dissent invoked three of her common federalism themes: deference, constitutional design, and complementary federalism.

1. Deference

Throughout her dissent, Justice Ginsburg chastised the Court for failing to defer to the Florida Supreme Court. "Rarely," she declared, "has this Court rejected outright an interpretation of state law by a state high court."[159] Yet three justices did just that by concluding that Florida had violated Article II of the Constitution. "Instead of respecting the state high court's province to say what the State's Election Code means," Justice Ginsburg observed, these justices "maintain[ed] that Florida's Supreme Court ha[d] veered so far from the ordinary practice of judicial review that what it did cannot properly be called judging."[160]

As Justice Ginsburg documented, this reading constituted an extraordinary slap at the Florida judges. Chief Justice Rehnquist, Justice Scalia, and Justice Thomas proffered a reasonable interpretation of Florida law, but their view was not the one adopted by Florida's own court. Their simple "disagreement with the Florida court's interpretation of its own State's law," Justice Ginsburg argued, "d[id] not warrant the conclusion that the justices of that court have legislated."[161] Her colleagues' contrary view impugned the integrity of Florida's Supreme Court, a suggestion that Justice Ginsburg was quick to challenge. "There is no cause here," she urged, "to believe that the members of Florida's high court have done less than 'their mortal best to discharge their oath of office,' and no cause to upset their reasoned interpretation of Florida law."[162]

Justice Ginsburg buttressed her deference argument by citing several lines of precedent. The Court, she observed, defers to statutory interpretations offered by federal agencies unless the agency transgresses a clear expression of congressional intent.[163] Deferring to a federal agency, but not a state's high court, affronted state autonomy. "Surely," Justice Ginsburg wrote, "the Constitution does not call upon us to pay more respect to a federal administrative agency's construction of federal law than to a state high court's interpretation of its own State's law."[164]

Similarly, Justice Ginsburg reminded her colleagues that when the Supreme Court construes state law to enforce a federal right, it affords a "full measure of respect" to state court interpretations of that law.[165] The Article II reasoning endorsed by three justices in *Bush v. Gore* conflicted with that tradition of deference.

The same lack of deference undermined the majority's equal protection holding. The recount ordered by the Florida courts might have been defective but, as Justice Ginsburg observed, the election process itself was imperfect.[166] Given widespread failures in voting methods and machine tabulation, "the recount adopted by the Florida court, flawed as it may be," was no "less fair or precise than the certification that preceded that recount."[167] Rather than impose an impossible standard of perfection, one that no other state could have met, Justice Ginsburg urged the Court to defer to Florida's reasonable attempts at vote tabulation.

The Court's greatest lack of deference, however, lay in its failure to allow the Florida courts an opportunity on remand to correct any flaws. Foreclosing that opportunity, the Court held that (a) Florida would have to certify its electoral votes by December 12, and (b) the looming deadline would preclude "orderly judicial review of any disputed matters that might arise."[168] Given those constraints, the Court determined, the recount had to cease.

As Justice Ginsburg noted, however, Florida was not bound by the December 12 deadline; it could have chosen to take more time to certify its votes. The Florida courts and election officials, furthermore, had shown impressive agility in handling the recount. A trial judge had promptly assumed supervision of the recount; even more impressive, "the Florida Supreme Court ha[d] produced two substantial opinions within 29 hours of oral argument."[169] Most important, Justice Ginsburg emphasized, "no one has doubted the good faith and diligence with which Florida election officials, attorneys for all sides of this controversy, and the courts of law have performed their duties."[170]

Given Florida's diligence, together with the deference owed a sovereign state, Justice Ginsburg saw no reason for the Supreme Court to prevent the state from attempting to satisfy the majority's equal protection mandate. The majority's "conclusion that a constitutionally adequate recount [would be] impractical" was not a ruling anchored in the constitutional text; it was a mere "prophecy."[171] If the majority had afforded proper deference to Florida, it would have at least remanded to the state courts for further proceedings.

2. Constitutional Design

Justice Ginsburg objected strenuously to the Article II argument advanced by Chief Justice Rehnquist, Justice Scalia, and Justice Thomas to defeat the Florida recount. Her colleagues' interpretation of Article II, Justice Ginsburg maintained, violated the constitutional design in two ways. First, it disregarded the maxim that federal courts must honor a state high court's construction of state law.[172] That concept, Justice Ginsburg explained, "reflects the core of federalism, on which all agree."[173] Overriding a state's interpretation of its own law denies that state's sovereignty, a clear violation of the federalist design.

Second, Article II itself strikes a careful balance between state and federal power. Section 1, clause 2 of the article explicitly gives the states a role in choosing the national executive: "Each State shall appoint, in such Manner as the Legislature thereof may direct, a Number of Electors" who will choose the president and vice president.[174] Chief Justice Rehnquist, Justice Scalia, and Justice Thomas read this provision stiffly, to give state legislatures *exclusive* control over the selection of electors. As Justice Ginsburg explained, this reading conflicts with the Constitution's spirit and text. The Constitution both recognizes "the basic principle that a State may organize itself as it sees fit"[175] and guarantees each state a "Republican Form of Government."[176] Under those circumstances, the Framers of Article II surely "understood that in a republican government, the judiciary would construe the legislature's enactments."[177]

Article II, in other words, confers authority on each "State," not just on the legislature. The legislature may "direct" the manner of choosing electors, but the courts must resolve disputes that arise from the selection process. That sequence constitutes the normal operation of a republican government. "The Chief Justice's solicitude for the Florida Legislature," Justice Ginsburg concluded, thus displaced "the more fundamental solicitude" that the Court owed to the sovereign state of Florida itself.[178]

Justice Ginsburg's reading of Article II fits the Constitution's text better than the construction offered by Chief Justice Rehnquist; her interpretation also embodies the deference ordinarily accorded states to organize their governmental processes as they choose. "Were the other Members of [the] Court as mindful as they generally are of our system of dual sovereignty," Justice Ginsburg asserted, they would have rejected the challenge to Florida's election process.[179]

3. Complementary Federalism
Justice Ginsburg buttressed her dissent by noting that even if the Court wasn't willing to defer to the Florida Supreme Court's prior rulings, it should at least have certified open questions of state law to that court. Certification, she noted, "'helps build a cooperative judicial federalism.'"[180] By urging her colleagues to pursue this device, Justice Ginsburg underscored the cooperation she seeks in federal-state relations. The majority, in contrast, was willing to forgo any possibility of collaboration with Florida.[181]

III. COHERENT FEDERALISM

As this brief review suggests, Justice Ginsburg espouses a coherent, principled concept of federalism. She roots her jurisprudence in the Constitution's design, which recognizes both national power and state autonomy. She also draws upon the Court's twentieth-century precedents, stressing how they created a healthy allocation of national and state power. Justice Ginsburg resolves federalism disputes with characteristic restraint, deferring to Congress when it flexes national powers and to state courts when they construe state law. Her preemption doctrine, requiring a clear expression of congressional intent to displace state law, similarly accommodates the interests of both state and national governments.

Justice Ginsburg fortifies these approaches with distinctive views of both the political process and federal-state partnerships. Her federalism jurisprudence incorporates a pragmatic view of how the political process informs the actions of Congress, state legislatures, and state courts. The Constitution trusts many decisions to the political branches, and Justice Ginsburg defends those assignments. At the same time, she understands the Court's duty to enforce the outer boundaries of constitutional constraints.

Justice Ginsburg has developed a particularly nuanced understanding of federal-state relationships. In addition to praising classic examples of cooperative federalism, such as the Medicaid program, she identifies other ways in which state regulation complements national work. States develop innovative programs that Congress imitates; they supplement national regulation; they perform roles specifically delegated by the Constitution; and they participate in traditional spending programs. In all of these ways, states remain a vital part of our government system.

These elements add up to a federalism jurisprudence that is both old and new. Justice Ginsburg draws upon long-standing precedent and constitutional design while articulating a vision of federal-state relations that is vibrant and forward-looking. Justice Ginsburg trusts voters and lawmakers at all levels to further the common good and, when necessary, to correct their mistakes. She understands the necessity of a strong hand on the national tiller while acknowledging the complementary role of autonomous states.

In her public speeches, Justice Ginsburg frequently credits the "way pavers" who opened doors for women and other newcomers in our profession.[182] Her federalism dissents are "way pavers" of a different sort: they point the way toward a thoughtful jurisprudence of federalism, one that accounts for state autonomy, national power, judicial restraint, and the political process. This is the federalism that a wise Court would seek for the future.

PART IV

THE JURIST

13

Reflections on the Confirmation Journey of Ruth Bader Ginsburg, Summer 1993

Robert A. Katzmann

Ruth Bader Ginsburg has been deservedly celebrated for her contributions as a Supreme Court Justice. For those of us in the lower courts who are guided by her opinions, we can only admire the justice's powerful analytic clarity, the graceful and succinct prose, the capacity to unpack complicated arguments in ways that are fair to all concerned, her collegial tone, and, to borrow a word from her lexicon, her many "pathmarking" contributions to the law's development. Of course, even if she had never served a day as a judge on any court, Ginsburg would have been a much heralded figure in our nation's history for her landmark advocacy on behalf of women's rights. In a life of extraordinary accomplishment, the justice has assumed iconic status for the American public. Greeting cards bear her likeness, operas are written about her, T-shirts with her images are popular gifts, Ruth Bader Ginsburg bobbleheads are hot commodities, a fan website records her wisdom. In a land where the loudest and flashiest often obtain the most celebrity attention, Ruth Ginsburg shares that stage of fame by dint of her intellect, achievements, and vision.

In the course of her Supreme Court confirmation process in the summer of 1993, the general American public first came to know Ruth Bader Ginsburg. What they observed – her character, her values – they liked, and the years since have only reinforced and deepened that connection. I witnessed her confirmation journey firsthand, an experience I will always treasure.

On being nominated by President Clinton on June 14, 1993, in a White House ceremony, Justice Ginsburg was thrust into the world of celebrity. "A Justice Grows in Brooklyn," the *New York Daily News* declared.

Immediately upon her nomination, Senator Daniel Patrick Moynihan, her very proud Senate sponsor, called me and asked if I might be special counsel pro bono to him and to then-Judge Ginsburg. I remember saying "yes" before he finished his sentence. I had written quite a lot about and worked on projects dealing with courts and Congress; I had a longtime, close association with

Senator Moynihan, who had been my professor in graduate school at Harvard, and I had been involved in a variety of projects with him in his Senate years. I also knew the Ginsburgs and, with Judge Ginsburg, had been involved in a pilot effort with the D.C. Circuit on statutory housekeeping.

On that first phone call, Senator Moynihan, concerned about the world of spin and handlers, said to me: "Make sure that she is allowed always to be herself." He need not have been worried because Ruth Bader Ginsburg was and always has been a person of independent mind and spirit. As each day passed in the summer of 1993, I got to know the Ginsburgs well, and my admiration and affection only deepened. Although the nominee really did not need any of my help, I had the privilege of being part of Team Ginsburg.

I was with Ruth Bader Ginsburg from the time of her nomination through the confirmation process, accompanying her on her visits with senators, beginning on June 15, when we met with Senate Judiciary Committee Chair Joseph Biden and Republican Ranking Member Orrin Hatch. I briefed her before our meetings with the senators as to what their interests and concerns might be. Sometimes those meetings would be meet-and-greet courtesy calls. Other times, those meetings provided an occasion for the senators to foreshadow issues on their minds, as when Republican Senator Larry Pressler of South Dakota indicated he would be asking the nominee about Indian tribal rights at the hearings. On still other occasions, a senator would use the meeting not to elicit a response from the nominee but to express a concern, as Senator Carl Levin did, about capital punishment. Judge Ginsburg spoke cordially with every senator with whom she met, and I thought, left a very positive impression as an authentic human being and as a master of judicial craft.

I well remember, as we made our rounds on the Hill, how tourists thronged to Ruth Bader Ginsburg and how friendly she was toward them. And I knew that the senators recognized her popularity, for it soon became routine for the senators we visited to have a photographer present. In a delightful moment, Republican Senator Charles Grassley, for instance, asked if then-Judge Ginsburg wouldn't mind attending an ice cream social in the Capitol, sponsored by his Iowa constituents – and she did, much to the thrill of those constituents. It was clear to all of us too, that women and girls especially welcomed her nomination.

Senator Moynihan wanted me to be his eyes and ears. He wanted me to be his representative in part because he wanted to communicate to his Senate colleagues the importance of Ginsburg's nomination to him and his commitment to her. As Senator Moynihan's representative, I participated in all of the White House meetings. Although he could attend only a few of our visits with senators because of the demands of being Finance Committee chair, his colleagues knew of his interest. I gave the senator a daily account of whom we saw and whom we were scheduled to see. Knowing that we had seen Senator X or were about to see Senator Y, he would have a word with Senator X and Senator Y on the Senate floor to reiterate his support and to keep a watchful eye. No senator was more respected by his colleagues than Senator Moynihan, and his wholehearted commitment to Ruth Ginsburg's confirmation was invaluable.

Throughout the process, at least once a day, I consulted with the brilliantly multi-talented Martin Ginsburg, whose keen sense of the big picture, attention to detail, and unerring judgment were always apparent. I savored my conversations with him, often laughing about some very funny and, at the same time, insightful comment that the nominee's husband would make.

In the period mid-June to mid-July 1993, the White House team, led by the savvy and experienced Associate White House Counsel Ronald Klain and Deputy White House Counsel Joel Klein, organized the daily schedule on the Hill, participated in Hill meetings, and oversaw confirmation strategy. Moreover, as part of the preparation process, the White House arranged for substantive briefings and mock questioning, in which White House staff and I played the role of particular senators. These sessions took place in the Old Executive Office Building, next to the White House, the building where Theodore Roosevelt and Franklin Roosevelt had offices when each was a young assistant secretary of the navy. Whether discussing complicated Supreme Court cases or the pressing issues of the day, Ruth Bader Ginsburg answered every question with comprehension, order, and aplomb. I had the sense, as I am sure the briefers did as well, that the nominee knew more than anyone in the room about the subjects at hand. Having been a distinguished law professor, scholar, litigator, and judge, there was little that anyone could teach her.

As testament to her principles and loyalty, I well recall Judge Ginsburg's insistence that in meetings with senators or in the hearings, she would not distance herself from her past life as a litigator at the Women's Rights Project at the ACLU, or her opinions, or any of the organizations with which she had been affiliated. She was ready to be challenged, alone, in front of a panel judging her in a highly televised and consequential setting.

Finally, some five weeks after nomination, on a typically humid summer day in Washington D.C., the day of the first confirmation hearing arrived, July 20, 1993. The nominee had met all of the senators on the Judiciary Committee and many of their colleagues. Judge Ginsburg entered room 216 of the Senate Hart Office Building, well in advance of the 10:10 AM start time. The unmistakable whiff of history charged the room. This was only the second woman to be questioned by the Senate panel for a seat on the highest bench of the land. Judge Ginsburg and Senator Moynihan sat side by side at the table. She seemed calm and ready; the senator, ebullient. Marty was right behind his wife. I was nearby too, as were family, friends, and members of the White House team. The room was packed and included numerous representatives of the media.

When her time came to deliver her opening statement, Judge Ginsburg did so in her characteristically precise, elegant prose, setting the tone for the confirmation hearings and offering a view of judging that guides me today:

> My approach, I believe, is neither "liberal" nor "conservative." Rather, it is rooted in the place of the judiciary – of judges – in our democratic society. The Constitution's preamble speaks first of We, the People, and then of their elected representatives. The Judiciary is third in line, and it is placed apart from the political fray so that its members can judge fairly, impartially, in accordance with the law and without fear about the animosity of any pressure group. In Alexander Hamilton's words: the mission of judges is "to secure a steady, upright, and impartial administration of the laws." I would add that the judge should carry out that function without fanfare, but with due care: she should decide the case before her without reaching out to cover cases not yet seen. She should be ever mindful, as Judge and then Justice Benjamin Nathan Cardozo said: "Justice is not to be taken by storm. She is to be wooed by slow advances."[1]

At her hearings, in a reassuring, measured cadence, she set forth a benchmark as to the kinds of questions she could answer. She noted in her opening statement that her writings as a law teacher, lawyer, and judge were the most reliable indicator of her attitude, outlook, approach and style:

> You have been supplied … with hundreds of pages about me, and thousands of pages I have penned – my writings as a law teacher, mainly about procedure; ten years of briefs filed when I was a courtroom advocate of the equal stature of men and women before the law; numerous speeches and articles on that same theme; thirteen years of opinions – well over 700 of them – decisions I made as a member of the U.S. Court of Appeals for the District of Columbia Circuit; several comments on the roles of judges and lawyers in our legal system…. I hope you will judge my qualifications principally on that written record spanning thirty-four years. I think of these proceedings much as I do of the division between the written record and briefs, on the one hand, and oral argument on the other hand, in appellate tribunals. The written record is by far the more important component in an appellate court's decision-making, but the oral argument often elicits helpful clarifications and concentrates the judges' minds on the character of the decision they are called upon to make.[2]

Acknowledging the legitimacy of the Senate's efforts to question her, Judge Ginsburg observed that she would "act injudiciously" were she to "say or preview" how she would cast her vote on questions the Supreme Court may be called on to decide. "Judges in our system," she said, "are bound to decide concrete cases, not abstract issues; each case is based on particular facts and its decision should turn on those facts and the governing law, stated and explained in light of the particular arguments the parties or their representatives choose to present."[3]

In three days of testimony, Judge Ginsburg was more than willing to explain how she approached problems and made decisions. Her responses revealed a mastery of the law that comes only with seasoned experience. Her testimony, as the report of the Senate Judiciary Committee noted,[4] offered insights into her views about freedom of speech and religion, separation of powers, statutory interpretation, criminal law and procedure, standing, gender discrimination, abortion, the role of the Supreme Court, and the scope of unenumerated rights. Nor did she hesitate to respond to queries about her writings, including her Madison Lecture critique of the rationale of *Roe v. Wade*.[5]

In many ways, Judge Ginsburg's exchanges were teaching moments, lessons for the public about how an eminent jurist approached judging. Consider, for example, the nominee's response to ranking Judiciary Committee member Senator Orrin Hatch of Utah:

SENATOR HATCH: What about this statement: The only legitimate way for a judge to go about defining the law is by attempting to discern what those who made the law intended.

JUDGE GINSBURG: I think all people could agree with that. But as I tried to say in response to the chairman's question, trying to divine what the Framers intended, I must look at that matter two ways. One is what they might have intended immediately for their day, and the other is their larger expectation that the Constitution would govern, as Cardozo said, not for the passing hour, but for the expanding future. And I know no better illustration of that than to take the words of the great man who wrote the Declaration of Independence. Thomas Jefferson said: "Were our state a pure democracy, there would still be excluded from our deliberations women who, to prevent depravation of morals and ambiguity of issues, should not mix promiscuously in gatherings of men." Nonetheless, I do believe that Thomas Jefferson, were he alive today, would say that women are equal citizens.... So I see an immediate intent about how an ideal is going to be recognized at a given time and place, but also a larger aspiration as our society improves. I think the Framers were intending to create a more perfect union that would become ever more perfect with time.

SENATOR HATCH: I think that is a good way of putting it.[6]

Her grasp of the law and of our constitutional system was apparent to all of the senators on the Judiciary Committee, and her qualifications were unquestioned. On the evening of the first day, Senator Moynihan told me that he felt the nominee's sure-handed performance would result in a quick, favorable Senate vote. Indeed, the firm support of both Biden and Hatch assured that her confirmation would be swift. On August 3, just eleven days after the hearings concluded, she was confirmed by a nearly unanimous vote, 96–3. A week later, she was sworn as Associate Justice of the Supreme Court, first at a private ceremony in the Supreme Court, and later in the East Room of the White House, by Chief Justice William Rehnquist, with a beaming Senator Moynihan in the front row and an equally beaming President Clinton at her side.

In Judge Ginsburg, I observed someone for whom the law was not about abstractions. Her career in the law was, and continues to be, about working to ensure that each of us can realize his or her potential. For her, life could entail the most difficult of challenges, both professional and personal, but she has always determined to meet them, to struggle through the obstacles to secure a better future for those of us here and now and those who follow. The enduring connection that she established with the American people who watched the confirmation hearings was based on their perception that, in an age too-often gripped by glitz and self-promotion, Ruth Bader Ginsburg was someone whose virtues were real.

For me, the most telling moment of the confirmation hearings came in response to a question from Senator Herbert Kohl as to how she'd like the American people to think of her. She answered quietly: "I would like to be thought of as a person who cares about people and does the best she can with the talent she has to make a contribution to a better world."[7]

That answer captures Justice Ginsburg's essence. I can think of a thousand ways that she has achieved and does achieve what she said that day. More than twenty years after her nomination to the Supreme Court, I can say that her status now as legend has not changed her. She is a person with a seemingly limitless capacity for friendship and kindness, in ways large and small, no matter the weighty burdens of her daily life; someone who places others before her own convenience; someone who, for instance, despite many demands on her time, made the effort in 1999 to come to New York City to swear me in on the circuit court; someone of conviction and enduring determination, fortified by a formidable intellect and prodigious work ethic; a person with a true sense of the aesthetic, of beauty and flair, taken by the simple pleasures that life has to offer, be it the aria *Nessun Dorma* or a horseback ride. To know her incomparable partner, Marty, and her accomplished children, Jane and James, and the rest of her family is to have a sense of what for her are life's blessings, and makes each of us appreciate what is truly important. Thank you, Ruth Bader Ginsburg.

14

Justice Ginsburg:
Demosprudence through Dissent

Lani Guinier

October Term 2006 was an unusual one for the Supreme Court. On seven occasions, more than any other term on record, a justice issued an oral dissent from the bench.[1] New York Times reporter Linda Greenhouse proclaimed that the term would also "be remembered as the time when Justice Ruth Bader Ginsburg found her voice, and used it."[2] The events of that year would indeed foreshadow Justice Ginsburg's emerging role as a forceful and passionate dissenter, an objecting voice within a Court that has been increasingly viewed as activist and divided.[3] As the legal community and media noted her two oral dissents that term, she affirmed her position going forward: "I will continue to dissent if, in my judgment, the court veers in the wrong direction when important issues are at stake."[4]

I have written previously[5] about how a dissent, at its best, represents an act of demosprudence. Demosprudence is a term Professor Gerald Torres and I coined to describe the process of making and interpreting law from an external – not just internal – "people-driven" perspective. That perspective emphasizes the role of informal democratic mobilizations and wide-ranging social movements that serve to make formal institutions, including those that regulate legal culture, more democratic. Demosprudence focuses on the ways that the demos (especially through social movements) can contribute to the meaning of law. The foundational hypothesis of demosprudence is that the wisdom of the people should help inform the lawmaking enterprise in a democracy. From this view, the Court gains a new source of democratic authority when its members engage ordinary people and other legislative authorities, such as Congress, in a productive dialogue about the potential role of "We the People"

I could not have written this essay without the amazingly able research – including the precise, finely tuned editing – of Lindsay McKenzie (Harvard Law School Class of 2015). I also benefited greatly from the timely and diligent assistance of a wonderfully talented undergraduate, Alexander Diaz (Harvard College 2014).

in lawmaking.[6] I highlight two instances in which reading her dissent from the bench reveals Justice Ginsburg's demosprudential orientation to the law.

LEDBETTER V. GOODYEAR TIRE & RUBBER CO.

America's first black president signed his first major piece of legislation on January 29, 2009: the Lilly Ledbetter Fair Pay Act.[7] Since the act carried Lilly Ledbetter's name, she fittingly stood beaming by President Obama's side during the signing ceremony.[8]

For nineteen years, however, this seventy-year-old grandmother had less reason to be joyful, working in supervisory blue-collar jobs in a Goodyear Tire and Rubber Plant in Gadsden, Alabama, earning 15 to 40 percent less than her male counterparts. This pay gap, which resulted from receiving smaller raises than the men, "added up and multiplied" over the years.[9] But Ledbetter did not discover the disparity until she was nearing retirement and "only started to get hard evidence of discrimination when someone anonymously left a piece of paper" in her mailbox listing the salaries of the men who held the same job.[10]

Ledbetter sued and a federal jury awarded her $223,776 in back pay and more than $3 million in punitive damages, finding that it was "more likely than not that [Goodyear] paid [Ledbetter] a[n] unequal salary because of her sex."[11] The Supreme Court overturned that verdict. The five-justice majority held that Ledbetter waived her right to sue by failing to file her complaint within 180 days of Goodyear's initial pay-setting decision.[12] In Ledbetter's words, the Court "sided with big business. They said I should have filed my complaint within six months of Goodyear's first decision to pay me less, even though I didn't know that's what they were doing."[13]

Justice Ruth Bader Ginsburg, on behalf of herself and three colleagues, dissented from the Court's decision.[14] A leading litigator and advocate for women's equality before taking her seat on the Court,[15] Justice Ginsburg took issue with five of her male colleagues. In May 2007, she read aloud the key elements of her written dissent from the bench – an act that, in her own words, reflects "more than ordinary disagreement."[16] Her oral dissent, which made the front page of the *Washington Post*,[17] signaled that something had gone "egregiously wrong."[18] In a stinging rebuke to the Court majority, she used the personal pronoun, speaking not to her colleagues but directly to the other "you's" in her audience – women who, despite suspecting something askew in their own jobs, were reluctant to rock the boat as the only women in male-dominated positions:

Indeed initially you may not know the men are receiving more for substantially similar work.... If you sue only when the pay disparity becomes steady and large enough to enable you to mount a winnable case, you will be cut off at the Court's threshold for suing too late.[19]

Justice Ginsburg's dissent reflected an acute sense, missing from the Court's opinion, of the circumstances surrounding women in male-dominated workplaces. In a job previously filled overwhelmingly by men, women "understandably may be anxious to avoid making waves."[20]

Justice Ginsburg was *courting* the people.[21] Her oral dissent and subsequent comments hinted at a democratizing form of judicial speech that, were it heard, could be easily understood by those outside the courtroom.[22] By speaking colloquially – using the personal pronoun "you" to address her audience – Justice Ginsburg signaled to ordinary women that the majority should not have the last word on the meaning of gender discrimination. Her goal was to engage an external audience in a conversation about our country's commitment to equal pay for equal work.[23]

While Justice Ginsburg spoke frankly to and about the Lilly Ledbetters of the world, her real target was Congress. Appalled by the Court's "cramped interpretation" of a congressional statute, Justice Ginsburg explicitly stated that the "ball again lies in Congress's court."[24] During a public conversation in September 2008, then-Harvard Law School Dean Elena Kagan asked Justice Ginsburg to describe her intended audience in Ledbetter. Ginsburg replied: "It was Congress. Speaking to Congress, I said, 'you did not mean what the Court said. So fix it.'"[25]

Democrats in Congress responded quickly. Initially called the Fair Pay Restoration Act, the House-passed bill would have eliminated the Court-sanctioned time limit.[26] That bill, however, died in the Senate, where Republicans – including John McCain – publicly denounced it as anti-business.[27]

As the initial Fair Pay Restoration Act languished in Congress, Lilly Ledbetter emerged as a real presence in the 2008 election campaign.[28] Despite her initial misgivings about partisan campaigning, she was infuriated by John McCain's refusal to support a congressional fix. She cut an ad for Barack Obama that had a "stratospheric effect" when poll-tested by *Fox News*'s political consultant Frank Luntz.[29] In August 2008, Ledbetter was a featured speaker at the Democratic National Convention in Denver.[30] There, as well as in her testimony before Congress, she acknowledged the significance of Justice Ginsburg's dissent both in affirming her concerns and directing attention to a legislative remedy.[31]

In her testimony before Congress, for example, Ledbetter echoed Justice Ginsburg's emphasis on the isolation many women feel when they first integrate the workplace.[32] Both Ledbetter and Justice Ginsburg used the pronoun "you" to speak directly to other women. At the same time that Ledbetter's story animated Justice Ginsburg's dissent, Justice Ginsburg's dissent amplified Ledbetter's own voice. Suitably emboldened, this Alabama grandmother went before Congress to speak directly to women about their shared fears of making waves in a male-dominated environment:

> Justice Ginsburg hit the nail on the head when she said that the majority's rule just doesn't make sense in the real world. You can't expect people to go around asking their coworkers how much they are making. Plus, even if you know some people are getting paid a little more than you, that is no reason to suspect discrimination right away. Especially when you work at a place like I did, where you are the only woman in a male-dominated factory, you don't want to make waves unnecessarily. You want to try to fit in and get along.[33]

Justice Ginsburg also continued to engage in a more public discourse about the Ledbetter case and her role as an oral dissenter. In an October 2007 speech posted on the Supreme Court website, she parodied the majority's reasoning: "'Sue early on,' the majority counseled, when it is uncertain whether discrimination accounts for the pay disparity you are beginning to experience, and when you may not know that men are receiving more for the same work. (Of course, you will likely lose such a less-than-fully baked case.)"[34] As reframed by Justice Ginsburg, Ledbetter's story was not about a negligent plaintiff who waited an unconscionably long time to sue; it was about an ordinary woman struggling to comprehend and eventually document the pay disparities in a work environment dominated by men. Justice Ginsburg frankly acknowledged the zigzag trajectory of change, especially given the real-world employment challenges such women face. In "propel[ling] change," her oral dissent was meant to "sound an alarm" that would be heard by members of Congress, Lilly Ledbetter, and women's rights advocates more generally. Her dissent was designed "to attract immediate public attention."[35]

Eventually social activists, legal advocacy groups, media translators, legislators, and "role-literate participants"[36] not only heard but also acted upon the alarm bells Ginsburg sounded. Marcia Greenberger of the National Women's Law Center was one of those "role-literate participants" who helped carry Justice Ginsburg's message forward. Greenberger characterized Ginsburg's oral dissent as a "clarion call" to the American people "that the Court is headed in the wrong direction."[37] Lilly Ledbetter became another such participant as her story, with Justice Ginsburg's assistance, helped ground and frame the discourse.[38] And for the first time in more than a decade, Congress pushed back against the Supreme Court. In January 2009, Lilly Ledbetter's name was enshrined in history when Congress passed and President Barack Obama signed the Lilly Ledbetter Fair Pay Act.[39]

In her *Ledbetter* dissent and subsequent comments, Justice Ginsburg was courting the people to change the law announced by the Supreme Court majority. In Robert Cover's "jurisgenerative" sense,[40] she claimed a space for citizens to advance alternative interpretations of the law. Her oral dissent and public remarks represented a set of demosprudential practices for instantiating and reinforcing the relationship between public engagement and institutional legitimacy.

SHELBY COUNTY V. HOLDER

Six years after *Ledbetter*, Justice Ginsburg again used her voice to sound the alarm when the Supreme Court handed down its decision in *Shelby County v. Holder*.[41] In June 2013, the year of the March on Washington's fiftieth anniversary – and two shy of the Voting Rights Act's own semi-centennial – the Court held that Section 4(b) of the Voting Rights Act, its preclearance formula, was unconstitutional.[42] That formula had been used successfully for nearly fifty years to identify which states and local jurisdictions were required to "preclear" with federal authorities any changes in their election processes, in order to prevent racial discrimination in voting. By invalidating the formula, the Court released all entities from these obligations.

Amidst a "sober and silent courtroom,"[43] Justice Ginsburg excoriated the majority in her fifth oral dissent that term, her third in two days.[44] While soft-spoken, her indignation was barely concealable.[45] But the part of the dispute that received most of her attention was not the Court's precedent, or even a purely legal issue – it was Congress's 2006 reauthorization of the act, and the words of Martin Luther King Jr. As in 2007, Justice Ginsburg spoke in the hope that those listening in and beyond the courtroom were getting roiled up to question and ultimately to challenge the majority opinion.

Justice Ginsburg's oral dissent in *Shelby* is an exercise in shrewd editing – it impressively expresses multiple arguments in truncated form, condensing thirty-seven pages of written dissent into ten minutes of oration.[46] As one example, her written dissent documents a painstaking account of failed voter protection before the Voting Right Act's passage. This history is collapsed parsimoniously into a single spoken line: "a mere century of disregard for the dictates of the Fifteenth Amendment."[47] The style of delivery is decidedly clipped; she poses short, pointed questions as a rhetorical way of highlighting issues that go unanswered by the majority.[48]

Her brief remarks from the bench do not, however, miss the occasion to provide real-life examples of voter discrimination. While Chief Justice Roberts frames the issue before the Court in a way that separates personal experiences of discrimination from the act's constitutionality,[49] minimizing their importance, Justice Ginsburg finds a way to use these incidents as a way to both respond to the majority's legal arguments and at the same time bring to the fore the human implications of the Court's decision. As both her oral and written dissents make clear, the case's dispositive question is "who decides whether, as currently operative, § 5 remains justifiable"[50] (or as shortened in her oral dissent, the "'who decides' question"),[51] and whether that decision was "rational."[52] The ugly specifics she provides – Mississippi's blocked attempt to resurrect its Jim Crow–era voter-registration system, and Texas's attack on early voting in a Latino district it had already tried to eliminate[53] – speak directly to Congress's rationality in reauthorizing the act.

Her written dissent drives the point home further, laying out six more "characteristic" examples of flagrant discrimination that were before Congress when it reauthorized the act in 2006.[54] Justice Ginsburg seizes the opportunity to emphasize Alabama's unique place in voter discrimination, surfacing a litany of its recent and offensive incidents. In 2010, an FBI wiretap investigation revealed Alabama state senators both referring to African Americans as "aborigines" and plotting to suppress from the ballot a referendum that would increase turnout.[55] The captured conversations, Ginsburg reminds us, "are shocking."[56] Such disturbing stories address the problems raised by the nature of Shelby County's facial challenge, but their purpose is also more visceral: they keep in the front of our minds the true consequences of the Court's ruling, its impact on the people in these communities. She also complicates the Court's rosy picture of voting rights by acknowledging "second-generation barriers."[57]

The majority opinion gives this side of the story short shrift. And the few examples detailed are held up as problems firmly in our Jim Crow past. Chief Justice Roberts cites seminal events of the civil rights movement only to wave farewell to a bygone era. The towns once made infamous by the "Freedom Summer" of 1964 and "Bloody Sunday" of 1965 are now governed by African American mayors[58] – this is emblematic of Roberts's arguments that we have entered a new age and that an understanding of current conditions of voter discrimination can be considered divorced from the history that created them. As with personal experiences of voter discrimination, the majority renders such backdrops unworthy of attention in deciding the issues before the Court. It concerns itself with narrow legal issues and places such considerations above the histories of people like congressman and civil-rights activist John Lewis, who lived through both events. Lewis, who prior to the ruling called the case one of the most important in a generation, said afterward that the Court had "stuck a dagger in the heart of the Voting Rights Act."[59]

In demanding that the coverage formula be justified by current conditions, the Court grants constitutional significance to its observation that "things have changed dramatically."[60] The statement bears resemblance to President Bush's 2003 "Mission Accomplished" moment.[61] Both are assertions of sole authority to evaluate conditions on the ground, without any acknowledgment of how the rights to make such appraisals are shared by multiple governing roles. Just as the president crowded out dissenting opinion on the war in Iraq, the Court's proclamation of victory leaves no room for alternative interpretations of the law offered by Congress, the activist community, victims of voter discrimination, or the lay public. These groups are silenced. The majority pays paltry lip service to the reality that "racial voter discrimination still exists."[62] Then it proceeds to announce – by judicial fiat – that racial voter discrimination is effectively over.

Justice Ginsburg embraces a more demosprudential view, rejecting the insistence that the Court alone may decide whether and how much racial discrimination still exists in voting. She reminds us powerfully of the role of nonjudicial actors, pointing repeatedly to Congress (directly mentioning it nineteen times in her oral dissent),[63] that, by the text and nature of the Civil War Amendments, should be accorded substantial deference.[64] Justice Ginsburg, in both her oral and written dissents, recognizes the central role played by the activist community in shaping the meaning of the Constitution and effecting social change. She quotes King: "The arc of the moral universe is long ... but it bends toward justice."[65] Yet the "steadfast commitment to see the task through to completion," she notes, is "disserved" by the Court's decision.[66] Invoking King (who went to jail simply for the right of others to vote),[67] and referencing the infamous, bloody march from Selma to Montgomery in 1965, she places the case squarely in a continuing struggle for voting rights and reminds us of the public's ongoing role in that movement's successes. Justice Ginsburg sees the Court as a participant in the long struggle for voting rights – with the potential to help or hinder that cause – not as an "objective" evaluator standing above it. Her position affirms the variety of roles in negotiating the meaning of law, an act that in turn legitimates the Court's constitutional role.[68]

Written opinions are not often neatly aligned with the goals of demosprudence. The latter is served by brevity, simplicity and colloquial language, often the mark of effective oral dissents. However, "the tools of demosprudence do not depend exclusively on orality to invite healthy discussion and stimulate public disagreements over the Constitution's meaning."[69] Written dissents, as *Shelby County* teaches, can still reflect the dissenter's willingness to "lift the curtains" behind a decision and involve others in the process of lawmaking.

Take history's role in the debate. While Justice Roberts criticizes Congress for living in the past, Justice Ginsburg's written dissent chides him for ignoring it.[70] History, she makes clear, has a crucial role to play in the Court's decision. "What's past is prologue,"[71] she cautions, quoting Shakespeare; "those who cannot remember the past are condemned to repeat it."[72] As such, Congress was entitled to consider the unique discriminatory history of covered states during its most recent reauthorization process,[73] just as people who may not be able to engage with the more traditional and complex doctrinal disputes at play are entitled to consult the country's history of voter discrimination. In other words, Justice Ginsburg follows the path charted by her oral dissent. She legitimates the consideration of nonlegal issues for the lay public, opening up the Court's disagreements to a wider audience by tapping into "rational, emotional, and psychic values that are anchored in an underlying set of communal commitments."[74]

Interestingly, Justice Ginsburg's oral dissent leaves out what has proven to be its written companion's most memorable line – the "umbrella" metaphor. She takes the Court to task for failing to engage with Congress's legislative record, which clearly demonstrates Section 5's continued effectiveness and its continued need. "Throwing out preclearance when it has worked and is continuing to work to stop discriminatory changes," Justice Ginsburg wrote, "is like throwing away your umbrella in a rainstorm because you are not getting wet."[75] Former Justice John Paul Stevens found this to be a clear and concise analogy for which the majority had no response,[76] and my colleague at Harvard Law School, Charles Ogletree, referenced it when summarizing his reaction to *Shelby County* in a *Washington Post* Op-Ed.[77] It ricocheted through the blogosphere – one commenter called it "pure gold."[78]

But the "umbrella" line was not simply a catchphrase for the legal community. It simplified the complex ramifications of the Court's ruling in a way that was clear and understandable to both role-literate activists and the broader public, providing ordinary people with a language to participate in a democratic conversation about voting rights, thus making it more likely for them to do so. It has been cited most often in voting rights discussions with wide audiences: Vice President Joe Biden's speech to the National Action Network[79] and a reception at the Naval Observatory during African American History Month.[80] It has been used by civil rights groups speaking to their constituencies,[81] and – recognizing its effectiveness and popularity – by Justice Ginsburg herself, in several interviews and appearances following the decision.[82] Her ability to use ordinary language that grabs the attention of the demos (which was on display earlier in the term[83]) is rivaled perhaps only by the language skills of Justice Scalia.

While she may have missed an opportunity to maximize the metaphor's reach by including it in her oral dissent, it seems that those who have gotten wind of her written points have gravitated toward this language.

While demosprudence is more concerned with practices and potential than it is with results, there are several reasons that the circumstances surrounding *Shelby County* present formidable challenges to repeating the successes of Justice Ginsburg's oral dissent in *Ledbetter*. In 2007, when *Ledbetter* was decided, the political environment was far more conducive to getting reform passed. Democrats controlled a majority of both chambers of Congress. The timing of the push for reform also coincided with the 2008 Democratic National Convention, and the resulting legislation landed on President Obama's desk during the first month of his presidential honeymoon. In short, the *Ledbetter* case presents a pitch-perfect example of a demosprudential dissent, of the Court enhancing its democratic legitimacy by engaging actors in a dialogue that heightens public engagement and accountability.

In *Ledbetter*, the nature of the "fix" was also different. The case turned on a narrow interpretive issue, where, as Justice Ginsburg explained in an interview, "it was very easy to fix the law, to make clear that Title VII meant what Lilly Ledbetter said it meant all along.... It's quite different from the Voting Rights Act. The Chief's opinion for the majority was that Congress got it wrong when it renewed the Act and thinking that it could renew it without changing the coverage formula."[84] She didn't have to say "I told you so" when asked about news that Texas and North Carolina would introduce strict voter identification laws that had previously been blocked by preclearance. She simply pointed, once more, to her umbrella metaphor: "We put down the umbrella because we weren't getting wet. But the storm is raging."[85]

The current situation is far more dire. The contemporary polarization in politics is considerable, and virtually every major piece of legislation is subject to congressional gridlock. Republicans also are likely to feel significant political pressure not to support a new coverage formula, pressure that may have cut in favor of previous reauthorizations given the act's revered status and popular support. The *Shelby County* majority was no doubt aware of such circumstances, yet it disingenuously spoke as if it "left room" for Congress to act.[86] Justice Ginsburg knew the truth. In a recent interview, she was not optimistic: "Will Congress rise above partisan strife to amend the act? I wish I could predict yes. But it is not likely given the inability in the House to take bipartisan action."[87] When asked on another occasion about the legislature's potential response, she lamented that it may not be "equipped to do anything about it."[88]

Nevertheless, significant reform efforts have been under way. A new bill, the Voting Rights Amendment Act of 2014, has been introduced in both chambers of Congress, seeking to meet the majority's task of implementing a preclearance formula that reflects current conditions.[89] The bill, despite acknowledged imperfections, has received support from many major civil rights groups and grassroots organizations.[90] Hank Sanders, a Harvard Law School graduate and an Alabama state senator for more than thirty years, continues to push for voting rights despite the Supreme Court's latest blow.[91] Senator Sanders notes that Justice Ginsburg's dissents have been "as clear and convincing as [those of] any Supreme Court justice that I can recall."[92] Believing in the central role Alabama plays in the history of voter discrimination and thus in its reform, Senator Sanders co-founded Save Ourselves Movement for Truth and Justice, a network of grassroots organizations dedicated to restoring voting rights after *Shelby County*.[93] At the time of this writing, Save Ourselves had embarked on "Marching to the 50th," a campaign kicked off by the Annual Bridge Crossing Jubilee in Selma – itself a major civil rights organizing occasion – and continuing with events in every state that was wholly subject to preclearance. The goals of the campaign are to restore the full strength of voter protections and register one million new voters by 2015, the fiftieth anniversary of the 1965 Selma-to-Montgomery marches and the subsequent passage of the Voting Rights Act. These are ambitious goals. Yet Senator Sanders draws inspiration from Justice Ginsburg: "she let us know that all of us are given the responsibility to fight in each of our arenas in any way we can."[94]

Justice Ginsburg herself, despite apprehensions, has made attempts to engage the broader citizenry in the reform dialogue. She gave a series of interviews following this past Supreme Court term[95] and has visited law schools[96] and bar associations around the country.[97] At a luncheon held at the Union League Club of Chicago, Justice Ginsburg addressed a number of recent cases, focusing on *Shelby County*, and even read from portions of her dissent. One attendee, a lawyer and member of the Illinois Bar's Standing Committee on Racial and Ethnic Minorities and the Law, was moved by her passion and recommended that the Bar further "explore the topic of voting rights law and the *Shelby* opinion.... It is a topic of undisputed importance as evidenced by the recent speech of one of the justices of the highest court in the land."[98]

Although the reform landscape still trembles from the shock of *Shelby County*, Justice Ginsburg has reached more people than she might have originally expected. Through her effective use of both oral and written dissents, Justice

Ginsburg has developed the architecture of demosprudence in today's Court. Her oral dissents in *Ledbetter* and *Shelby County* are shining examples of how judges (and other legal actors) can affirm the power and legitimacy of the demos, simply by speaking to it and with it. Such a contribution – as with the legacy of Ginsburg herself – will penetrate through the ages, enhancing our democracy in ways we may never fully appreciate.

15

Oral Argument as a Bridge between the Briefs and the Court's Opinion

Tom Goldstein

A Supreme Court oral argument is an odd beast. Unlike at many other courts, in which oral argument represents the one time in which overworked judges can really focus on the issue, facts, and arguments of the parties, oral argument at the Supreme Court is not particularly important to the case's outcome. The reasons are many. The Supreme Court's docket is small – around eighty cases heard a year – allowing the justices the luxury of being able to focus deeply on each case. Each justice has four clerks, often among the brightest legal minds of their ages, to assist. The Court tends to restrict the issues presented to those that, in the main, involve broad legal principles rather than intricate factual disputes that tend to get cumbersome in briefs.

By the time issues reach the Supreme Court, they have been through two rounds of judicial decision, helping clarify and crystallize the issue. And, at the Supreme Court, the issues get not one but two rounds of briefing (one at the cert stage and one at the merits stage), plus a plethora of amicus filings, all written by an increasingly specialized Supreme Court bar.

Finally, because the justices vote on a case within one or two days after the oral argument (for Monday and Tuesday arguments, the vote occurs on Wednesday; for Wednesday arguments, the vote occurs on Friday), the justices tend to be prepared for the vote before argument. The end result of all this is that by the time the case reaches oral argument, the justices have had the best preparation possible, and they have devoted significant and deep thought to the issue. Oral argument rarely changes which side wins or loses.

Yet the crossfire of questions from the justices can be notoriously intense in a quasi-public setting, a rare display from an otherwise quite secretive court. If oral argument rarely changes the outcome, why such spectacle and effort? I hope to explore this question, with particular attention to one of the best questioners on the Court, Justice Ginsburg.

Any effort to describe how justices approach oral argument inevitably requires invoking illustrations and anecdotes. I am fortunate to have argued more than thirty cases before the Court. Not surprisingly, I'm most familiar with those cases, and so I draw upon that experience here. In my experience, there are three main models for how justices ask questions at oral argument, each defined primarily by its motivation.

The first type of question is used as an opportunity to articulate a justice's views of the case in an attempt to persuade the other members of the Court. This is a product of the Court's unusual procedures. Each of the nine chambers functions as essentially its own law firm. Although each justice extensively discusses a case within her own chambers, it is rare for the justices to talk among themselves prior to oral argument. So the oral argument presents the first chance for the justices to persuade each other about how the case should be decided.

Although the likelihood of persuasion is low, oral argument may be the only chance. When justices vote on the case during their private conference, they speak in order of seniority. The chief justice introduces the case and announces his vote. Then the next most senior justice – currently, Justice Scalia – adds any further points he believes are relevant and votes. And so on down the line. By the time the most junior justices speak, the die in the case has been cast. (While a justice is free to change her vote any time before the opinion is released, that happens rarely.)

Not surprisingly, the more junior justices are among the most likely to use the oral argument to highlight important points for their colleagues. Consider a close, ideologically divisive case from the perspective of Justices Alito, Sotomayor, and Kagan. Each recognizes the importance of the vote of their more senior colleague, Justice Kennedy, who is generally the Court's ideological center. By the time each of them says anything in the Court's private conference, Kennedy will have explained his views and already voted. It will be too late.

Justice Ginsburg asks few of these questions. Having served on the Court for more than two decades, Justice Ginsburg seems to have concluded that the oral argument is unlikely to change a case's outcome. As a relatively senior justice, it is also less essential that she regularly use the argument as an opportunity to call her colleagues' attention to a particular issue in the case.

A second type of question is posed to the side the justice is leaning toward voting against. A justice might pose these questions aggressively, relentlessly questioning the side with which she disagrees, sometimes with an audible edge of disbelief in her voice. This mode of interrogation goes far beyond highlighting a single issue. The justice may simply be incredulous, or may hope that it will become apparent that the litigant's position is insupportable. Most of the justices take this approach occasionally on a question about which they are passionate or with an advocate who has proved particularly frustrating. In her earliest time on the Court, though much less so now, Justice Sotomayor was regularly aggressive in her questions in cases raising issues with which she had particular experience or of which she cared greatly about the outcome.

A justice may pose a less aggressive question to the side against whom she intends to vote as a way to test the justice's own views in the case and give the side she plans to vote against a chance to respond. The goal here is to shore up the justice's strong sense – based on the briefs – of how the case should come out by seeing whether the justice has missed something important, or potentially whether the lawyer has thought up an important answer after submitting the briefing. Justice Breyer, for example, uses this approach most clearly, laying out the key arguments of the side he thinks should prevail. He will say to the other lawyer something like this: "Your opponent makes three points, which are that ... I want to make sure you have the chance to respond. Why do you say they are not right?" Justice Kennedy has a similar approach, but he will generally focus on the one point he thinks is most important. And until he gets an answer to that question, he will return to it.

Justice Ginsburg tends to use this milder manner of question. An unusually high proportion of Justice Ginsburg's questions are friendly. They give the lawyer an open-ended opportunity to respond. She rarely asks a hypothetical that tests the boundary of a party's rule and requires a yes or no answer. Instead, she tends to focus her questions on the scope of the parties' proposed rules and the practical consequences of the case. For example, in a case involving whether the petitioner would be deported for a minor drug offense, she asked counsel for the government what results would follow from a holding that marijuana offenses did not trigger deportation. The Court's opinion explained that the government's claim that its immigration authority would be significantly curtailed was seriously overstated.[1] Still, Justice Ginsburg knows how to ask an aggressive question when she cares deeply about an issue, and she tends to do so in a way that gets right to the point. For example, in a case involving the application of the Americans with Disabilities Act to foreign-flagged cruise ships, she asked the defendant's counsel about whether it was subject to other civil rights protections – such as prohibitions on race discrimination.[2] And in a case involving the Age Discrimination in Employment Act, she repeatedly pushed back at arguments that would have the consequence of narrowing the parallel language in the seminal employment-discrimination provisions of Title VII.[3]

Although no concrete data exist, most justices tend to use this type of question, testing the side against whom the justice is leaning. Justice Ginsburg, however, is more balanced than most of her colleagues. My review of the thirty-one cases I have argued before her since 1988 reveals that in eleven, she asked each side roughly the same number of questions (the number was either the same or off by only one). In twelve, she asked more questions of the side she eventually voted against; in eight, she did the reverse. This highly unusual balance suggests that Justice Ginsburg deploys the other types of questions more regularly than do her colleagues. That strikes me as the mark of a particularly skillful questioner.

Justice Ginsburg's balance leads to the third model, which is the most valuable to the Court as a whole and which appears to most reflect Justice Ginsburg's distinctive approach to oral argument. In my experience, for Justice Ginsburg, the argument seems to play the role of a bridge between the period in which the Court reaches its likely conclusions based on the briefing and the point at which it prepares the opinion with its reasoning. Most of her questions serve the institutional role of raising issues that will help the opinion's eventual author craft the ruling. In other words, her questions often strive to persuade her colleagues not necessarily on the ultimate outcome but rather on how the opinion gets shaped.

For example, Justice Ginsburg often shows concern with how the Court will craft an opinion by asking about how the case relates to prior precedent. In a case involving whether the plaintiffs could file suit where they lived rather than where they had been injured, she repeatedly asked how that broad theory of jurisdiction could be reconciled with prior decisions holding that a foreign defendant can be sued only in states in which it has purposefully availed itself. She then wrote the opinion finding that jurisdiction was lacking, citing those precedents.[4] By contrast, in a case involving whether strip-searches of arrestees violate the Fourth Amendment, she asked several questions about the precedent cited by the government but ultimately voted in favor of holding that the search was unconstitutional.[5]

Justice Ginsburg also will identify cases that she thinks could be decided on narrower grounds than the parties propose. In a case presenting the issue of whether courts must defer to agency interpretations of vague jurisdictional statutes, she questioned whether the case could be decided by simply concluding that the underlying statute was not actually vague at all. The Court ultimately did not take that narrower approach to resolving the case. But it presented an important possibility that had to be addressed.[6]

A specific application of questions that have the Court's opinion in mind are those that seek to resolve an uncertainty about an important fact or a party's position. These questions are relatively rare because the briefs generally clarify the issues sufficiently by the time of the argument. Nevertheless, the occasions in which such questions are needed are extremely important.

When there is some ambiguity in a party's position – and thus some uncertainty about the argument the Court must confront in its opinion – Justice Ginsburg is the most likely to raise it. For example, in the strip-search case, she asked repeatedly what types of offenses would give rise to a basis to conduct such a search. The answer to that question was essential to the Court's effort to set forth a rule that prisons could apply in practice.

Justice Ginsburg also takes special care with the record, more so than most of her colleagues. She is the justice most likely to focus on a particular fact that can be important to the outcome. For example, in the immigration case, she asked what the record showed about the drugs. No doubt, she already knew that it demonstrated that the petitioner had possessed a trivially small amount of marijuana. But it was the one fact that most persuasively illustrated the unnecessary harshness of the government's position.[7]

Other times, the record may be unclear. Thus in a case involving whether the First Amendment prohibits the government from restricting the use of pharmacy records for solicitation, she asked both parties whether the government permitted the same records to be used for other purposes. It did. The Court's eventual opinion relied on those other uses to show that the government was unconstitutionally discriminating against the use of the records for commercial speech.[8]

Justice Ginsburg is also quick to note when she is concerned that an attorney is overstating or misstating the record. In a death penalty case, she noted that contrary to the government's suggestion at argument, the prosecutor at trial had claimed to the jury that the defendant was a drug dealer.[9]

As this brief analysis suggests, Justice Ginsburg employs a variety of types of questions in ways that make oral argument enormously helpful for the Court as a whole. But of equal import is her demeanor. She is unfailingly kind. Even in the rare case that she has the daggers out for a party, her tone is always measured and she begins with the polite honorific to the lawyer "Mr." or "Ms." Her tiny size and quiet voice – combined with the bad acoustics of the courtroom – can mislead visitors to argument into underestimating the justice. It is not a mistake that the advocates make.

16

Fire and Ice: Ruth Bader Ginsburg, the Least Likely Firebrand

Dahlia Lithwick

Ruth Bader Ginsburg is so frequently referred to as the "Thurgood Marshall of Women's Rights" that it's nearly become a legal cliché. And in some sense the comparison is perfectly appropriate: as head and founder of the ACLU's Women's Rights Project, Ginsburg devised and oversaw a brilliant and subtle litigation strategy that achieved – in just a few short years – extraordinary outcomes for women's equality under the law. Unsurprisingly, she modeled much of the legal work and analysis on the blueprint laid out by Marshall in his tenure at the National Association for the Advancement of Colored People (NAACP). But visitors to oral argument at the Supreme Court – particularly those who grew up with a mental picture of Ginsburg as a kind of supercharged cross between Thurgood Marshall and Gloria Steinem – often remark that the soft-spoken, mild-mannered Ginsburg is nothing like the feminist firebrand they were expecting.

There's something about her early advocacy work with the ACLU, and the inevitable comparisons to Marshall, that leads us to imagine Ginsburg as an outspoken '70s era, bra-burning women's libber. We might imagine a Justice Ginsburg who regales her judicial colleagues, as Marshall used to, with lengthy discursions about the injustices of her life back in the bad old pre-equality days, and one who pens searing opinions that channeled Susan B. Anthony. Yet the public encounters with the diminutive, soft-spoken Ginsburg are hard to reconcile with that image. Even when she was an ACLU litigator, Ginsburg was quiet and scholarly, even if the injustices she worked to correct were deeply felt and personally resonant. And that is why the truth about Ginsburg is far more compelling: the realities of her early life, the nature of her legal project, and her own precise, understated temperament have combined to make her appear more Ninja Librarian than Raging Gender Warrior. Ginsburg is indeed a feminist firebrand, but she is, both by choice and necessity, a firebrand made of ice.

Ginsburg's early life reveals the extent to which she – despite her early promise of academic brilliance and unlimited ambition – was forced to adopt a dual role from a young age. In his 2009 book, *Equal: Women Reshape American Law*, Fred Strebeigh describes a young Ginsburg at Cornell who was "scary smart" yet found it necessary to hide her grinding work ethic by studying in campus bathrooms.[1] Ginsburg spent a remarkable amount of time trying to "pass" as an ordinary girl of the 1950s and '60s. In 2014, we can squint back at history and nearly forget that she was one of only nine women in her class of 500 at Harvard. She felt the necessity to conceal her true reasons for attending Harvard Law School when questioned by then-dean Erwin Griswold about why she was taking a slot that should go to a man. (She told him she wanted to be able to understand the work of her husband – who was a year ahead of her at the Law School.)[2] Ginsburg felt the need to hide her own pregnancy in her first years teaching at Rutgers law school.

Ruth Bader Ginsburg was not a product of the women's lib movement she went on to lead. For one thing, she was a lawyer, first and foremost, not a politician. Moreover, by the time she argued her first case at the U.S. Supreme Court, Ginsburg was nearly forty years old. Her law students were the openly fierce ones, forever "ready to rumble," and once staging a protest to demand that a women's bathroom be carved out of part of an existing men's room at Columbia.[3] But if her students were of the generation that "let it all hang out," Ginsburg was of the generation that held it all fiercely in. She was bookish, reserved, understated. One of her first students who came to work for her at the ACLU erroneously described Ginsburg as an "ice woman."[4] That is because women who grew up in the '50s were usually ice women by necessity.

Unlike Marshall, what drew Ginsburg to a life in the law, and to law school itself, was not a pervasive experience of gender discrimination. For much of her early life, she took gender bias as a given. Injustice struck her in another manner. Ginsburg came of age during the red scare of the 1950s, and what drove her to the study of law was the career-wrecking bravery of people in the entertainment industry and unions, who were willing to stand up to Joseph McCarthy. As she explained in an interview conducted in 2011, "There were brave lawyers who were standing up for those people, and reminding our Senate, 'Look at the Constitution, look at the very First Amendment. What does it say? It says we prize, above all else, the right to think, to speak, to write, as we will, without Big Brother over our shoulders' and my notion was, if lawyers can be helping us get back in touch with our most basic values, that's what I want to be."[5] In short, Ginsburg arrived at the legal epicenter of the gender-rights revolution in a perfectly sideways fashion. She came to law school hoping to emulate the brave lawyers of the McCarthy era, she became a specialist in civil procedure, and she taught women's law for the most benign reasons: her students asked her to teach a class and she became interested.

Unlike Thurgood Marshall, who used his legendary powers as a raconteur to help others understand what it would have been like to grow up in the Jim Crow South, Ginsburg tended to keep her stories of second-class gender treatment to herself. Not inclined to share the tales of her own rejections, slights, put-downs and lost opportunities,[6] Ginsburg fought to change what she saw as a fundamentally gender-biased legal apparatus, using the language of strict scrutiny, compelling interest, and suspect classification. Her weapons were precedent, the strategic mind of a brigadier general and a mastery of facts. Even her pathbreaking legal approach – litigating principally cases on behalf of men who were victims of laws rooted in gender stereotypes – was nothing like Thurgood Marshall's more blatant plea for justice for African Americans. The utterly radical nature of Ginsburg's legal agenda was perennially masked in perfectly rational argument and analysis. Logic, not fireworks, was the reason she won five of six anti-discrimination cases she argued before the Supreme Court.

Ginsburg is also reserved by temperament. Marna Tucker, who served on President Jimmy Carter's nominating commission once said that when Ginsburg first got to Washington, she was deemed so reserved that if you were seated next to her at a dinner party, the way to make small talk with her was to "ask her about her children or the law."[7] Nor is Ginsburg a radical liberal jurist in any sense, regardless of her early stewardship of the ACLU's women's rights project. Texas senator John Cornyn asserted at John Roberts's confirmation hearings that Ginsburg had "supported taxpayer funding for abortion, constitutional right to prostitution and polygamy ... and she opposed Mother's and Father's Days as discriminatory occasions."[8] Yet the truth is that Ginsburg was never as far to the left as her critics liked to believe. A study by *Legal Times* of her voting patterns in her twelve years on the federal Court of Appeals for the District of Columbia shows her voting more often with her Republican colleagues than the Democrats: according to Ruth Marcus at the *Washington Post*: "In cases that divided the court, she joined most often with then-Judge Kenneth W. Starr and Reagan appointee Laurence H. Silberman; in split cases, she agreed 85 percent of the time with then-Judge Robert H. Bork – compared with just 38 percent of the time with her fellow Carter appointee, Patricia M. Wald."[9]

Nor did Ginsberg rest her early legal analysis in emotion or in appeals to social science. She advanced her legal theory like a supercomputer: with stripped-down analysis of the case law and doctrine. Her performance in her early days as an oral advocate was anything but passionate, fiery, or flamboyant. After she argued *Reed v. Reed*,[10] her first case at the U.S. Supreme Court,

Justice Harry L. Blackmun, known for awarding letter grades and comments to the oral advocates who appeared before him, wrote of Ginsburg: "C+. Very Precise Female."[11]

It was both perfectly accurate and also absurdly unperceptive. Precision and dispassionate logic were the most effective techniques Ginsburg had before the Court. The nine men she was attempting to persuade each believed themselves to be huge supporters of women. They cherished their wives and spoiled their daughters, after all. Some, like William J. Brennan, were even able to write lofty prose about women's equality while holding antiquated views about women in private.[12] Had Ginsburg run at the court in a frenzy of '70s-era feminist outrage, she would have terrified even the most liberal of the justices. As she herself put it, in a 2009 interview about working with men, "it will be welcomed much more if you have a gentle touch than if you are aggressive."[13] So she came at them like a Pentium chip. And it worked.

When Ginsburg was elevated to the high court in 1993, President Bill Clinton introduced her to the nation as "the Thurgood Marshall of gender equality law."[14] But what most court watchers actually saw in Ginsburg was in fact closer to a new John Paul Stevens. She was scholarly, even-tempered, and soft-spoken. She asked a lot of questions in her first years on the bench, but in both her opinion writing and demeanor, she remained level and understated. Even when she was absolutely maddened by court decisions with which she disagreed, she was careful to keep her tone cordial and collegial. Even when the court handed down the fractious and angry 5–4 decision in *Bush v. Gore*,[15] Ginsburg held her tongue. As her former clerk, Goodwin Liu, now a California Supreme Court justice, explained to the *New York Times* in 2007: "I was struck by how much of an institutional citizen she was, how attuned to the wishes of her colleagues and to not giving offense."[16] Ginsburg herself always offered the same advice about what to do when one encounters offensive ideas: "Don't react in anger…. Regard every encounter as an opportunity to teach someone."[17]

In part, Ginsburg was able to keep her inner feminist firebrand in check because for the first several years at the high court, she always had the luxury of being the second woman. She was – right from the outset – unburdened by the scenario she most resented: being the "lone woman" in any setting, when "every eye is on you."[18] Ginsburg may have chuckled at the fact that oral advocates routinely addressed her as Justice O'Connor, and vice versa[19] (in 1993, the National Association of Women Judges had T-shirts made for the two jurists that read, "I'm Sandra, not Ruth," and "I'm Ruth, not Sandra")[20] but she was always able to point to the fact that she and O'Connor had dramatically

different personal styles and legal philosophies as evidence that there was no
unitary women's viewpoint at the Court.

But that all changed in 2005, when O'Connor retired and left Ginsburg as
the lone woman at the high court. O'Connor, who never considered herself
an outspoken feminist, said that she was "very disappointed that the vacancy I
created was not filled by a woman."[21] And as time passed, Ginsburg appeared
to agree. Suddenly, in small and nearly imperceptible ways, Ginsburg began
to voice her frustrations, and she started to sound very different from the quiet,
collegial Ginsburg we thought we knew.

First, there were the dissents. The first came in the 2007 term, in the Court's
so-called partial-birth abortion case of *Gonzalez v. Carhart*, which upheld, for
the first time, an abortion restriction at least in part on the grounds that women
may come to regret their abortions in later years. The decision, authored by
Justice Anthony Kennedy, upheld the federal Partial-Birth Abortion Ban Act
just seven years after striking down a substantially similar state law; a shift
attributable chiefly to the departure of Sandra Day O'Connor from the court
and the arrival of Samuel Alito. Ginsburg was more than willing to pull aside
the curtain of judicial reserve and note in her dissent that the court was now
"differently composed than it was when we last considered a restrictive abortion regulation."[22] But the tone of her dissent also went far beyond what her
listeners were accustomed to. It opened with "Today's opinion is alarming."[23]
Salon's Rebecca Traister described it as "incandescent, shimmering with rage
and steely reason."[24] Ginsburg took the extra, highly uncharacteristic step of
reading it aloud from the bench. And in that dissent Ginsburg made no effort
to conceal her outrage at Kennedy's assumption that regret for one's abortion
justifies the court's intervention:

> The Court invokes an antiabortion shibboleth for which it concededly has no
> reliable evidence: Women who have abortions come to regret their choices,
> and consequently suffer from "[s]evere depression and loss of esteem."
> Because of women's fragile emotional state and because of the "bond of love
> the mother has for her child," the Court worries, doctors may withhold infor-
> mation about the nature of the intact D&E procedure. The solution the
> Court approves, then, is not to require doctors to inform women, accurately
> and adequately, of the different procedures and their attendant risks. Instead,
> the Court deprives women of the right to make an autonomous choice, even
> at the expense of their safety. This way of thinking reflects ancient notions
> about women's place in the family and under the Constitution – ideas that
> have long since been discredited.[25]

In a subsequent interview Ginsburg characterized Kennedy's opinion even
more tartly: "The poor little woman, to regret the choice that she made.

Unfortunately there is something of that in *Roe*. It's not about the women alone. It's the woman in consultation with her doctor. So the view you get is the tall doctor and the little woman who needs him."[26] It hardly warrants mentioning that Ginsburg, who at her bulkiest weighs 100 pounds, tends not to have a lot of patience for faux solicitude for any arguments involving "little women."

The other case that triggered a rather intense burst of feminist outrage in the usually sanguine Ginsburg came later that same term with the fair pay case of *Ledbetter v. Goodyear Tire & Rubber Co.* (2007), in which the Court held that pay discrimination claims could not be brought against employers more than 180 days after an alleged act of discrimination.[27] In the 5–4 ruling, penned by Justice Samuel Alito, the Court reversed a rule allowing victims of pay discrimination to sue for as long as they continued to receive discriminatory paychecks. Lilly Ledbetter had worked at Goodyear Tire for almost twenty years but had no evidence that she was being paid less than her male co-workers for much of that time. When she finally realized what had happened and filed suit, she prevailed in the trial court, but the suit was tossed out by the Supreme Court because she had not challenged each paycheck's discrimination within a 180-day period. Ginsburg's reaction was one of absolute wonderment: her male colleagues seemed to have no idea whatsoever about how pay discrimination actually happened in the real world; they seemingly had no notion at all of the ways salaries may remain unknown to workers and how pay disparities aggregate over time. The Court, Ginsburg said, as she announced her dissent, "does not comprehend, or is indifferent to, the insidious way in which women can be victims of pay discrimination. Today's decision counsels: Sue early on, when it is uncertain whether discrimination accounts for the pay disparity you are beginning to experience."[28] Her language (again) suggested that her male colleagues have absolutely no inkling of how women – nearly all women in her view – experience pay discrimination. Most important, Justice Ginsburg expressly called upon Congress to correct the Court's decision.[29] It did.[30]

This change in tone did not go undetected by feminists who had been waiting to hear echoes of Ginsburg's early ACLU activism at the Supreme Court. Indeed, 2007 became the year, according to veteran Supreme Court correspondent Linda Greenhouse, "when Justice Ruth Bader Ginsburg found her voice, and used it."[31] Cynthia Fuchs Epstein, a sociologist and a longtime friend of Ginsburg's, described the transition in this way: "Her style has always been very ameliorative, very conscious of etiquette.... She has always been regarded as sort of a white-glove person, and she's achieved a lot that way. Now she is seeing that basic issues she's fought so hard for are in jeopardy, and she

is less bound by what have been the conventions of the court."[32] USA *Today*'s
Joan Biskupic characterized the change in Ginsburg's tone in a similar vein:
"In 2006, oral arguments and the justices' behind-the-scenes discussions on
how disputes should be resolved have had a different tone. In the strip-search
case and others this term, Ginsburg has revealed a woman's point of view that
was strikingly at odds with those of many of her colleagues."[33]

In my view, the sea change came with a relatively inconsequential case
about student privacy that made its way to the Supreme Court in April of 2009.
Thirteen-year-old Savana Redding was an honor student at Safford Middle
School, just outside Tucson, Arizona. She had been strip-searched by school
administrators looking for hidden prescription-strength ibuprofen, based on
a tip from a classmate that the child was selling drugs. So with no call to her
mother, two female staff members made Savana strip down to her bra and
underwear, then shake them out to prove she wasn't hiding any contraband
headache medicine. In an affidavit, Redding stated: "The strip search was the
most humiliating experience I have ever had. I held my head down so that
they could not see that I was about to cry." A federal appeals court found that
the strip-search was both "traumatizing" and unconstitutional.[34] The Supreme
Court granted cert.

Something about the facts of the Redding case led the justices to conduct
oral argument that April morning with less than the usual level of decorum.
Justice Antonin Scalia and Chief Justice John Roberts quizzed counsel over
whether it was constitutionally better to search inside or outside a student's
underwear first. Scalia suggested that once you've searched everywhere else,
"by God, the drugs must be in her underpants." Then Justice Stephen Breyer
began to muse aloud whether the search of Savana Redding was terribly different from a policy having her "change into a swimming suit or your gym
clothes," because, as he explained "I'm trying to work out why this is a major
thing to say, strip down to your underclothes, which children do when they
change for gym?"[35]

Justice Ginsburg was becoming visibly annoyed that her colleagues were
treating the search of a teenage girl as something midway between an inconvenience and a punch line. She broke in angrily to insist that this was nothing
at all like changing for gym class, pointing out that "what was done in the case
… it wasn't just that they were stripped to their underwear. They were asked
to shake their bra out, to – to shake, stretch the top of their pants and shake
that out."[36] Ginsburg honestly couldn't believe her colleagues thought this
was trivial.

But Breyer, undeterred, mused aloud: "In my experience when I was 8 or 10
or 12 years old, you know, we *did* take our clothes off once a day, we changed

for gym, OK? And in my experience, too, people did sometimes stick things in my underwear." The whole courtroom cracked up. "Or not *my* underwear," Breyer tried to clarify, to the mounting giggles of the spectators. "Whatever. Whatever. I was the one who did it? I don't know. I mean, I don't think it's beyond human experience."[37]

One surprising aspect of the *Redding* argument was the extent to which the normally reserved press corps explicitly worked these facts in their reports to show Ginsburg's isolation that day. As Nina Totenberg, National Public Radio's veteran court correspondent put it in her report of the *Redding* arguments that same evening, "Ginsburg seemed to all but shout, boys may like to preen in the locker room, but girls, particularly teenage girls, do not."[38] Ginsburg herself was unwilling to allow the issue to go unaired, or to let the decision play out privately in conferences and draft opinions. So while the *Redding* decision was still pending, she gave an unprecedented interview to another female journalist, Joan Biskupic, at *USA Today*, saying of her colleagues, "They have never been a 13-year-old girl.... It's a very sensitive age for a girl. I didn't think that my colleagues, some of them, quite understood." And then she added, "The differences between male and female justices are ... seldom in the outcome." Pause. Then quixotically: "It is sometimes in the outcome."[39]

In the same interview, Ginsburg also said in the strongest terms that the court needed a second woman. She explained that it wasn't simply that she sometimes felt marginalized as the lone woman on the bench, but also because the image of a lone woman on the high court would confuse and undermine young people visiting the court. "Young women are going to think," she explained, "Can I really aspire to that kind of post?"[40] She added that Sandra Day O'Connor would have likely sided with her in the Lilly Ledbetter case and another case from that term regarding workplace discrimination toward pregnant employees: "As often as Justice O'Connor and I have disagreed," she said, "because she is truly a Republican from Arizona, we were together in all the gender discrimination cases.... I have no doubt that she would have understood Lilly Ledbetter's situation."[41] And while she claims to agree with Justice O'Connor's longtime posture that a wise old man and a wise old woman tend to arrive at the same legal conclusions, Ginsburg was ever becoming more inclined to say things like this of wise old women: "Maybe there's a little more empathy.... Anybody who has been discriminated against, who comes from a group that's been discriminated against, knows what it's like."[42]

Just two weeks after the *Redding* interview with Biskupic, President Barack Obama announced his nomination of Judge Sonia Sotomayor to fill the vacancy created when Justice David Souter stepped down. And when the court handed down *Safford v. Redding* shortly thereafter, the search was deemed unconstitutional by an 8–1 vote, and nobody was laughing anymore.

It was almost as though something had finally snapped in the sole female justice. As if she had grown tired of laughing along with the guys after a lifetime of ignoring the laughter, and even, sometimes, feeling forced to laugh along, as she had once done with Dean Griswold at Harvard. As Ginsburg described it in an interview later that summer, her male colleagues had failed utterly to imagine the world from the vantage point of a thirteen-year-old high school girl: "I think many of [the male justices] first thought of their own reaction. It came out in various questions. You change your clothes in the gym, what's the big deal?"[43] One had the sense, almost, that Ginsburg had choked down the vocal outrage in the 1970s, but she just couldn't quite bring herself to do it again in the new millennium. Or as Goodwin Liu, her former law clerk, who now sits on the California Supreme Court put it to the *New York Times*, "Here she is, the one woman of a nine-member body, describing the get-along imperative and the desire not to make waves felt by the one woman among 16 men.... It's as if after 15 years on the court, she's finally voicing some complaints of her own."[44]

And Ginsburg, who had been unfailingly collegial about the men who shared the bench with her, began to openly reminisce about earlier experiences in her lifetime, moments in which she had felt marginalized or belittled. Remarkably, she began to talk about some of these episodes, in some cases complaining for the first time about events that had occurred decades earlier. So, for example, she explained Joan Biskupic in May 2009 that without Justice O'Connor present at case conferences, she felt like the court had reverted to a sort of Mad Men era of discourse: "I don't know how many meetings I attended in the '60s and '70s where I would say something," she explained, "and I thought it was a pretty good idea. Then somebody else would say exactly what I said. Then people would become alert to it and respond to it." Ginsburg reported a similar phenomenon during conferences on the Court – a phenomenon she had not experienced as dramatically with the more senior, more conservative Justice O'Connor as an ally. There were times, Ginsburg said, "when I will say something – and I don't think I'm a confused speaker – and it isn't until somebody else says it that everyone will focus on the point."[45]

It seemed that Ginsburg wasn't just finding a strong feminist voice in order to correct for existing injustices. She was also finding the way to speak about the slights and slurs she had been unwilling to discuss publicly as a younger lawyer. She openly expressed the view that she and O'Connor shared "certain sensitivities that our male colleagues lack." She started to talk about the years in which she had been talking, and nobody really listened.

In important ways, Ginsburg remained her usual grim, stoic self, even as she began to write the way ACLU lawyers dream of. She was, for instance, back on the bench, and in fighting form, a mere eighteen days after undergoing major surgery for pancreatic cancer in 2009.[46] The following day, she attended a joint session of Congress purely because, as she said, "I wanted people to see that the Supreme Court isn't all male."[47] Ginsburg would, a year later, also be back on the bench to read a dissent less than twenty-four hours after the death of her husband.[48] And yet again in the 2010 term, Ginsburg penned another sizzling dissent in yet another discrimination case, this time, involving gender-discrimination claims by a massive class of female Wal-Mart employees who alleged that they were passed over for promotions, mistreated by male managers, underpaid, and systematically disadvantaged because of their sex. The plaintiffs described harrowing gender stereotyping and discrimination in the workplace and attempted to remedy this pattern as a class. But in another familiar pattern, the high court in 2011 voted 5–4 that the women of Wal-Mart could not bring this suit as a class action.[49] And in an increasingly familiar pattern Ginsburg's dissent called them out for legal eloquence masking real-world cluelessness: "Managers, like all humankind, may be prey to biases of which they are unaware," she wrote. "The risk of discrimination is heightened when those managers are pre-dominantly of one sex, and are steeped in a corporate culture that perpetuates gender stereotypes."[50]

It's hard to identify precisely what changed for Ginsburg in the years after O'Connor's retirement, when, for a time, she became the lone voice of Everywoman at the high court. And even as she has been joined by Sonia Sotomayor and Elena Kagan, she has remained the fiercest defender of the lines she drew in the sand as a litigator decades ago. In part, she seems unwilling to give up ground that was so hard fought in the '70s. In part she seems ever more incredulous that we continue to fight the battles of the '60s and '70s, and perhaps also incredulous at a generation of young women who don't recall that the battle was fought at all. But, more profoundly, Ginsburg seems disinclined to sit back and be polite when her colleagues diminish or disregard the real experiences of women, experiences she herself had, and sometimes even played down, in her own life. "Every working woman of my generation had an experience comparable to Lilly Ledbetter, or the women of Wal-Mart," Ginsburg told me in an interview in 2012. "Ask a man about Lilly Ledbetter's experience, and he may comprehend it, but he may not have firsthand experience."[51] Increasingly, she sees it as her responsibility to hold these experiences up to the light, so that her male colleagues can understand something that requires little explanation if you have ever been employed while female in the United States of America: that unfairness persists; that it is pervasive. And that she doesn't want to talk about it in polite whispers anymore.

Ginsburg has spent a lifetime positioned midway between genteel intellectualism and daily acts of sexism. She has made a career of marrying the two, and she did so in a way that was far more effective, given the era, than acting out at the extremes. She is, and has always been, trained to two very different roles. "My mother told me two things constantly," she told a group of Duke Law School students in 2005. "One was to be a lady and the other was to be independent."[52] She has managed to make a substantial and indeed historic contribution to American legal history by doing both. And for anyone who wishes for the more radical, inflammatory, civil rights version of Ruth Bader Ginsburg at the Court, my suggestion is just this: she's already there. You just need to listen more closely.

Ginsburg, Optimism, and Conflict Management

Scott Dodson

As editor of this volume, I find myself in the enviable position of now possessing a wealth of perspectives on Ruth Bader Ginsburg. I hope to use that position to offer a very brief synthesis of the insights from these chapters and to pose some concluding reflections.

Ginsburg has always been difficult to quantify, and she herself has eschewed ideological labels. In perhaps the most revealing self-identification of judicial philosophy, Ginsburg once wrote that she strives to emulate "independent-thinking individuals with open, but not drafty, minds, individuals willing to listen and, throughout their days, to learn."[1]

We should listen to her. The contributors to this book underscore her own assessment. Nina Totenberg emphasizes the importance of Ginsburg's personal relationships – with her mother, her mother-in-law, her husband, and her colleagues – and the ways she has been touched by everyday life: school, marriage, career, pregnancy, family, friends, cancer, and death. Herma Hill Kay shows Professor Ginsburg's influence on Justice Ginsburg and her success integrating academia, advocacy, and judging. Linda K. Kerber both microscopes and telescopes *Reed v. Reed*, illustrating how Ginsburg's advocacy for gender equality in the 1970s affected the specific individuals involved in that case and the larger social movement toward greater women's rights. Complementing Kerber, Neil S. Siegel and Reva B. Siegel take a juridical approach to *Struck v. Secretary of Defense*, connecting Ginsburg's advocacy to the development of her gender-equality jurisprudence and her rejection of the separate-spheres social construct. And, in yet a third view of Ginsburg the advocate, Joan C. Williams unearths Ginsburg's representation of men during her advocacy for gender equality and picks up that mantle to argue for a provocative next step in eradicating gender discrimination in the workplace: focusing on men.

Part I of the book thus reveals a coherent foundation upon which Ruth Bader Ginsburg is built. She is an understated but committed intellectual who saw, firsthand, both the harms of socialized inequality and the benefit the law can work to rectify those harms. During these years, she honed a professor's and advocate's tools of deep research, sensitivity to the law's real-world impact, clear and reasoned argument, and goal-oriented strategy. To get there, she drew on her own experiences, she highlighted social effects, she blazed new paths when necessary, and she used the power of forceful argument.

The following two sets of chapters build upon that foundation by framing Ginsburg's jurisprudence in a number of doctrinal areas. The first set focuses on rights and remedies. Stephen B. Cohen bridges the gap by introducing *Judge* Ginsburg, on the D.C. Circuit, where she wrote one of her first opinions articulating her commitment to effective school desegregation. Cary Franklin then flips that coin, weaving Ginsburg's best-known case, *VMI*, into a jurisprudential narrative that links her gender-equality principles to the legacy of *Brown v. Board of Education*, with implications for the modern affirmative-action cases in school admissions. Lisa Kern Griffin then applies this Fourteenth Amendment jurisprudence to Ginsburg's criminal justice cases, finding the latter indicative of a measured, fact-intensive approach that favors due process rights of fairness, dignity, and equality over substantive rights and results. Aziz Z. Huq helps explain that criminal justice account by positioning Ginsburg's opinions within the confines and pathologies of a rigid justice system that leaves little room for ideological decision making.

The second set of doctrinal chapters focuses on structure. I see Ginsburg's approach to subject-matter jurisdiction as an attempt to inject pragmatism, caution, and mindfulness into the doctrine, with special sensitivity to the cost pressures on private litigants. Paul Schiff Berman details the way Ginsburg accommodates interjurisdictional conflicts, arguing that she strives to create space for different sovereigns to engage and debate with each other. And Deborah Jones Merritt echoes that accommodationist approach in core cases involving federalism and congressional power.

Parts II and III thus illuminate Justice Ginsburg's jurisprudence in key doctrinal areas. They show her drawing from her earlier experiences to employ different strategies for enhancing equality: playing a more aggressive, leadership role in developing the law of gender and race discrimination while influencing the procedural protections of the criminal justice doctrine in more modest and subtle – perhaps the only achievable – ways. Her structure-based opinions reflect a jurist dedicated to anti-formalist appreciation of the systemic consequences of jurisdictional boundaries and to efforts to facilitate intersystem and intrasystem dialogue and cooperation.

The final chapters reflect upon Justice Ginsburg outside her legal opinions. Judge Katzmann reflects on her poise and appeal during that most politically sensitive of appointment processes: a Supreme Court confirmation. Lani Guinier views her as oral dissenter, using the power of the spoken word (no matter how dimunitive the body from which it issues) to reach a wider audience, thereby extending the influence of her views beyond written opinions. Tom Goldstein sets out a typology of oral-argument questioning and characterizes Justice Ginsburg's questions as those that most help influence the way a majority opinion is written, even if she is in dissent. And finally, Dahlia Lithwick brings her story full circle, reflecting upon Ginsburg's passion in various stages of her life and demonstrating that that passion, though deceptively quiet, is alive and well.

Part IV thus completes the picture of Ruth Bader Ginsburg. These chapters document her judicial temperament – which is perhaps best described oxymoronically: passionate but dispassionate. The fire is there, but it is delivered not through fanfare or aggression but through the prism of reason, perspective, and clear-sightedness, and always with savvy. These chapters, too, show Justice Ginsburg employing various strategies for navigating her way forward and for pushing her vision.

As a whole, these diverse chapters confirm that Ginsburg is a product of listening and learning from her own history. Growing up a Jewish woman in an age that privileged Christian men, she listened with skepticism to the majoritarian, separate-spheres justifications for that era's social structures. She saw and heard the real impact of social inequality. Yet she also appreciated the unflagging ability of society to change, to evolve for the better. In many ways, the jurisprudence that developed is one of optimism – of the essential belief that the law can lead to a better life. The law is not an end of itself but a means of enabling a progressive society to flourish. There are limits, to be sure. Ginsburg well understands the constraints of the law, and she respects the limited role of the judicial branch. But, ultimately, she seems to believe that judges can and should strive to make the legal system a positive agent for good. And even when she is on the dissenting side of an opinion, she does not give up but rather uses oral argument to help shape the Court's opinions and, as a last resort, uses her own pen to project optimism that her view will one day prevail.

Yet Ginsburg is no ivory-tower optimist. She uses her considerable skills, honed over the years, to make that optimism a reality. One of those skills is an astute sense of conflict management. Law is conflict. So is life. But not all conflict is the same. Some conflict is productive and should be cultivated. The ability of the law to create space for and give voice to various law-speaking institutions has the potential to turn conflict into healthy conversation – and even beneficial cooperation – while at the same time highlighting the humility of each institution. Just as the law-school classroom is not a one-way lecture hall but a multivocal learning experience, so too do opportunities for institutional actors to engage with each other and with private interests enliven and enhance the law. Perhaps this is one reason Ginsburg has criticized *Roe v. Wade* for reaching too far; the decision shut down healthy (and progressing) debate, ultimately backfiring by giving abortion opponents an enduring target. Congress, the courts, the states, the parties, and even society at large all have a role to play in the articulation and development of legal norms, and those norms will develop best if all are able to speak and to listen to each other.

At the same time, other conflicts are harmful and demand resistance. Social conflict, arising from social inequality, should be resolved rather than fomented. Ginsburg's assertive gender-equality jurisprudence has helped level the playing field for all citizens: men, women, black, white, gay, straight. She has not hesitated to use the power of the pulpit – through opinions, dissents, oral dissents, and even media appearances – to combat deleterious conflict. Yet she has spoken less forcefully in the criminal justice arena, in which she has pushed for equal-access and due-process gains in a more measured approach, cognizant of the true limits of what a justice can do in today's criminal justice system. Her work in these areas thus reflects her facility in appraising and approaching conflict with the appropriate sensitivity to its varied contexts.

Finally, some conflict is neither good nor bad but rather is an indelible feature of relationships. This conflict is not to be resolved but rather to be managed. She has always effectively handled the press, and she skillfully navigated her Supreme Court confirmation. By all accounts, her marriage to Marty Ginsburg was a thing of beauty, despite their different personalities. Her relationship with Justice Scalia, who in many ways is her ideological and political antipode on the Court, is close. They wage their jurisprudential battles during oral argument and in the footnotes of the *Supreme Court Reporter,* and, having done so, they then leave their differences there and welcome the joy of sharing their common love of music and good company.

Perhaps this is why Ginsburg is so difficult to characterize. Her judging is neither principally originalist nor purposivist, neither truly liberal nor conservative, neither purely pragmatist nor formalist, neither wholly activist nor deferential. As she herself seems to see it, she defies the usual labels. Rather, her judging appears to be a blend of different approaches and philosophies, depending on the particular conflict at issue. Though she recognizes and appreciates the conflict, she does not shy away from it. Perhaps, then, she deserves an unconventional label. Perhaps she should be regarded not for a single manifestation of her jurisprudence (if that were even possible) but rather for its motivation. Perhaps she is Ginsburg the optimist.

Notes

1 NOTES ON A LIFE

1 Brief for Appellant, 1971 WL 133596, Reed v. Reed, 404 U.S. 71 (1971).
2 U.S. CONST. amend. XIV, § 1.
3 The Court ultimately denied the petition. *See* Comm'r of Internal Revenue v. Moritz, 412 U.S. 906 (1973).
4 Weinberger v. Weisenfeld, 420 U.S. 636 (1975). The Court adopted Ginsburg's proposal to cover both sexes equally rather than strike the provision as unconstitutional.
5 Robert Barnes, *The Question Facing Ruth Bader Ginsburg: Stay or Go?*, WASH. POST MAGAZINE (Oct. 4, 2013), available at http://www.washingtonpost.com/lifestyle /magazine/the-question-facing-ruth-bader-ginsburg-stay-or-go/2013/10/04 /4d789e28-1574-11e3-a2ec-b47e45e6f8ef_story.html
6 N.W. Austin Muni. Util. Dist. No. 1 v. Holder, 557 U.S. 193 (2009).
7 Shelby Cnty. v. Holder, 133 S. Ct. 2612, 2651 (2013) (Ginsburg, J., dissenting).
8 550 U.S. 618.
9 Pub. L. 111–2, 123 Stat. 5 (2009).
10 Tr. of Oral Arg. at 45, Safford Unified Sch. Dist. No. 1 v. Redding, 557 U.S. 364 (2009), available at http://www.supremecourt.gov/oral_arguments/argument _transcripts/08-479.pdf
11 *Id.* at 45–46. For an audio recording of the oral argument, see http://www.oyez.org /cases/2000-2009/2008/2008_08_479
12 The Court also held that the school officials were immune from liability, a holding from which Ginsburg dissented.
13 United States v. Virginia, 518 U.S. 515 (1996).
14 *Id.* at 533, 550.
15 558 U.S. 310 (2010).

2 RUTH BADER GINSBURG:
LAW PROFESSOR EXTRAORDINAIRE

1 Herma Hill Kay, *Ginsburg, Ruth Bader, 1933–*, 1 ENCYCLOPEDIA OF THE SUPREME COURT OF THE UNITED STATES 337–42 (David Tanenhaus ed. 2008).

2 She has since been joined by another female law-professor-turned-justice: Elena Kagan. Six male justices have held tenured appointments at law schools, including most recently Stephen Breyer.

3 Edith Lampson Roberts, *Ruth Bader Ginsburg, in* THE SUPREME COURT JUSTICES: ILLUSTRATED BIOGRAPHIES, 1789–1995, at 531–32 (Clare Cushman ed., 2d ed. 1995). The narrative in this part of the text generally follows that in Herma Hill Kay, *Ruth Bader Ginsburg, Professor of Law,* 104 COLUM. L. REV. 1, 7–19 (2004) with updates and additional material as noted throughout.

4 *Justice Ruth Bader Ginsburg '59,* Columbia Law School Report, Spring 1994, at 9.

5 Ruth Bader Ginsburg, Gillian Metzger & Abbe Gluck, *A Conversation with Justice Ruth Bader Ginsburg,* 25 COLUM. J. GENDER & L. 6, 7 (2013).

6 ERWIN N. GRISWOLD, OULD FIELDS, NEW CORNE: THE PERSONAL MEMOIRS OF A TWENTIETH CENTURY LAWYER 171 (1992) (reporting that the vote in favor of admitting women was "about three to one").

7 Gerald Gunther, *Ruth Bader Ginsburg: A Personal, Very Fond Tribute,* 20 U. HAW. L. REV. 583, 583 (1988).

8 Columbia Report, *supra* note 4, at 9.

9 Ruth Bader Ginsburg, *Remarks for Columbia University Reception* (June 21, 1994) (on file with the *Columbia Law Review*).

10 Roberts, *supra* note 3, at 531–32.

11 RUTH BADER GINSBURG & ANDERS BRUZELIUS, CIVIL PROCEDURE IN SWEDEN (1965).

12 *See* Kay, *supra* note 3, at 10.

13 Ruth Bader Ginsburg, *Remarks for First Meeting of Alumnae of Columbia Law School* (Mar. 11, 1996) (on file with the *Columbia Law Review*); Mitchel Ostrer, *Columbia's Gem of the Motion: A Profile of Ruth Bader Ginsburg,* JURIS. DR., Oct. 1977, at 34, 36.

14 Ruth Bader Ginsburg, *Remarks for Rutgers* (Apr. 11, 1995) (on file with the *Columbia Law Review*).

15 *Id.*

16 *Id.*

17 Ruth Bader Ginsburg, *Judgments in Search of Full Faith and Credit: The Last-in-Time Rule for Conflicting Judgments,* 82 HARV. L. REV. 798 (1969) (clarifying the priory to be accorded to inconsistent final state court judgments).

18 Ginsburg, Metzger & Gluck, *supra* note 5, at 8.

19 This material is taken from the forthcoming book, HERMA HILL KAY, THE FIRST FEW AND THOSE WHO FOLLOWED: A HISTORY OF WOMEN LAW PROFESSORS IN THE UNITED STATES DURING THE TWENTIETH CENTURY (TENTATIVE TITLE) © HERMA HILL KAY.

20 339 U.S. 629 (1950). At its December 1951 annual meeting, the AALS adopted Art. 6, § 6–1 (1-a), which required member schools to provide "equality of opportunity in legal education without discrimination or segregation on the ground of race or color."

21 Interview with Dean Frank T. Read, February 16, 2001 (copy on file with the author).

22 *See* Frank T. Read & Elisabeth S. Petersen, *Sex Discrimination in Law School Placement,* 18 WAYNE L. REV. 639, 652–53 (1972). The current provision is Art. 6,

§ 6–3 (a), "Diversity: Nondiscrimination and Affirmative Action," which reads "A member school shall provide equality of opportunity in legal education for all persons, including faculty and employees with respect to hiring, continuation, promotion and tenure, applicants for admission, enrolled students, and graduates, without discrimination or segregation on the ground of race, color, religion, national origin, sex, age, disability, or sexual orientation." 2009 AALS Handbook at 37.

23 Committee Reports, 1970 Proc. Ass'n Am. L. Schs. (pt. 2) 76, 160 n.2 (recording amendment to Approved Association Policy). The amendment had been proposed by the newly created Special Committee on Women in Legal Education, of which one of the pre-1960s women law professors, Ellen Peters of Yale, was a member. Special Committees, 1969 Proc. Ass'n Am. L. Schs. (pt. 2) 233, 234. Professor Ginsburg was appointed to the renamed 1971 Special Committee on Equality of Opportunity for Women in Legal Education. Special Committees, 1970 Proc. Ass'n Am. L. Schs. (pt. 2) 261, 261.

24 Ginsburg, *supra* note 13.

25 *See infra* text at notes 32–36 (Casebook), 37–38 (ACLU), and 39–51 (ERA).

26 Equal Employment Opportunity Act of 1972, Pub. L. No. 92–261 § 3, 86 Stat. 103, 103–04 (codified as amended at 42 U.S.C. §2000e-1(a) (2000)).

27 *See supra* note 22.

28 This dual requirement may help explain Professor Soia Mentschikoff's concerns that member schools would be so anxious to hire "their woman" to the faculty that they would not pay sufficient attention to the qualifications of the chosen candidates. Interview with Judge Ruth Bader Ginsburg, Sept. 22, 1991 (transcript on file with the *Columbia Law Review*).

29 Ginsburg, *supra* note 13.

30 See Lesley Oelsner, *Columbia Law Snares a Prize in the Quest for Women Professors*, N.Y. TIMES, Jan. 26, 1972, at 39 (reporting that "In a new accelerating competition among the nation's law schools, Columbia University has just scored a major coup: its law school, to its undisguised glee, has just bid for and won a woman for the job of full professor – the first in its 114-year history, ... The glee comes in part because the woman, Ruth Bader Ginsburg, is what the school's dean, Michael Sovern, calls 'so distinguished a scholar,' that her credentials and honors would stand out in any catalogue of professors").

31 *Id.* Oelsner noted that Ginsburg's appointment came as the University of Michigan Law School dean, Theodore St. Antoine, says, at a time when many of the country's best law schools have been "scrambling" for women, often for the same one. Most have no women at any rung of the professional ladder, and, according to other sources, the woman Columbia got was among those being scrambled for.

32 Ginsburg, *supra* note 9. Myers's description of the meeting is found in Carol H. Meyer, *The First Activist Feminist I Ever Met*, 9 AFFILIA 85, 85 (1994) (adding that "I also have a strong memory of Ginsburg – a diminutive woman with black hair, tied with a huge bow. Ginsburg was gracious and funny and clearly in command as she told us her purpose for bringing us together.")

33 This subsection is drawn from Herma Hill Kay, *Claiming a Space in the Law School Curriculum: A Casebook on Sex-Based Discrimination*, 25 COLUM. J.L. & GENDER 54, 54–58 (2013).

34 Other related books included LEO KANOWITZ, SEX ROLES IN LAW AND SOCIETY:
    CASES AND MATERIALS (1973) (containing text excerpts from LEO KANOWITZ,
    WOMEN AND THE LAW: THE UNFINISHED REVOLUTION (1969)); and BARBARA A.
    BABCOCK ET AL., SEX DISCRIMINATION AND THE LAW: CAUSES AND REMEDIES
    (1975).
35 AALS Symposium on the Law School Curriculum and the Legal Rights of Women,
    Advance Notice, 1972.
36 Kenneth M. Davidson, Ruth Bader Ginsburg & Herma Hill Kay, TEXT, CASES AND
    MATERIALS ON SEX-BASED DISCRIMINATION at XI (1974) (citing Margaret Mead,
    MALE AND FEMALE 39 (1949), and Simone de Beauvoir, THE SECOND SEX at xvi
    (1949)).
37 *Id.* at XII–XIII.
38 Reed v. Reed, 404 U.S. 71 (1971); Frontiero v. Richardson, 411 U.S. 677 (1973);
    Comm'r v. Moritz, 469 F.2d 466 (10th Cir. 1972), *cert. denied*, 412 U.S. 906 (1973);
    see also Martin D. Ginsburg, *Distinguished Service Award Presentation*, 25 A.B.A.
    SEC. OF TAX'N NEWS Q. 7 (Summer 2006) (recounting that he had called *Moritz*
    to his wife's attention and insisted that she read it, despite her usual aversion to tax
    cases).
39 Both Ginsburg and Davidson left as co-authors after the first edition. I edited the sec-
    ond and third editions alone; Professor Marty West of the U.C. Davis Law School
    joined me as a co-author for the fourth through the sixth editions, and Professor Tristin
    K. Green is my co-author for the most recent, seventh, edition that appeared in 2012.
40 S.J. Res. 21, 68th Cong. (1923).
41 *See* CARL N. DEGLER, AT ODDS: WOMEN AND THE FAMILY IN AMERICA FROM THE
    REVOLUTION TO THE PRESENT 359 (1980); Ruth Bader Ginsburg, *The Need for the
    Equal Rights Amendment*, 59 A.B.A. J. 1013 (1973).
42 117 Cong. Rec. 35,814–15 (Oct. 12, 1971) (statement of Rep. Griffiths).
43 *See* Ruth Bader Ginsburg, *Let's Have ERA as a Signal*, 63 A.B.A. J. 70, 70 (1977);
    Ginsburg, *supra* note 40.
44 Ruth Bader Ginsburg, *The Equal Rights Amendment Is the Way*, 1 HARV. WOMEN'S
    L.J. 19, 20 (1978) (editor's introduction).
45 Ginsburg, *supra* note 40, at 1013.
46 *Id.* at 1017–18.
47 Ginsburg, *supra* note 42, at 73.
48 Ginsburg, *supra* note 43, at 21 (footnotes omitted).
49 Equal Rights Amendment Extension: Hearings on S.J. Res. 134 Before the
    Subcomm. on the Constitution of the Comm. on the Judiciary, 95th Cong. 265–71
    (1978) (statement of Professor Ruth Bader Ginsburg).
50 *Id.* at 269.
51 H.R. J. Res. 638, 95th Cong. (1978), approved by the House of Representatives on
    August 15, 1978, 124 Cong. Rec. 26,193–203 (Aug. 15, 1978), and by the Senate on
    October 6, 1978, 124 Cong. Rec. 34,314–15 (Oct. 6, 1978).
52 *See* Ruth Bader Ginsburg, *Ratification of the Equal Rights Amendment: A Question
    of Time*, 57 TEX. L. REV. 919, 936 (1979) (footnotes omitted).
53 Kay, *supra* note 1, at 337 (discussing a sample of Ginsburg's notable opinions
    through the October 2007 Term).
54 518 U.S. 515 (1996).

55 *Id.* at 532–33.
56 550 U.S. 618 (2007).
57 *Id.* at 645, 661 (Ginsburg, J., dissenting).
58 *Id.* at 661 (Ginsburg, J., dissenting).
59 Pub. L. No. 111–2, § 3, 42 U.S.C. § 20003–5(3)(A).
60 550 U.S. 124 (2007).
61 530 U.S. 914 (2000).
62 *Id.* at 159–60.
63 *Carhart II*, 550 U.S. at 170, 191 (Ginsburg, J., dissenting).
64 The Court's subsequent unanimous personal jurisdiction decision in Walden v. Fiore, 134 S. Ct. 1115, 1126 (2014), did not break new ground but rather was decided under "well established principles of personal jurisdiction" that require the necessary "minimum contacts" to uphold jurisdiction be those between the "defendant, the forum, and the litigation," not simply those between the defendant and the plaintiffs or third parties, and they must be created by the defendant himself.
65 131 S. Ct. 2846 (2010).
66 131 S. Ct. 2780 (2010).
67 134 S. Ct. 746 (2014).
68 *Id.* at 763 (Sotomayor, J., concurring).
69 *Goodyear Tires*, 131 S. Ct. at 2850.
70 *Id.* at 2853–54.
71 *Id.* at 2852.
72 *Id.* at 2857.
73 *McIntyre*, 131 S. Ct. at 2790 (plurality opinion of Kennedy, J.)
74 *Id.* at 2792 (Breyer, J., concurring).
75 *Id.* at 2793.
76 *Id.* at 2794 (Ginsburg, J. dissenting) (quoting Russell J. Weintraub, *A Map Out of the Personal Jurisdiction Labyrinth*, 28 U.C. DAVIS L. REV. 531, 555 (1995)).
77 *Id.* at 2804. *International Shoe* had held (as Justice Kennedy acknowledged in *McIntyre*) that "a court may subject a defendant to judgment only when the defendant has sufficient contacts with the sovereign 'such that the maintenance of the suit does not offend traditional notions of fair play and substantial justice.'" *Int'l Shoe*, 326 U.S. at 316.
78 134 S. Ct. 746 (2014).
79 95 U.S. 714 (1877).
80 326 U.S. 310 (1945).
81 342 U.S. 437 (1952).
82 *Daimler*, 134 S. Ct. at 753–758.
83 *Id.* at 753–58, nn.8, 10, 16, & 20. The crux of their disagreement over precedent is found in their opposing interpretations of Perkins v. Benguet Consolidated Mining Co., 342 U.S. 437 (1952).
84 Herma Hill Kay, *Chief Justice Traynor and Choice of Law Theory*, 35 HASTINGS L.J. 747 (1984).
85 Garrett Epps, *Don't Tell Ruth Ginsburg to Retire*, THE ATLANTIC (Mar. 2013), available at http://www.theatlantic.com/national/print/2014/03/don't-tell-ruth-ginsburg-to-retire/284479/

3 BEFORE *FRONTIERO* THERE WAS *REED*

1 *See* W. Va. St. Bd. of Educ. v. Barnette, 319 U.S. 624 (1943).
2 For recent contemplation of the legacy of Brown v. Board of Education, 347 U.S. 483 (1954), see, e.g., MARTHA MINOW, IN *BROWN'S* WAKE: LEGACIES OF AMERICA'S EDUCATIONAL LANDMARK (2010); GARY ORFIELD & SUSAN E. EATON, DISMANTLING DESEGREGATION: THE QUIET REVERSAL OF *BROWN V. BOARD OF EDUCATION* (1996). For a detailed narrative history, see RICHARD KLUGER, SIMPLE JUSTICE: THE HISTORY OF *BROWN V. BOARD OF EDUCATION* AND BLACK AMERICA'S STRUGGLE FOR EQUALITY (1975).
3 *See* Minor v. Happersett, 88 U.S. 162 (1875).
4 U.S. CONST. art. IV, § 2.
5 U.S. CONST. amend. XIV, § 1.
6 *See* Bradwell v. Illinois, 83 U.S. 130 (1873).
7 *See* Minor v. Happersett, 88 U.S. 162 (1875).
8 Reed v. Reed, 465 P.2d 635 (Idaho 1970). I have considered this case at some length in Linda K. Kerber, *Sally Reed Demands Equal Treatment, in* DAYS OF DESTINY 441–51 (Alan Brinkley & James McPherson eds. 2001). Some of what follows is taken from this essay.
9 IDAHO CODE §§ 15–312, -314 (1975).
10 EEOC v. Rhode Island, 549 F. Supp. 60, 66 (1982).
11 BETTY FRIEDAN, THE FEMININE MYSTIQUE (1963).
12 Telephone interviews with Allen Derr (Nov. 2000, Dec. 2000, Jan. 2001).
13 Reed v. Reed, 465 P.2d 635, 638 (Idaho 1970).
14 83 U.S. 130.
15 208 U.S. 412.
16 335 U.S. 464.
17 368 U.S. 57.
18 I have discussed these matters at length in LINDA K. KERBER, NO CONSTITUTIONAL RIGHT TO BE LADIES: WOMEN AND THE OBLIGATIONS OF CITIZENSHIP (1998).
19 Ruth B. Cowan, *Women's Rights through Litigation: An Examination of the American Civil Liberties Union Women's Rights Project, 1971–1976,* 8 COLUM. HUM. RIGHTS L. REV. 380 (1976).
20 Interview with Ruth Bader Ginsburg (Feb. 26, 1991).
21 For both an audio recording and a written transcript of the oral argument, see http://www.oyez.org/cases/1970-1979/1971/1971_70_4/
22 *Id.*
23 *Id.* For the historical context of *Goesaert*, see Amy Holman French, *Mixing It Up: Michigan Barmaids Fight for Civil Rights,* 40 MICH. HIST. REV. 1 (2014).
24 368 U.S. 57, 62.
25 Brief for the Appellant, 1971 WL 133596, Reed v. Reed, 404 U.S. 71 (1971).
26 For a succinct treatment of the effort to pass the Equal Rights Amendment, see DAVID KYVIG, EXPLICIT AND AUTHENTIC ACTS: AMENDING THE U.S. CONSTITUTION, 1776–1995 (1996). For the struggle over the ERA in a single state, see DONALD MATHEWS & JANE SHERRON DE HART, SEX, GENDER AND THE POLITICS OF ERA: A STATE AND A NATION (1990).

27   362 U.S. 525.

28   Sail'er Inn, Inc. v. Kirby, 5 Cal. 3d 1 (1971). For an account of this case, see FRED STREBEIGH, EQUAL: WOMEN RESHAPE AMERICAN LAW (2009). Wendy Williams is now Professor Emerita at Georgetown University Law Center.

29   *Supra* note 21.

30   Ruth Bader Ginsburg & Barbara Flagg, *Some Reflections on the Feminist Legal Thought of the 1970s*, 1989 U. CHI. LEGAL F. 9; Ruth Bader Ginsburg, *Women as Full Members of the Club: An Evolving American Ideal*, 6 HUMAN RTS. 2 (1977).

31   *Transcript of Interview of U.S. Supreme Court Associate Justice Ruth Bader Ginsburg, April 10, 2009*, 70 OHIO ST. L.J. 805, 812 (2009).

32   411 U.S. 677.

33   420 U.S. 636.

34   518 U.S. 515.

35   538 U.S. 721.

36   The oral argument transcript is available at http://www.supremecourt.gov/oral _arguments/argument_transcripts/09-5801.pdf. The Court affirmed the Ninth Circuit's judgment by a tie vote without accompanying opinions. Flores-Villar v. United States, 131 S. Ct. 2312 (2011). It is likely that the question will present itself again.

37   William B. Turner, *The Gay Rights State: Wisconsin's Pioneering Legislation to Prohibit Discrimination Based on Sexual Orientation*, 22 WIS. WOMEN'S L.J. 91 (2007).

38   Defense of Marriage Act, Pub. L. 104–199, 110 Stat. 2419 (Sept. 21, 1996).

39   Goodridge v. Dep't of Pub. Health, 440 Mass. 309 (2003).

40   518 U.S. 515 (1996).

41   *Goodridge*, 440 Mass. 309. I have written about Marshall's originality in Linda K. Kerber, *A Voice that Echoes*, BOSTON GLOBE (May 23, 2009).

42   It has been all too easy to forget that the logic of equal protection was not uniformly embraced at the time. The *Goodridge* decision set off celebrations of civil disobedience as mayors in San Francisco; Portland, Oregon; and other cities issued marriage licenses, but it also set off a firestorm of protest: every one of these marriages was nullified by state courts and Marshall was personally attacked for "unprincipled judicial activism" that jeopardized the integrity of her court.

43   United States v. Windsor, 133 S. Ct. 2675, 2693–95 (2013).

44   410 U.S. 113 (1973).

45   417 U.S. 484 (1974) (Brennan, J., dissenting, joined by Douglas and Marshall, JJ.).

46   These statistics are available through the Guttmacher Institute, at http://www .guttmacher.org/in-the-know/abortion-providers.html

47   550 U.S. 124.

48   *Id.* at 169–71 (Ginsburg, J., dissenting) (emphasis in original). I have reflected on these matters in Linda K. Kerber, *Why Diamonds Really Are a Girl's Best Friend*, 153 PROCEEDINGS AM. PHIL. SOC'Y 56 (Mar. 2009).

49   *Id.* at 171–72 (Ginsburg, J., dissenting) (citing Planned Parenthood of S.E. Pa. v. Casey, 505 U.S. 833 (1992)).

50   Allen Derr died in 2013 at the age of eighty-five.

4 *STRUCK BY STEREOTYPE*

1 *Nomination of Ruth Bader Ginsburg to Be Associate Justice of the Supreme Court of the United States: Hearing before the S. Comm. on the Judiciary*, 103d Cong. 206 (1993) (statement of Judge Ginsburg) [hereinafter *Ginsburg Hearings*].

2 *See* Brief for the Petitioner, Struck v. Sec'y of Def., 409 U.S. 1071 (1972) (No. 72–178), 1972 WL 135840. Melvin Wulf, Joel Gora, Brenda Feigen Fasteau, and Robert Czeisler also worked on the case and signed the brief, but it is evident that Ginsburg's distinctive voice pervades the brief.

3 Struck v. Sec'y of Def., 409 U.S. 1071 (1972).

4 *See id.* at 1071 (vacating and remanding for consideration of mootness in light of the government's change in position).

5 404 U.S. 71 (1971). *Reed* invalidated under the Equal Protection Clause an Idaho law that gave automatic preference to men over women as administrators of estates. *Id.* at 77.

6 410 U.S. 113 (1973).

7 411 U.S. 677 (1973).

8 417 U.S. 484 (1974).

9 Brief for the Petitioner, *supra* note 2, at 4, 10–11.

10 For examples of other feminist lawyers of the era who challenged pregnancy discrimination as sex discrimination, see Reva B. Siegel, *Constitutional Culture, Social Movement Conflict and Constitutional Change: The Case of the De Facto ERA*, 94 Calif. L. Rev. 1323, 1385–86 (2006).

11 Justice Ginsburg has used this or similar language in a variety of settings, both on and off the Court. *See, e.g.*, Gonzales v. Carhart, 550 U.S. 124, 171–72 (2007) (Ginsburg, J., dissenting); United States v. Virginia (*VMI*), 518 U.S. 515, 532 (1996).

12 Neil S. Siegel, *Equal Citizenship Stature: Justice Ginsburg's Constitutional Vision*, 43 New Eng. L. Rev. 771 (2010) (symposium honoring the jurisprudence of Justice Ginsburg).

13 Brief for the Petitioner, *supra* note 2, at 7.

14 *Id.* at 9 (emphasis added) (quoting United States *ex rel.* Robinson v. York, 281 F. Supp. 8, 19 (D. Conn. 1968), and Griggs v. Duke Power Co., 401 U.S. 424, 432 (1971)).

15 For one account of Ginsburg's legal strategy, see Deborah L. Markowitz, *In Pursuit of Equality: One Woman's Work to Change the Law*, 11 Women's Rts. L. Rep. 73 (1989).

16 *VMI*, 518 U.S. 515.

17 *Id.* at 534 (citing Goesaert v. Cleary, 335 U.S. 464, 467 (1948)).

18 *See, e.g.*, Judith Baer, *Advocate on the Court: Ruth Bader Ginsburg and the Limits of Formal Equality*, in Rehnquist Justice: Understanding the Court Dynamic 216, 231 (Earl M. Maltz ed. 2003); *see also infra* note 81 and accompanying text. See *infra* Part III for a discussion of substantive (i.e., antisubordination) versus formal (i.e., anti-classification) views of equality.

19 Brief for the Petitioner, *supra* note 2, at 8–9.

20 *See* Geduldig v. Aiello, 417 U.S. 484, 496–97 n.20 (1974)

21 *See* Brief for the Petitioner, *supra* note 2, at 10.

22 *See infra* Part IV.
23 This chapter takes the facts from the Brief for the Petitioner, *supra* note 2, at 3–7. Justice Ginsburg has recounted the story of *Struck* on several occasions. *See* Ruth Bader Ginsburg, *Remarks for the Celebration of 75 Years of Women's Enrollment at Columbia Law School*, 102 COLUM. L. REV. 1441, 1447 (2002); Ruth Bader Ginsburg, *Speaking in a Judicial Voice*, 67 N.Y.U. L. REV. 1185, 1200–02 (1992); Ruth Bader Ginsburg, Assoc. Justice, Supreme Court of the U.S., Advocating the Elimination of Gender-Based Discrimination: The 1970s New Look at the Equality Principle, Address at the University of Cape Town, South Africa (Feb. 10, 2006) [hereinafter Ginsburg, Advocating], *available at* http://www.supremecourtus.gov/publicinfo/speeches/sp_02-10-06.html. She also discussed *Struck* at her Supreme Court confirmation hearing. *See, e.g., Ginsburg Hearings, supra* note 1, at 205–06; *see also infra* Part II.
24 Brief for the Petitioner, *supra* note 2, at 3.
25 *Id.*
26 *Id.* at 3–4.
27 *Id.* at 4.
28 *See id.* The regulation stated:

> The commission of any woman officer will be terminated with the least practical delay when it is determined that one of the conditions in a or b *below* exist . . .
>
> a. Pregnancy:
>   (1) *General*:
>
>   (a) A woman will be discharged from the service with the least practical delay when a determination is made by a medical officer that she is pregnant.
>   . . .
>
> b. Minor Children:
>   (1) *General*. The commission of any woman officer will be terminated with the least practical delay when it is established that she: . . .
>   (d) Has given birth to a living child while in a commissioned officer status.

Air Force Reg. 36–12(40) (1970). A 1971 amendment to the regulation provided that "Discharge Action will be cancelled if Pregnancy is Terminated." *Id.* at 1376 (quoting Part I.C of 1971 Amendments to Regulations).
29 Brief for the Petitioner, *supra* note 2, at 56.
30 *See id.* at 4.
31 Struck v. Sec'y of Def., 460 F.2d 1372, 1374, 1377 (9th Cir. 1971).
32 *See, e.g.,* Brief for the Petitioner, *supra* note 2, at 55 ("Parenthood among servicemen is not deterred, indeed additional benefits are provided to encourage men who become fathers to remain in service." (citations omitted)).
33 *See infra* Part II.
34 Ginsburg, Advocating, *supra* note 23. It is unclear why Griswold feared a Supreme Court decision on the merits in *Struck*. Perhaps he perceived governmental coercion of abortion as an inadvisable context in which to vindicate the federal government's asserted interests in the area of pregnancy discrimination. *Cf.* Janice Goodman, Rhonda Copelon Schoenbrod & Nancy Stearns, Doe *and* Roe, *Where Do We Go from Here?*, 1 WOMEN'S RTS. L. REP. 20, 35 (1974) (discussing *Struck* as a case arising "in the area of coercion").

35 Memorandum Suggesting Mootness, Struck v. Sec'y of Def., 409 U.S. 1071
   (1972) (No. 72–178). For Ginsburg's response to the motion, see Opposition to
   Memorandum for the Respondents Suggesting Mootness, Struck, 409 U.S. 1071
   (No. 72–178).

36 Struck, 409 U.S. at 1071.

37 Reva B. Siegel, Comments, in WHAT ROE V. WADE SHOULD HAVE SAID: THE NATION'S
   TOP LEGAL EXPERTS REWRITE AMERICA'S MOST CONTROVERSIAL OPINION 244, 245
   (Jack M. Balkin ed. 2005). For another account of Struck, see Siegel, supra note 15,
   at 1385 & n.169.

38 Geduldig v. Aiello, 417 U.S. 484, 496–97 (1974) (holding that the Equal Protection
   Clause permitted California to exclude from its disability insurance program the
   risk of disability resulting from normal pregnancy).

39 Ginsburg Hearings, supra note 1, at 205.

40 Id. at 206.

41 Brief for the Petitioner, supra note 2, at 14 (emphasis added).

42 Id. at 20.

43 Id. at 35.

44 Id. at 20.

45 Id. at 36. Ginsburg also observed that mandatory discharge puts a pregnant woman
   at a competitive disadvantage with men, "for it deprives her of opportunity for training and work experience during pregnancy and, in many cases, for a prolonged
   period thereafter." Id.

46 Id. at 37; see also id. ("Loss of her job and accumulated benefits profoundly affect
   the choices open to her. No position awaits her after childbirth and she is apt to
   encounter discrimination in locating new employment, this time because she is a
   mother. If she defers return to the labor force for an extended period, her skills will
   have grown rusty and, upon attempted re-entry, she will face a further barrier: this
   time her age as well as her sex and limited work experience will count against her."
   (footnote omitted)).

47 Id. at 55.

48 Id. at 48.

49 Id. at 50–51 (citation and internal quotation marks omitted); see also id. at 52 ("The
   discriminatory treatment required by the challenged regulation ... reflects the discredited notion that a woman who becomes pregnant is not fit for duty, but should
   be confined at home to await childbirth and thereafter devote herself to child care."
   (footnote omitted)).

50 See supra text accompanying note 50; cf. Brief for Petitioner, supra note 2, at 50–51
   ("The regulation arbitrarily establishes a presumption of unfitness, distinguishing
   irrationally between pregnancy and far more debilitating physical conditions that
   do not occasion automatic discharge, and differentiating capriciously between a
   female and male who surrenders a child for adoption.").

51 Id. at 38; see also id. at 38–45 (discussing, inter alia, Hoyt v. Florida, 368 U.S. 57
   (1961); Goesaert v. Cleary, 335 U.S. 464 (1948); Muller v. Oregon, 208 U.S. 412 (1908);
   and Bradwell v. Illinois, 83 U.S. (16 Wall.) 130 (1873)). A similar sentence appears in
   her brief in Frontiero. See Brief of ACLU as Amicus Curiae at 34–35, Frontiero v.
   Richardson, 411 U.S. 677 (1973) (No. 71–1694) ("Presumably well-meaning exaltation of woman's unique role as wife and mother has, in effect, denied women equal

opportunity to develop their individual talents and capacities and has impelled them to accept a dependent, subordinate status in society."). Ginsburg "worked on *Frontiero* and *Struck* simultaneously." Letter from Ruth Bader Ginsburg, Assoc. Justice, Supreme Court of the U.S., to Neil S. Siegel (Mar. 31, 2009) (on file with authors).

52 Brief for the Petitioner, *supra* note 2, at 30–32.

53 *Id.* at 26–27 (footnote omitted).

54 *Id.* at 52 ("Imposition of this outmoded standard upon petitioner unconstitutionally encroaches upon her right to privacy in the conduct of her personal life.").

55 381 U.S. 479 (1965).

56 405 U.S. 438 (1972).

57 Brief for the Petitioner, *supra* note 2, at 54 (quoting *Baird*, 405 U.S. at 453).

58 *Id.* at 55 ("Parenthood among servicemen is not deterred, indeed additional benefits are provided to encourage men who become fathers to remain in service.").

59 *Id.*

60 *Id.* at 56.

61 *Id.*

62 *Id.* (footnote omitted).

63 *Ginsburg Hearings*, *supra* note 1, at 206.

64 A wide range of scholars have discussed the antisubordination understanding of equal protection. *See* Owen M. Fiss, *Groups and the Equal Protection Clause*, 5 Phil. & Pub. Aff. 107, 151 (1976); Catherine A. MacKinnon, *Difference and Dominance: On Sex Discrimination*, in Feminism Unmodified: Discourses on Life and Law 32, 38 (1987); Athena D. Mutua, *The Rise, Development and Future Directions of Critical Race Theory and Related Scholarship*, 84 Denv. U. L. Rev. 329, 336 (2006); Reva B. Siegel, *Equality Talk: Antisubordination and Anticlassification Values in Constitutional Struggles over Brown*, 117 Harv. L. Rev. 1470, 1472–76 (2004); *see also* Jack M. Balkin & Reva B. Siegel, *The American Civil Rights Tradition: Anticlassification or Antisubordination?*, 58 U. Miami L. Rev. 9, 10 (2003); Jill Elaine Hasday, *The Principle and Practice of Women's "Full Citizenship": A Case Study of Sex-Segregated Public Education*, 101 Mich. L. Rev. 755, 769–79 (2002).

65 Brief for the Petitioner, *supra* note 2, at 34.

66 *Id.* at 27; *see also* text accompanying notes 14, 52. On the antisubordination principle, see Siegel, *supra* note 65, at 1472–73 (defining "the antisubordination principle" as "the conviction that it is wrong for the state to engage in practices that enforce the inferior social status of historically oppressed groups").

67 518 U.S. 515, 533–34 (1996).

68 Brief for the Petitioner, *supra* note 2, at 15.

69 For a classic focus on the purposes, effects, and social meanings of a practice as determinative under equal protection analysis, see Charles L. Black Jr., *The Lawfulness of the Segregation Decisions*, 69 Yale L.J. 421 (1960).

70 163 U.S. 537, 551 (1896) ("We consider the underlying fallacy of the plaintiff's argument to consist in the assumption that the enforced separation of the two races stamps the colored race with a badge of inferiority. If this be so, it is not by reason of anything found in the act, but solely because the colored race chooses to put that construction upon it.").

71 83 U.S. (16 Wall.) 130, 139 (1872). The Court upheld the exclusion of women from the practice of law. *Id.* at 139. In a concurring opinion, Justice Bradley wrote that "the paramount destiny and mission of woman are to fulfil the noble and benign offices of wife and mother. This is the law of the Creator." *Id.* at 141 (Bradley, J., concurring). "Although the method of communication between the Creator and the jurist is never disclosed," Ginsburg wrote in her *Struck* brief, "'divine ordinance' has been a dominant theme in decisions justifying laws establishing sex-based classifications." Brief for the Petitioner, *supra* note 2, at 39.

72 Brief for the Petitioner, *supra* note 2, at 35.

73 Similarly, Justice Ginsburg viewed a 2007 sex discrimination case from the perspective of the victim. *See* Ledbetter v. Goodyear Tire & Rubber Co., 550 U.S. 618, 643–46 (2007) (Ginsburg, J., dissenting) (citation omitted).

74 *See Ginsburg Hearings, supra* note 1, at 206 ("The main emphasis was on her equality as a woman, vis-a-vis a man who was equally responsible for the conception."); *id.* ("I did think about it, first and foremost, as differential treatment of the woman, based on her sex.").

75 *See id.* at 205 ("It has never in my mind been an either/or choice, never one rather than the other; it has been both."); *id.* at 206 ("At no time did I regard it as an either/or, one pocket or the other issue."). Throughout her career, Ginsburg reasoned about abortion in equality as well as liberty frames. *See* Reva B. Siegel, *Equality and Choice: Sex Equality Perspectives on Reproductive Rights in the Work of Ruth Bader Ginsburg*, 25 Colum. J. Gender & L. 63 (2013).

76 *See* Goodman et al., *supra* note 35, at 35 (discussing reproductive freedom as the right to decide whether to have or not to have children without state interference, and describing *Struck* as a case about "coercion"). For an account of the feminist reproductive rights claims of the era, see, for example, Reva B. Siegel, *Sex Equality Arguments for Reproductive Rights: Their Critical Basis and Evolving Constitutional Expression*, 56 Emory L.J. 815 (2007). "In these early briefs, liberty talk and equality talk were entangled as emanations of different constitutional clauses." *Id.* at 823.

77 *See, e.g.,* Brief for the Petitioner, *supra* note 2, at 52 ("The discriminatory treatment required by the challenged regulation … reflects the discredited notion that a woman who becomes pregnant is not fit for duty, but should be confined at home to await childbirth and thereafter devote herself to child care. Imposition of this outmoded standard upon petitioner unconstitutionally encroaches upon her right to privacy in the conduct of her personal life." (footnote omitted)).

78 *See* Reva B. Siegel, *Dignity and the Politics of Protection: Abortion Restrictions under Casey/Carhart*, 117 Yale L.J. 1694, 1738–45, 1763–66 (2008) (developing this insight); *id.* at 1744–45 ("Concern that restrictions on women's liberty can communicate meanings about women's social standing lies at the heart of the sex discrimination cases, especially those cases invalidating laws that deny women autonomy to make decisions about their family roles.").

79 Justice Ginsburg has more recently reemphasized the close link between constitutional equality and constitutional liberty in the area of reproductive rights. *See, e.g.,* Gonzales v. Carhart, 550 U.S. 124, 170–72, 184–86 (2007) (Ginsburg, J., dissenting) (so arguing and citing equal protection sex discrimination cases as support for the abortion right).

80 *See, e.g.*, Baer, *supra* note 18, at 216, 231; David Cole, *Strategies of Difference: Litigating for Women's Rights in a Man's World*, 2 L. & INEQUALITY 33, 55 (1984). Ginsburg has herself summarized much of the criticism. *See* Ruth Bader Ginsburg & Barbara Flagg, *Some Reflections on the Feminist Legal Thought of the 1970s*, 1989 U. CHI. LEGAL F. 9, 17.

81 *See, e.g.*, Craig v. Boren, 429 U.S. 190 (1976); Weinberger v. Wiesenfeld, 420 U.S. 636 (1975); Moritz v. Comm'r of Internal Revenue, 469 F.2d 466 (10th Cir. 1972).

82 For an account of these developments in race discrimination law, see generally Fiss, *supra* note 65; Siegel, *supra* note 65, at 1535–38. One of the authors has explored the implications in sex discrimination law. *See* Reva B. Siegel, *"The Rule of Love": Wife Beating as Prerogative and Privacy*, 105 YALE L.J. 2117, 2188–95 (1996) (showing how the Court's rejection of disparate impact claims in *Washington v. Davis*, 426 U.S. 229 (1976), and *Personnel Administrator v. Feeney*, 442 U.S. 256 (1979), shielded from equal protection scrutiny "facially neutral" practices (such as domestic violence policies) that have long played a role in subordinating women).

83 Brief for the Petitioner, *supra* note 2, at 38–45.

84 *Id.* at 50–51 (citation and internal quotation marks omitted).

85 *See* Cary Franklin, *The Anti-Stereotyping Principle in Constitutional Sex Discrimination Law*, 85 N.Y.U. L. REV. 1, 3–4 (2010).

86 Fiss, *supra* note 65, at 157.

87 CATHERINE A. MACKINNON, SEXUAL HARASSMENT OF WORKING WOMEN: A CASE OF SEX DISCRIMINATION 117 (1979).

88 347 U.S. 483 (1954). For discussions of debates about the meaning of *Brown*, see Christopher W. Schmidt, *Brown and the Colorblind Constitution*, 94 CORNELL L. REV. 203, 231–37 (2008); Neil S. Siegel, *Race-Conscious Student Assignment Plans: Balkanization, Integration, and Individualized Consideration*, 56 DUKE L.J. 781, 830–33, 841–43 (2006); Siegel, *supra* note 65, at 1532–44.

89 *See generally* LINDA GREENHOUSE & REVA SIEGEL, BEFORE ROE V. WADE: VOICES THAT SHAPED THE ABORTION DEBATE BEFORE THE SUPREME COURT'S RULING (2012) (reproducing feminist arguments for abortion rights from 1969 to 1973 that invoke both privacy and equality and analyze the regulation of abortion as part of the regulation of motherhood).

90 For a discussion of these two points, see *infra* Part IV.

91 *See* Craig v. Boren, 429 U.S. 190, 197 (1976).

92 Particularly in light of how current cultural battle lines have been drawn, it is illuminating to see Justice Ginsburg's voice deployed in the service of both the equal citizenship stature of women and one particular woman's religiously based opposition to procuring an abortion. It may be ironic that Ginsburg's views on sex discrimination and abortion first developed in this setting, but it is a reminder that Americans today agree about more than they may realize.

93 Brief for the Petitioner, *supra* note 2, at 26 ("In addition to the two commonly differentiated review standards, some of the decisions of this Court suggest an intermediate standard.").

94 *Id.* at 29 n.24.

95 *See, e.g., id.* at 46 ("In 1971, two legal scholars – both of them male – examined the record of the judiciary in sex discrimination cases; they concluded that the

performance of American judges in this area 'can be succinctly described as ranging from poor to abominable.'").

96 Brief for the Petitioner, *supra* note 2, at 54 n.55 (*"Griswold* alone, or in conjunction with *Baird*, has been cited in numerous lower court decisions holding that women have a right to determine for themselves, free from unwarranted governmental intrusion, whether or not to bear children" (citing Roe v. Wade, 314 F. Supp. 1217 (N.D. Tex. 1970))).

97 *See, e.g., supra* note 58 and accompanying text.

98 *See* United States v. Windsor, 133 S. Ct. 2675 (2013); Lawrence v. Texas, 539 U.S. 558 (2003); Romer v. Evans, 517 U.S. 620 (1996).

99 *See* Geduldig v. Aiello, 417 U.S. 484, 496 (1974).

100 Robert C. Post & Reva B. Siegel, *Legislative Constitutionalism and Section Five Power: Policentric Interpretation of the Family and Medical Leave Act,* 112 YALE L.J. 1943, 2042 n.309 (2003).

101 Consider, for example, the likely prospects of an attempt to repeal the PDA, which responded to *Geduldig* and *General Electric Co. v. Gilbert,* 429 U.S. 125, 136 (1976) (holding that a disability benefit plan excluding disabilities related to pregnancy was not sex-based discrimination within the meaning of Title VII). For a discussion of the PDA's role in shaping popular and judicial understandings of sex discrimination, see Reva B. Siegel, *"You've Come a Long Way, Baby": Rehnquist's New Approach to Pregnancy Discrimination in Hibbs,* 58 STAN. L. REV. 1871, 1897–98 (2006).

102 For a discussion of these developments from the perspective of legal doctrine, see Neil S. Siegel & Reva B. Siegel, *Pregnancy and Sex Role Stereotyping, from Struck to Carhart,* 70 OHIO ST. L.J. 1095 (2009).

103 538 U.S. 721 (2003). Commentators have noted the magnitude of Chief Justice Rehnquist's shift in position from his early days on the Court to *VMI* and then to *Hibbs. See, e.g.,* Linda Greenhouse, *Introduction: Learning to Listen to Ruth Bader Ginsburg,* N.Y. CITY L. REV. 213, 218–19 (2004); Deborah Jones Merritt & David M. Lieberman, *Ruth Bader Ginsburg's Jurisprudence of Opportunity and Equality,* 104 COLUM. L. REV. 39, 47 (2004); Siegel, *supra* note 103, at 1871–98.

104 29 U.S.C. § 2612(a)(1)(c) (2006).

105 *Hibbs,* 538 U.S. at 740.

106 *Id.* at 738.

107 *Id.* at 734.

108 *Id.* at 736 (quoting *The Parental and Medical Leave Act of 1986: J. Hearing before the Subcomm. on Labor-Mgmt. Relations and the Subcomm. on Labor Standards of the H. Comm. on Educ. and Labor,* 99th Cong., 2d Sess., 100 (1986) (statement of Women's Legal Defense Fund)).

109 *See id.* at 731 & n.5.

110 For further discussion of *Geduldig,* see *supra* note 8 and accompanying text.

111 Geduldig v. Aiello, 417 U.S. 484, 496 n.20 (1974). For a discussion of the Court's reasoning in *Hibbs,* see generally Siegel, *supra* note 103, at 1889–91.

112 For further elaboration of this reading of *Geduldig,* see generally Siegel & Siegel, *supra* note 104.

113 417 U.S. at 496–97 n.20. The *Gedulgig* decision reasoned:
    While it is true that only women can become pregnant it does not follow that every legislative classification concerning pregnancy is a sex-based classification

like those considered in [*Reed* and *Frontiero*]. Normal pregnancy is an objectively identifiable physical condition with unique characteristics. *Absent a showing that distinctions involving pregnancy are mere pretexts designed to effect an invidious discrimination against the members of one sex or the other,* lawmakers are constitutionally free to include or exclude pregnancy from the coverage of legislation such as this on any reasonable basis, just as with respect to any other physical condition.

    Id. (emphasis added). This much quoted passage from *Geduldig* is often read as denying that pregnancy discrimination is sex discrimination. In fact, the passage in question reasons that pregnancy discrimination is not always sex discriminatory or invidious, but sometimes may be. In the years since its decision in *Geduldig*, the Court has come to recognize that gender bias in the regulation of pregnancy is more prevalent than perhaps it first believed.

114 *See* Brief for Appellees, Geduldig v. Aiello, No. 73–640, 1974 WL 185752 (1974), at *38 ("The issue for courts is not whether pregnancy is, in the abstract, sui generis, but whether the legal treatment of pregnancy in various contexts is justified or invidious. The 'gross, stereotypical distinctions between the sexes' ... are at the root of many laws and regulations relating to pregnancy" (quoting Frontiero v. Richardson, 411 U.S. 677, 685 (1973))).

115 A notable recent decision ignoring the links between pregnancy and sex-stereotyping that *Hibbs* emphasized is *Coleman v. Court of Appeals of Maryland*, 132 S. Ct. 1327 (2012) (denying that Congress had power under the Fourteenth Amendment to provide money damages against state actors for breach of the self-care provisions of the Family and Medical Leave Act). In an impassioned dissent, Justice Ginsburg pointed out that Congress included medical (or "self-care") leave in the FMLA to provide leave for pregnancy in a form that both men and women could take, hoping in this way to minimize stereotyping against young female applicants for employment. *Id.* at 1345 (Ginsburg J., dissenting). For a recent analysis of the decision, see Reva B. Siegel, *Equality's Frontiers: How Congress's Section 5 Power Can Secure Transformative Equality (As Justice Ginsburg Illustrates in Coleman)*, 122 YALE L.J. ONLINE 267 (2013), http://www.law.yale.edu/documents/pdf/Faculty/Siegel_Equalityfrontiers.pdf

116 *See* Brief for Petitioner, *supra* note 2, at 54 n.55; *see also* text accompanying note 98. For subsequent discussions, see generally Ruth Bader Ginsburg, *Sex Equality and the Constitution*, 52 TUL. L. REV. 451 (1978); Ruth Bader Ginsburg, *Some Thoughts on Autonomy and Equality in Relation to Roe v. Wade*, 63 N.C. L. REV. 375 (1985).

117 Roe v. Wade, 410 U.S. 113, 163, 164 (1973).

118 505 U.S. 833 (1992).

119 *Id.* at 876 (plurality opinion) ("In our view, the undue burden standard is the appropriate means of reconciling the State's interest with the woman's constitutionally protected liberty").

120 *See, e.g., id.* at 852, 856, 897. For analysis of the significance of the equality reasoning in *Casey*, see generally Neil S. Siegel & Reva B. Siegel, *Equality Arguments for Abortion Rights*, 60 UCLA L. REV. DISCOURSE 160 (2013).

121 550 U.S. 124, 159 (2007). For a critique, see Neil S. Siegel, *The Virtue of Judicial Statesmanship*, 86 TEX. L. REV. 959, 1014–30 (2008).

122 *Carhart*, 550 U.S. at 171 (Ginsburg, J., joined by Stevens, Souter, and Breyer, JJ., dissenting) (citing Reva Siegel, *Reasoning from the Body: A Historical Perspective on Abortion Regulation and Questions of Equal Protection*, 44 STAN. L. REV. 261 (1992), and Sylvia Law, *Rethinking Sex and the Constitution*, 132 U. PA. L. REV. 955, 1002–28 (1984)); *see also, e.g.*, Siegel, *supra* note 77, at 837–38 (situating Justice Ginsburg's opinion in *Carhart* in a survey of sex-equality arguments for reproductive rights).

123 *See* Gen. Elec. Co. v. Gilbert, 429 U.S. 125 (1976); Geduldig v. Aiello, 417 U.S. 484 (1974).

124 A Colloquy, Proceedings of the Forty-Ninth Judicial Conference of the District of Columbia Circuit (May 24, 1988), *in* 124 F.R.D. 241, 338 (1989).

125 Nev. Dep't of Human Res. v. Hibbs, 538 U.S. 721 (2003).

5 BEYOND THE TOUGH GUISE

1 Peter J. Rubin, *Justice Ruth Bader Ginsburg: A Judge's Perspective*, 70 OHIO ST. L.J. 825, 825 (2009); *see also* Michael James Confusione, *Ruth Bader Ginsburg and Justice Thurgood Marshall: A Misleading Comparison*, 26 RUTGERS L.J. 887 (1995) (reporting that President Clinton made the comparison in his announcement of her nomination).

2 Tony Mauro, *Ginsburg Nominated: "Thurgood Marshall of Gender Equality Law,"* USA TODAY, June 15, 1993.

3 *See, e.g.*, Judith Baer, *Advocate on the Court: Ruth Bader Ginsburg in the Limits of Formal Equality*, *in* REHNQUIST JUSTICE: UNDERSTANDING THE COURT DYNAMIC 16 (Earl M. Maltz ed. 2003).

4 *See* CATHARINE A. MACKINNON, FEMINISM UNMODIFIED: DISCOURSES ON LIFE AND LAW (1988).

5 Neil S. Siegel & Reva B. Siegel, *Struck by Stereotype: Ruth Bader Ginsburg on Pregnancy Discrimination as Sex Discrimination*, 59 DUKE L.J. 771 (2010); *see also* Neil S. Siegel, *Equal Citizenship Stature: Justice Ginsburg's Constitutional Vision*, 43 NEW ENG. L. REV. 799 (2009).

6 Brief of Amicus Curiae for the Appellant, 1972 WL 133598, Reed v. Reed, 404 U.S. 71 (1971).

7 *Id.* at 11.

8 *Id.* at 12.

9 *Id.* at 13–15.

10 Brief of Amicus Curiae for the Appellants, Frontiero v. Richardson, 411 U.S. 677 (1972).

11 *Id.* at 13 (quoting ALFRED, LORD TENNYSON, LOCKSLEY HALL (1842)). For other statements in the brief, see *id.* at 14 ("In the pre-Civil War South, white women ranked as chief slave of the harem."); *id.* at 18 ("Activated by feminists of both sexes, legislatures and courts have begun to recognize and respond to the subordinate position of women in our society, and the second-class status our institutions historically have imposed upon them.").

12 Brief of Amicus Curiae for the Petitioner at 27, 1972 WL 135840, Struck v. Sec'y of Defense, 409 U.S. 1071 (1972).

13 *Id.* at 29.

14 *Id.* at 30. Although the constant analogies to race today seem dicey, they seemed less so in the 1970s, when Pauli Murray, a black feminist, championed the race-sex analogy. *See* Pauli Murray & Mary O. Eastwood, *Crow and the Law: Sex Discrimination and Title VII*, 34 Geo. Wash. L. Rev. 232 (1965–1966), *see also* America Civil Liberties Union (ACLU), *Tribute: The Legacy of Ruth Bader Ginsburg and WRP Staff, (March 7, 2006),* available at http://www.aclu.org /womens-rights/tribute-legacy-ruth-bader-ginsburg-and-wrp-staff. And remember that, at this point, Ginsburg and company were lobbying hard to persuade the Court to apply strict scrutiny (developed in the context of race) to sex.

15 *Id.* at 38 (quoting Elizabeth Janeway, Man's World, Women's Place: A Study in Social Mythology (1971)).

16 *Id.*

17 *Id.* at 41.

18 Brief of Amicus Curiae for the Appellants at 4, 1973 WL 172384, Kahn v. Shevin, 416 U.S. 351 (1973).

19 *Id.* at 17 n.11; *cf.* MacKinnon, *supra* note 4, at 45.

20 *Id.* at 18.

21 *Id.* at 25.

22 Thurgood Marshall, by contrast, understood that change needed to come at a structural level. *See, e.g.*, Cal. Fed. Sav. & Loan Ass'n v. Guerra, 479 U.S. 272, 289 (1987) ("The entire thrust behind [the Pregnancy Discrimination Act] is to guarantee women the basic right to participate fully and equally in the workforce, without denying them the fundamental right to full participation in family life."). Marshall's formulation neatly explains why treating women "the same" entailed upholding their right to pregnancy disability leave; his language parsimoniously deconstructs the masculine norm that "real" workers do not bear children.

23 Brief Amicus Curiae for the Appellant, 1979 WL 199959, Wengler v. Druggists Mut. Ins. Co., 446 U.S. 142 (1979).

24 *Id.* at 3.

25 *Id.* at 10.

26 *Id.* at 19.

27 *Id.* at 36.

28 *Id.* at 45.

29 MacKinnon, *supra* note 4, at 5.

30 Catharine A. MacKinnon, The Sexual Harassment of Working Women (1979).

31 Catharine A. MacKinnon, *Pornography as Defamation and Discrimination*, 71 B.U. L. Rev. 793 (1991).

32 Catharine A. MacKinnon, Are Women Human? And Other International Dialogues (2006).

33 MacKinnon, *supra* note 4, at 50.

34 *Id.*

35 Reed v. Reed, 404 U.S. 71 (1971) (challenging statute that gave automatic prefer-ence to men over women in administering relatives' estates); Struck v. Dept. of Defense, 409 U.S. 1071 (1972) (challenging Air Force officer's discharge because she got pregnant); Frontiero v. Richardson, 411 U.S. 677 (1973) (challenging

military program that offered medical and other benefits automatically to the wives of service members, but required husbands to prove dependence); Weinberger v. Wiesenfeld, 420 U.S. 636 (1975) (challenging social security survivors program that limited eligibility to widows); Edwards v. Healy, 421 U.S. 772 (1975) (challenging system that allowed women to opt out of jury service, on grounds of their family responsibilities); Liberty Mut. Ins. Co. v. Wetzel, 424 U.S. 737 (1974) (challenging denial of pregnancy benefits in comprehensive insurance scheme); Vorchheimer v. Sch. Dist. of Philadelphia, 424 U.S. 737 (1976) (challenging all-boys public school in a brief stressing the career benefits to girls of attending the school); Califano v. Goldfarb, 430 U.S. 199 (1977) (challenging social security survivors' benefits program that required surviving males, but not females, to prove dependence); Nashville Gas Co. v. Satty, 434 U.S. 136 (1977); City of Los Angeles v. Manhart, 435 U.S. 702 (1978) (challenging pension system that charged women more than men on the grounds they live longer; for analysis of how this relates to separate spheres, see Joan C. Williams, Reshaping the Work-Family Debate: Why Men and Class Matter, 129–30 (2010)); Califano v. Wescott, 443 U.S. 76 (1979) (challenging AFDC-U program, which offered benefits to the families of unemployed men but not to unemployed women); Wengler v. Druggists Mut. Ins. Co., 446 U.S. 142 (1979) (challenging workers' comp law that offered automatic death benefits to wives but required husbands to prove incapacity or dependency); Orr. v. Orr, 440 U.S. 268 (1979) (challenging alimony law that limited alimony to women). The two cases I could find that the Women's Rights Project wrote briefs for that did not deconstruct separate spheres were Craig v. Boren, 429 U.S. 190 (1976), and Coker v. Georgia, 433 U.S. 584 (1974) – and Ginsburg made clear that she did not support the bringing of the lawsuit in Craig v. Boren, and only got involved to protect the gains attained in other cases.

36 Motion for Leave to File Brief of Amicus Curiae, 1976 WL 194246, Craig v. Boren, 429 U.S. 190 (1976) (arguing that the beer statute reinforced an imagery of women as passive and men as active risk-takers); Brief of Amicus Curiae for the Petitioner, 1976 WL 181482, Coker v. Georgia, 433 U.S. 584 (1976) (challenging the death penalty for rape, which stressed that rule's linkage with the tradition of women as property (and racism)).

37 Susan H. Williams & David C. Williams, *Sense and Sensibility: Justice Ruth Bader Ginsburg's Mentoring Style as a Blend of Rigor and Compassion*, 1998 U. Hawai'i L. Rev. 589, 593.

38 MacKinnon, *supra* note 4, at 11.

39 *Id.* at 41.

40 *Id.* at 91.

41 *Id.* at 92.

42 *Id.* at 45.

43 Cary Franklin, *The Anti-Stereotyping Principle in Constitutional Sex Discrimination Law*, 85 N.Y.U. L. Rev. 83, 97–105 (2010). Justice Ginsburg views reproductive rights through the same prism, namely with the concern that laws limiting reproductive rights may impede a woman's ability "to participate equally in the economic and social life of the Nation." Mickey Kaus, *Moderate Threat*, New Republic, July 12, 1993 (quoting Justice Ginsburg).

44 Franklin, *supra* note 43, at 100.

45 *Id.* at 101.
46 Ruth Bader Ginsburg, *Some Thoughts on the 1980's Debate over Special versus Equal Treatment of Women*, 4 L. & INEQUALITY 143, 146 (1986).
47 Brief of Amicus Curiae for the Appellee at 12, 1974 WL 186057, Weinberger v. Wiesenfeld, 420 U.S. 636 (1974).
48 *Id.* at 22.
49 Franklin, *supra* note 43, at 101–02; *see also* Ruth Bader Ginsburg, *Gender and the Constitution*, 44 U. CIN. L. REV. 1, 1 (1975) (quoting Palme that "in order that women shall be emancipated ... men must also be emancipated").
50 Emily Bazelon, *The Place of Women on the Court*, N.Y. TIMES, July 12, 2009; *see also* Michael J. Klarman, *Social Reform Litigation and Its Challenges: An Essay in Honor of Justice Ruth Bader Ginsburg*, 32 HARV. J.L. & GENDER 251, 266 (2009).
51 David Von Drehle, *Redefining Care with a Simple Careful Assault*, WASH. POST, July 19, 1993; *see also* Jeffrey Rosen, *The New Look of Liberalism on the Court*, N.Y. TIMES, Oct. 5, 1997, at 60 ("This is my dream of the way the world should be ... when fathers take equal responsibility for the care of their children, that's when women will truly be liberated.")
52 Brief of Amicus Curiae for the Appellants at 4, 1973 WL 172384, Kahn v. Shevin, 416 U.S. 351 (1973).
53 *Id.* at 12, 13.
54 Brief of Amicus Curiae for the Appellant at 14, 1978 WL 206698, Orr v. Orr, 440 U.S. 268 (1978).
55 *Id.* at 27.
56 518 U.S. 515 (1996).
57 538 U.S. 721 (2003).
58 I have to admit that Justice Ginsburg herself does not agree. *See Remarks of Ruth Bader Ginsburg*, 7 N.Y. CITY L. REV. 221, 236 (2004) ("The Virginia Military Academy case was very satisfying because I regard it ... [as] the culmination of the litigation in which I was engaged in the 1970s.").
59 *Hibbs*, 538 U.S at 725.
60 *See, e.g.*, Hennifer Yatkis Dukart, *Geduldig Reborn: Hibbs as a Success(?) of Justice Ruth Bader Ginsburg's Sex-Discrimination Strategy*, 93 CALIF. L. REV. 541, 544–55 (2005).
61 Others have made the same observation. *See, e.g., id.*; Linda Greenhouse, *Learning to Listen to Ruth Bader Ginsburg*, 7 N.Y. CITY L. REV. 213, 218 (2004).
62 WILLIAMS, *supra* note 35, at 118.
63 Ruth Bader Ginsburg & Barbara Flagg, *Some Reflections on the Feminist Legal Thought of the 1970s*, 1989 U. CHI. LEGAL F. 9, 18 (praising "legislation like the Family and Medical Leave Act, a measure that takes women at work as the model..., but spreads out to shelter others: men and women who need time off not only to care for a newborn, but to attend to a seriously ill child, spouse, elderly parent or self"); *cf.* WILLIAMS, *supra* note 35, at 77–108 (discussing the need to deconstruct masculine workplace norms and replace them with norms that include the traditional life patterns of women).
64 Ginsburg, *supra* note 49, at 29.
65 *Id.* at 28–34.
66 *Id.* at 29.

67 *Id.* at 30.
68 *Id.*
69 *Id.*
70 *Id.* at 38.
71 *Id.* at 44.
72 Joan C. Williams, Unbending Gender: Why Family and Work Conflict and What To Do About It (2000).
73 Ginsburg, *supra* note 49, 44 (1975).
74 *Id.*
75 Williams, *supra* note 35, at 115–16.
76 Nev. Dept. of Human Res. v. Hibbs, 538 U.S. 721 (2003); *see also* Reva B. Siegel, *"You've Come a Long Way, Baby": Rehnquist's New Approach to Pregnancy Discrimination in Hibbs*, 58 Stan. L. Rev. 1871 (2006).
77 29 U.S.C. §§ 2601–54.
78 *Hibbs*, 538 U.S. at 725.
79 *Id.* at 730, 733.
80 *Id.* at 731.
81 *Id.* at 736.
82 *Id.*
83 *See* N.C. Rehnquist, *Chief Justice's Wife Dies at 62*, Wash. Post, Oct. 18, 1991, at C5; Alan J. Borsuk, *The Rehnquist Difference*, Milwaukee J. Sentinel, June 27, 2004, at 1A; Katharine B. Silbaugh, *Is the Work-Family Conflict Pathological or Normal under the FMLA?: The Potential of the FMLA to Cover Ordinary Work-Family Conflicts*, 15 Wash. U. J.L. & Pol'y 193, 208 (2004); Herman Obermayer, *The William Rehnquist You Didn't Know*, A.B.A. J. (Mar. 1, 2010), available at http://www.abajournal.com/magazine/article/the_william_rehnquist_you_didnt_know/
84 Alice H. Eagly & Valerie Steffen, *Gender Stereotypes Stem from the Distribution of Women and Men into Social Roles*, 46 J. Personality & Soc. Psych. 735–54 (1984).
85 For a comprehensive data-based analysis, see The Stalled Gender Revolution, http://www.vanneman.umd.edu/endofgr/cpsempfam.html
86 Joseph Vandello et al., *Precarious Manhood*, 95 J. Personality & Soc. Psych. 1325, 1326 (2008).
87 *Id.* at 1327.
88 *Id.*
89 Nicholas Townsend, The Package Deal: Marriage, Work and Fatherhood in Men's Lives (2002).
90 Marianne Cooper, *Being the "Go-To Guy": Fatherhood, Masculinity, and the Organization of Work in Silicon Valley*, in Families at Work: Expanding the Bounds 5 (Naomi Gerstel et al. eds. 2002).
91 *Id.* at 7.
92 *Id.* at 9.
93 *Id.*
94 Joseph A. Vandello et al., *When Equal Isn't Really Equal: The Masculine Dilemma of Seeking Work Flexibility*, 69 J. Soc. Issues 303, 311 (2013).
95 *Id.* at 309–10.
96 *Id.* at 314.
97 *Id.*

98 *Id.* 314–15.
99 Laurie A. Rudman & Kris Mescher, *Penalizing Men Who Request a Family Leave: Is Flexibility Stigma a Femininity Stigma?*, 69 J. Soc. Issues 322, 336 (2013).
100 *Id.* at 327.
101 *Id.* at 336.
102 *Id.*
103 Jennifer L. Berdahl & Sue H. Moon, *Workplace Mistreatment of Middle Class Workers Based on Sex, Parenthood, and Caregiving*, 69 J. Soc. Issues 341, 354 (2013).
104 *Id.* at 353.
105 Joan C. Williams, Tough Guise: Violence, Media and the Crisis in Masculinity (1999).
106 Debra Meyerson et al., *Disrupting Gender, Revising Leadership, in* Women & Leadership: The State of Play and Strategies for Change 453, 461 (Barbara Kellerman & Deborah L. Rhode eds. 2007).
107 *Id.* at 456.
108 *Id.*
109 *Id.* at 459.
110 *Id.*
111 *Id.* at 460. For a more theoretical examination of this gender norm, see Ronald F. Levant, *Toward the Reconstruction of Masculinity, in* Toward a New Psychology of Men 91 (Ronald F. Levant & Williams S. Pollack eds. 2003).
112 Meyerson, *supra* note 106, at 461.
113 *Id.* at 462; Vandello et al., *supra* note 86, at 1326.
114 Meyerson, *supra* note 106, at 465.

6 "seg academies," taxes, and judge ginsburg

1 656 F.2d 820 (D.C. Cir. 1981), *rev'd sub nom.* Allen v. Wright, 468 U.S. 737 (1983).
2 On the other hand, Justice Ginsburg's Supreme Court opinions concerning taxation have generally involved arcane and narrow procedural issues to the exclusion of the substantive problems generally occupying both academic and practicing tax lawyers. Her thirteen opinions, listed alphabetically, include Ballard v. C.I.R., 544 U.S. 40 (2005); Barclays Bank PLC v. Franchise Tax Bd., 512 U.S. 298 (1994); City of Sherrill v. Oneida Indian Nation of N.Y., 544 U.S. 197 (2005); Hibbs v. Winn, 542 U.S. 88 (2004); Jefferson Cnty. v. Acker, 527 U.S. 423 (1999); Kawashima v. Holder, 132 S. Ct. 1166 (2012) (Ginsburg, J., dissenting); Levin v. Commerce Ene., Inc., 560 U.S. 413 (2010); Lunding v. N.Y. Tax Appeals Tribunal, 522 U.S. 287 (1998) (Ginsburg, J., dissenting); Montana v. Crow Tribe of Indians, 523 U.S. 696 (1998); NFIB v. Sibelius, 567 U.S. 1 (2012) (Ginsburg, J., concurring & dissenting); N.W. Airlines, Inc. v. Cnty. of Kent, 510 U.S. 355 (1994); Okla. Tax Comm'n v. Chickasaw Nation, 515 U.S. 450 (1995); United States v. Williams, 514 U.S. 527 (1995); Wagnon v. Prairie Band Potawatomi Nation, 546 U.S. 95 (2005) (Ginsburg, J., dissenting).
3 Act of Aug. 27, 1894, ch. 349, § 32, 28 Stat. 509, 556. The exemption was reenacted in the Corporation Income Tax of 1909, Act of Aug. 5, 1909, ch. 6, § 38, 36 Stat. 112,

and in the Revenue Act of 1913, Act of Oct. 3, 1913, ch. 16, § 2(G), 38 Stat. 172. The current version is I.R.C. § 501(c).

4   This tax allowance originated with a floor amendment to the Revenue Act of 1917. 55 Cong. Rec. 6728 (1917) (remarks of Sen. Hollis). The current version is I.R.C. §§ 170, 501(c)(3).

5   I.R.C. §§ 3121(k), 3306(c)(8).

6   347 U.S. 483 (1954).

7   *See generally* DAVID NEVIN & ROBERT E. BILLS, THE SCHOOLS THAT FEAR BUILT (1976); Katherine Griffith Terjen, *Close-up on Segregation Academies*, NEW SOUTH (Fall 1972), at 50.

8   *See* Note, *The Judicial Role in Attacking Racial Discrimination in Tax-Exempt Private Schools*, 93 HARV. L. REV. 378 (1979).

9   *See generally* Proposed IRS Revenue Procedure Affecting Tax-Exemption of Private Schools: Hearings before the Subcommittee on Oversight of the House Committee on Ways and Means, 96th Cong., 1st Sess. (1979) [hereinafter "Implementation Hearings"].

10 *See* NEVIN & BILLS, *supra* note 7, at 15. Payroll taxes, however, were the focus of the litigation in Bob Jones University v. United States, 639 F.2d 147, 149 (4th Cir. 1980), and Goldsboro Christian Schools, Inc., v. United States, No. 80–1473, at 2 (4th Cir. Feb. 24, 1981).

11 *See* Implementation Hearings, *supra* note 9, at 254 (statement of Jerome Kurtz).

12 *See* BORIS I. BITTKER & LAWRENCE LOKKEN, FEDERAL TAXATION OF INCOME, ESTATES AND GIFTS ¶ 35.1.3 (2013).

13 *See id.*

14 1979-1 C.B. 108.

15 Oppewal v. Comm'r, 468 F.2d 1000 (1st Cir. 1972). *Oppewal* was followed in Haak v. United States, 451 F. Supp. 1087 (W.D. Mich. 1978).

16 A description of the controversy can be found in 126 Cong. Rec. S16, at 228–36 (Dec. 11, 1980).

17 *See id.* at 231–34.

18 *Id.* at 233–34.

19 *Id.* at 228–31.

20 Until 1965, exempt status was routinely granted to private schools without regard to practices of racial discrimination. In the mid-1960s, however, the IRS decided to reexamine this policy in the light of Brown v. Board of Education and later Supreme Court decisions invalidating state aid to segregated private schools. From October 15, 1965, to August 2, 1967, a freeze was maintained on applications for exempt status "filed by private schools apparently found to be operated on a seg-regated basis." Green v. Kennedy, 309 F. Supp. 1127, 1130 (D.D.C. 1970). In 1967, after an internal review, the IRS concluded that it lacked authority to withhold exemptions except where the school already received other substantial state assis-tance, such as tuition grants or the use of public facilities. IRS News Release, Aug. 2, 1967, *reprinted in* 1967 Stand. Fed. Tax Rep. (CCH) ¶ 6734.

21 The named defendant, David Kennedy, was secretary of the treasury. After he was replaced by John Connally, the case was retitled Green v. Connally and is commonly referred to by that name.

22 28 U.S.C. §§ 2282, 2284 (1976).

23 *Green*, 309 F. Supp. 1127.

24 IRS News Releases, July 10 and July 19, 1970, *reprinted in* 7 Stand. Fed. Tax Rep. (CCH) ¶¶ 6790, 6814 (1970).

25 330 F. Supp. 1150 (D.D.C. 1971).

26 *Id.* at 1157–59.

27 *Id.* at 1160.

28 *Id.* at 1161.

29 *Id.* at 1163.

30 *Id.*

31 *Id.* at 1164–65.

32 *Id.* at 1170–71.

33 *Id.*

34 *Id.* at 1174.

35 404 U.S. 997 (1971), *sub nom.* Coit v. Green.

36 Bob Jones Univ. v. United States, 639 F.2d 147 (4th Cir. 1980); Goldsboro Christian Schs., Inc, v. United States, No. 80–1473 (4th Cir. Feb. 24, 1981); Prince Edward Sch. Found. v. United States, No. 79–1622 (D.C. Cir. June 30, 1980); Wright v. Regan, 656 F.2d 820 (D.C. Cir. 1981).

37 Pub. L. No. 94–568, 90 Stat. 2697 (1976).

38 Congress added Section 501(i) to reverse a judicial decision that upheld tax exemptions for these groups in McGlotten v. Connally, 338 F. Supp. 448 (D.D.C. 1972).

39 S. Rep. No. 1318, 94th Cong., 2d Sess., 7–8 & n.5 (1976); H.R. Rep. No. 1353, 94th Cong., 2d Sess., 8 & n.5 (1976).

40 U.S. Department of the Treasury Press Release, "Treasury Establishes New Tax-Exempt Policy," Jan. 8, 1982, *reprinted in* Administration's Change in Federal Policy Regarding the Tax Status of Racially Discriminatory Private Schools: Hearing before the House Committee on Ways and Means, 97th Cong., 2d Sess., 607–08 (1982) [hereinafter "Policy Change Hearings"].

41 639 F.2d 147 (4th Cir. 1980).

42 No. 80–1473 (4th Cir. Feb. 24, 1981).

43 Memorandum for the United States, *reprinted in* Policy Change Hearings, *supra* note 40, at 612–14.

44 *See* Bernard Wolfman, *Law, Cut on a Bias*, N.Y. TIMES, Jan. 19, 1982, at A27; Joseph Kraft, *A Con Job*, WASH. POST, Jan. 21, 1982, at A19; Anthony Lewis, *Shucks, It's Only the Law*, N.Y. TIMES, Jan. 21, 1982, at A23; *Pirouetting on Civil Rights*, TIME, Jan. 25, 1982, at 24.

45 White House Press Release, "Statement by the President," Jan. 12, 1982, *reprinted in* Policy Change Hearings, supra note 40, at 620.

46 Steven R. Weisman, *Reagan Acts to Bar Tax Break to Schools in Racial Bias Cases*, N.Y. TIMES, Jan. 19, 1982, at A1.

47 Wright v. Regan, No. 80–1124 (D.C. Cir. Feb. 18, 1982).

48 Stuart Taylor Jr., *Schools Tax Issue Put to High Court in Shift by Reagan*, N.Y. TIMES, Feb. 26, 1982, at A1.

49 461 U.S. 574 (1983).

50 Stuart Taylor Jr., *U.S. Drops Rule on Tax Penalty for Racial Bias*, N.Y. TIMES, Jan. 9, 1982, at A1. The average segregated school was estimated to enroll 200 students. *See generally supra* note 7 (citing sources). Even if that estimate is doubled, the

111 schools denied exemptions would be expected to enroll no more than 50,000 students.

51 Terjen, *supra* note 7, at 50.

52 Note, *Segregation Academies and State Action*, 82 YALE L.J. 1436, 1448 (1973).

53 Implementation Hearings, *supra* note 9 at 479 (statement of E. Richard Larson).

54 *Id.* at 5 (statement of Jerome Kurtz); Staff of Subcommittee on Oversight of the House Committee on Ways and Means, Report on IRS's Proposed Revenue Procedure Regarding the Tax-Exempt Status of Private Schools, 96th Cong., 1st Sess., 40 & nn.3–4 (Committee Print 1979) [hereinafter "Staff Report"].

55 The temporary *Green* order, issued the previous January, offered no guidance on implementation. Green v. Kennedy, 309 F. Supp. 1127 (D.D.C. 1970).

56 IRS News Releases, *supra* note 24, ¶¶ 6790, 6814.

57 330 F. Supp. 1150, 1179 (D.D.C. 1971).

58 1972-2 C.B. 834.

59 Implementation Hearings, *supra* note 9, at 4 (statement of Jerome Kurtz).

60 1975-2 C.B. 587–88. The second requirement of publicity through the mass media is, however, relaxed for three kinds of schools. A church-related school drawing at least 75 percent of its students from the sponsoring religious denomination may announce its anti- discrimination policy in a church newspaper. A school drawing a substantial percentage of students from a large geographical area may demonstrate reasonable efforts to inform students of its policy. A school with a meaningful number of minority students is entirely exempt. *Id.* at 588–89.

61 The positions of the Civil Rights Commission, the Ford Justice Department, and the Carter Justice Department are reported in Implementation Hearings, *supra* note 9, at 221–35, 237–51, 1175–87. A staff report expressed general agreement with their conclusions, Staff Report, *supra* note 54, at 21.

62 According to Rep. Sam Gibbons:

Not surprisingly, this [has] proved inadequate. It was a bit like asking the average American taxpayer to simply mail in a check for his taxes, along with an affirmation that the amount enclosed was correct, without requiring any specific figures or documentation.

Implementation Hearings, *supra* note 9, at 1.

63 The case was originally docketed as Wright v. Simon, No. 76–1426 (D.D.C. July 30, 1976).

64 Proposed Rev. Proc., 43 Fed. Reg. 37296 (1978).

65 Brumfield v. Dodd, 425 F. Supp. 528 (E.D. La. 1976); Norwood v. Harrison, 382 F. Supp. 921 (D. Miss. 1974).

66 Proposed Rev. Proc., *supra* note 64, § 3.03.

67 *Id.* § 4.02.

68 Staff Report, *supra* note 54, at 40.

69 Proposed Rev. Proc., *supra* note 64.

70 *Id.*

71 *See* Implementation Hearings, *supra* note 9; Staff Report, *supra* note 54, at 1–8.

72 Implementation Hearings, *supra* note 9; Staff Report, *supra* note 54, at 1–8; Hearings before the Subcommittee on Taxation and Debt Management Generally of the Senate Committee on Finance, 96th Cong., 1st Sess. (1979).

73 Treasury, Postal Service, and General Government Appropriations Act of 1980, Pub. L. No. 96–74, § 615, 93 Stat. 559, 577 (1979).

74 *Id.* § 103, 93 Stat. at 5–62.

75 The restrictions remained in force during the 1981 and 1982 fiscal years because Treasury funds were provided through continuing resolutions, which automatically carried through any restrictions on appropriations enacted in the previous fiscal year. Continuing Appropriations for Fiscal Year 1981, Pub. L. No. 96–369, 94 Stat. 1351 (1980); Continuing Appropriations for Fiscal Year 1981, Pub. L. No. 96–536, 94 Stat. 3166 (1980); Continuing Appropriations for Fiscal Year 1982, Pub. L. No. 97–51, 95 Stat. 958 (1981); Continuing Appropriations for Fiscal Year 1982, Pub. L. No. 97–85, 95 Stat. 1098 (1981); Continuing Appropriations for Fiscal Year 1982, Pub. L. No. 97–92, 95 Stat. 1183 (1981).

76 The two riders did not alter either the *Green* construction of the Internal Revenue Code or the existing requirement that exempt private schools announce a non-discrimination policy. The sponsors stated that their purpose was only to prevent implementation of the new enforcement rules. Thus, neither bill prohibited the spending of appropriated funds to enforce the 1975 Revenue Procedure. Policy Change Hearings, *supra* note 40, at 691–92, 701.

77 The case was then docketed as Wright v. Miller, 480 F. Supp. 790 (D.D.C. 1979).

78 426 U.S. 26 (1976).

79 *Id.* at 42–43.

80 480 F. Supp. at 793 n.1.

81 Green v. Miller, No. 1355–69 (D.D.C. May 5, 1980), *amended*, June 2, 1980.

82 Continuing Appropriations for Fiscal Year 1982, Pub. L. No. 97–51, *supra* note 64.

83 656 F.2d 820 (D.C. Cir. 1981).

84 *Id.* at 823–825.

85 *Id.* at 826.

86 *Id.*

87 *Id.* at 828.

88 413 U.S. 455 (1973).

89 417 U.S. 556 (1974).

90 656 F.2d at 829.

91 413 U.S. at 457.

92 *Id.* at 471.

93 417 U.S. at 556.

94 *Id.* at 568. The proceedings were remanded to the District Court for findings as to whether the nonexclusive "use of zoos, museums, parks, and other recreational facilities by private school groups in common with others … involves the government so directly as to violate the equal protection clause." *Id.* at 570. Four justices would have declared unconstitutional, without remand, the nonexclusive use of facilities, such as athletic fields, that relieve [the schools] of the expense of maintaining their own facilities" or are used "for events that are part of the school curriculum." *Id.* at 576–82.

95 656 F.2d at 828.

96 468 U.S. 737 (1984).

97 *Id.* at 758.

98 *Id.* at 759.
99 *Id.* at 766.
100 *Id.* at 767.
101 *Id.* at 774.
102 *Id.* at 795.
103 Carla Crowder, *Private White Academies Struggle in Changing World*, BIRMINGHAM NEWS, Oct. 27, 2002, *available at* http://www.al.com/specialreport /birminghamnews/?blackbelt16.html
104 *Id.*
105 Sarah Carr, *In Southern Towns, "Segregation Academies" Are Still Going Strong*, ATLANTIC, Dec. 13, 2012, *available at* http://www.theatlantic.com /national/archive/2012/12/in-southern-towns-segregation-academies-are-still-going -strong/266207/
106 *Id.*
107 518 U.S. 515 (1996).
108 *Id.*, Transcript of Oral Argument at 45.
109 518 U.S. at 598 (Scalia, J., dissenting).
110 Bob Jones Univ. v. United States, 461 U.S. 574, 598 (1983).
111 Brief for Twenty Six Private Women's Colleges as Amici Curiae Supporting Petitioner, *VMI*, 518 U.S. 515, 1995 WL 702837, at *23, *25.
112 *VMI*, 518 U.S. at 532 n.6.
113 *Id.* at 533 n.7.
114 Husband of Justice Ruth Bader Ginsburg for fifty-six years until his death in 2010, Professor Martin David Ginsburg was an internationally renowned tax expert and probably the greatest authority ever on the law of corporate taxation.
115 TAM 7744007, 1977 WL 50659.
116 Martin Ginsburg, *Sex Discrimination and the IRS: Public Policy and the Charitable Deduction*, 10 TAX NOTES 27 (Jan. 14, 1980).
117 *Id.*
118 *Id.*

7 A MORE PERFECT UNION

1 347 U.S. 483 (1954).
2 *Presidential Proclamation – 60th Anniversary of* Brown v. Board of Education, May 15, 2014, http://www.whitehouse.gov/the-press-office/2014/05/15/presidential -proclamation-60th-anniversary-brown-v-board-education
3 *Id.*
4 Sheryl Gay Stolberg, *Mrs. Obama, in Speech, Cites Growing Divisions*, N.Y.TIMES, May 17, 2014, at A14.
5 Arne Duncan, *Progress and Challenges 60 Years after* Brown v. Board, HOMEROOM: THE OFFICIAL BLOG OF THE U.S. DEP'T OF ED., May 15, 2014, http://www.ed.gov /blog/?guest_author_name=Arne+Duncan
6 *Id.*
7 *Id.*
8 Parents Involved in Cmty. Sch. v. Seattle Sch. Dist. No. 1, 551 U.S. 701, 747 (2007).

9 *See* Shelby Cnty. v. Holder, 133 S. Ct. 2612 (2013).

10 *Id.* at 2628.

11 *Id.* at 2625.

12 *Id.* at 2629.

13 This view is perhaps best, and certainly most succinctly, summed up in Chief Justice Roberts's recent observation that "the way to stop discrimination on the basis of race is to stop discriminating on the basis of race." *Parents Involved*, 551 U.S. at 748.

14 518 U.S. 515 (1996).

15 *Id.* at 520.

16 *Id.* at 522.

17 *Id.* (noting that "only about 15% of VMI cadets enter career military service" (internal quotation marks omitted; alteration in original)).

18 *Id.* at 520, 523 (noting that "VMI has the largest per-student endowment of all public undergraduate institutions in the Nation" primarily "because its alumni are exceptionally close to the school").

19 *Id.* at 520 (noting that "VMI has notably succeeded in its mission to produce leaders; among its alumni are military generals, Members of Congress, and business executives"); *id.* at 552 (discussing the "network of business owners, corporations, VMI graduates and non-graduate employers … interested in hiring VMI graduates" (internal quotation marks omitted; alteration in original)).

20 *Id.* at 523.

21 *See* Br. for the Pet'r at 5, *VMI*, 518 U.S. 515.

22 *Id.* at 24–25.

23 *See* Br. for the Resp. at 17, *VMI*, 518 U.S. 515.

24 *Id.* at 43–44. For a fascinating account of the fear that co-education would disrupt physical closeness between male cadets at what was the nation's only other all-male public military academy, see Susan Faludi, *The Naked Citadel*, New Yorker, Sept. 5, 1994, at 62.

25 *VMI*, 518 U.S. at 541 (quoting testimony by one of Virginia's expert witnesses (internal quotation marks omitted)).

26 *Id.* at 526.

27 *Id.* 526–27 (describing the proposed Virginia Women's Institute for Leadership, which did not have a military format, did not require its students to eat together or wear uniforms, and generally eschewed the "adversarial method").

28 *See* Jason Farago, *Ruth Bader Ginsburg: The Supreme Court's Leading Lady Shouldn't Leave Yet*, Guardian, Aug. 2, 2013, http://www.theguardian.com/commentisfree/2013/aug/02/ruth-bader-ginsburg-supreme-court-20-years

29 Owen M. Fiss, *Groups and the Equal Protection Clause*, 5 Phil. & Pub. Aff. 107, 108 (1976).

30 *Id.*

31 *VMI*, 518 U.S. at 523 (citing a finding to this effect by the district court (internal quotation marks omitted)). The idea of a "critical mass," which Ginsburg introduced here, has gone on to play an important role in the Court's affirmative action jurisprudence. *See* Grutter v. Bollinger, 539 U.S. 306, 330–33 (2003).

32 *Id.* at 540. Neither party in this case contested that such accommodations would be required, and the district court found, as a matter of fact, that admitting women to VMI would require the school to make such changes. *Id.*

33 *Id.* at 533 n.7 (noting that "it is the mission of some single-sex schools 'to dissipate, rather than perpetuate, traditional gender classifications,'" but ultimately declining to reach the question of whether states can provide "separate but equal" undergraduate institutions for men and women (quoting Brief of Twenty-Six Private Women's Colleges as Amici Curiae Supporting Petitioner, *VMI*, 518 U.S. 515)).

34 *Id.* (internal quotation marks omitted).

35 *Id.* at 531.

36 *Id.* at 531 n.5.

37 *Id.* at 531, 543–44.

38 *Id.* at 536–39.

39 *See id.* at 536 n.9 (noting that these stereotypes often took a rather literal form, as numerous "authorities" in the nineteenth century argued that education would interfere with women's reproductive functions and incapacitate them for wife- and motherhood).

40 *Id.* at 566 (Scalia, J., dissenting).

41 *Id.*

42 *Id.* at 533–34.

43 *Id.* at 557.

44 *Id.* at 546 (noting that after VMI admitted its first African American cadets, in 1968, the student body stopped singing "Dixie" and saluting the Confederate flag and the tomb of General Robert E. Lee at ceremonies and sports events).

45 *Id.* at 558.

46 *Id.* at 576 (Scalia, J., dissenting); *see id.* at 570 ("To reject the Court's disposition today ... [i]t is only necessary to apply honestly the test the Court has been applying to sex-based classifications for the past two decades.").

47 *Id.* at 574.

48 *Id.* at 574–75 (suggesting that the stringent scrutiny to which the Court subjected VMI's all-male admissions policy is "particularly out of place because it is perfectly clear that, if the question of the applicable standard of review for sex-based classifications were to be regarded as an appropriate subject for reconsideration, the stronger argument would be not for elevating the standard to strict scrutiny, but for reducing it to rational-basis review").

49 *See, e.g., id.* at 531, 533, 534, 545, 546, 556. This language was not new. Courts had been using it in sex discrimination cases since at least the early 1980s. *See* Mississippi Univ. for Women v. Hogan, 458 U.S. 718, 724 (1982) (asserting that a party seeking to uphold government action based on sex must establish an "exceedingly persuasive justification" for such action). Nonetheless, the Court's avoidance of the term "intermediate scrutiny" in favor of "exceedingly persuasive justification," and its observation that strict scrutiny had "thus far" been reserved to cases involving race, *VMI*, 518 U.S. at 533 n.6, was enough to raise questions about the level of scrutiny the Court actually applied in this case. *See, e.g.,* Cass R. Sunstein, *The Supreme Court, 1995 Term – Foreword: Leaving Things Undecided,* 110 HARV. L. REV. 4, 75 (1996) (asserting that "the Court did not merely restate the intermediate scrutiny test but pressed it closer to strict scrutiny" and that "after *United States v. Virginia,* it is not simple to describe the appropriate standard of review" in cases involving sex-based state action).

50 *See* Geduldig v. Aiello, 417 U.S. 484, 496 n.20 (1974) ("The lack of identity between [pregnancy] and gender as such ... becomes clear upon the most cursory analysis.

[Pregnancy discrimination] divides [humanity] into two groups – pregnant women and nonpregnant persons. While the first group is exclusively female, the second includes members of both sexes.").

51 *VMI*, 518 U.S. at 533.

52 *Id.*

53 *Id.*

54 *Id.*

55 *Id.*

56 For more on *VMI*'s innovative approach to "real differences" between men and women, see Cary Franklin, *The Anti-Stereotyping Principle in Constitutional Sex Discrimination Law*, 85 N.Y.U. L. REV. 83, 143–46 (2010). Most scholars have interpreted *Geduldig* as holding that pregnancy discrimination does not constitute discrimination on the basis of sex. Reva Siegel has pointed out, however, that the holding in *Geduldig* was narrower than this. *Geduldig* held that "not … *every* legislative classification concerning pregnancy is a sex-based classification like those considered in *Reed* … and *Frontiero*," the first cases in which the Court invalidated sex-based state action under the Equal Protection Clause. *See* Geduldig v. Aiello, 417 U.S. 484, 496 n.20 (1974) (emphasis added). As Siegel notes, this holding leaves open the possibility that *some* legislative classifications involving pregnancy are sex-based classifications like those considered in *Reed* and *Frontiero*. *See* Reva B. Siegel, *You've Come a Long Way, Baby: Rehnquist's New Approach to Pregnancy Discrimination in Hibbs*, 58 STAN. L. REV. 1871, 1873 (2006). Thus, we might read Ginsburg's discussion of the regulation of "real differences" in *VMI* not as contradicting *Geduldig*, but as clarifying when, in fact, such regulation runs afoul of legal prohibitions of sex discrimination.

57 Indeed, Ginsburg observes in *VMI* that after the school integrated, it "established a program on 'retention of black cadets' designed to offer academic and social-cultural support to 'minority members of a dominantly white and tradition-oriented student body,'" and that the school "maintains a 'special recruitment program for blacks.'" *VMI*, 518 U.S. at 546 n.6 (quoting U.S. v. Va., 766 F. Supp. 1407, 1436–37 (W.D. Va. 1991)). This does not constitute a holding, but it is certainly a strong suggestion that Ginsburg believes these programs to be constitutional for the same reasons she suggests in *VMI* that sex-specific accommodations and recruitment programs are constitutional: they aim to integrate formerly segregated institutions, break down stereotypes, and distribute opportunities to groups that have previously been denied them.

58 This essay focuses on the applications of Ginsburg's constitutional reasoning in *VMI* to the context of race, but race is not the only context to which she has applied these ideas. *See, e.g.*, Samuel R. Bagenstos, *Justice Ginsburg and the Judicial Role in Expanding "We the People": The Disability Rights Cases*, 104 COLUM. L. REV. 49, 56 (2004) (arguing that "the critique of paternalism that lies at the core of disability rights thinking has much in common with – and was surely influenced by – the women's movement's own attack on paternalistic practices that limited women's opportunities, an attack exemplified by … Ginsburg's litigation agenda throughout the 1970s," and that her judicial opinions have, not coincidentally, done more than any of her colleagues' to promote the full citizenship stature of people with disabilities).

59 *See, e.g.*, Gratz v. Bollinger, 539 U.S. 244, 299–300 & nn. 4–5 (2003) (Ginsburg, J., dissenting); Grutter v. Bollinger, 539 U.S. 306, 345–46 (2003) (Ginsburg, J., concurring).

60 *See, e.g., Gratz*, 539 U.S. at 299–301 (Ginsburg, J., dissenting) (discussing racial disparities in a wide range of social contexts and asserting that "'bias both conscious and unconscious ... keeps up barriers that must come down if equal opportunity and nondiscrimination are ever genuinely to become this country's law and practice'" (quoting Adarand Constructors, Inc. v. Peña, 515 U.S. 200, 274 (1995) (Ginsburg, J., dissenting)).

61 *Id.* (Ginsburg, J., dissenting) (internal quotation marks omitted).

62 *Id.* at 298 (Ginsburg, J., dissenting).

63 *Id.* (Ginsburg, J., dissenting).

64 *Id.* (Ginsburg, J., dissenting) (internal quotation marks omitted).

65 133 S. Ct. 2612 (2013).

66 *Id.* at 2631 (striking down §4 of the act, which contained the coverage formula the federal government had long used as a basis for subjecting jurisdictions to preclearance requirements).

67 *Id.* at 2628.

68 *Id.* at 2642 (Ginsburg, J., dissenting) (quoting WILLIAM SHAKESPEARE, THE TEMPEST act 2, sc. 1).

69 *Id.* (Ginsburg, J., dissenting) (quoting 1 GEORGE SANTAYANA, THE LIFE OF REASON 284 (1905)).

70 *Id.* (Ginsburg, J., dissenting).

71 Gratz v. Bollinger, 539 U.S. 244, 302 (2003) (Ginsburg, J., dissenting); *see also* Grutter v. Bollinger, 539 U.S. 306, 344 (2003) (Ginsburg, J., concurring).

72 *Gratz*, 539 U.S. at 301 (quoting Norwalk Core v. Norwalk Redevelopment Agency, 395 F.2d 920, 931–32 (2d Cir. 1968)).

73 Adarand Constructors, Inc. v. Peña, 515 U.S. 200, 275 (1995) (Ginsburg, J., dissenting).

74 *Id.* (Ginsburg, J., dissenting).

75 *See* Ruth Bader Ginsburg & Barbara Flagg, *Some Reflections on the Feminist Legal Thought of the 1970s*, 1989 U. CHI. LEGAL F. 9, 11 (recalling that reading all available material on women and the law in 1970 "proved not to be a burdensome venture" as "so little had been written, one could manage it all in a matter of weeks"). The first sex discrimination casebooks – including one authored by Ginsburg herself – did not appear until several years later. *See* Linda K. Kerber, *Writing Our Own Rare Books*, 14 YALE J.L. & FEMINISM 429, 430–31 (2002).

76 *See* Franklin, *supra* note 56, at 108–10 (discussing early legal feminists' development of the race-sex analogy).

77 Green v. New Kent Cnty. Sch. Bd., 391 U.S. 430, 440 (1968).

78 *Id.* at 440, 442 (internal quotation marks omitted).

79 402 U.S. 1 (1971).

80 *Id.* at 16.

81 401 U.S. 424 (1971).

82 *Id.* at 431.

83 *See* Reva B. Siegel, *The Supreme Court, 2012 Term – Foreword: Equality Divided*, 127 HARV. L. REV. 1, 14 (2013) (observing that "during the 1970s, when plaintiffs

brought equal protection challenges to public employment selection criteria with a racially exclusionary impact, at least eight federal courts of appeals employed disparate impact frameworks in adjudicating these lawsuits, all importing to the constitutional context the liability rule that had been set down in *Griggs*"). Ultimately, the Supreme Court declined to import to the contextual context the liability rule in *Griggs*. *See* Personnel Adm'r of Mass. v. Feeney, 442 U.S. 256 (1979); Washington v. Davis, 426 U.S. 229 (1976). These cases departed from an understanding that had been quite prevalent until that point.

84 416 U.S. 351 (1974).

85 416 U.S. 312 (1974).

86 For further discussion of the challenges Ginsburg faced as a result of the coinciding grants of certiorari in *Kahn* and *DeFunis*, see SERENA MAYERI, REASONING FROM RACE: FEMINISM, LAW, AND THE CIVIL RIGHTS REVOLUTION 87–90 (2011).

87 *See, e.g.*, Br. for Appellants at 4, *Kahn*, 416 U.S. 351 (differentiating genuine "affirmative action measures tailored narrowly and specifically to rectify the effects of past discrimination" from "generalized provisions based on gender stereotypes of the variety here").

88 *Kahn*, 416 U.S. at 355–56.

89 After *Kahn*, the Court issued a series of decisions invalidating apparently benign forms of sex-based state action on the ground that they reinforced traditional stereotyped conceptions of men's and women's sex and family roles. For further discussion of these cases, see Franklin, *supra* note 56, at 132–38. The Court deemed *DeFunis* moot because the plaintiff was set to graduate from law school by the time the justices began their deliberations. *DeFunis*, 416 U.S. at 319–20.

90 Adarand Constructors, Inc. v. Peña, 515 U.S. 200, 275 (1995) (Ginsburg, J., dissenting) (quoting *id.* at 245 (Stevens, J., dissenting)).

91 Gratz v. Bollinger, 539 U.S. 244, 302 (2003) (Ginsburg, J., dissenting) (quoting U.S. v. Jefferson Cnty. Bd. of Ed., 372 F.2d 836, 876 (5th Cir. 1966) (Wisdom, J.)).

92 *Id.* at 301 (Ginsburg, J., dissenting).

8 BARRIERS TO ENTRY AND JUSTICE GINSBURG'S CRIMINAL PROCEDURE JURISPRUDENCE

1 *See* Kathleen M. Sullivan, *Constitutionalizing Women's Equality*, 90 CALIF. L. REV. 735, 739 (2002) ("American women's equality is a story of creative interpretation of the Equal Protection Clause and of advocates' bravado ... [l]ed with inventiveness and strategic brilliance by now-Justice Ruth Bader Ginsburg.").

2 *See* Christopher Slobogin, *Justice Ginsburg's Gradualism in Criminal Procedure*, 70 OHIO ST. L.J. 867, 870 (2009).

3 *See, e.g.*, United States v. Virginia, 518 U.S. 515 (1996).

4 Neil S. Siegel, *"Equal Citizenship Stature": Justice Ginsburg's Constitutional Vision*, 43 NEW. ENG. L. REV. 799, 825 (2009).

5 *See generally* Sarah E. Valentine, *Ruth Bader Ginsburg: An Annotated Bibliography*, 7 N.Y. CITY L. REV. 391 (2004). *See also* Slobogin, *supra* note 2, at 870 ("To date, no one has taken a sustained look at Justice Ginsburg's approach to decision-making in the area of criminal procedure.").

6 Perry v. New Hampshire, 132 S. Ct. 716 (2012).

7 *Id.* at 730.

8 Connick v. Thompson, 131 S. Ct. 1350 (2011).

9 *Id.* at 1370–87 (Ginsburg, J., dissenting).

10 Slobogin, *supra* note 2, at 870.

11 Siegel, *supra* note 4, at 801.

12 *See* Slobogin, *supra* note 2, at 876; *see also id.* at 887 (stating that some of Justice Ginsburg's criminal procedure decisions may have been lost opportunities and that "a bit more willingness to push the envelope might be worthwhile even for a judge who tends to [be] gradualist").

13 Her record is, however, in keeping with her resistance to affixing "conservative" or "liberal" labels to jurisprudential trends, which she has pointed out tends to be the practice of unsuccessful litigants. *See generally* Ruth Bader Ginsburg, *Interpretations of the Equal Protection Clause*, 9 HARV. L. & POL'Y REV 41 (1986).

14 Justice Ginsburg has written that "measured motions" seem right "for constitutional as well as common law adjudication," and that "doctrinal limbs too swiftly shaped" "may prove unstable." Ruth Bader Ginsburg, *Speaking in a Judicial Voice*, 67 N.Y.U. L. REV. 1185, 1198 (1992); *see also* Pamela S. Karlan, *Some Thoughts on Autonomy and Equality in Relation to Ruth Bader Ginsburg*, 70 OHIO ST. L.J. 1085, 1086 (2009).

15 Ginsburg, *supra* note 14, at 1209.

16 Slobogin, *supra* note 2, at 867.

17 *Nomination of Ruth Bader Ginsburg to Be Associate Justice of the Supreme Court of the United States: Hearing before the S. Comm. on the Judiciary*, 103d Cong. 56 (1993) (statement of Judge Ruth Bader Ginsburg) (internal quotation marks omitted).

18 Roe v. Wade, 410 U.S. 113 (1973).

19 Ruth Bader Ginsburg, *Some Thoughts on Autonomy and Equality in Relation to Roe v. Wade*, 63 N.C. L. REV. 375, 376 (1985); *see also* Adam Liptak, *Court Is 'One of Most Activist,' Ginsburg Says, Vowing to Stay*, N.Y. TIMES, Aug. 24, 2013, at A1 (recounting Justice Ginsburg's view that the Court moved too fast in *Roe* because the decision "'gave the anti-abortion forces a single target to aim at'").

20 *See* Miranda v. Arizona, 384 U.S. 436 (1966); Gideon v. Wainwright, 372 U.S. 335 (1963); Mapp v. Ohio, 367 U.S. 643 (1961).

21 *See, e.g.,* Herring v. United States, 555 U.S. 135, 157 (2009) (Ginsburg, J., dissenting).

22 Slobogin, *supra* note 2, at 879.

23 Perry v. New Hampshire, 132 S. Ct. 716 (2012).

24 *Id.* at 730.

25 *Id.* at 718 (quoting Neil v. Biggers, 409 U.S. 188, 201 (1972)) (internal quotation marks omitted).

26 *See, e.g.,* BRANDON GARRETT, CONVICTING THE INNOCENT 145 (2011).

27 United States v. Jones, 132 S. Ct. 945, 956 (2012) (Sotomayor, J., concurring).

28 Berghuis v. Thompkins, 560 U.S. 370, 400–01 (2010) (Sotomayor, J., dissenting).

29 *Perry*, 132 S. Ct. at 730–40 (Sotomayor, J., dissenting).

30 *See* Crawford v. Washington, 541 U.S. 36, 68–69 (2004); *see also* Michigan v. Bryant, 131 S. Ct. 1143, 1177 (2011) (Ginsburg, J., dissenting).

31 *Perry*, 132 S. Ct. at 728.

32 *See id.* at 726. Justice Ginsburg noted that the "crucial element of police overreaching" was missing, and therefore that the Due Process Clause was not implicated. *Id.* (quoting Colorado v. Connelly, 479 U.S. 157, 163, 167 (1986)).

33 Kentucky v. King, 131 S. Ct. 1849 (2011).

34 *See id.* at 1864 (Ginsburg, J., dissenting) ("The Court today arms the police with a way routinely to dishonor the Fourth Amendment's warrant requirement in drug cases. In lieu of presenting their evidence to a neutral magistrate, police officers may now knock, listen, then break the door down, nevermind that they had ample time to obtain a warrant."); *see also* Arkansas v. Sullivan, 532 U.S. 769, 773 (2001) (Ginsburg, J., concurring) (agreeing that officers' subjective intentions are irrelevant for probable cause analysis but urging reconsideration in the event of an "epidemic of unnecessary minor-offense arrests"); Minnesota v. Carter, 525 U.S. 83, 108 (1998) (Ginsburg, J., dissenting) ("Human frailty suggests that today's decision will tempt police to pry into private dwellings without warrant, to find evidence incriminating guests who do not rest there through the night.").

35 *See* Howes v. Fields, 132 S. Ct. 1181, 1195 (2012) (Ginsburg, J., concurring in part and dissenting in part).

36 Florida v. J.L., 529 U.S. 266, 274 (2000).

37 *See* Fernandez v. California, 134 S. Ct. 1126, 1140 (2013) (Ginsburg, J., dissenting).

38 Herring v. United States, 555 U.S. 135, 155 (2009) (Ginsburg, J., dissenting); *see also* Arizona v. Evans, 514 U.S. 1, 30 (1995) (Ginsburg, J., dissenting) (asserting that deterrence is an empirical question rather than a "logical" one).

39 *Cf.* Smith v. Massachusetts, 543 U.S. 462, 476 (2005) (Ginsburg, J., dissenting) ("As a trial unfolds, a defendant must be accorded a timely, fully informed opportunity to meet the State's charges. I would so hold as a matter not of double jeopardy, but of due process.").

40 Perry v. New Hampshire, 132 S. Ct. 716, 721 (2012).

41 *See, e.g.,* Rivera v. Illinois, 556 U.S. 148, 162 (2009) (holding that the erroneous denial of a peremptory challenge does not violate the Constitution because the defendant "received precisely what due process required: a fair trial before an impartial and properly instructed jury"); Vermont v. Brillon, 556 U.S. 81, 82 (2009) (attributing a public defender's trial delay to the defendant because a "contrary conclusion could encourage appointed counsel to delay proceedings by seeking unreasonable continuances, hoping thereby to obtain a dismissal of the indictment on speedy-trial grounds").

42 In the discrimination decisions as well, however, Justice Ginsburg has emphasized entitlements themselves less than the question of whether a disqualification applies to one group but not another. *See, e.g.,* United States v. Virginia, 518 U.S. 515 (1996).

43 *See* Crawford v. Washington, 541 U.S. 36 (2004); Apprendi v. New Jersey, 530 U.S. 466 (2000).

44 Justice Kagan is the exception.

45 *See* Joyce A. Baugh, *Ruth Bader Ginsburg: A Judge's Judge and a Lawyer's Lawyer, in* Supreme Court Justices in the Post-Bork Era: Confirmation Politics and Judicial Performance 61–80 (2002).

46 In 1954, the Court included Chief Justice Earl Warren, a former governor of California; Hugo L. Black, a former United States Senator; Felix Frankfurter, a

former law professor; William O. Douglas, who had served as chairman of the Securities and Exchange Commission; and Robert H. Jackson, who had been the United States Attorney General. *See* Adam Liptak, *Judging a Court with Ex-Judges Only*, N.Y. TIMES, Feb. 17, 2009, at A14.

47 *See, e.g.*, Lee Epstein, et al. *Circuit Effects: How the Norm of Federal Judicial Experience Biases the U.S. Supreme Court*, 157 U. PA. L. REV. 833, 853–64 (2009).

48 Linda Greenhouse, *Justices on the Job*, N.Y. TIMES, July 24, 2013, http://opinionator .blogs.nytimes.com/2013/07/24/justices-on-the-job/

49 *See* David L. Shapiro, *Justice Ginsburg's First Decade: Some Thoughts about Her Contributions in the Fields of Procedure and Jurisdiction*, 104 COLUM. L. REV. 21, 21–22 (2004) (discussing Justice Ginsburg's "lawyerly" approach and narrow focus on analyzing the particular context and the facts at hand).

50 *See* Wendy W. Williams, *Ruth Bader Ginsburg's Equal Protection Clause: 1970–80*, 25 COLUM. J. GENDER & L. 41, 41 (2013).

51 Kowalski v. Temser, 543 U.S. 125, 144 (2004) (Ginsburg, J., dissenting); *see id.* at 139–40 (objecting to the Court's conclusion that attorney lacked standing to sue on behalf of indigent criminal defendants because of the "incapacities under which these defendants labor and the complexity of the issues their cases may entail").

52 As Neil Siegel writes, "a Justice whose basic approach to constitutional law is oriented around the ideal of essential human dignity, of full human stature, might be expected to respond skeptically to a President's assertion that there are, in effect, no judicially enforceable constitutional limits on his authority to declare someone an 'enemy combatant' and to indefinitely detain the individual or try him before a military commission." Siegel, *supra* note 4, at 831 (citing Boumediene v. Bush, 553 U.S. 723 (2008), Hamdan v. Rumsfeld, 548 U.S. 557 (2006), Hamdi v. Rumsfeld, 542 U.S. 507 (2004), Rasul v. Bush, 542 U.S. 466 (2004), and Rumsfeld v. Padilla, 542 U.S. 426 (2004)); *see also* Slobogin, *supra* note 2, at 875 (noting that Justice Ginsburg voted for the petitioner in "every one of the cases contesting the Bush Administration's attempts to exempt its war on terrorism from federal court jurisdiction"); *cf.* Weiss v. United States, 510 U.S. 163, 194 (1994) (Ginsburg, J., concurring) ("The care the Court has taken to analyze petitioner's claims demonstrates once again that men and women in the Armed Forces do not leave constitutional safeguards and judicial protection behind when they enter military service.").

53 *See, e.g.*, Smith v. Massachusetts, 543 U.S. 462, 475–80 (2005) (Ginsburg, J., dissenting); Shafer v. South Carolina, 532 U.S. 36, 54–55 (2001); *see also, e.g.*, Gray v. Netherland, 518 U.S. 152, 171–86 (1995) (Ginsburg, J., dissenting); Simmons v. South Carolina, 512 U.S. 154, 174–75 (1994) (Ginsburg, J., concurring).

54 *See, e.g.*, Bullcoming v. New Mexico, 131 S. Ct. 2705, 2709–19 (2011); Michigan v. Bryant, 131 S. Ct. 1143, 1176–77 (2011) (Ginsburg, J., dissenting); Cunningham v. California, 549 U.S. 270, 293 (2007).

55 *See generally* Carol S. Steiker, *Raising the Bar: Maples v. Thomas and the Sixth Amendment Right to Counsel*, 127 HARV. L. REV. 468 (2013).

56 Alabama v. Shelton, 535 U.S. 654 (2002).

57 *See id.* at 674.

58 Halbert v. Michigan, 545 U.S. 605 (2005).

59 *Id.* at 621 (quoting Griffin v. Illinois, 351 U.S. 12, 24 (1956) (Frankfurter, J., concurring in judgment)) (internal quotation marks omitted).

60 *See id.*

61 Kowalski v. Temser, 543 U.S. 125, 142 (2004) (Ginsburg, J., dissenting).

62 Nichols v. United States, 511 U.S. 738, 765–66 (1994) (Ginsburg, J., dissenting).

63 Pliler v. Ford, 542 U.S. 225, 235–37 (2004) (Ginsburg, J., dissenting).

64 Steiker, *supra* note 55, at 471.

65 *Id.* at 471 (discussing Harrington v. Richter, 131 S. Ct. 770 (2011), Vermont v. Brillon, 556 U.S. 81 (2009), Halbert v. Michigan, 545 U.S. 605 (2005), Rompilla v. Beard, 545 U.S. 374 (2005), Wiggins v. Smith, 539 U.S. 510 (2003), and Alabama v. Shelton, 535 U.S. 654 (2002)).

66 Maples v. Thomas, 132 S. Ct. 912 (2012).

67 *Id.* at 917.

68 *See also* Lee v. Kenna, 534 U.S. 362, 366 (2002) (holding a state rule requiring a writing and specific showing to seek a continuance insufficient to bar federal habeas review because "caught in the midst of a murder trial and unalerted to any procedural defect in his presentation, defense counsel could hardly be expected to divert his attention from the proceedings rapidly unfolding in the courtroom and train, instead, on preparation of a written motion and affidavit").

69 *Brillon*, 556 U.S. 81.

70 *Id.* at 94 (internal quotation marks and citation omitted). Justice Ginsburg has not, however, been similarly supportive of the right to proceed pro se. *See* Slobogin, *supra* note 2, at 874.

71 Justice Ruth Bader Ginsburg, In Pursuit of the Public Good: Lawyers Who Care, the Joseph L. Rah, Jr. Lecture at the Univ. of the D.C., David A. Clarke Sch. of Law (Apr. 9, 2001) (transcript available at http://www.supremecourt.gov/publicinfo /speeches/ viewspeeches.aspx?Filename=sp_04-09-01a.html).

72 *See* Florida v. Nixon, 543 U.S. 175, 190 (2004); *see also* Maples v. Thomas, 132 S. Ct. 912 (2012) (critiquing counsel's performance). Nor has Justice Ginsburg been forgiving of attorneys who make their own procedural errors. She once wrote that there was no need for a windfall when "counsel was not misled by any trial court statements or actions; rather, he neglected to follow plain instructions." Carlisle v. United States, 517 U.S. 416, 436 (1996) (Ginsburg, J., concurring).

73 *See The Supreme Court 2006 Term – Leading Cases*, 121 Harv. L. Rev. 225, 230 (2007); *cf.* J.E.B. v. Alabama, 511 U.S. 127, 151 (1994) (holding that peremptory challenges to exclude jurors based on gender violate the Equal Protection Clause).

74 *See* Jones v. United States, 527 U.S. 373, 413 (1999) (Ginsburg, J., dissenting) (arguing that juries should not be presented with choices "clouded by … misinformation," and that this jury was wrongly instructed that the defendant could receive a sentence other than life imprisonment if a death sentence was not imposed); Romano v. Oklahoma, 512 U.S. 1, 19 (1994) (Ginsburg, J., dissenting) (maintaining that the jury should not be relieved of responsibility for imposition of the death penalty); *cf.* Perry v. New Hampshire, 132 S. Ct. 716, 728–29 (2012) (explaining that careful jury instructions addressing the flaws in eyewitness identifications can educate and empower the jury).

75 Apprendi v. New Jersey, 530 U.S. 466 (2000).

76 *Id.* at 475–76.

77 *See* Ring v. Arizona, 536 U.S. 584, 602 (2002).

78 *See* Cunningham v. California, 549 U.S. 270, 293 (2007).

79 United States v. Booker, 543 U.S. 220 (2005).

80 *Id.* at 244.

81 Connick v. Thompson, 131 S. Ct. 1350 (2011).

82 *Id.* at 1355.

83 Other suppressed evidence in the case concerned a financial reward that the informant received from the victim's family and an eyewitness whose description of the perpetrator did not match Thompson. *Id.* at 1371–72 (Ginsburg, J., dissenting).

84 Once the blood evidence surfaced, a former prosecutor also came forward to report that five years earlier, one of the original prosecutors on the Thompson case confessed to withholding evidence, after he learned that he was dying of cancer. *Id.* at 1374–75.

85 Brady v. Maryland, 373 U.S. 83 (1963).

86 *Id.* at 91–92.

87 *Connick*, 131 S. Ct. at 1359 (citing Monell v. Dep't of Soc. Servs. of N.Y., 436 U.S. 658, 692 (1978)).

88 Canton v. Harris, 489 U.S. 378 (1989).

89 *Id.* at 388.

90 *See* Smith v. Cain, 132 S. Ct. 627 (2012); Kyles v. Whitley, 514 U.S. 419 (1995).

91 *Connick*, 131 S. Ct. at 1366. According to Justice Scalia's concurrence in *Connick*, *Canton* describes the *only* case in which a deliberate indifference claim could be premised on a single violation: the extreme circumstance of arming police officers untrained in the permissible use of deadly force. *Id.* at 1367–70 (Scalia, J., concurring).

92 *Id.* at 1387 (Ginsburg, J., dissenting).

93 *Id.* at 1366 (Scalia, J., concurring). Similar "excavations" by Justice Ginsburg do not always yield the conclusion that procedures were unfair. In her opinion for the Court in *Skilling v. United States*, for example, Justice Ginsburg engaged in an extensive analysis of the trial publicity and the voir dire questions themselves to determine that neither a presumption of prejudice nor actual bias prevented a fair trial in Enron's home venue of Houston. 130 S. Ct. 2896, 2907 (2010). Justice Sotomayor disagreed, concluding that prejudicial information about the Enron case was "deeply ingrained in the popular imagination." *Id.* at 2943 (Sotomayor, J., dissenting).

94 *Connick*, 131 S. Ct. at 1370 (Ginsburg, J., dissenting).

95 *See* Susan A. Bandes, *The Lone Miscreant, The Self-Training Prosecutor, and Other Fictions: A Comment on* Connick v. Thompson, 80 FORDHAM L. REV. 715, 721 (2011).

96 *Connick*, 131 S. Ct. at 1380 n.14, 1387 (Ginsburg, J., dissenting).

97 *Id.* at 1384; *see also* Bandes, *supra* note 95, at 726 (noting that there were thirteen additional pieces of evidence which, "once in [Thompson's] possession, helped [him] win an acquittal in his murder retrial").

98 *Connick*, 131 S. Ct. at 1382 (Ginsburg, J., dissenting).

99 *Id.* at 1384.

100 Bandes, *supra* note 95, at 717.

101 *Connick*, 131 S. Ct. at 1370 (Ginsburg, J., dissenting).

102 *Id.* at 1385.

103 *Id.*

104 Banks v. Dretke, 540 U.S. 668, 695 (2004).

105 *See* Neil S. Siegel & Reva B. Siegel, Struck *by Stereotype*, this volume.

106 Hon. Ruth Bader Ginsburg, *The Role of Dissenting Opinions*, 95 MINN. L. REV. 1, 3 (2010).

107 *Id.* at 8; *see also* Ruth Bader Ginsburg, *Remarks on Writing Separately*, 65 WASH. L. REV. 133, 142–44 (1990); Nancy Gertner, *Dissenting in General: Herring v. United States in Particular*, 127 HARV. L. REV. 433, 433 (2013).

108 Justice Ruth Bader Ginsburg, The 20th Annual Leo and Berry Eizenstat Memorial Lecture: The Role of Dissenting Opinions (Oct. 21, 2007) (transcript available at http://www.supremecourt.gov/publicinfo/speeches/sp_10-21-07.html).

109 *Id.*

110 *Id.*

111 Ledbetter v. Goodyear Tire & Rubber Co., 550 U.S. 618 (2007), *superseded by statute*, Lily Ledbetter Fair Pay Act of 2009, Pub. L. No. 111–2, 123 Stat. 5 (codified at 42 U.S.C. § 2000e-5(e)(3) (2012)).

112 *Id.* at 645 (Ginsburg, J., dissenting).

113 *Id.*; *cf.* Libretti v. United States, 516 U.S. 29, 54 (Ginsburg, J., concurring) (noting that one cannot waive a jury trial right of which one is not fully aware).

114 *See, e.g.*, John Thompson, *The Prosecution Rests, but I Can't*, N.Y. TIMES, Apr. 10, 2011, at WK11 (maintaining that Thompson was not concerned about money damages but rather about accountability for the prosecutors involved, particularly given the 4,000 prisoners serving life without parole in Louisiana who do not have lawyers to seek post-conviction relief).

115 *See generally, e.g.*, Hadar Aviram, *Legally Blind: Hyperadversarialism, Brady Violations, and the Prosecutorial Organizational Culture*, 87 ST. JOHN'S L. REV. 1 (2013); Darryl K. Brown, *Defense Counsel, Trial Judges, and Evidence Production Protocols*, 45 TEX. TECH. L. REV. 133 (2012); Bruce A. Green, *Federal Criminal Discovery Reform: A Legislative Approach*, 64 MERCER L. REV. 639 (2013); Janet Moore, *Democracy and Criminal Discovery Reform After Connick and Garcetti*, 77 BROOK. L. REV. 1329 (2012); Ellen Yaroshesky, *New Orleans Prosecutorial Disclosure in Practice after* Connick v. Thompson, 25 GEO. J. LEGAL ETHICS 913 (2012).

116 *See* Linda Greenhouse, *Oral Dissents Give Ginsburg a New Voice on Court*, N.Y. TIMES, May 31, 2007, at A1.

117 *See* Fisher v. Univ. of Texas, 133 S. Ct. 2411, 2432–33 (2013) (Ginsburg, J., dissenting); Gonzalez v. Carhart, 550 U.S. 124, 169–71 (2007) (Ginsburg, J., dissenting). Some see positive incrementalism on substantive commitments – such as the death penalty – as well. *See* Slobogin, *supra* note 2, at 878–79 (citing Kennedy v. Louisiana, 554 U.S. 407 (2008), Roper v. Simmons, 543 U.S. 551 (2005), and Atkins v. Virginia, 536 U.S. 304 (2002)). Indeed, Justice Ginsburg herself stated in a 2013 interview with New York radio station WQXR: "If I had my way there would be no death penalty. But the death penalty for now is the law, and I could say 'Well, I won't participate in those cases,' but then I can't be an influence." Interview by Marilyn Horne with Justice Ruth Bader Ginsburg, WQXR 105.9 FM (Feb. 2, 2013).

118 *Fisher*, 133 S. Ct. 2411.

119 *See id.* at 2433 (Ginsburg, J., dissenting) ("'I have several times explained why government actors, including state universities, need not blind themselves to the

still lingering, every day evident, effects of centuries of law-sanctioned inequality.'" (quoting Gratz v. Bollinger, 539 U.S. 244, 298 (2003) (Ginsburg, J., dissenting))).

120 *Carhart*, 550 U.S. 124.

121 *Id.* at 169–71 (2007) (Ginsburg, J., dissenting). *See generally* Reva B. Siegel, *The Right's Reasons: Constitutional Conflict and the Spread of Women-Protective Antiabortion Argument*, 57 DUKE L.J. 1641 (2008).

122 *Carhart*, 550 U.S. at 169 (Ginsburg, J., dissenting).

123 *See* Vicki C. Jackson, Lee v. Kemna: *Federal Habeas Corpus and State Procedure*, 127 HARV. L. REV. 445, 448–49 (2013) ("In opinions across areas including gender equality, race equality, and reproductive freedom, Justice Ginsburg's attention to the facts is a welcome font of common law judicial sensibility.").

124 Vance v. Ball State Univ., 133 S. Ct. 2434 (2013).

125 *Id.* at 2455–66 (Ginsburg, J., dissenting).

126 *Id.* at 2434 (majority opinion).

127 *Id.*

128 Shelby Cty. v. Holder, 133 S. Ct. 2612 (2013).

129 *Id.* at 2650 (Ginsburg, J., dissenting).

130 *See* Ledbetter v. Goodyear Tire & Rubber Co., 550 U.S. 618, 645 (2007) (Ginsburg, J., dissenting), *superseded by statute*, Lily Ledbetter Fair Pay Act of 2009, Pub. L. No. 111–2, 123 Stat. 5 (codified at 42 U.S.C. § 2000e-5(e)(3) (2012)).

131 *See Vance*, 133 S. Ct. at 2434 (Ginsburg, J., dissenting) ("The Court today strikes from the supervisory category employees who control the day-to-day schedules and assignments of others, confining the category to those formally empowered to take tangible employment actions.").

132 *See Shelby Cty.*, 133 S. Ct. at 2634 (Ginsburg, J., dissenting) ("Although the VRA wrought dramatic changes in the realization of minority voting rights, the Act, to date, surely has not eliminated all vestiges of discrimination against the exercise of the franchise by minority citizens.").

133 *See* Connick v. Thompson, 131 S. Ct. 1350, 1370 (2011) (Ginsburg, J., dissenting); *cf.* Transcript of Oral Argument at 29, Smith v. Cain, 132 S. Ct. 627 (2012) (No. 10–8145) (statement of Justice Ginsburg) ("But how could it not be material? Here is the only eyewitness.... Are you really urging that the prior statements were immaterial?").

134 *Connick*, 131 S. Ct. at 1370 (Ginsburg, J., dissenting).

135 Ruth Bader Ginsburg, *Remarks of Ruth Bader Ginsburg at CUNY School of Law*, 7 N.Y. CITY L. REV. 221, 238 (2004).

136 *See* Siegel, *supra* note 4, at 816 ("Affording 'equal dignity' to all Americans, including historically marginalized groups, constitutes the central purpose of Justice Ginsburg's constitutional vision.").

137 *Id.* at 804.

138 Karlan, *supra* note 14, at 1091; *see also* Siegel & Siegel, *supra* note 105 (explaining that Justice Ginsburg argued in sex discrimination cases both that "restricting women's liberty may be a means to the end of communicating inequality" and that "discriminating against women may diminish their opportunities to fashion fulfilling lives").

139 *See* Reva B. Siegel, *Sex Equality Arguments for Reproductive Rights: Their Critical Basis and Evolving Constitutional Expression*, 56 EMORY L.J. 815, 823 (2007) ("In

these early briefs, liberty talk and equality talk were entangled as emanations of different constitutional clauses."); *see also* Siegel, *supra* note 4, at 840–41.

140 M.L.B. v. S.L.J., 519 U.S. 102 (1996).

141 *Id.* at 120; *see also* Martha Minow, M.L.B. v. S.L.J., 519 U.S. 102 (1996), 127 HARV. L. REV. 461, 467 (2013).

142 *M.L.B.,* 519 U.S. at 120.

143 *Id.*

144 *See* Ginsburg, *supra* note 19, at 384 (reasoning that an autonomy-based abortion right "places restraints, not affirmative obligations, on government").

145 This would be true, for example, in cases concerning funding for the right to counsel. *See* Karlan, *supra* note 14, at 1092.

146 *Id.* at 1091 (citing *M.L.B.,* 519 U.S. at 120).

147 *See, e.g.,* Deborah Jones Merritt & David M. Lieberman, *Ruth Bader Ginsburg's Jurisprudence of Opportunity and Equality,* 104 COLUM. L. REV. 39, 45 (2004) (stating that Justice Ginsburg has "extended her commitment to opportunity and equality far beyond gender discrimination").

9 A LIBERAL JUSTICE'S LIMITS

1 Ruth Bader Ginsburg, *Speaking in a Judicial Voice,* 67 N.Y.U. L. REV. 1185, 1198 (1992).

2 Wendy W. Williams, *Ruth Bader Ginsburg's Equal Protection Clause,* 25 COLUM. J. GENDER & L. 41, 41 (2013).

3 United States v. Virginia, 518 U.S. 515, 533–34 (1996).

4 Ruth Bader Ginsburg, *Gender and the Constitution,* 44 U. CIN. L. REV. 1 (1975).

5 *See generally* Frontiero v. Richardson, 411 U.S. 677, 687–88 (1973) (discussing the relationship between questions of sex equality under the Fourteenth Amendment and the then-pending Equal Rights Amendment); *see also* Ruth Bader Ginsburg, *Ratification of the Equal Rights Amendment: A Question of Time,* 57 TEX. L. REV. 919, 919 (1979); JANE J. MANSBRIDGE, WHY WE LOST THE ERA (1986).

6 Ginsburg, *supra* note 1, at 1206.

7 *Id.* at 1204.

8 Greenlaw v. United States, 554 U.S. 237, 244 (2008) (citation and quotation marks omitted).

9 Justice Ginsburg was a student in Prof. Sacks's 1957 Legal Process Section. Ruth Bader Ginsburg, *In Memoriam: Albert M. Sacks,* 105 HARV. L. REV. 16, 17 (1991); *see also* Henry Paul Monaghan, *Doing Originalism,* 104 COLUM. L. REV. 32, 35 (2004).

10 Ginsburg, *supra* note 1, at 1193, 1198.

11 Moreover, the counter majoritarian fallacy rests on a classical fallacy of composition, the claim that for a system to be democratic, each of its components must be democratic. The installation of permanent technocratic control over monetary policy in the United States is evidence of that point. In any case, the Court is hardly the least democratic element of the American constitutional order. For a more wide-ranging critique, see SANFORD LEVINSON, OUR UNDEMOCRATIC

CONSTITUTION: WHERE THE CONSTITUTION GOES WRONG (AND HOW WE THE
PEOPLE CAN CORRECT IT) (2006)

12 ALEXANDER BICKEL, THE LEAST DANGEROUS BRANCH: THE SUPREME COURT AT
THE BAR OF POLITICS 23 (1962).

13 CASS R. SUNSTEIN, RADICALS IN ROBES: WHY EXTREME RIGHT-WING COURTS ARE
WRONG FOR AMERICA 29–30 (2005).

14 John F. Manning, *Justice Ginsburg and the New Legal Process*, 127 HARV. L. REV.
455, 459 (2013).

15 Jason J. Czarmezki, William K. Ford & Lori A. Ringhand, *An Empirical
Examination of the Confirmation Hearings of the Justices of the Rehnquist Court*, 24
CONST. COMMENTARY 127, 140 tbl.B (2007).

16 Christopher Slobogin, *Justice Ginsburg's Gradualism in Criminal Procedure*, 70
OHIO ST. L.J. 865, 879 (2009).

17 *See, e.g.*, Shady Grove Orthopedic Assocs., P.A. v. Allstate Ins. Co., 559 U.S. 393,
437–45 (2010) (Ginsburg, J., dissenting); Bush v. Gore, 531 U.S. 98, 136 (2000)
(Ginsburg, J., dissenting); Gasperini v. Ctr. for Humanities, Inc., 518 U.S. 415,
428–29 (1996) (Ginsburg, J., dissenting).

18 *See, e.g.*, Slobogin, *supra* note 16, at 877 (noting that Justice Ginsburg had written
only four of sixty-one Fourth Amendment decisions issued in the study period).
Another important gap here is cases concerning plea bargaining. *See, e.g.*, Missouri
v. Frye, 132 S. Ct. 1399 (2012); Lafler v. Cooper, 132 S. Ct. 1376 (2012).

19 *See, e.g.*, David A. Sklansky, *Cocaine, Race, and Equal Protection*, 47 STAN. L.
REV. 1283, 1284 (1995) (arguing that the "equal protection rules developed by the
Supreme Court … systematically ignore, and lead judges and others to ignore, …
evidence of at least unconscious racism on the part of Congress").

20 I use "liberal" in the colloquial sense of left-of-center; in this context, its meaning
coincides with the classical liberal commitment of individual liberty and a small state.
Contrary to folk wisdom, however, Justice Ginsburg's votes are not wholly asymmetrical in favor of criminal defendants. A 2009 study found that she voted for the government in 110 of 266 criminal procedure cases. Slobogin, *supra* note 16, at 871.

21 Ginsburg, *supra* note 1, at 1206.

22 For a recent example of the Court's tin ear to the effects of continuing gender stereotyping, see Coleman v. Ct. of App. of Md., 132 S. Ct. 1327 (2012).

23 *See* IAN AYRES, PERVASIVE PREJUDICE? UNCONVENTIONAL EVIDENCE OF RACE AND
GENDER DISCRIMINATION (2001) (collecting evidence).

24 *See* Ginsburg, supra note 9, at 17–18; Neil A. Lewis, *Rejected as Clerk, Chosen as
Justice: Ruth Joan Bader Ginsburg*, N.Y. TIMES, June 15, 1993, at A1.

25 *See* ANNA L. HARVEY, VOTES WITHOUT LEVERAGE: WOMEN IN AMERICAN ELECTORAL
POLITICS 1920–1970 (1998) (charting the relative weakness of women voters' influence in the decades after passage of the Nineteenth Amendment).

26 For a history of the politicization of crime in the late 1900s, see Cornell W.
Clayton & J. Mitchell Pickerill, *The Politics of Criminal Justice: How the New
Rights Shaped the Rehnquist Court's Criminal Justice Jurisprudence*, 94 GEO. L.J.
1385 (2005).

27 William J. Stuntz, *The Pathological Politics of Criminal Law*, 100 MICH. L. REV. 505,
510 (2001) (identifying a "deeper politics of criminal law – that are steadily making
criminal law both larger and less relevant – [that] shows no signs of changing").

28 The usual meaning of crisis focuses on an abrupt and singular event, but this is not its sole meaning. See Reinhart Koselleck, *Crisis*, 67 J. HIST. IDEAS 357 (2006).

29 Christopher Muller, *Northward Migration and the Rise of Racial Disparity in American Incarceration, 1880–1950*, 118 AM. J. SOC. 281, 282–83 (2012).

30 Pew Ctr. on the States, *Prison Count 2010*, at 2 (2010), *available at* http://www .pewtrusts.org/uploadedFiles/wwwpewtrustsorg/Reports/sentencing_and _corrections/Prison_Count_2010.pdf

31 Loïc Waquant, *From Slavery to Mass Incarceration*, 13 NEW LEFT REV. 41, 41 (2002). For trend data, see Muller *supra* note 29, at 282–83.

32 KATHERINE BECKETT, MAKING CRIME PAY: LAW AND ORDER IN CONTEMPORARY AMERICAN POLITICS (1997).

33 This is persuasively documented by Judge Shira Scheindlin in *Floyd v. City of New York*, – F. Supp. 2d –, 2013 WL 4046209 (S.D.N.Y. Aug 13, 2013); *see also* Lynn Langton & Matthew Durose, U.S. Department of Justice Bureau of Justice Statistics, *Police Behavior during Traffic and Street Stops, 2011* (2013) (documenting racial disparities in national-level policing data for 2011).

34 See Samuel R. Gross & Michael Shaffer, *Exonerations in the United States, 1989–2012* (June 2013) (documenting 873 exonerations, but estimating that the rate of false convictions is much higher).

35 Alexandra Natapoff, *Misdemeanors*, 85 S. CAL. L. REV. 1313, 1316 (2012).

36 *See, e.g.*, Am. Bar Ass'n Standing Comm. on Legal Aid & Indigent Defendants, *Gideon's Broken Promise: America's Continuing Quest for Equal Justice: A Report on the American Bar Association's Hearings on the Right to Counsel in Criminal Proceedings* (2004), *available at* http://www.americanbar.org/groups/legal_aid _indigent_defendants/initiatives/indigent_defense_systems_improvement /gideons_broken_promise.html

37 Eve Brensike Primus, *A Structural Vision of Habeas Corpus*, 98 CALIF. L. REV. 1, 16–23 (2010).

38 The history is wonderfully limned in GEORGE FISHER, PLEA BARGAINING'S TRIUMPH: A HISTORY OF PLEA BARGAINING IN AMERICA (2003).

39 Ronald M. George, *Challenges Facing an Independent Judiciary*, 80 N.Y.U. L. REV. 1345, 1353 (2005).

40 Anne R. Traum, *Mass Incarceration at Sentencing*, 64 HASTINGS L.J. 423, 446–47 (2013).

41 Marie Gottschalk, *The Past, Present, and Future of Mass Incarceration in the United States*, 10 CRIMINOLOGY & PUB. POL. 483, 489 (2011).

42 DONALD BRAMAN, DOING TIME ON THE OUTSIDE: INCARCERATION AND FAMILY LIFE IN URBAN AMERICA (2007).

43 The landmark study is Robert Sampson et al., *Neighborhoods and Violent Crime: A Multilevel Study of Collective Efficacy*, 277 SCIENCE 918 (1997).

44 JEFF MANZA & CHRISTOPHER UGGEN, LOCKED OUT: FELON DISENFRANCHISEMENT AND AMERICAN DEMOCRACY (2006).

45 BRUCE WESTERN, PUNISHMENT AND INEQUALITY IN AMERICA 11–33 (2006).

46 James D. Unnever & Francis T. Cullen, *The Social Sources of Americans' Punitiveness: A Test of Three Competing Models*, 48 CRIMINOLOGY 99, 119 (2010).

47 The Court's effect appears to be long term, rather than short term. Joshua Daniel Ura, *Backlash and Legitimation: Macro Political Responses to Supreme Court*

Decisions, 58 AM. POL. SCI. J. 110, 120 (2013) (identifying short-term negative and long-term positive effects of the Court's endorsement of a policy position on public support for the same position).

48 KEITH E. WHITTINGTON, POLITICAL FOUNDATIONS OF JUDICIAL SUPREMACY: THE PRESIDENCY, THE SUPREME COURT, AND CONSTITUTIONAL LEADERSHIP IN U.S. HISTORY (2007).

49 For demonstration of relationship between welfare and crime policy via state-by-state analysis, see Katherine Beckett & Bruce Western, *Governing Social Marginality*, 3 PUNISHMENT & SOC. 43, 45 (2001). For theoretical consideration of its connection to the construction of markets, see BERNARD E. HARCOURT, THE ILLUSION OF FREE MARKETS (2011) (developing an account of "neoliberal penality").

50 I have explored this idea in another context. *See* Aziz Z. Huq, *Standing for the Structural Constitution*, 99 VA. L. REV. 1435 (2013).

51 In original jurisdiction cases, the Court can appoint a special master to engage in fact finding. *See* Anne-Marie C. Carstens, *Lurking in the Shadows of Judicial Process: Special Masters in the Supreme Court's Original Jurisdiction Cases*, 86 MINN. L. REV. 625 (2002). In one instance in 1794, the Court even presided over a jury trial. *See* Lochlan F. Shelfer, *Special Juries in the Supreme Court*, 123 YALE L.J. 208 (2013).

52 *Cf.* Douglas Laycock, *Federal Interference with State Prosecutions: The Need for Prospective Relief*, 1977 SUP. CT. REV. 193 (developing the reasons that raising a federal defense in a criminal prosecution is not a full substitute for prospective injunctive relief).

53 For an example of a federal court entertaining relief in respect to a criminal statute before enforcement against the plaintiff, see *Steffel v. Thompson*, 415 U.S. 452 (1974).

54 *See generally* H.W. PERRY JR., DECIDING TO DECIDE: AGENDA SETTING IN THE UNITED STATES SUPREME COURT (1991).

55 Stuntz, *supra* note 27, at 512; *see also* Erik Luna, *The Overcriminalization Phenomenon*, 54 AM. U. L. REV. 703 (2005).

56 By and large, the Supreme Court has declined opportunities to generate a constitutional body of substantive criminal law. For an argument that the Court should have taken this path, see William J. Stuntz, *The Uneasy Relationship between Criminal Procedure and Criminal Justice*, 107 YALE L.J. 1, 6 (1997).

57 *See* Michigan v. Long, 463 U.S. 1032 (1983). *But see* Henry Paul Monaghan, *Supreme Court Review of State-Court Determinations of State Law in Constitutional Cases*, 103 COLUM. L. REV. 1919 (2003) (suggesting a somewhat broader scope of Supreme Court ancillary jurisdiction).

58 Susan R. Klein & Ingrid B. Grobey, *Debunking Claims of Over-Federalization of Criminal Law*, 62 EMORY L.J. 1, 7 (2012). That said, the content of federal criminal law may be more troubling than the content of state criminal law. The former is said to be "out of kilter with any sense of moral proportion: minor infractions are often treated as serious crimes, and all crimes, both serious and trivial, are punished with remarkable severity." Stephen F. Smith, *Proportionality and Federalization*, 91 VA. L. REV. 879, 883 (2005).

59 See WILLIAM J. STUNTZ, THE COLLAPSE OF AMERICAN CRIMINAL JUSTICE 260–65 (2011). Stuntz's argument is importantly (and in my view successfully) challenged as

a historical account in Stephen J. Schulhofer, *Criminal Justice, Local Democracy, and Constitutional Rights*, 111 MICH. L. REV. 1045 (2013). The account nonetheless identifies a powerful analytic possibility.

60 510 U.S. 135, 149 (1994).

61 *Id.* at 147–48. *But see* United States v. Hayes, 555 U.S. 415, 429 (2009) (Ginsburg, J.) (declining to invoke the rule of lenity). For a classic study of how lenity is invoked, see John C. Jeffries, *Lenity, Vagueness, and the Construction of Penal Statutes*, 71 VA. L. REV. 189, 198–200 (1985).

62 531 U.S. 12, 24–25 (2000).

63 561 U.S. 358 (2010).

64 Elizabeth R. Sheyn, *Criminalizing the Denial of Honest Services after Skilling*, 2011 WISC. L. REV. 27, 43.

65 William J. Stuntz, *The Political Constitution of Criminal Justice*, 119 HARV. L. REV. 780, 783 (2006).

66 Another example of this strategy is the narrow construction of the federal arson statute developed, partly on federalism grounds, by Justice Ginsburg in *Jones v. United States*, 329 U.S. 848 (2000).

67 *See* Richard L. Hasen, *End of the Dialogue? Political Polarization, the Supreme Court, and Congress*, 86 S. CAL. L. REV. 205 (2013).

68 Mapp v. Ohio, 367 U.S. 643 (1961). The Court subjected the federal government to the exclusionary rule in *Weeks v. United States*, 232 U.S. 383 (1914).

69 Henry J. Friendly, *The Bill of Rights as a Code of Criminal Procedure*, 53 CALIF. L. REV. 929, 951–53 (1965).

70 Akhil Reed Amar, *Fourth Amendment First Principles*, 107 HARV. L. REV. 757 (1994).

71 *See* Davis v. United States, 131 S. Ct. 2419, 2423–24 (2011); Herring v. United States, 555 U.S. 135, 148 (2009); Arizona v. Evans, 514 U.S. 1, 12–16 (1995); Illinois v. Krull, 480 U.S. 340, 352–53 (1987).

72 *See Herring*, 555 U.S. at 148–57 (Ginsburg, J., dissenting); *Evans*, 514 U.S. at 23–34 (Ginsburg, J., dissenting).

73 *Evans*, 514 U.S. at 29 n.5 (Ginsburg, J., dissenting); *Herring*, 555 U.S. at 153 (Ginsburg, J., dissenting).

74 For a stark example of this, see *Hudson v. Michigan*, 547 U.S. 586, 599 (2006) (concluding that there is "increasing evidence that police forces across the United States take the constitutional rights of citizens seriously" given the availability of training and the fact that "modern police forces are staffed with professionals"). I cannot resist noting that Justice Scalia, who is often resistant to the idea of updating constitutional rules to fit contemporary circumstances, authored this argument in favor of narrowing Fourth Amendment protections in light of contingent institutional developments.

75 131 S. Ct. 1849, 1864 (2011) (Ginsburg, J., dissenting).

76 517 U.S. 806 (1996).

77 For another example, see Fernandez v. California, 571 U.S. – (2014) (Ginsburg, J., dissenting).

78 Stone v. Powell, 428 U.S. 465 (1975).

79 Worse, "when the Court chips away at law development in civil cases, it points to the continuing availability of law development using other remedies, such as the

exclusionary rule. When the Court chips away at the exclusionary rule, it points to the continuing availability of law development with other remedies, including civil liability." Orin S. Kerr, *Fourth Amendment Remedies and Development of the Law: A Comment on Camreta v. Greene and Davis v. United States,* 2011 CATO SUP. CT. REV. 237, 254 (2011).

80 Arizona v. Evans, 514 U.S. 1, 26 (1995) (Ginsburg, J., dissenting).

81 For a good overview of what is known about such programs, see LUKE HARDING, THE SNOWDEN FILES (2014). For a useful, if tiresomely cheerleading, introduction to big data, see VIKTOR MAYER-SCHONBERGER & KENNETH CUKIER, BIG DATA: A REVOLUTION THAT WILL TRANSFORM HOW WE LIVE, WORK, AND THINK (2013).

82 *See* Latif v. Holder, 686 F.3d 1122, 1130 (9th Cir. 2012); Ibrahim v. Dep't of Homeland Sec., 669 F.3d 983, 999 (9th Cir. 2012); *see generally* Anya Bernstein, *The Hidden Costs of Terrorist Watchlists,* 61 BUFF. L. REV. 461 (2013).

83 *See, e.g.,* United States v. Jones, 132 S. Ct. 945, 949–53 (2012) (Scalia, J.).

84 Apprendi v. New Jersey, 530 U.S. 466, 490 (2000). In *Apprendi,* the defendant pleaded guilty to a crime that carried a sentence of between five and ten years. The sentencing court found that the crime was a racially motivated hate crime, and imposed a "sentence enhancement" that carried the sentence to twelve years. The Court subsequently clarified that "the relevant 'statutory maximum' is not the maximum sentence a judge may impose after finding additional facts, but the maximum he may impose without any additional findings [beyond what a jury found or a plea entailed]." Cunningham v. California, 549 U.S. 270, 275 (2007) (citation omitted).

85 Ring v. Arizona, 536 U.S. 584 (2002).

86 543 U.S. 220 (2005).

87 Justice Ginsburg did pen an opinion extending *Booker* to California's determinative sentencing regime, but again declined to explain her *Booker* vote. *Cunningham,* 549 U.S. 270.

88 555 U.S. 160 (2009).

89 552 U.S. 85 (2007).

90 Gall v. United States, 552 U.S. 38 (2007) (holding that appellate courts may not treat the fact that a sentence departs from a guidelines range as a basis for presuming that it is unreasonable); Rita v. United States, 551 U.S. 338 (2007) (holding that appellate courts may presume within-guideline sentences to be reasonable). Justice Ginsburg has also dissenting from the holding that *Apprendi* error is not structural in nature. Washington v. Recuenco, 548 U.S. 212, 219 (2006) (Ginsburg, J., dissenting).

91 For empirical evidence, see Crystal Yang, *Have Inter-Judge Sentencing Disparities Increased in an Advisory Guidelines Regime? Evidence from* Booker, – N.Y.U. L. REV. – (forthcoming); Ryan W. Scott, *Inter-Judge Sentencing Disparity after Booker: A First Look,* 63 STAN. L. REV. 1 (2010).

92 Aziz Z. Huq, *Habeas and the Roberts Court,* 81 U. CHI. L. REV. – (forthcoming).

93 Wainwright v. Sykes, 433 U.S. 72, 90 (1977).

94 Halbert v. Michigan, 545 U.S. 605 (2005). This is consistent with her larger concern with access to counsel. *See, e.g.,* Alabama v. Shelton, 535 U.S. 654, 674 (2002).

95 Banks v. Dretke, 540 U.S. 668 (2004).

96 131 S. Ct. 1289 (2011).

97 *Id.* at 1296. This includes claims that a defendant falls into a class that cannot constitutionally be punished. *See* Doug Lieb, *Can Section 1983 Help Prevent the Execution of Mentally Retarded Prisoners*, 121 YALE L.J. 1571 (2012).

98 Maples v. Thomas, 132 S. Ct. 912, 922 (2012).

99 For an account of these cases and their effect on post-conviction relief more generally, see Huq, *supra* note 92.

100 *Maples*, 132 S. Ct. at 917–18.

101 *Id.* at 929 (Alito, J., concurring); *id.* at 934 (Scalia, J., dissenting).

102 *See* Carol Steiker, *Raising the Bar:* Maples v. Thomas *and the Sixth Amendment Right to Counsel* 73–74 (Feb. 2013), available at http://dash.harvard.edu/bitstream /handle/1/10582558/Steiker.pdf?sequence=1

103 Vermont v. Brillon, 556 U.S. 81, 93–94 (2009).

104 131 S. Ct. 1350, 1367 (2011) (Ginsburg, J. dissenting).

105 DONALD HOROWITZ, THE COURTS AND SOCIAL POLICY (1977); GERALD ROSENBERG, THE HOLLOW HOPE: CAN COURTS BRING ABOUT SOCIAL CHANGE? (1991)

106 ROSENBERG, *supra* note 105, at 10–21.

107 HOROWITZ, *supra* note 105, at 41–49.

108 For critical discussion of the Court's Eleventh Amendment jurisprudence, see John F. Manning, *The Eleventh Amendment and the Reading of Precise Constitutional Texts*, 113 YALE L.J. 1663 (2004).

109 DAVID GARLAND, THE CULTURE OF CONTROL: CRIME AND SOCIAL ORDER IN CONTEMPORARY SOCIETY 57 (2001)

110 Ginsburg, supra note 1, at 1193.

111 *Id.*

112 For an exploration of the Court's supervisory authority, see Amy Coney Barrett, *The Supervisory Power of the Supreme Court*, 106 COLUM. L. REV. 324 (2006).

113 Thomas Keck, *Party, Policy, or Duty, Why Does the Supreme Court Invalidate Federal Statutes*, 101 AM. POL. SCI. REV. 321, 323 (2007).

114 *See, e.g.*, Pearson v. Callahan, 555 U.S. 223 (2009).

115 For a cataloging of instances in which the Court has expressed such concerns, see Marin Levy, *Judging the Flood of Litigation*, 80 U. CHI. L. REV. 1007, 1037–59 (2012).

116 It would be circular to insist that the habeas statute's standard of review in 28 U.S.C. §2254(d)(1) constrains federal habeas courts. As Justice Stevens demonstrated in *Terry Williams v. Taylor*, it is perfectly possible to gloss that provision to leave large discretion in federal judicial hands. 529 U.S. 362, 385–88 (2000) (opinion of Stevens, J.). Judicial constructions, not congressional commands, have strangled the post-conviction writ to almost a nullity. The question then is how to explain those constrictive readings of the law.

117 See, *e.g.*, Schiro v. Landrigan, 550 U.S. 465, 499 (2007) (Stevens, J., dissenting) ("In the end, the Court's decision can only be explained by its increasingly familiar effort to guard the floodgates of litigation."); Harris v. Reed, 489 U.S. 255, 282 n.6 (1989) (Kennedy, J., dissenting) (expressing concern about the "burden on federal courts" from increased litigation).

118 Skinner v. Switzer, 131 S. Ct. 1289, 1299 (2011).

119 *See* Maples v. Thomas, 132 S. Ct. 912, 922 (2012) (focusing on abandonment rather than negligence or gross negligence); Wendy Zorana Zupac, *Mere Negligence or*

Abandonment? Evaluating Claims of Attorney Misconduct after Maples v. Thomas, 122 YALE L.J. 1328, 1357–58 (2013).

120 Kate Stith, *The Arc of the Pendulum: Judges, Prosecutors, and the Exercise of Discretion*, 117 YALE L.J. 1420, 1425 (2008).

121 *Id.* at 1478–80 (noting that "the remedy in *Booker* ... opens the possibility of an evolving sentencing law that draws on the judgment and experience of sentencing judges themselves").

122 *See* sources cited in note 91. It is important to note that "the vast majority of sentences outside the Guidelines are given at the government's request." Rachel E. Barkow, *Sentencing Guidelines at the Crossroads of Politics and Experience*, 160 U. PA. L. REV. 1599, 1624 (2012).

123 Stephanos Bibas & Susan Klein, *The Sixth Amendment and Criminal Sentencing*, 30 CARDOZO L. REV. 775, 789 (2008) ("The steady stream of judge-induced downward departures ... confirms that district judges like to reduce sentences.").

124 In other instances, Justice Ginsburg has written to affirm a broad view of white-collar criminal law. *See* United States v. O'Hagan, 521 U.S. 642 (1997) (permitting criminal liability under §10(b) of the 1934 Securities Exchange Act based on the misappropriation of material, nonpublic information).

125 JOHN HAGAN, WHO ARE THE CRIMINALS? THE POLITICS OF CRIME POLICY FROM THE AGE OF ROOSEVELT TO THE AGE OF REAGAN (2012).

126 Hon. Jed Rakoff, *The Financial Crisis: Why Have No High-Level Executives Been Prosecuted?*, N.Y. REV. BOOKS, Jan 9, 2014.

127 *Compare* HAGAN, *supra* note 125, at 2 (developing a "class and race inequality" justification for differential treatment of different genres of crime), *with* Susan P. Shapiro, *Collaring the Crime, not the Criminal: Reconsidering the Concept of White Collar Crime*, 55 AM. SOC. REV. 346 (1990) (favoring a cost-related account).

128 William J. Stuntz, *The Virtues and Vices of the Exclusionary Rule*, 20 HARV. J.L. & PUB. POL'Y 443, 443–44 (1997).

129 *See* Daryl J. Levinson, *Making Government Pay: Markets, Politics, and the Allocation of Constitutional Costs*, 67 U. CHI. L. REV. 345, 370–71 (2000).

130 City of Los Angeles v. Lyons, 461 U.S. 95, 105–06 (1983).

131 Imagine, for example, judicial orders to increase taxes to fund criminal defense and adjudication.

10   A REVOLUTION IN JURISDICTION

1 *See* Scott Dodson, *Justice Souter and the Civil Rules*, 88 WASH. U. L. REV. 289, 290–91 (2010).

2 *See, e.g.*, Tr. of Oral Arg. at 18, Ashcroft v. Iqbal, No. 07-1015, 2008 WL 5168319, at *13–15 (2009) ("I can't remember my civil procedure course.").

3 *See* Howard M. Wasserman, *The Roberts Court and the Civil Procedure Revival*, 31 REV. LITIG. 313, 314–17 (2012).

4 *See* Stephen B. Burbank & Sean Farhang, *Litigation Reform: An Institutional Approach*, 162 U. PA. L. REV. (forthcoming) (arguing that the Court has been using procedural rulings to limit private enforcement of substantive public law).

5 Laura Krugman Ray, *Justice Ginsburg and the Middle Way*, 68 Brook. L. Rev. 629, 639 (2003). Justice Ginsburg is no longer alone. Justice Elena Kagan taught the subject as a law professor, and Justice Sonia Sotomayor dealt daily with the Federal Rules of Civil Procedure as a district judge. *See* Mike Dorf, *Judicial Experience*, Dorf on Law (May 19, 2010), *available at* http://www.dorfonlaw.org/2010/05 /judicial-experience.html

6 Ruth Bader Ginsburg & Anders Bruzelius, Civil Procedure in Sweden (1965).

7 *See Transcript of Interview of U.S. Supreme Court Associate Justice Ruth Bader Ginsburg*, April 10, 2009, 70 Ohio St. L.J. 805, 806–07 (2009). The great Benjamin Kaplan praised it as an "excellent book" that "takes its place in the small library of English-language writings about foreign procedure that can claim intellectual distinction." Benjamin Kaplan, *Civil Procedure in Sweden*, 79 Harv. L. Rev. 629, 460–61 (1965).

8 Ruth Bader Ginsburg, *In Celebration of Jack Friedenthal*, 78 Geo. Wash. L. Rev. 1 (2009).

9 Ruth Bader Ginsburg, *In Memoriam: Benjamin Kaplan*, 124 Harv. L. Rev. 1349 (2011).

10 Ruth Bader Ginsburg, *Tribute to Arthur Miller*, 67 N.Y.U. Ann. Surv. Am. L. 1 (2011).

11 Ruth Bader Ginsburg, *The Work of Professor Allan Delker Vestal*, 70 Iowa L. Rev. 13 (1984).

12 Ruth Bader Ginsburg, *In Memory of Herbert Wechsler*, 100 Colum. L. Rev. 1359 (2000).

13 Ruth Bader Ginsburg, *Charlie's Letters*, 79 Tex. L. Rev. 3 (2000); Ruth Bader Ginsburg, *In Celebration of Charles Alan Wright*, 76 Tex. L. Rev. 1581 (1998).

14 *See* Tobias Barrington Wolff, *Ruth Bader Ginsburg and Sensible Pragmatism in Federal Jurisdictional Policy*, 70 Ohio St. L.J. 839, 840 (2009).

15 *See id.*

16 *See* David L. Shapiro, *Justice Ginsburg's First Decade: Some Thoughts about her Contributions in the Fields of Procedure and Jurisdiction*, 104 Colum. L. Rev. 21, 21 (2004).

17 *Id.* at 21–22.

18 *See* Mark A. Hall, *The Jurisdictional Nature of the Time to Appeal*, 21 Ga. L. Rev. 399, 408 (1986) (noting the "sanctity" of federal subject-matter jurisdiction).

19 Mansfield, Coldwater & Lake Mich. Ry. v. Swan, 111 U.S. 379, 382 (1884).

20 Perry Dane, *Jurisdictionality, Time, and the Legal Imagination*, 23 Hofstra L. Rev. 1, 5 (1994) ("In modern Anglo-American legal doctrine, legal issues are either 'jurisdictional' or 'non-jurisdictional.'").

21 *See* Scott Dodson, *Mandatory Rules*, 61 Stan. L. Rev. 1, 4–5 (2008).

22 *See id.* at 2 ("Whether a rule is jurisdictional or not affects both litigants and the courts in important ways."); Peter J. Rubin, *Justice Ruth Bader Ginsburg: A Judge's Perspective*, 70 Ohio St. L.J. 825, 830 (2009) ("The importance of cabining claims of a jurisdictional bar to those cases in which the bar truly is jurisdictional is quite profound.").

23 361 U.S. 220 (1960). That careless use had begun much earlier in the Courts of Appeals, however. *See* Dane, *supra* note 20, at 39 n.102 (reporting "thousands of

cases," with the earliest usage, "in more or less its present meaning," dating back
to 1900); Hall, *supra* note 18, at 399 n.2 & 411 (citing cases and tracing its first exact
usage to 1926).

24 *Robinson*, 361 U.S. at 220–22.

25 *Id.* at 224, 226, 229.

26 *See* Hall, *supra* note 18, at 410–11. To be sure, the Court was not entirely consistent
in its opinions on jurisdictionality. Foman v. Davis, 371 U.S. 178 (1962), held that
the failure in the notice to specify what judgment was appealed is a nonjurisdictional defect. And Schacht v. United States, 398 U.S. 58, 64 (1970), stated: "The
procedural rules adopted by the Court for the orderly transaction of its business are
not jurisdictional." Nevertheless, the phrase "mandatory and jurisdictional" continued to spread among the lower courts and in other Supreme Court opinions.
A few commentators objected, perhaps laying some foundation for later changes.
See Dane, *supra* note 20, at 39–40 (arguing that jurisdictionality does not equate
to rigidity or inflexibility and suggesting that there is less to the "mandatory and
jurisdictional" doublet than one might think); Hall, *supra* note 18, at 400 (arguing that the subject-matter jurisdiction of the appellate courts is defined by the
finality of the district court's judgment, not the timing of a notice of appeal and
suggesting that the "mandatory and jurisdictional" moniker is merely an emphasis
of rigidity).

27 434 U.S. 257 (1978).

28 *Id.* at 264.

29 459 U.S. 56 (1982) (per curiam).

30 *Id.* at 62 (quoting *Browder*, 434 U.S. at 264).

31 487 U.S. 312 (1988).

32 *Id.* at 318.

33 *See, e.g.*, Atchison, Topeka & Santa Fe Railway Co. v. Interstate Commerce
Comm'n, 851 F.2d 1432, 1438 (D.C. Cir. 1988) (noting "the continuing proclivity
of courts to type statutes of limitations as 'jurisdictional,' and therefore unyielding,
or 'non-jurisdictional,' therefore supple – open to waiver, estoppel, or equitable
tolling arguments"). Ginsburg has said that her appellate opinions, along with her
academic writings, are a "reliable indicator" of her jurisprudence. Nomination of
Ruth Bader Ginsburg to be Associate Justice of the Supreme Court of the United
States: Hearings before the Senate Committee on the Judiciary, 103d Cong. 51, 52
(1993).

34 781 F.2d 935 (D.C. Cir. 1986).

35 *Id.* at 941 & n.10.

36 *Id.* at 943 (Ginsburg, J., dissenting).

37 *Id.* at 945 n.4 (Ginsburg, J., dissenting).

38 880 F.2d 506 (D.C. Cir. 1989).

39 *Id.* at 509.

40 *Id.* at 526–29 (Ginsburg, J., concurring).

41 *Id.* at 529 (Ginsburg, J., concurring).

42 *Id.* at 553 (Silberman, J., dissenting).

43 AFL-CIO v. OSHA, 905 F.2d 1568, 1571 (D.C. Cir. 1990).

44 For example, because the D.C. Circuit long ago had held the statutory deadline
for aggrieved agency complainants to seek review to be "jurisdictional in nature,"

NRDC v. NRC, 666 F.2d 595, 602 (D.C. Cir. 1981), Ginsburg consistently adhered to that characterization as a circuit judge, though she did so in the form of per curiam decisions that made clear that binding precedent dictated the result, *see, e.g.,* Spannus v. FEC, 990 F.2d 643, 644 (D.C. Cir. 1993) (per curiam); LaRouche v. FEC, 990 F.2d 641, 642 (D.C. Cir. 1993) (per curiam); Ene. Probe v. NRC, 872 F.2d 436, 437 (D.C. Cir. 1989) (per curiam).

45 517 U.S. 416 (1996).

46 *Id.* at 434 (Ginsburg, J., concurring).

47 *Id.* at 435 (Ginsburg, J., concurring).

48 523 U.S. 83 (1998).

49 *Id.* at 90 (quoting United States v. Canness, 85 F.3d 661, 663 n.2 (D.C. Cir. 1996)).

50 *Id.* at 91.

51 532 U.S. 757 (2001).

52 *Id.* at 760 ("For want of a signature on a timely notice, the appeal is not automatically lost.").

53 *Id.* at 767.

54 540 U.S. 443 (2004).

55 *Id.* at 446–47.

56 28 U.S.C. § 2075.

57 *Id.*

58 *Kontrick,* 540 U.S. at 453 (quoting Owen Equip. & Erection Co. v. Kroger, 437 U.S. 365, 370 (1978)).

59 *Id.* at 454–55.

60 *Id.* at 458.

61 541 U.S. 401 (2004).

62 *Id.* at 413.

63 *Id.*

64 546 U.S. 12 (2005) (per curiam).

65 *Id.* at 16.

66 *Id.* at 18.

67 *Id.* at 19.

68 *Id.* at 18–19.

69 *Id.* at 18.

70 546 U.S. 500 (2006).

71 *Id.* at 516.

72 *Id.* at 510.

73 *Id.* at 511 (quoting Steel Co. v. Citizens for a Better Envt., 523 U.S. 83, 91 (1998)).

74 *Id.* at 510 (internal quotation marks omitted).

75 *Id.* at 514–15. Howard Wasserman has been one of the leading proponents of distinguishing between merits and subject-matter jurisdiction. Howard M. Wasserman, *The Demise of "Drive-By" Jurisdictional Rulings,* 105 Nw. U. L. Rev. 947 (2011) [hereinafter Wasserman, *Demise*]; Howard M. Wasserman, *Jurisdiction, Merits, and Substantiality,* 42 Tulsa L. Rev. 579 (2007). For another prominent take, see Kevin M. Clermont, *Jurisdictional Fact,* 91 Cornell L. Rev. 973 (2006).

76 *Arbaugh,* 546 U.S. at 513–16.

77 *Id.* at 515 (quoting Zipes v. Trans World Airlines, Inc., 455 U.S. 385, 394 (1982)).

78 551 U.S. 205 (2007).

79 *Id.* at 206–07.
80 *Id.* at 209.
81 *Id.* at 210 n.2.
82 *Id.*
83 *Id.* at 213–14.
84 Perhaps Souter was assigned the dissent because Ginsburg was already drafting a dissent from the March arguments. *See* Wilkie v. Robbins, 551 U.S. 537 (2007) (Ginsburg, J., concurring & dissenting).
85 *Bowles*, 551 U.S. at 216 (Souter, J., dissenting).
86 *Id.* at 216 (Souter, J., dissenting).
87 *Id.* at 218 (Souter, J., dissenting).
88 *Id.* at 219 (Souter, J., dissenting).
89 *See, e.g.*, Elizabeth Chamblee Burch, *Nonjurisdictionality or Inequity*, 102 Nw. U. L. Rev. Colloquy 64 (2007); Perry Dane, *Sad Time: Thoughts on Jurisdictionality, the Legal Imagination, and Bowles v. Russell*, 102 Nw. U. L. Rev. Colloquy 164 (2008); Scott Dodson, *The Failure of Bowles v. Russell*, 43 Tulsa L. Rev. 631 (2008) [hereinafter Dodson, *Failure*]; Scott Dodson, *Jurisdictionality and Bowles v. Russell*, 102 Nw. U. L. Rev. Colloquy 42 (2007) [hereinafter Dodson, *Jurisdictionality*]. *But see* E. King Poor, *The Jurisdictional Time Limit for an Appeal: The Worst Kind of Deadline – Except for All Others*, 102 Nw. U. L. Rev. Colloquy 151 (2008) (defending *Bowles*).
90 552 U.S. 130 (2008).
91 *Id.* at 134.
92 *Id.* at 140 (Stevens, J., dissenting) (joined by Justice Ginsburg).
93 *See* Scott Dodson, *Three Muted Cheers for* John R. Sand & Gravel, Civ. Proc. & Fed. Courts Blog (Jan. 8, 2008), *available at* http://lawprofessors.typepad.com /civpro/2008/01/dodson-three-mu.html).
94 *John R. Sand*, 552 U.S. at 134. For commentary on the significance of this terminology, see Dodson, *supra* note 93 ("The Court framed the issue in this case (and, retrospectively, in cases like Bowles) as whether the limits are 'more absolute' rather than whether they are 'jurisdictional.'"), *available at* http://lawprofessors .typepad.com/civpro/2008/01/dodson-three-mu.html); Wasserman, *Demise*, *supra* note 75, at 964 ("Importantly, however, the Court avoided explicitly labeling the limitations issue as jurisdictional, instead calling it a 'more absolute' limitations statute.... *John R. Sand* recognized and applied Dodson's category of special, absolute, mandatory but still nonjurisdictional legal rules.").
95 558 U.S. 67 (2009).
96 *Id.* at 71.
97 *Id.* at 81.
98 *Id.* at 85.
99 *Id.* at 82.
100 559 U.S. 154 (2010).
101 *Id.* at 157.
102 131 S. Ct. 1197 (2011).
103 *Id.* at 1202.
104 132 S. Ct. 641 (2012).
105 *Id.* at 646 (citing 28 U.S.C. §§ 2253(c)(2)-(3)).

106 133 S. Ct. 817 (2013).

107 *Id.* at 821–22.

108 *See, e.g., id.* at 824 ("Tardy jurisdictional objections can therefore result in a waste of adjudicatory resources and can disturbingly disarm litigants."); *Henderson*, 131 S. Ct. at 1202 ("Because the consequences that attach to the jurisdictional label may be so drastic, . . . [w]e have urged that a rule should not be referred to as jurisdictional unless it governs a court's adjudicative capacity, that is, its subject-matter or personal jurisdiction.").

109 Wasserman, *Demise, supra* note 75, at 947.

110 Ex parte McCardle, 74 U.S. (7 Wall.) 506, 514 (1868).

111 Mansfield, Coldwater & Lake Mich. Ry. v. Swan, 111 U.S. 379, 382 (1884).

112 902 F.2d 84 (D.C. Cir. 1990).

113 *Id.* at 88.

114 523 U.S. 83 (1998).

115 *Id.* at 94.

116 *Id.* at 94–95.

117 *Id.* at 101.

118 526 U.S. 574 (1999).

119 *Id.* at 577.

120 *Id.* at 584–85.

121 *Id.* at 584.

122 *Id.* at 579.

123 *Id.* at 588.

124 Scott C. Idleman, *The Emergence of Jurisdictional Resequencing in the Federal Courts*, 87 CORNELL L. REV. 1, 9 (2001).

125 *See* Kevin M. Clermont, *Sequencing the Issues for Judicial Decisionmaking: Limitations from Jurisdictional Primacy and Intrasuit Preclusion*, 63 FLA. L. REV. 301, 304–06, 328–29 (2011); Peter B. Rutledge, *Decisional Sequencing*, 62 ALA. L. REV. 1, 3–4, 7 (2010); *cf.* Heather Elliot, *Jurisdictional Resequencing and Restraint*, 43 NEW ENG. L. REV. 725 (2009) (applauding resequencing as a doctrine of judicial restraint); Alan M. Trammell, *Jurisdictional Sequencing*, 47 GA. L. REV. 1099, 1103 (2013) (developing "a theory of jurisdictional sequencing based on the dichotomy between conduct rules and allocative rules"). *But cf.* Clermont, *supra*, at 324–25 (criticizing *Ruhrgas's* preclusion discussion); Idleman, *supra* note 124, at 9 (criticizing *Ruhrgas* on legitimacy grounds).

126 549 U.S. 422 (2007).

127 *Id.* at 425.

128 *Id.* at 431 (internal quotation marks omitted).

129 *Id.* at 432–33.

130 519 U.S. 61 (1996).

131 *Id.* at 64.

132 *Id.*

133 Prior cases had held jurisdictional defects to be curable before final judgment, but the Court had never considered a "cure" case in which the defect was properly and timely objected to by the party opposing federal jurisdiction. *See, e.g.*, Grubbs v. Gen. Elec. Credit Corp., 405 U.S. 699 (1972); Am. Fire & Cas. Co. v. Finn, 341 U.S. 6 (1951).

134 *Caterpillar*, 519 U.S. at 73 ("The *jurisdictional* defect was cured, *i.e.*, complete diversity was established before the trial commenced. Therefore, the Sixth Circuit erred in resting its decision on the absence of subject-matter jurisdiction. But a statutory flaw – Caterpillar's failure to meet the Sec. 1441(a) requirement that the case be fit for federal adjudication at the time the removal petition is filed – remained in the unerasable history of the case.").

135 *Id.* at 76.

136 It also is Ginsburgian in its honest discussion of precedent, in which the Court carefully lays out the prior holdings and shows where the instant case breaks new ground. *Id.* at 71–74.

137 541 U.S. 567 (2004).

138 *Id.* at 568–69.

139 *Id.* at 590–94 (Ginsburg, J., dissenting).

140 Wasserman, *Demise*, *supra* note 75.

141 It is worth pointing out that her decisions in these areas can be said to have increased the scope of federal judicial power by relieving courts from limitations on their subject-matter jurisdiction. She has made similar efforts elsewhere. *See, e.g.*, Marshall v. Marshall, 547 U.S. 293 (2006) (narrowing the probate exception to federal jurisdiction).

142 *See* Wolff, *supra* note 14, at 841; Elijah Yip & Eric K. Yamamato, *Justice Ruth Bader Ginsburg's Jurisprudence of Process and Procedure*, 20 U. Haw. L. Rev. 647, 650 (1998).

143 551 U.S. 205 (2007).

144 *See* Dodson, *supra* note 21, at 8.

145 *See id.*

146 *See* Scott Dodson, *Hybridizing Jurisdiction*, 99 Calif. L. Rev. 1439 (2011).

147 *See id.* at 1459.

148 *See* Dodson, *supra* note 21, at 6.

149 *See id.* at 11–15; Dodson, *Failure*, *supra* note 89, at 632, 647; Dodson, *Jurisdictionality*, *supra* note 89, at 46–48.

150 *See, e.g.*, Sebelius v. Auburn Reg. Med. Ctr., 133 S. Ct. 817, 827–28 (2013) (holding a limit nonjurisdictional but immune from equitable tolling); Greenlaw v. United States, 554 U.S. 237, 245, 252 (2008) (holding the cross-appeal rule to be "unyielding" based on long-standing treatment and declining to determine its jurisdictional status); Kontrick v. Ryan, 540 U.S. 443, 456, 457 & n.12 (2004) (recognizing that a nonjurisdictional rule can be immune from equitable exceptions, judicial discretion, or party stipulation); *cf.* Hallstrom v. Tillamook Cnty., 493 U.S. 20 (1989) (holding a statutory deadline mandatory but declining to resolve its jurisdictional character).

151 *See, e.g.*, Day v. McDonough, 547 U.S. 198, 205 (2006) ("A statute of limitations defense, the State acknowledges, is not 'jurisdictional,' hence courts are under no *obligation* to raise the time bar sua sponte." (emphasis in original)).

152 552 U.S. 130 (2008).

153 *See* Ray, *supra* note 5, at 647; *e.g.*, Reed Elsevier, Inc. v. Muchnick, 559 U.S. 154, 172–74 (2010) (Ginsburg, J., concurring) (struggling to faithfully reconcile *Arbaugh* and *Bowles*).

154 *See* Evan Tsen Lee, *The Dubious Concept of Jurisdiction*, 54 Hastings L.J. 1613, 1628 (2003) (calling the concept of jurisdiction "dubious" but nevertheless

asserting that "banishing the term 'jurisdiction' from our legal lexicon is out of the question" in part because "centuries of Anglo-American jurisprudence are built on the notion that something called 'jurisdiction' is a predicate for moving forward in adjudication").

155 Wood v. Milyard, 132 S. Ct. 1826, 1834–35 (2012); *Day*, 547 U.S. at 202 (2006). These opinions rely heavily on a case that predated Ginsburg's presence on the Supreme Court, Granberry v. Greer, 481 U.S. 129 (1987).

156 Wood, 132 S. Ct. at 1832 n.4 ("A waived claim or defense is one that a party has knowingly and intelligently relinquished; a forfeited plea is one that a party has merely failed to preserve…. That distinction is key to our decision in Wood's case."); *id.* at 1833 n.5 (stressing that only forfeitures – not waivers – could be overlooked).

157 *See* Scott Dodson, *Party Subordinance in Federal Litigation*, 83 GEO. WASH. L. REV. 1 (2014).

11 RUTH BADER GINSBURG AND THE INTERACTION OF LEGAL SYSTEMS

1 *See* RUTH BADER GINSBURG & ANDERS BRUZELIUS, CIVIL PROCEDURE IN SWEDEN (1965).

2 For a brief summary of legal pluralism scholarship, see Paul Schiff Berman, *The New Legal Pluralism*, 5 ANN. REV. L. & SOC. SCI. 225 (2009).

3 *See, e.g.*, JOHN NEVILLE FIGGIS, CHURCHES IN THE MODERN STATE (1913).

4 *See, e.g.*, Frederic William Maitland, *Trust and Corporation, in* MAITLAND: SELECTED ESSAYS 141 (Hazeltine et al. eds., 1936).

5 *See, e.g.*, Leopold Pospisil, *Modern and Traditional Administration of Justice in New Guinea*, 19 J. LEGAL PLURALISM & UNOFFICIAL L. 93 (1981).

6 *See, e.g.*, ROBERT C. ELLICKSON, ORDER WITHOUT LAW: HOW NEIGHBORS SETTLE DISPUTES (1991); Christine Jolls et al., *A Behavioral Approach to Law and Economics*, 50 STAN. L. REV. 1471 (1998).

7 *See, e.g.*, PAUL SCHIFF BERMAN, GLOBAL LEGAL PLURALISM: A JURISPRUDENCE OF LAW BEYOND BORDERS (2012); NICO KRISCH, BEYOND CONSTITUTIONALISM: THE PLURALIST STRUCTURE OF POSTNATIONAL LAW (2010); Sally Engle Merry, *International Law and Sociolegal Scholarship: Toward a Spatial Global Legal Pluralism*, 41 STUDIES IN L., POLITICS & SOC'Y 149 (2008).

8 *See, e.g.*, ERIN RYAN, FEDERALISM AND THE TUG OF WAR WITHIN (2011); Robert B. Ahdieh, *Dialectical Regulation*, 38 CONN. L. REV. 863 (2006); Robert A. Schapiro, *Toward a Theory of Interactive Federalism*, 91 IOWA L. REV. 243 (2005).

9 Ahdieh, *supra* note 8, at 867.

10 For example, debates in the United States about judicial citation of foreign authority have often centered around delineating when it is permissible and when impermissible to reference foreign or international law. *See, e.g.*, Melissa A. Waters, *Creeping Monism: The Judicial Trend toward Interpretive Incorporation of Human Rights Treaties*, 107 COLUM. L. REV. 628 (2007). Similarly, theories of jurisdiction and choice of law have long sought to provide a single answer to the question of which law should apply to a cross-border dispute. *Compare* Pennoyer v. Neff, 95

U.S. 714 (1877) (holding that states have complete authority within their territorial boundaries but no authority outside those boundaries), *with* Int'l Shoe Co. v. Washington, 326 U.S. 310, 316 (1945) (establishing a test for determining whether an assertion of personal jurisdiction comports with the due process clause of the U.S. Constitution on the basis of whether the defendant had sufficient contacts with the relevant state "such that the maintenance of the suit does not offend 'traditional notions of fair play and substantial justice'" (quoting Milliken v. Meyer, 311 U.S. 457, 463 (1940))); *compare also* Restatement (First) of Conflict of Laws § 378 (1934) ("The law of the place of wrong determines whether a person has sustained a legal injury."), *with* Restatement (Second) of Conflict of Laws § 6 cmt. c (1971) (providing a more flexible inquiry aimed at determining the place with the "most significant relationship" to the dispute in question).

11 *See* Schapiro, *supra* note 8.

12 Ahdieh, *supra* note 8, at 867.

13 *See* Berman, *supra* note 7, at 236–43.

14 Robert M. Cover, *The Uses of Jurisdictional Redundancy: Interest, Ideology, and Innovation*, 22 Wm. & Mary L. Rev. 639 (1981).

15 *See id.*

16 *Id.* at 682.

17 *See* Judith Resnik, *Law's Migration: American Exceptionalism, Silent Dialogues, and Federalism's Multiple Ports of Entry*, 115 Yale L.J. 1564 (2006).

18 *See* Judith Resnik, *Afterword: Federalism's Options*, 14 Yale L. & Pol'y Rev. 465, 473–74 (1996) ("My point is not only that particular subject matter may go back and forth between state and federal governance but also that the tradition of allocation itself is one constantly being reworked; periodically, events prompt the revisiting of state or federal authority, and the lines move.").

19 *See* Robert M. Cover, *The Supreme Court, 1982 Term – Foreword: Nomos and Narrative*, 97 Harv. L. Rev. 4, 53 (1983).

20 *See id.* at 11–15.

21 *See* Judith Resnik, *Living Their Legal Commitments: Paideic Communities, Courts, and Robert Cover (An Essay on Racial Segregation at Bob Jones University, Patrilineal Membership Rules, Veiling, and Jurisgenerative Practices)*, 17 Yale J.L. & Human. 17, 25 (2005) ("[Cover] wanted the state's actors ... to be uncomfortable in their knowledge of their own power, respectful of the legitimacy of competing legal systems, and aware of the possibility that multiple meanings and divergent practices ought sometimes to be tolerated, even if painfully so.").

22 Ruth B. Ginsburg, *Judgments in Search of Full Faith and Credit: The Last-in-Time Rule for Conflicting Judgments*, 82 Harv. L. Rev. 798 (1969).

23 U.S. Const. art. IV, § 1 ("Full faith and credit shall be given in each state to the public acts, records, and judicial proceedings of every other state. And the Congress may by general laws prescribe the manner in which such acts, records, and proceedings shall be proved, and the effect thereof.").

24 Ginsburg, *supra* note 22, at 828.

25 *Id.* at 829.

26 *Id.*

27 *Id.* at 830.

28 516 U.S. 367 (1996).

29 *See id.* at 388 (Ginsburg, J., concurring & dissenting).
30 *See id.* (Ginsburg, J., concurring & dissenting).
31 *See id.* at 399 (Ginsburg, J., concurring & dissenting).
32 522 U.S. 222 (1998).
33 *Id.* at 236 n.9.
34 *Id.* at 228–29.
35 *See id.*
36 *See id.* at 237 n.11.
37 *Id.* at 230.
38 *Id.* at 233.
39 *Id.* at 238.
40 *Id.*
41 547 U.S. 293 (2006).
42 *Id.* at 311–12.
43 *Id.* at 312.
44 *See* Karen O'Connor & Barbara Palmer, *The Clinton Clones: Ginsburg, Breyer, and the Clinton Legacy*, 84 JUDICATURE 262, 265 (2001).
45 *See* Russell A. Miller, *Clinton, Ginsburg, and Centrist Federalism*, 85 IND. L.J. 225, 226–27 (2010).
46 518 U.S. 515 (1996).
47 *See* Russell A. Miller, *In a Dissenting Voice: Justice Ginsburg's Federalism*, 43 NEW ENG. L. REV. 771, 774 (2009) ("In the shadow of [Ginsburg's] progressive gender equity jurisprudence resides a commitment to state autonomy, a position generally viewed as the prerogative of the right. This belies the claims of conservative commentators and empirical scholars who view Justice Ginsburg as one of the Court's most consistently liberal and activist justices.").
48 512 U.S. 415, 418 (1994).
49 *Id.*
50 *Id.* at 439 (Ginsburg, J., dissenting) (quoting OR. REV. STAT. 30.925 (1991)).
51 *Id.* at 440–41 (Ginsburg, J., dissenting) (quoting OR. REV. STAT. 30.925(3) (1991)).
52 *Id.* at 436 (Ginsburg, J., dissenting).
53 *Id.* (Ginsburg, J., dissenting).
54 517 U.S. 559 (1996).
55 *Id.* at 607 (Ginsburg, J., dissenting).
56 *Id.* at 610 (Ginsburg, J., dissenting).
57 *Id.* at 611 (Ginsburg, J., dissenting).
58 *Id.* (Ginsburg, J., dissenting).
59 *Id.* at 613 (Ginsburg, J., dissenting).
60 *Id.* (Ginsburg, J., dissenting).
61 *Id.* (Ginsburg, J., dissenting) (emphasis in original).
62 522 U.S. 156 (1997).
63 *Id.* at 175 (Ginsburg, J., dissenting).
64 *Id.* at 174.
65 *Id.* at 176 (Ginsburg, J., dissenting).
66 *See id.* at 176–80 (Ginsburg, J., dissenting).
67 *Id.* at 176–77 (Ginsburg, J., dissenting).
68 *Id.* at 176 (Ginsburg, J., dissenting).

69 *Id.* at 175 (Ginsburg, J., dissenting).
70 463 U.S. 1032 (1983).
71 *See id.* at 1040–41.
72 Ginsburg's position regarding *Michigan v. Long* echoes the concerns origi-
    nally expressed by Justice Stevens in *Long* itself. *See id.* at 1065–72 (Stevens, J.,
    dissenting).
73 Arizona v. Evans, 514 U.S. 1, 24 (1995) (Ginsburg, J., dissenting).
74 *Id.* at 30 (Ginsburg, J., dissenting).
75 514 U.S. 549 (1995).
76 529 U.S. 598 (2000).
77 I am grateful to Scott Dodson for suggesting this particular encapsulation of my
    views regarding Ginsburg's federalism jurisprudence.
78 518 U.S. 415 (1996).
79 304 U.S. 64 (1938).
80 *Gasperini*, 518 U.S. at 423.
81 N.Y. C.P.L.R. §5501(c) (McKinney 1995).
82 U.S. Const. amend. VII.
83 *Gasperini*, 518 U.S. at 450 (Scalia, J., dissenting).
84 *See id.* at 432–35.
85 *Id.* at 419.
86 *See id.* at 437–39.
87 *See id.* at 419.
88 559 U.S. 393 (2010).
89 *Id.* at 398–406.
90 *Id.* at 437 (Ginsburg, J., dissenting).
91 *Id.* (Ginsburg, J., dissenting).
92 *Id.* (Ginsburg, J., dissenting).
93 *Id.* at 446–47 (Ginsburg, J., dissenting).
94 513 U.S. 219 (1995).
95 *Id.* at 238 (O'Connor, J., concurring & dissenting).
96 *Id.* at 235 (Stevens, J., concurring & dissenting).
97 *Id.* at 222.
98 *Id.* at 221–22 (quoting 49 U.S.C. § 1305(a)(1) (1978)).
99 *Id.* at 228.
100 *Id.* at 228–29.
101 *See, e.g.*, Richard D. Freer, *Some Thoughts on the State of Erie after Gasperini*, 76
    Tex. L. Rev. 1637 (1998) (criticizing the decision).
102 *See* Ruth Bader Ginsburg, *"A Decent Respect to the Opinions of [Human]kind"*:
    The Value of a Comparative Perspective in Constitutional Adjudication, 26 Am. U.
    Int'l L. Rev. 927, 927 (2011).
103 *See id.*
104 *Id.*
105 *Id.* at 929.
106 *Id.* at 931.
107 *Id.* at 933–34.
108 *Id.* at 934.
109 *See id.*

110 *See generally* Berman, *supra* note 7.

111 542 U.S. 241 (2004).

112 *Id.* at 261–62.

113 *See id.* at 261 ("A foreign nation may limit discovery within its domain for reasons peculiar to its own legal practices, culture, or traditions – reasons that do not necessarily signal objection to aid from United States federal courts.").

114 *See id.* at 262.

115 *See id.* at 264–65.

116 *See id.*

117 *See generally, e.g.*, KAL RAUSTIALA, DOES THE CONSTITUTION FOLLOW THE FLAG? (2009).

118 887 F.2d 275, 307–08 (D.C. Cir. 1989) (Ginsburg, J., concurring & dissenting) (alteration in original) (citation and internal quotation marks omitted).

119 *Id.* at 308 (Ginsburg, J., concurring & dissenting) (internal quotation marks omitted).

120 524 U.S. 666, 701–02 (1998) (Ginsburg, J., dissenting).

121 *See DKT Mem'l Fund*, 887 F.2d at 308 (Ginsburg, J., concurring & dissenting).

122 United States v. Tiede, 86 F.R.D. 227, 247–51 (U.S. Ct. Berlin 1979).

123 *Id.* at 244.

124 For example, Indian law scholar Carole Goldberg summarized Ginsburg's statements concerning Indian law during her confirmation hearings to become a Supreme Court justice as follows:

> Specifically, each time [Senator Larry Pressler] asked her how she would resolve an Indian law dispute, she maintained that she would look to Congress for guidance, and rule as Congress has directed in the exercise of its "plenary power" over Indian affairs. Whether the question involved the scope of tribal sovereignty, the extent of the federal trust responsibility to the tribes, or the powers of states within Indian country, her answer was the same: "The courts will do what Congress instructs."

Carole Goldberg, *Finding the Way to Indian Country: Justice Ruth Bader Ginsburg's Decisions in Indian Law Cases*, 70 OHIO ST. L.J. 1003, 1008–09 (2009) (quoting Nomination of Ruth Bader Ginsburg to Be Associate Justice of the Supreme Court of the United States: Hearing Before the S. Comm. on the Judiciary, 103d Cong. 233–35 (1993) (questioning by Sen. Pressler) (internal footnotes omitted).

125 *See* Goldberg, *supra note* 124 at 1005–07. My discussion of Ginsburg's role in the ACLU deliberations regarding the *Martinez* case is derived from Goldberg's account.

126 436 U.S. 49 (1978).

127 *Id.* at 49.

128 ALVIN ZIONTZ, A LAWYER IN INDIAN COUNTRY: A MEMOIR 177 (2009).

129 *See* Goldberg, *supra* note 124, at 1006 ("Ruth Bader Ginsburg's unyielding stance on *Martinez* suggests that she may have formed a view that Indian law and civil rights law invariably conflict.").

130 520 U.S. 438 (1997).

131 480 U.S. 9 (1987).

132 *See* Goldberg, *supra* note 124, at 1023–24.

133 *Id.* at 1024.

134   544 U.S. 197 (2005).
135   Treaty of Canandaigua with the Six (Iroquois) Nations, art. III, 7 Stat. 44 (Nov. 11, 1794).
136   *See* 25 U.S.C. §§ 174–202.
137   *City of Sherrill*, 544 U.S. at 205–06.
138   Goldberg, *supra* note 124, at 1028.
139   County of Oneida v. Oneida Indian Nation, 470 U.S. 226 (1985); Oneida Indian Nation v. County of Oneida, 414 U.S. 661 (1974).
140   *City of Sherill*, 544 U.S. at 211–12.
141   Goldberg, *supra* note 124, at 1029.
142   18 U.S.C. § 1151(a) (2012).
143   See Solem v. Bartlett, 465 U.S. 463, 472 (1984).
144   *See* Goldberg, *supra* note 124, at 1029.
145   *City of Sherill*, 544 U.S. at 216–17.
146   *See* Goldberg, *supra* note 124, at 1030.
147   *See id.* at 1031.
148   *City of Sherill*, 544 U.S. at 216 n.11.
149   *Id.* at 202, 203, 213, 215, 216 n.11, 221.
150   Goldberg, *supra* note 124, at 1031.
151   546 U.S. 95 (2005).
152   *Id.* at 131 (Ginsburg, J., dissenting).
153   554 U.S. 316 (2008).
154   *Id.* at 343 (Ginsburg, J., concurring & dissenting) (quoting maj. op. at 320).
155   *Id.* (Ginsburg, J., concurring & dissenting) (quoting Plains Commerce Bank v. Long Family Land & Cattle Co., 491 F.3d 878, 887 (8th Cir. 2007)).
156   Goldberg, *supra* note 124, at 1035.

12   THE ONCE AND FUTURE FEDERALIST

1   *See* Gibbons v. Ogden, 22 U.S. (9 Wheat.) 1 (1824); *see also* Wickard v. Filburn, 317 U.S. 111, 121–25 (1942) (describing history of commerce clause decisions).
2   Nat'l Fed'n of Indep. Bus. v. Sebelius, 132 S. Ct. 2566, 2585 (2012) (opinion of Roberts, C.J.); *see also* McCulloch v. Maryland, 17 U.S. (4 Wheat.) 316, 405 (1819) ("The question respecting the extent of the powers actually granted [to the national government] is perpetually arising, and will probably continue to arise, as long as our system shall exist.").
3   For discussions of this "revolution," see, *e.g.*, Erwin Chemerinsky, *The Federalism Revolution*, 31 N.M. L. Rev. 7 (2001); Allison H. Eid, *Federalism and Formalism*, 11 Wm. & Mary Bill Rts. J. 1191 (2003); Calvin Massey, *Federalism and the Rehnquist Court*, 53 Hastings L.J. 431 (2002); Nicole Huberfeld et al., *Plunging into Endless Difficulties: Medicaid and Coercion in National Federation of Independent Business v. Sebelius*, 93 B.U. L. Rev. 1 (2013).
4   *See* Laura Krugman Ray, *Justice Ginsburg and the Middle Way*, 68 Brook. L. Rev. 629, 631 (2003) ("[Justice Ginsburg] locates her work within a tradition of what she calls 'way pavers,' judges who are responsible for preparing the ground for those who follow.").
5   132 S. Ct. 2566 (2012).

6 133 S. Ct. 2612 (2013).

7 U.S. CONST. art. I, § 8, cl. 3.

8 *Sebelius*, 132 S. Ct. at 2615 (Ginsburg, J., concurring & dissenting).

9 *Id.* (Ginsburg, J., concurring & dissenting).

10 *Id.* (Ginsburg, J., concurring & dissenting) (quoting 2 THE RECORDS OF THE FEDERAL CONVENTION OF 1787, at 131 (Max Farrand ed. 1966)).

11 NLRB v. Jones & Laughlin Steel Corp., 301 U.S. 1, 37 (1937).

12 Gonzales v. Raich, 545 U.S. 1, 17 (2005).

13 In addition to *Sebelius*, discussed here, see United States v. Morrison, 529 U.S. 598 (2000); Printz v. United States, 521 U.S. 898 (1997); United States v. Lopez, 514 U.S. 549 (1995); New York v. United States, 505 U.S. 144 (1992). In 2005, on the other hand, the Court upheld congressional power to prohibit intrastate use of marijuana for medical purposes. Gonzales v. Raich, 545 U.S. 1 (2005). Scholars have differed on how significantly *Raich* affects the reach of *Morrison*, *Lopez*, and other more restrictive Commerce Clause decisions. *Compare, e.g.*, George D. Brown, *Counterrevolution? – National Criminal Law after Raich*, 66 OHIO ST. L.J. 947 (2005) (*Raich* halted further expansion of the new federalism, but did not roll back previous decisions), *with, e.g.*, Ilya Somin, *Gonzales v. Raich: Federalism as a Casualty of the War on Drugs*, 15 CORNELL J.L. & PUB. POL'Y 507, 508 (2006) ("*Raich* represents a major – possibly even terminal – setback for efforts to impose meaningful judicial constraints on Congress' Commerce Clause powers").

14 132 S. Ct. 2566 (2012).

15 Pub. L. No. 111–148, 124 Stat. 119.

16 26 U.S.C. § 5000A(a) (2012).

17 *See Sebelius*, 132 S. Ct. at 2585 (opinion of Roberts, C.J.) (discussing Congress's rationale for the individual mandate).

18 *See Sebelius*, 132 S. Ct. at 2585–93 (opinion of Roberts, C.J.); *id.* at 2642, 2644–50 (joint dissent of Justices Scalia, Kennedy, Thomas, and Alito). Justice Thomas added a brief individual dissent in which he "adhere[d] to [his] view that 'the very notion of a "substantial effects" test under the Commerce Clause is inconsistent with the original understanding of Congress' powers and with this Court's early Commerce Clause cases.'" *Id.* at 2677 (Thomas, J., dissenting) (quoting *Morrison*, 529 U.S. at 627 (Thomas, J., concurring)).

19 *Id.* at 2585 (opinion of Roberts, C.J.) (emphasis added) (quoting United States v. Darby, 312 U.S. 100, 118–119 (1941)); *id.* at 2644–47 (joint dissent).

20 *Id.* at 2643 (opinion of Roberts, C.J.); *see also id.* at 2587 (opinion of Roberts, C.J.) ("Construing the Commerce Clause to permit Congress to regulate individuals precisely because they are doing nothing would open a new and potentially vast domain to congressional authority. Every day individuals do not do an infinite number of things.").

21 *Id.* at 2646–47 (opinion of Roberts, C.J.) (quoting McCulloch v. Maryland, 17 U.S. (4 Wheat.) 316, 421, (1819)).

22 *Id.* at 2643 (opinion of Roberts, C.J.). The four justices who authored the joint dissent used even more colorful language. "If Congress can reach out and command even those furthest removed from an interstate market to participate in the market," these justices predicted, "then the Commerce Clause becomes a font of unlimited power, or in Hamilton's words, 'the hideous monster whose devouring jaws ... spare neither sex nor age, nor high nor low, nor sacred nor profane.'" *Id.* at

2646 (joint dissent) (quoting THE FEDERALIST No. 33, at 202 (Alexander Hamilton) (Clinton Rossiter ed., 1961)).

23 *Id.* at 2593–2600 (opinion of Roberts, C.J.); *id.* at 2609, 2629 (Ginsburg, J., concurring & dissenting) (joined by Breyer, Sotomayor & Kagan, JJ.).

24 *See* Timothy Sandefur, *So It's a Tax, Now What? Some of the Problems Remaining after NFIB v. Sebelius*, 17 TEX. REV. L. & POL. 203, 212–13 (2013) (summarizing debate over whether *Sebelius*'s Commerce Clause distinction is holding or dictum).

25 Throughout this section, I refer to the five justices who rebuffed Congress's Commerce Clause authority as the "majority" or "Commerce Clause majority." Although a different majority upheld the legislation under the Spending Clause, a majority of five justices emphatically rejected Congress's Commerce Clause power.

26 *Sebelius*, 132 S. Ct. at 2609, 2616 (Ginsburg, J., concurring & dissenting) (quoting Gonzales v. Raich, 545 U.S. 1, 17 (2005)). The justices on both sides of the Commerce Clause debate also discussed the role of the Necessary and Proper Clause in supporting Congress's power. I do not explore those differences here.

27 *Id.* at 2609 (Ginsburg, J., concurring & dissenting).

28 *Id.* (Ginsburg, J., concurring & dissenting).

29 *Id.* (Ginsburg, J., concurring & dissenting).

30 *Id.* at 2622 (Ginsburg, J., concurring & dissenting).

31 *Id.* (Ginsburg, J., concurring & dissenting).

32 317 U.S. 111 (1942).

33 *Sebelius*, 132 S. Ct. at 2622–23 (Ginsburg, J., concurring & dissenting).

34 *Id.* at 2573, 2587, 2589 (opinion of Roberts, C.J.).

35 *Id.* at 2622 (Ginsburg, J., concurring & dissenting).

36 *Id.* at 2616 (Ginsburg, J., concurring & dissenting).

37 *Id.* at 2609 (Ginsburg, J., concurring & dissenting).

38 *Id.* at 2611 (Ginsburg, J., concurring & dissenting) (citing 42 U.S.C. § 18091(2) (Supp. IV 2010)).

39 *Id.* at 2611 (Ginsburg, J., concurring & dissenting).

40 *Id.* (Ginsburg, J., concurring & dissenting) (quoting 42 U.S.C. § 18091(2)(F) (Supp. IV 2010)).

41 *Id.* (Ginsburg, J., concurring & dissenting) (citing 42 U.S.C. § 18091(2) (Supp. IV 2010)).

42 *Id.* at 2617 (Ginsburg, J., concurring & dissenting).

43 *Id.* at 2619 (Ginsburg, J., concurring & dissenting).

44 *Id.* (Ginsburg, J., concurring & dissenting).

45 *Id.* (Ginsburg, J., concurring & dissenting) (internal cross-reference omitted).

46 *See id.* at 2615–16 (Ginsburg, J., concurring & dissenting) (discussing origin of the Commerce Clause).

47 *Id.* at 2615 (Ginsburg, J., concurring & dissenting) (quoting 2 THE RECORDS OF THE FEDERAL CONVENTION OF 1787, at 131 (Max Farrand ed., 1966)).

48 *Id.* (Ginsburg, J., concurring & dissenting) (quoting Letter from James Madison to Edmund Randolph (Apr. 8, 1787), in 9 PAPERS OF JAMES MADISON 368, 370 (Robert A. Rutland & William M. E. Rachal eds., 1975)).

49 *Id.* at 2615 n.3 (Ginsburg, J., concurring & dissenting) (quoting Alexander Hamilton, *The Continentalist No. V, in* 3 THE PAPERS OF ALEXANDER HAMILTON 75, 78 (Harold C. Syrett ed., 1962)).

50 *Id.* at 2612 (Ginsburg, J., concurring & dissenting).

51 *Id.* (Ginsburg, J., concurring & dissenting).

52 *Id.* (Ginsburg, J., concurring & dissenting).

53 *Id.* (Ginsburg, J., concurring & dissenting) (quoting Brief for Health Care for All, Inc. et al. as Amici Curiae Supporting Petitioners at 4, Dep't of Health & Human Serv. v. Florida, 132 S. Ct. 1133 (2012) (No. 11–398)).

54 *Id.* at 2614 (Ginsburg, J., concurring & dissenting) (quoting Brief for American Association of People with Disabilities et al. as Amici Curiae supporting Petitioners at 9, Dep't of Health & Human Serv. v. Florida, 132 S. Ct. 1133 (2012) (No. 11–398)).

55 *Id.* at 2614 (Ginsburg, J., concurring & dissenting).

56 *Id.* at 2609 (Ginsburg, J., concurring & dissenting).

57 *Id.* at 2612 (Ginsburg, J., concurring & dissenting).

58 *Id.* at 2609 (Ginsburg, J., concurring & dissenting).

59 *Id.* at 2643 (joint dissent).

60 *Id.* at 2646 (joint dissent) (quoting The Federalist No. 33, at 202 (Alexander Hamilton) (Clinton Rossiter ed., 1961)).

61 *Id.* at 2588 (opinion of Roberts, C.J.).

62 *Id.* at 2624 (Ginsburg, J., concurring & dissenting).

63 *Id.* (Ginsburg, J., concurring & dissenting).

64 *See id.* at 2625 (Ginsburg, J., concurring & dissenting) (Justices Scalia, Thomas, Kennedy, and Alito "assert[ed], outlandishly …").

65 *Id.* at 2623 (Ginsburg, J., concurring & dissenting) (quoting Seven–Sky v. Holder, 661 F.3d 1, 19 (D.C. Cir. 2011)).

66 *Id.* at 2623 n.8 (Ginsburg, J., concurring & dissenting).

67 U.S. CONST. art. I, § 8, cl. 1.

68 Older adults will continue to receive benefits through the nationally administered Medicare program. *See Sebelius*, 132 S. Ct. at 2581–82 (opinion of Roberts, C.J.).

69 To start, Congress promised to cover 100 percent of these costs; coverage would then decline to 90 percent by 2020. *Id.* at 2632 (Ginsburg, J., concurring & dissenting).

70 42 U.S.C. § 1396c (2012).

71 Justices Breyer and Kagan joined the Chief Justice's opinion finding the Medicaid expansion unconstitutional; the joint dissenters also found the expansion unconstitutional.

72 132 S. Ct. at 2630 (Ginsburg, J., concurring & dissenting) (emphasis original).

73 *Id.* at 2634 (Ginsburg, J., concurring & dissenting) (quoting South Dakota v. Dole, 483 U.S. 203, 211 (1987)).

74 *Id.* (Ginsburg, J., concurring & dissenting).

75 *Id.* (Ginsburg, J., concurring & dissenting) (quoting *Dole,* 483 U.S. at 207–08, 210).

76 *Id.* at 2636 (Ginsburg, J., concurring & dissenting).

77 *Id.* at 2640 (Ginsburg, J., concurring & dissenting) (quoting *Sebelius*, 132 S. Ct. at 2602) (opinion of Roberts, C.J.))

78 *Id.* (Ginsburg, J., concurring & dissenting).

79 *Id.* (Ginsburg, J., concurring & dissenting).
80 *Id.* at 2641 (Ginsburg, J., concurring & dissenting) (citing Baker v. Carr, 369 U.S. 186, 217 (1962)).
81 *Id.* at 2630 (Ginsburg, J., concurring & dissenting).
82 *Id.* at 2641 (Ginsburg, J., concurring & dissenting).
83 *Id.* at 2630 (Ginsburg, J., concurring & dissenting).
84 *Id.* at 2629 (Ginsburg, J., concurring & dissenting).
85 *Id.* at 2629 (Ginsburg, J., concurring & dissenting).
86 *Id.* at 2632 (Ginsburg, J., concurring & dissenting).
87 *Id.* at 2633 n.17 (Ginsburg, J., concurring & dissenting).
88 U.S. Const. amend. XIII, § 2; U.S. Const. amend. XIV, § 5; U.S. Const. amend. XV, § 2.
89 *Ex parte* Virginia, 100 U.S. 339, 345 (1879) (emphasis added).
90 South Carolina v. Katzenbach, 383 U.S. 301, 326 (1966).
91 *Id.* at 337.
92 *Id.* at 326.
93 *Id.* at 324.
94 *Id.*
95 *See* Shelby Cnty. v. Holder, 133 S. Ct. 2612, 2620 (2013) (describing reauthorizations of the Voting Rights Act).
96 Georgia v. United States, 411 U.S. 526 (1973); City of Rome v. United States, 446 U.S. 156 (1980); Lopez v. Monterey Cnty., 525 U.S. 266 (1999).
97 133 S. Ct. 2612 (2013).
98 *Id.* at 2621 (quoting N.W. Austin Mun. Util. Dist. No. One v. Holder, 557 U.S. 193, 202 (2009)).
99 *Id.* at 2622 (quoting *N.W. Austin*, 557 U.S. at 203).
100 *Id.* at 2623.
101 *Id.* at 2636 (Ginsburg, J., dissenting).
102 *Id.* at 2638 (Ginsburg, J., dissenting).
103 *Id.* at 2644 (Ginsburg, J., dissenting).
104 *Id.* (Ginsburg, J., dissenting)
105 383 U.S. 301, 326 (1966).
106 *Shelby Cnty.*, 133 S. Ct. at 2648 (Ginsburg, J., dissenting) (quoting South Carolina v. Katzenbach, 383 U.S. at 328–29) (emphasis added by Ginsburg, J.).
107 557 U.S. 193 (2009).
108 133 S. Ct. at 2649 (Ginsburg, J., dissenting).
109 *Id.* (Ginsburg, J., dissenting). In addition to attacking the majority's disregard of precedent, Justice Ginsburg challenged its equal sovereignty discussion on substantive grounds. The sparsely reasoned holding, she pointed out, "is capable of much mischief" because "Federal statutes that treat States disparately are hardly novelties." *Id.* (Ginsburg, J.).
110 *Id.* (Ginsburg, J., dissenting); *see also id.* at 2638 (Ginsburg, J., dissenting) ("The Court has repeatedly affirmed the statute's constitutionality and Congress has adhered to the very model the Court has upheld.").
111 *Id.* at 2644 (Ginsburg, J., dissenting).
112 *Id.* at 2632 (Ginsburg, J., dissenting) (footnote omitted).
113 *See id.* at 2635–36 (Ginsburg, J., dissenting).

114 *See id.* at 2639–44 (Ginsburg, J., dissenting).

115 *Id.* at 2644 (Ginsburg, J., dissenting).

116 *Id.* at 2630 (quoting *N.W. Austin*, 557 U.S. at 204); *see also id.* at 2621 ("We expressed serious doubts about the Act's continued constitutionality."); *id.* at 2627 ("By 2009, however, we concluded that the 'coverage formula raise[d] serious constitutional questions.'" (quoting *N.W. Austin*, 557 U.S. at 204)).

117 *Id.* at 2631.

118 *Id.*

119 *Id.* at 2648 (Ginsburg, J., dissenting). Justice Ginsburg also chided the majority for declaring the coverage provision facially unconstitutional, rather than judging the provision as applied to Shelby County. "By what right," she asked, "given its usual restraint, does the Court even address Shelby County's facial challenge to the VRA?" *Id.* at 2644 (Ginsburg, J., dissenting).

120 *Id.* at 2637 (Ginsburg, J., dissenting).

121 *Id.* (Ginsburg, J., dissenting)

122 *Id.* at 2622–24.

123 *Id.* at 2624.

124 *Id.* at 2634 (Ginsburg, J., dissenting).

125 *Id.* at 2624.

126 *Id.* at 2634 (Ginsburg, J., dissenting) (emphasis added).

127 *Id.* at 2641 n.5 (Ginsburg, J., dissenting) (discussing South Carolina v. United States, 898 F. Supp. 2d 30 (D.D.C. 2012)).

128 *Id.* at 2633 (Ginsburg, J., dissenting).

129 *Id.* at 2626.

130 *Id.* at 2635 (Ginsburg, J., dissenting).

131 *Id.* at 2652 (Ginsburg, J., dissenting).

132 Bush v. Gore, 531 U.S. 98 (2000) (per curiam).

133 *See, e.g.*, Michael S. Greve & Jonathan Klick, *Preemption in the Rehnquist Court: A Preliminary Empirical Assessment*, 14 SUP. CT. ECON. REV. 43, 84–88 (2006); Russell A. Miller, *Clinton, Ginsburg, and Centrist Federalism*, 85 IND. L.J. 225, 271–76 (2010); Ernest A. Young, *The Rehnquist Court's Two Federalisms*, 83 TEX. L. REV. 1 (2004).

134 552 U.S. 312 (2008).

135 *Id.* at 320.

136 Pub. L. No. 94–295, 90 Stat. 539. The statute included a preemption clause, which is codified at 21 U.S.C. § 360k.

137 552 U.S. at 315.

138 *Id.* at 334 (Ginsburg, J., dissenting) (quoting Cipollone v. Liggett Grp., Inc., 505 U.S. 504, 516 (1992)).

139 *Id.* (Ginsburg, J., dissenting) (quoting Rice v. Santa Fe Elevator Corp., 331 U.S. 218, 230 (1947)).

140 *Id.* at 345 (Ginsburg, J., dissenting). In addition to favoring national authority, the Court in *Riegel* demonstrated distaste for common-law tort actions against manufacturers of medical devices. *See, e.g., id.* at 325 (majority opinion) ("A jury … sees only the cost of a more dangerous design, and is not concerned with its benefits; the patients who reaped those benefits are not represented in court."); *id.* at 326 (noting Congress's possible concern for "those who would suffer without

new medical devices if juries were allowed to apply the tort law of 50 States to all innovations").

141 *Id.* at 334 (Ginsburg, J., dissenting) (quoting N.Y. State Conf. of Blue Cross & Blue Shield Plans v. Travelers Ins. Co., 514 U.S. 645, 655 (1995)).

142 *Id.* at 335 (Ginsburg, J., dissenting) (quoting Bates v. Dow Agrosciences LLC, 544 U.S. 431, 449 (2005)).

143 *Id.* at 333 (Ginsburg, J., dissenting).

144 U.S. CONST. art. VI, cl. 2.

145 552 U.S. at 336 (Ginsburg, J., dissenting).

146 *Id.* at 340 (Ginsburg, J., dissenting).

147 *Id.* at 344–45 (Ginsburg, J., dissenting).

148 *Id.* at 345 (Ginsburg, J., dissenting).

149 *Id.* at 337 (Ginsburg, J., dissenting) (quoting Margaret Jane Porter, *The Lohr Decision: FDA Perspective and Position*, 52 FOOD & DRUG L.J. 7, 11 (1997)) (internal quotation marks omitted).

150 *Id.* (Ginsburg, J., dissenting) (quoting Margaret Jane Porter, *The Lohr Decision: FDA Perspective and Position*, 52 FOOD & DRUG L.J. 7, 11(1997)) (internal quotation marks omitted). The FDA changed its position for the *Riegel* litigation, a shift that Justice Ginsburg regarded with skepticism. *Id.* at 338 n.8 (Ginsburg, J., dissenting).

151 *Id.* at 345 (Ginsburg, J., dissenting).

152 *Id.* at 338 (Ginsburg, J., dissenting) (quoting Medtronic Inc. v. Lohr, 518 U.S. 470, 487 (1996) (plurality opinion)).

153 531 U.S. 98 (2000) (per curiam).

154 *Id.* at 103; *id.* at 129, 133–34 (Souter, J., dissenting); *id.* at 144–46 (Breyer, J., dissenting). Justices Souter and Breyer each identified fewer Equal Protection violations than the majority did, but they agreed that at least one aspect of Florida's recount procedure violated the clause.

155 *Id.* at 110. Justices Souter and Breyer each concluded that although the Florida procedure violated the Equal Protection Clause, the Court should give the state court a chance to remedy the defect on remand. *Id.* at 129, 134–35 (Souter, J., dissenting); *id.* at 144, 146–47 (Breyer, J., dissenting).

156 U.S. CONST. art. II, § 1, cl. 2.

157 *See supra* notes 88–131 and accompanying text.

158 The ruling in *Bush v. Gore* bears a paradoxical relationship to the Court's federalism decisions in *New York v. United States*, 505 U.S. 144 (1992), and *Printz v. United States*, 521 U.S. 898 (1997). The latter two cases express an "autonomy" theory of federalism, which forbids national actions that "tamper with the independent relationship between a state government and its voters." Deborah Jones Merritt, *Three Faces of Federalism: Finding A Formula for the Future*, 47 VAND. L. REV. 1563, 1571 (1994). That autonomy principle should have restrained the Court from interfering with Florida's election process. I do not discuss *New York*, *Printz*, or the autonomy principle further here. These cases represent a narrow strain of the Court's federalism jurisprudence, and Justice Ginsburg was not on the Court when it decided *New York*, the key case in this genre. She dissented from the Court's holding in *Printz*, but did not write separately.

159 531 U.S. at 139 (Ginsburg, J., dissenting).

160 *Id.* at 135–36 (Ginsburg, J., dissenting).
161 *Id.* at 136 (Ginsburg, J., dissenting).
162 *Id.* (Ginsburg, J., dissenting) (citation omitted) (quoting Sumner v. Mata, 449 U.S. 539, 549 (1981)).
163 *Id.* (Ginsburg, J., dissenting) (citing Chevron U.S.A. Inc. v. Natural Res. Defense Council, Inc., 467 U.S. 837, 843 (1984)).
164 *Id.* (Ginsburg, J., dissenting).
165 *Id.* at 137 (Ginsburg, J., dissenting).
166 *Id.* at 143 (Ginsburg, J., dissenting).
167 *Id.* (Ginsburg, J., dissenting).
168 *Id.* at 110 (per curiam).
169 *Id.* at 144 (Ginsburg, J., dissenting).
170 *Id.* (Ginsburg, J., dissenting).
171 *Id.* (Ginsburg, J., dissenting).
172 *Id.* at 142 (Ginsburg, J., dissenting).
173 *Id.* (Ginsburg, J., dissenting).
174 U.S. CONST. art. II, § 1, cl. 2.
175 531 U.S. at 141 (Ginsburg, J., dissenting).
176 U.S. CONST., art. IV, § 4.
177 531 U.S. at 141 (Ginsburg, J., dissenting).
178 *Id.* at 142 (Ginsburg, J., dissenting).
179 *Id.* at 142–43 (Ginsburg, J., dissenting).
180 *Id.* at 139 (Ginsburg, J., dissenting) (quoting Lehman Bros. v. Schein, 416 U.S. 386, 391 (1974)).
181 Certification would have slowed resolution of the controversy but, as Justice Ginsburg pointed out, the Florida Supreme Court had issued its opinions with remarkable speed. *See supra* note 169 and accompanying text. It might have been possible for the lower court to respond to certified questions with similar efficiency.
182 *See, e.g.*, Ruth Bader Ginsburg, *Remarks on Women's Progress at the Bar and on the Bench*, 89 CORNELL L. REV. 801, 805 (2004); Ruth Bader Ginsburg & Laura W. Brill, *Women in the Federal Judiciary: Three Way Pavers and the Exhilarating Change President Carter Wrought*, 64 FORDHAM L. REV. 281, 281 (1995); Ruth Bader Ginsburg, *In Memoriam: Albert M. Sacks*, 105 HARV. L. REV. 16, 17 (1991). Justice Ginsburg has also spoken of "way pavers" who "inspired students and involved them in pro bono work." Ruth Bader Ginsburg, *In Pursuit of the Public Good: Lawyers Who Care*, 52 ME. L. REV. 301, 304 (2000). Professor Laura Krugman Ray preceded me in using the phrase "way paver" to describe Justice Ginsburg's own jurisprudence. *See* Ray, *supra* note 4, at 631.

13 REFLECTIONS ON THE CONFIRMATION JOURNEY OF RUTH BADER GINSBURG, SUMMER 1993

1 Hearings before the Committee on the Judiciary, United States Senate, Nomination of Ruth Bader Ginsburg, to Be Associate Justice of the Supreme Court of the United States, 103d Cong., 1st Sess. (1994) (opening statement of Ruth Bader Ginsburg).

2 *Id.*
3 *Id.*
4 Senate Judiciary Committee, Nomination of Ruth Bader Ginsburg to Be an Associate Justice of the Supreme Court of the United States, S. Exec. Rep. No. 6, 103d Cong. 1st Sess. (1993).
5 *Id.*
6 *Id.*
7 *Id.*

14 JUSTICE GINSBURG:
DEMOSPRUDENCE THROUGH DISSENT

1 Jeff Bleich et al., *Dissenting from the Bench*, OR. ST. B. BULL. (Oct. 2008), http:// www.osbar.org/publications/bulletin/08oct/dissenting.html
2 Linda Greenhouse, *Oral Dissents Give Ginsburg a New Voice*, N.Y. TIMES, May 31, 2007, at A1.
3 Adam Liptak, *How Activist Is the Supreme Court?*, N.Y. TIMES, Oct. 12, 2013, http:// www.nytimes.com/2013/10/13/sunday-review/how-activist-is-the-supreme-court .html ("Justice Ginsburg's impression [of the Court's activism] fits with a popular perception of the court."); David Paul Kuhn, *The Incredible Polarization and Politicization of the Supreme Court*, THE ATLANTIC, June 29, 2012, http://www .theatlantic.com/politics/archive/2012/06/the-incredible-polarization-and -politicization-of-the-supreme-court/259155/ (noting that "The Roberts Court has decided more cases by a 5-to-4 ruling (about 21.5 percent) than any Court before it, though only by a narrow margin.").
4 *No Turning the Clock Back on Abortion, Justice Ginsburg Says*, WASH. POST, Oct. 22, 2007, at A5. At the time, Justice Ginsburg had only issued "six oral dissents over 14 years on the Court." *Id.*
5 Portions of this chapter track my argument in Lani Guinier, *Courting the People: Demosprudence and the Law/Politics Divide*, 89 B.U. L. REV. 539 (2009). The concept of demosprudence is developed in Lani Guinier, *The Supreme Court, 2007 Term – Foreword: Demosprudence through Dissent*, 122 HARV. L. REV. 4 (2008) [hereinafter Guinier, *Foreword*].
6 Guinier, *Foreword*, *supra* note 5, at 40–41.
7 Lilly Ledbetter Fair Pay Act of 2009, Pub. L. No. 111–2, 123 Stat. 5 (2009).
8 *See* Richard Leiby, *A Signature with the First Lady's Hand in It*, WASH. POST, Jan. 29, 2009, at C1.
9 *Justice Denied? The Implications of the Supreme Court's* Ledbetter v. Goodyear *Employment Discrimination Decision: Hearing before the H. Comm. on Educ. & Labor*, 110th Cong. 10 (2007) [hereinafter *Hearing*] (statement of Lilly Ledbetter); *see also* Lilly Ledbetter, *Address to the Democratic National Convention* (Aug. 26, 2008), http://www.demconvention.com/lily-ledbetter/
10 *Hearing*, *supra* note 9. Ledbetter's salary was $3,727 a month. The salary of the lowest paid man, with far less seniority, was $4,286.
11 Ledbetter v. Goodyear Tire & Rubber Co., 550 U.S. 618, 643–44 (2007) (Ginsburg, J., dissenting) (quoting record from below).

12 *Id.* at 621 (majority opinion).

13 Ledbetter, *supra* note 9.

14 *Ledbetter*, 550 U.S. at 643 (Ginsburg, J., dissenting).

15 In an interview with the ACLU, Ginsburg's co-counsel described the first case Ginsburg argued before the Court: "I've never heard an oral argument as unbelievably cogent as hers.... Not a single Justice asked a single question; I think they were mesmerized by her." *Tribute: The Legacy of Ruth Bader Ginsburg & WRP Staff*, AM. CIV. LIBERTIES UNION (Mar. 7, 2006), http://www.aclu.org/womensrights /gen/24412pub20060307.html

16 Justice Ruth Bader Ginsburg, *The 20th Annual Leo and Berry Eizenstat Memorial Lecture: The Role of Dissenting Opinions* (Oct. 21, 2007), http://www .supremecourtus.gov/publicinfo/speeches/sp_10-21-07.html

17 Robert Barnes, *Over Ginsburg's Dissent, Court Limits Bias Suits*, WASH. POST, May 30, 2007, at A1 ("Speaking for the three other dissenting justices, Ginsburg's voice was as precise and emotionless as if she were reading a banking decision, but the words were stinging."). Barnes noted that Justice Ginsburg's oral dissent was a "usually rare practice that she has now employed twice in the past six weeks to criticize the majority for opinions that she said undermine women's rights." *Id.*

18 Ruth Bader Ginsburg, *Celebration Fifty-Five: A Public Conversation between Dean Elena Kagan '86 and Justice Ruth Bader Ginsburg '56–'58 at the Harvard Law School Women's Leadership Summit* (Sept. 20, 2008) (from notes taken by and on file with author); *see also* Ginsburg, *supra* note 16 ("A dissent presented orally ... garners immediate attention. It signals that, in the dissenters' view, the Court's opinion is not just wrong, but importantly and grievously misguided.").

19 Oral Dissent of Justice Ginsburg at 4:25, Ledbetter v. Goodyear Tire & Rubber Co., 550 U.S. 618 (2007), available at http://www.oyez.org/cases/2000 -2009/2006/2006_05_1074/opinion; *see also* Guinier, *Foreword*, *supra* note 5.

20 Oral Dissent, *Ledbetter*, supra note 19, at 8:30–8:37.

21 By "courting" I mean enlisting or inspiring rather than wooing or currying favor with.

22 Guinier, *Foreword*, *supra* note 5, at 40.

23 *Cf.* Timothy R. Johnson, Ryan C. Black & Eve M. Ringsmuth, *Hear Me Roar: What Provokes Supreme Court Justices to Dissent from the Bench?*, 92 MINN. L. REV. 1560, 1568–73 (2009) (finding that Supreme Court Justices use their oral dissents strategically to signal strong disagreement as well as the need for action by third parties to change the majority decision). As was her practice, Justice Ginsburg handed out her bench announcement right after the delivery of her oral dissent. Her press-release-style opening paragraphs in her opinions are intended to help reporters under tight deadlines get it right.

24 Oral Dissent, *Ledbetter*, *supra* note 19, at 10:17–10:58; *see also* Guinier, *Foreword*, *supra* note 5, at 41 n.179.

25 Ginsburg, *supra* note 18.

26 H.R. 2831, 110th Cong. (2007).

27 The initial bill passed the House in July 2007, but never came up for a vote in the Senate. GovTrack, H.R. 2831: Lilly Ledbetter Fair Pay Act of 2007, http://www .govtrack.us/congress/bill.xpd?bill=h110-2831 (last visited Mar. 17, 2009); *see also*

Carl Hulse, *Republican Senators Block Pay Discrimination Measure*, N.Y. Times, Apr. 24, 2008, at A22.

28 *Morning Edition: Fair Pay Law Strikes a Blow for Equal Pay* at 4:12, Nat'l Pub. Radio (Jan. 29, 2009), http://www.npr.org/templates/player/mediaPlayer.html?action=1&t=1&islist=false&id=99995431&m=99995549 (describing Ledbetter's prominent role and reporting that Ledbetter's husband, a retired National Guard Sergeant Major, voted for a Democratic president for the first time in fifty years when he cast his ballot for Barack Obama).

29 *Id.* at 3:07–3:18. In the ad, Ledbetter says, "John McCain opposed a law to give women equal pay for equal work. And he dismissed the wage gap, saying women just need education and training. I had the same skills as the men at my plant. My family needed that money."

30 Ledbetter, *supra* note 9.

31 *Hearing*, *supra* note 9.

32 *Id.* at 11.

33 *Id.* at 10; *see also* Ledbetter v. Goodyear *Equal Pay Hearing: Lilly Ledbetter*, YouTube http://www.youtube.com/watch?v=jRpYoUu5XH0 (last visited Mar. 10, 2009).

34 Ginsburg, *supra* note 16.

35 *Id.*; *see also* Johnson, Black & Ringsmuth, *supra* note 23, at 1563. Justice Ginsburg's willingness to participate in a more expansive conversation is not entirely unexpected, given her view that conversation should run both ways. "If we don't listen we won't be listened to." Ginsburg, *supra* note 18.

36 Guinier, *Foreword*, *supra* note 5, at 52 n.232 ("Role-literate participants are those people, not just judges, who see themselves as agents, interpreters, or movement leaders, and who understand the various ways that they are able to object to and/or potentially influence constitutional decisions by the courts."); *see also* Interview with Reva Siegel (Sept. 22, 2008) (whose use of the term "role-literate" was inspirational).

37 Mother Jones, *Ginsburg's Famous White Gloves Finally Come Off*, http://www.motherjones.com/mojoblog/archives/2007/05/4556_ginsburgs_famou.html (May 31, 2007, 22:19 PST) (quoting Marcia Greenberger).

38 Justice Ginsburg's dissent and Lilly Ledbetter's public statements converge on a common explanation for Ledbetter's delay in filing her lawsuit, an explanation that influenced both the media coverage and the Obama campaign's framing of the case. *See* Adam Liptak, *Justices Hear Bias Case on Maternity, Pensions, and Timing*, N.Y. Times, Dec. 11, 2008, at B7; Sheryl Gay Stolberg, *Obama Signs Equal-Pay Legislation*, N.Y. Times, Jan. 29, 2009, http://www.nytimes.com/2009/01/30/us/politics/30ledbetterweb.html?hp. Their mutually reinforcing explanation for Ledbetter's delay in filing her lawsuit, their joint outreach to Congress, and their success in sparking favorable media coverage of the new legislation became key talking points on conservative blogs. *See, e.g.*, Posting of Hans Bader, OpenMarket. org (Mar. 4, 2009, 15:29), http://www.openmarket.org/2009/03/04/distorting-the-news-to-obamas-advantage/; Posting of Orin Kerr, Volokh Conspiracy (Mar. 9, 2009, 16:18), http://volokh.com/posts/1236629897.shtml; Posting of Ed Whelan, Nat'l Rev. Online (Mar. 9, 2009, 13:51), http://bench.nationalreview.com/post/?q=YzA0Zjk1MzViMWUwMWNlYWEwZTkyYTIzYmY3MzAxYWE. Indeed, Lilly

Ledbetter soon came to symbolize a populist message. Ledbetter not only was present at the signing ceremony for the bill named in her honor, but also sat with First Lady Michelle Obama during President Obama's first address to a joint session of Congress. Michael Falcone, *Guests of the First Lady, Reflecting Main Themes of the Speech*, N.Y. TIMES, Feb. 25, 2009, at A16.

39 Lilly Ledbetter Fair Pay Act of 2009, Pub. L. No. 111–3, 123 Stat. 5 (2009). The act passed the Senate with "Yea" votes from every present Democrat and all four female Republicans. U.S. Senate Roll Call Votes, 111th Cong., 1st Sess., http://www.senate.gov/legislative/LIS/roll_call_lists/roll_call_vote_cfm.cfm?congress=111&session=1&vote=00014 (last visited Mar. 17, 2009).

40 *See generally* Robert M. Cover, *The Supreme Court, 1981 Term – Foreword: Nomos and Narrative*, 97 HARV. L. REV. 4 (1983) (conceptualizing the law as normative in nature).

41 Shelby Cnty. v. Holder, 133 S. Ct. 2612 (2013).

42 *Id.* at 2631.

43 Mark Walsh, *A "view" from the Court: June 25, 2013*, SCOTUSBLOG (June 25, 2013), http://www.scotusblog.com/2013/06/a-view-from-the-court-june-25-2013/

44 Richard Wolf, *Ginsburg's dedication undimmed after 20 years on court*, USA TODAY (Aug. 1, 2013), http://www.usatoday.com/story/news/nation/2013/07/31/ginsburg-female-justices-no-shrinking-violets-/2606239/. Justice Ginsburg also issued an oral dissent in *Fisher v. Univ. of Tex.*, 133 S. Ct. 2411 (2013), and a "combined" oral dissent in *Univ. of Tex. S.W. Med. Ctr. v. Nassar*, 133 S. Ct. 2513 (2013), and *Vance v. Ball State Univ.*, 133 S. Ct. 2434 (2013), which is technically counted as a single oral dissent. *See* Rob Silverblatt, *Justice Ginsburg's Record-Breaking Day*, USA TODAY (June 25, 2013), http://www.usnews.com/news/articles/2013/06/25/justice-ginsburgs-record-breaking-day

45 *See* Dana Milbank, *Roberts' Cynical Treatment of MLK in Voting Ruling*, WASH. POST (June 25, 2013), http://www.washingtonpost.com/opinions/dana-milbank-robertss-cynical-treatment-of-mlk-in-voting-ruling/2013/06/25/31c99360-dddb-11e2-b797-cbd4cb13f9c6_story.html, (noting that her oral dissent was "quietly spoken but powerfully worded").

46 Oral Dissent of Justice Ginsburg, Shelby Cnty. v. Holder, 133 S. Ct. 2612 (2013), http://www.oyez.org/cases/2010-2019/2012/2012_12_96

47 *Id.* at 00:19.

48 In addressing the difficulties of Shelby County's mounting of a facial challenge, for example, Justice Ginsburg asked sharply: "By what right does the Court address the county's claim?" Oral Dissent, *Shelby Cnty.*, *supra* note 46, at 7:17.

49 The Court concedes that "voting discrimination still exists; no one doubts that." *Shelby Cnty.*, 133 S. Ct. at 2619. Yet it keeps a laser-focus on data such as voter registration, turnout, and minority representation in elected office, and it demands a high correlation between these data and jurisdictions covered by the preclearance formula.

50 *Id.* at 2632 (Ginsburg, J., dissenting).

51 Oral Dissent, *Shelby Cnty.*, *supra* note 46, at 1:41.

52 *Id.* at 1:17.

53 *Id.* at 5:01.

54 *Shelby Cnty.*, 133 S. Ct. at 2640–41 (Ginsburg, J., dissenting).

55 *Id.* at 2647 (Ginsburg, J., dissenting).

56 *Id.* (Ginsburg, J., dissenting).

57 Oral Dissent, *Shelby Cnty.*, *supra* note 46, at 5:51.

58 *Shelby Cnty.*, 133 S. Ct. at 2626.

59 *John Lewis and Others React to the Supreme Court's Voting Rights Act Ruling,*
    WASH. POST (June 25, 2013), http://www.washingtonpost.com/opinions/john
    -lewis-and-others-react-to-the-supreme-courts-voting-rights-act-ruling/2013/06/25
    /acb96650-ddda-11e2-b797-cbd4cb13f9c6_story.html

60 *Id.*

61 In a televised speech, President Bush, in front of a banner that read "Mission
    Accomplished," announced to the nation: "Major combat operations in Iraq have
    ended. In the battle of Iraq, the United States and our allies have prevailed." *See*
    Office of Press Secretary, *President Bush Announces Major Combat Operations in
    Iraq Have Ended* (May 1, 2003), http://georgewbush-whitehouse.archives.gov/news
    /releases/2003/05/20030501-15.html (last visited Mar. 3, 2014). The speech has since
    been significantly criticized as brash and premature, as significantly more American
    troops died after the speech was given than before. *See* James Wright, *10 Years After
    "Mission Accomplished," the Risks of Another Intervention,* THE ATLANTIC (May
    1, 2013), http://www.theatlantic.com/international/archive/2013/05/10-years-after
    -mission-accomplished-the-risks-of-another-intervention/275446/ (noting the pre-
    speech death toll at 139, and the 4,335 lives lost after it).

62 *Shelby Cnty.*, 133 S. Ct. at 2619.

63 *See* Oral Dissent, *Shelby Cnty.*, *supra* note 46.

64 *Id.* at 1:59. Congress's decision that more time was needed to eviscerate the scourge
    of discrimination in voting, she also noted, should also warrant the Court's "unstint-
    ing approbation." *Shelby Cnty.*, 133 S. Ct. at 2633 (Ginsburg, J., dissenting).

65 Oral Dissent, *Shelby Cnty.*, *supra* note 46, at 9:59.

66 *Id.* at 10:15.

67 *See* LANI GUINIER, LIFT EVERY VOICE: TURNING A CIVIL RIGHTS SETBACK INTO A
    NEW VISION OF SOCIAL JUSTICE 175 (1998) (quoting from King's letter to the *New
    York Times* in February 1965 describing the dramatic appeal of the conditions in
    Alabama): "This is Selma, Alabama," Dr. King wrote. "There are more Negroes in
    jail with me," he continued, "than there are on the voting rolls."

68 The invocation of King's words is an example of how demosprudence can "reframe
    our understanding of the important role that mobilized or engaged constituencies
    play in legitimating the Court's constitutional role." Guinier, *Foreword, supra* note
    5, at 54.

69 *Id.* at 55.

70 *Shelby Cnty.*, 133 S. Ct. at 2642 (Ginsburg, J., dissenting).

71 *Id.* (Ginsburg, J., dissenting).

72 *Id.* (Ginsburg, J., dissenting) (quoting G. SANTAYANA, THE LIFE OF REASON 284
    (1905)).

73 *See id.* at 2638 (Ginsburg, J., dissenting).

74 *See* Guinier, *Foreword, supra* note 5.

75 *Shelby Cnty.*, 133 S. Ct. at 2650 (Ginsburg, J., dissenting).

76 John Paul Stevens, *The Court & the Right to Vote: A Dissent,* N.Y. REV. BOOKS
    (Aug. 15, 2013), http://www.nybooks.com/articles/archives/2013/aug/15/the-court
    -right-to-vote-dissent/

77 Ogletree, *supra* note 60, http://www.washingtonpost.com/opinions/john-lewis-and
-others-react-to-the-supreme-courts-voting-rights-act-ruling/2013/06/25/acb96650
-ddda-11e2-b797-cbd4cb13f9c6_story.html (as Professor Ogletree reminds us, "five
justices have chosen to rip out what Rep. John Lewis has called the "heart and
soul" of the Voting Rights Act.")

78 Ross Guberman, *The Supreme Writer on the Court: The Case for Roberts*, VOLOKH
CONSPIRACY (July 8, 2013), http://www.volokh.com/2013/07/08/the-supreme-writer
-on-the-court-the-case-for-roberts/ (posting a comment from user "Somewhere in
Middle America" evaluating the writing of several justices).

79 Kirk Hanneman, *Biden Agrees with Ginsburg on Voting Rights Act* (Jan. 20, 2014),
http://blog.fednews.com/blog/2014/01/20/biden-agrees-with-ginsburg-on-voting
-rights-act/

80 Jenee Desmond Harris, *Biden on Voting Rights and Black History: 'Hatred
Never Goes Away'*, ROOT.COM (Feb. 26, 2014), http://www.theroot.com/articles
/culture/2014/02/joe_biden_on_voting_rights_hatred_never_goes_away.html

81 Deborah Vagins & Laughlin McDonald, *Supreme Court Put a Dagger in the Heart
of the Voting Rights Act*, ACLU.ORG (July 2, 2013), https://www.aclu.org/blog/voting
-rights/supreme-court-put-dagger-heart-voting-rights-act. NAACP Legal Defense
and Education Fund, *Protecting Voters in the Wake of the Supreme Court's Ruling
in* Shelby County, Alabama v. Holder, NAACPLDF.ORG, http://www.naacpldf
.org/files/case_issue/Key%20Points%20and%20Action%20Items,%20Shelby%20
County,%20Alabama%20v.%20Holder.pdf

82 *See* Liptak, *supra* note 3.

83 The response to Justice Ginsburg's umbrella line paralleled the public's reaction to an earlier metaphor she coined during oral arguments for *United States v.
Windsor*, when she described the union accorded to gays whose marriage was legal
but diminished by the Defense of Marriage Act as "skim milk marriage." Transcript
of Oral Argument at 71, *Windsor*, 133 S.Ct. 2675, (No. 12–307), *available at* http://
www.supremecourt.gov/oral_arguments/argument_transcripts/12-307_jnt1.pdf.
Justice Ginsburg's colorful phrase appeared constantly in the months leading up
to the *Windsor* decision, picked up not just by traditional news outlets such as the
Washington Post, but by BuzzFeed, a "social news and entertainment" website
directed toward a nonlegal audience. Chris Geidner, *The Moment When Justice
Ginsburg Took Aim to Kill DOMA – It's All about Skim Milk*, BuzzFEED (Mar. 27,
2013, 4:58 PM), http://www.buzzfeed.com/chrisgeidner/the-moment-when-justice
-ginsburg-took-aim-to-kill-doma

84 The Takeaway with John Hockenberry, *Justice Ginsburg Part II: Gender, the Second
Amendment, Immigration & More* (Sept. 17, 2013), http://www.thetakeaway.org
/story/second-amendment-outdated-justice-ginsburg-says/

85 Interview with Jeffrey Rosen, *Justice Ginsburg on Supreme Court Rulings and
Political Activism* at 27:38 (Sept. 6, 2013), http://www.c-span.org/video/?314892-1
/justice-ginsburg-supreme-court-rulings-political-activism

86 *See* Richard L. Hasen, Shelby County *and the Illusion of Minimalism*, WM. &
MARY BILL RTS. J. (forthcoming) (noting that the majority's decision "willfully
ignores political realities").

87 Brooke Donald, *At Stanford, Justice Ginsburg Says Collegiality Is Not Swayed
by Bitter Battles* (Sept. 18, 2013), http://news.stanford.edu/news/2013/september
/ginsburg-law-talk-091813.html

88 Liptak, *supra* note 3.

89 GovTrack, H.R. 3899: Voting Rights Amendment Act of 2014, https://www.govtrack
.us/congress/bills/113/hr3899 (last visited Mar. 20, 2014).

90 *See* NAACP Legal Defense and Education Fund's Voting Rights Amendment
Act of 2014 webpage, http://www.naacpldf.org/case-issue/voting-rights-amendment
-act-2014; ACLU online petition, *Congress: Pass the Voting Rights Amendment
Act of 2014*, https://www.aclu.org/secure/congress-repair-voting-act; Leadership
Conference for Civil and Human Rights, VRA for Today, http://vrafortoday.org/

91 While a supporter of a legislative fix to *Shelby County*, Senator Sanders takes issue
with the current form of the Voting Rights Amendment Act of 2014, which proposes a preclearance formula that does not fully capture discriminatory voter ID
laws and consent decrees, among other things. *See Summary of the Voting Rights
Amendment Act of 2014, Introduced January 16, 2014*, ADVANCEMENT PROJECT, http://
www.advancementproject.org/pages/summary-of-the-voting-rights-amendment
-act-of-2014-introduced-january-16-20 (last visited Apr. 7, 2014).

92 Interview with Hank Sanders (Mar. 5, 2014).

93 *See* Saving Ourselves (S.O.S.), *Marching to the 50th, available at* http://
sosmovement.net/marching-to-the-50th/

94 Interview, *supra* note 92.

95 *See* Liptak, *supra* note 3; *see also* Hockenberry, *supra* note 84, and Interview, *supra*
note 92.

96 *See* Donald, *supra* note 87.

97 Daniel Saeedi, *Voting Rights in America: A Lunch with Justice Ginsburg*, 24:2
CHALLENGE NEWSLETTER (Jan. 2014), http://www.isba.org/committees/minorities
/newsletter/2014/01/votingrightsinamericaalunchwithjust

98 *Id.*

15 ORAL ARGUMENT AS A BRIDGE BETWEEN THE BRIEFS AND THE COURT'S OPINION

1 Tr. of Oral Arg. at 59–60, Moncrieffe v. Holder, 133 S. Ct. 1678 (2013).

2 Tr. of Oral Arg. at 33, Spector v. Norwegian Cruise Lines, 545 U.S. 119 (2005).

3 Tr. of Oral Arg. at 29, 51, Smith v. City of Jackson, 544 U.S. 228 (2003).

4 Tr. of Oral Arg. at 40–41, Walden v. Fiore, 134 S. Ct. 1115 (2014).

5 Tr. of Oral Arg. at 3, 14, 26, 55, Florence v. Board of Chosen Freeholders, 132 S. Ct.
1510 (2012).

6 Tr. of Oral Arg. at 5, 7, 23, 51, City of Arlington v. FCC, 133 S. Ct. 1863 (2013).

7 Tr. of Oral Arg. at 5, Moncrieffe v. Holder, 133 S. Ct. 1678 (2013).

8 Tr. of Oral Arg. at 11, Sorrell v. IMS Health v. Schneider, 131 S. Ct. 2653 (2011).

9 Tr. of Oral Arg. at 38–39, Cone v. Bell, 556 U.S. 449 (2009).

16 FIRE AND ICE: RUTH BADER GINSBURG, THE LEAST LIKELY FIREBRAND

1 FRED STREBEIGH, EQUAL: WOMEN RESHAPE AMERICAN LAW 12 (2009).

2 *Id.* at 36.

3 *Id.* at 66.

4 *Id.* at 20.

5 Julie Taboh, *Supreme Court Justice Continues Equality Fight*, VOICE OF AMERICA NEWS (Dec. 14, 2011).

6 STREBEIGH, *supra* note 1, at 35.

7 Stephanie Francis Ward, *Family Ties: The Private and Public Lives of Justice Ruth Bader Ginsburg*, A.B.A. J. (Oct. 2010).

8 Ruth Marcus, *The Ginsburg Fallacy*, WASH. POST (Nov. 15, 2005).

9 *Id.*

10 404 U.S. 71 (1971).

11 STREBEIGH, *supra* note 1, at 55.

12 David J. Garrow, *Justice William Brennan, a Liberal Lion Who Wouldn't Hire Women*, WASH. POST (Oct. 17, 2010).

13 Emily Bazelon, *The Place of Women on the Supreme Court*, N.Y. TIMES MAGAZINE (July 7, 2009).

14 William J. Clinton, *Remarks Announcing the Nomination of Ruth Bader Ginsburg to Be a Supreme Court Associate Justice* (June 14, 1993), *available at* http://www.presidency.ucsb.edu/ws/?pid=46684

15 531 U.S. 98 (2000).

16 Linda Greenhouse, *Oral Dissents Give Ginsburg a New Voice on Court*, N.Y. TIMES (May 31, 2007).

17 David Crary, *Ginsburg Questions 1973 Abortion Ruling's Timing*, ASSOCIATED PRESS (Feb. 10, 2012).

18 Bazelon, *supra* note 13.

19 Jacob Gershman, *Ginsburg Recalls Days When She Used to Be Confused with O'Connor*, WALL ST. J. (Dec. 17, 2013).

20 Ruth Bader Ginsburg, *A Woman's Voice May Do Some Good*, POLITICO (Sept. 25, 2013).

21 Joan Biskupic, *Retired Justice O'Connor Has a Lot on Her Docket*, USA TODAY (June 15, 2005).

22 550 U.S. 124 (2007) (Ginsburg, J., dissenting).

23 *Id.* at 170.

24 Rebecca Traister, *Hell Hath No Fury like Ruth Bader Ginsburg*, SALON.COM (Feb. 6, 2009).

25 STREBEIGH, *supra* note 1, at 183–85.

26 Bazelon, *supra* note 13.

27 550 U.S. 618 (2007).

28 Opinion Announcement, *Ledbetter*, 550 U.S. 618, *available at* http://www.oyez.org/cases/2000-2009/2006/2006_05_1074/opinion

29 *Ledbetter*, 550 U.S. at 661 (Ginsburg, J., dissenting) ("Once again, the ball is in Congress' court. As in 1991, the Legislature may act to correct this Court's parsimonious reading of Title VII.").

30 Lilly Ledbetter Fair Pay Act of 2009, Pub. L. 111–2, 123 Stat. 5 (2009).

31 Greenhouse, *supra* note 16.

32 *Id.*

33 Joan Biskupic, *Ginsburg: Court Needs Another Woman*, USA TODAY (May 5, 2009).

34 Redding v. Stafford Unified Sch. Dist. No. 1, 531 F.3d 1071 (9th Cir. 2008).
35 Tr. of Oral Arg. at 27–28, 44–45, Safford Unified Sch. Dist. No. 1 v. Redding, 557 U.S. 364 (2009), available at http://www.supremecourt.gov/oral_arguments /argument_transcripts/08-479.pdf
36 *Id.* at 45.
37 *Id.* at 58.
38 Nina Totenberg, *Court Hears School Strip Search Case*, Nat'l Pub. Radio (Apr. 21, 2009), *available at* http://www.npr.org/templates/story/story.php?storyId =103334943
39 Biskupic, *supra* note 33.
40 *Id.*
41 *Id.*
42 Richard Wolf, *Ginsburg's Dedication Undimmed after 20 Years on the Court*, USA Today (Aug. 1, 2013).
43 Bazelon, *supra* note 13.
44 Greenhouse, *supra* note 16.
45 Biskupic, *supra* note 33.
46 Tony Mauro, *Justice Ginsburg Back on the Bench*, Blog of the Legal Times (Feb. 23, 2009).
47 Biskupic, *supra* note 33.
48 Nina Totenberg, *Martin Ginsburg's Legacy: Love of Justice*, NPR.org (July 3, 2010).
49 Wal-Mart Stores, Inc. v. Dukes, 133 S. Ct. 2541 (2011).
50 *Id.* at 2564 (Ginsburg, J., dissenting).
51 Interview with Ruth Bader Ginsburg (2012).
52 Kate Stamell, *Supreme Court Justice Praises Women in Law at Duke speech*, The Chronicle (Feb. 1, 2005).

GINSBURG, OPTIMISM, AND CONFLICT MANAGEMENT

1 Ruth Bader Ginsburg, *Interpretations of the Equal Protection Clause*, 9 Harv. J.L. & Pub. Pol'y 41, 45 (1986).

Index